Domestic Abuse: Law and P

Eighth Edition

Domestic Abuse: Law and Practice

Eighth Edition

Roger Bird

LexisNexis®

LexisNexis® UK & Worldwide

United Kingdom — RELX (UK) Limited trading as LexisNexis®, 1–3 Strand, London WC2N 5JR and 9–10 St Andrew Square, Edinburgh EH2 2AF

LNUK Global Partners — LexisNexis® encompasses authoritative legal publishing brands dating back to the 19th century including: Butterworths® in the United Kingdom, Canada and the Asia-Pacific region; Les Editions du Juris Classeur in France; and Matthew Bender® worldwide. Details of LexisNexis® locations worldwide can be found at www.lexisnexis.com

Published by LexisNexis®

A CIP Catalogue record for this book is available from the British Library.

ISBN 978-1-7847-3467-1

9 781784 734671

ISBN for this volume: 9781784734671

Printed and bound in Great Britain by Hobbs the Printers, Hampshire SO40 3WX

Visit LexisNexis at http://www.lexisnexis.co.uk

Preface

During the recent debates on the Domestic Abuse Bill 2020 many politicians have given the impression that the existing law contained no protection against such abuse and that urgent action was required to provide such protection. One distinguished former member of the cabinet even said, on Radio 4, that the new provisions would enable a victim of abuse to remain in the family home whereas in the past she had been required to leave and enable the perpetrator to remain.

Readers of this book will already be aware that the court's ability to eject a perpetrator of abuse from his home has existed and been regularly exercised at least since 1970 and the first chapter of this book contains a brief history of Parliament's attempts to improve the powers and procedures of the courts since then. The new Bill is therefore a further attempt to build on those foundations and to provide more protection against the scourge of domestic abuse which has, if anything, worsened over the past year.

Having said that, the new Bill is clearly an improvement on the previous law and is to be welcomed for that reason. Referring again to the history in chapter one, what is notable is the increasing tendency over recent years for the state and public authorities to take over the task of providing protection and punishing breaches of the law. What began as the responsibility of individual victims and their lawyers is now squarely a duty laid on the police and other public bodies. The law cannot change human nature but can do its best to continually improve the ways in which excesses are contained and to learn from the experience of earlier attempts.

For the time being the new law and remedies will exist side by side with the old law and I have done my best in this edition to explain how they may overlap.

The law is as at the date below.

Roger Bird
October 2020

Contents

Abbreviations

ChA 1989	Children Act 1989
CASA 2010	Crime and Security Act 2010
CCR	County Court Rules
CPR	Civil Procedure Rules 1998
DVCVA 2004	Domestic Violence, Crime and Victims Act 2004
DVMPA 1976	Domestic Violence and Matrimonial Proceedings Act 1976
FLA 1996	Family Law Act 1996
FPR	Family Procedure Rules 2010
MCA 1973	Matrimonial Causes Act 1973
MHA 1983	Matrimonial Homes Act 1983
PD	Practice Direction (of the Civil Procedure Rules 1998 or the Family Procedure Rules 2010)
PHA 1997	Protection from Harassment Act 1997
RSC	Rules of the Supreme Court

Table of Statutes

H

L

Table of Statutory Instruments

Table of Cases

K

L

M

N

P

Chapter 1

INTRODUCTION TO THE DOMESTIC ABUSE BILL 2020

1.1 Domestic abuse, or domestic violence as it used to be called, is not a new problem. It has always existed and the law has tried to provide remedies for the victims in various forms. The court has always had an inherent jurisdiction to protect the victims of abuse, and this jurisdiction was often invoked before successive governments tried to codify such protection in statutory form[1]. The 2020 Bill is the latest of these attempts and will be considered in detail in this book at the same time as explaining the existing law. This 'side by side' approach is necessary because, as is explained in the next chapter, much of the existing law is not to be repealed, at least for the time being, but will run in parallel with the new law which will come into force at a time to be decided. This chapter will try to bring together the essential features of the new Act in one place, but readers will also find that the new law is referred to from time to time in the rest of the book.

Before the Bill is considered in detail, however, a very brief outline of previous statutory measures may be helpful to show how we have reached the present position.

1 See eg *Gurasz v Gurasz* [1970] p 11.

DOMESTIC VIOLENCE AND MATRIMONIAL PROCEEDINGS ACT 1976

1.2 The Domestic Violence and Matrimonial Proceedings Act 1976 (DVMPA 1976) was the first statute to try specifically to provide remedies for what is now called domestic abuse. It provided that a county court could grant an injunction containing one or more of several provisions, such as restraining one party from molesting another, and excluding them from the family home[1]. This protection was available where the parties were or had been married or had lived together in the same household as husband and wife[2]. Where actual bodily harm had been used or was threatened a power of arrest could be attached to any order[3]. The Act contained no specific guidelines as to how the court should exercise its jurisdiction.

1 DVMPA 1976, s 1(1).
2 DVMPA 1976, s 2(2).
3 DVMPA 1976, s 2(1).

MATRIMONIAL HOMES ACT 1983

1.3 The Matrimonial Homes Act 1983 (MHA 1983) was designed to deal with rights of occupation of a home and was intended to complement the provisions of the DVMPA 1976 and remedy gaps in the protection it provided. The purpose of the Act was to protect the rights of occupation of a party and, where appropriate, to restrict or even terminate the rights of occupation of other parties. It contained specific guidelines as to how the jurisdiction of the court should be exercised, directing the court to 'make such order as it thinks just and reasonable having regard to the conduct of the spouses in relation to each other and otherwise, to their respective needs and financial resources, to the needs of any children and to all the circumstances of the case'[1]. The MHA 1983 only applied where the parties were married.

1 MHA 1983, s 1(3).

DOMESTIC PROCEEDINGS AND MAGISTRATES' COURTS ACT 1978

1.4 The Domestic Proceedings and Magistrates' Courts Act 1978 (DPMCA 1978) conferred on magistrates' courts powers similar to but not identical with those contained in the DVMPA 1976. An important difference was that the magistrates' court had no power to commit to prison for breach of an undertaking.

The effect of these statutory measures was that there was considerable litigation over what certain words and phrases in the various Acts might, or might not, mean. Judges gratefully seized on the new statutes to provide justification for making orders to prevent domestic violence and it was sometimes argued that the courts had gone too far and exceeded their powers. Two important cases resulting from this were *Richards v Richards*[1] in which the House of Lords stressed the requirement on courts to have strict regard to the wording of the statute, and *G v G (Ouster Ex Parte Application)*[2] which dealt with the powers of the court to make orders on applications without notice. These and other developments led the Law Commission to examine the topic and it concluded, unsurprisingly, that one of the principal problems was that the law was contained in three separate statutes. There was confusion about how to exercise the discretionary jurisdiction and it was anomalous that unmarried couples were at a disadvantage compared with married couples[3]. The Commission therefore made the recommendations for a unified jurisdiction contained in a draft Bill. This recommendation was accepted by the government and formed the basis of the Family and Domestic Violence Bill 1995 (FDVB).

1 [1984] AC 174.
2 [1990] 1 FLR 395.
3 See Law Com Report 'Domestic Violence and Occupation of the Family Home' Law Com No 207.

FAMILY AND DOMESTIC VIOLENCE BILL 1995

1.5 The FDVB was introduced in 1995 and attracted all-party support, although there was strong opposition from some quarters over who might be entitled to make applications under these provisions, it being alleged in some quarters that the Bill was contrary to 'family values'. At the eleventh hour, when the Bill had completed its parliamentary passage but before receiving Royal Assent, a significant body of Parliamentary dissent arose and the government decided that, as there was insufficient time to deal with potential amendments, the Bill should be abandoned.

PART IV FAMILY LAW ACT 1996

1.6 However, all was not lost. The provisions of the FDVB were introduced as Pt IV of the Family Law Act 1996 (FLA 1996), which received Royal Assent on 4 July 1996. The main provisions of the FLA were concerned with divorce law reform, and provided for some very convoluted and apparently contradictory procedures, and in 1997 the government of the day decided that it would be too difficult to bring it into force. However, Pt IV survived, and formed the basis of the law, with some modifications, for the next 20 years.

Part IV provided for a unified jurisdiction of courts, and introduced the concepts of 'matrimonial home rights.' It also introduced 'associated persons' which was the term used to define those entitled to make applications under the Act. Powers of arrest were retained and a new procedure for warrants of arrest was introduced. The two main classes of order were non-molestation orders and occupation orders, and all courts retained jurisdiction to punish offenders for breaches of their orders. It should be noted, however, that there was still no statutory definition of domestic violence or abuse.

DOMESTIC VIOLENCE, CRIME AND VICTIMS ACT 2004

1.7 In 2004 the Domestic Violence, Crime and Victims Act (DVCVA 2004) introduced an important change to Pt IV of the FLA 1996. Breaches of non-molestation orders now became a criminal and arrestable offence and had to be dealt with by magistrates' courts under their criminal jurisdiction. County courts lost their jurisdiction to attach powers of arrest to non-molestation orders and to punish breaches. The definition of 'associated persons' was broadened to include same sex couples.

CONSULTATION PAPER

1.8 That was the legal position when the government's paper *Transforming the Response to Domestic Abuse*[1] was published in January 2019. This paper arose out of consultation which was promised in the conservative party's election manifesto in 2017. The consultation had asked the public and interested organisation to comment on how to achieve various objectives such promoting awareness and transforming the justice system.

The response to the consultation identified nine measures which needed to be incorporated in statutory form to improve the court process and protection for victims. These included provision for a statutory definition of domestic abuse, establishment of the office of Domestic Abuse Commissioner, a new Domestic

Abuse Protection Notice (DAPN) and Domestic Abuse Protection Order (DAPO), restrictions on cross-examination of victims by perpetrators, a new statutory presumption that complainants of an offence involving behaviour that amounts to domestic abuse are eligible for special measures in the criminal courts and various other measures. This will be the subject matter of the Act which will now be considered.

1 CP 15 (see https://assets.publishing.service.gov.uk/government/uploads/system/uploads/attachment_data/file/772247/Transforming_the_response_to_domestic_abuse_-_consultation_response_and_draft_bill_-print.pdf).

THE DOMESTIC ABUSE BILL 2020

1.9 The Bill was first introduced in 2019 but for various political reasons failed to complete its parliamentary progress on several occasions. It was again introduced in February 2020, completed its Report Stage and Third Reading in July, and was voted through by the House of Commons. The First Reading in the House of Lords took place on 7 July and the Second Reading is yet to be scheduled. In later chapters key aspects of the new provisions will be examined but here it may be appropriate to deal with one of the most important changes, namely the definition of domestic abuse.

Main features of the Domestic Abuse Bill 2020

Domestic abuse defined

1.10 As has been explained above, there has previously been no statutory definition of domestic abuse, or domestic violence as it used to be called. There have been various attempts, by judges and others, to provide a satisfactory definition, and, as will be seen in **Chapter 3**, attempt to define this by Practice Direction, but there has never been one form of words designed to be all-embracing. The Bill clearly wishes to put this beyond any doubt. The consultation paper had asked for comments on a proposed definition of domestic abuse and suggested one answer. There was widespread public support for the suggested definition.

Accordingly, s 1 of the Bill, after stating that this section defines what is meant by 'domestic abuse', continues as follows:

> '(2) Behaviour by a person ("A") towards another person ("B") is "domestic abuse" if—
> (a) A and B are each aged 16 or over and are personally connected, and
> (b) the behaviour is abusive.
>
> (3) Behaviour is "abusive" if it consists of any of the following—
> (a) physical or sexual abuse;
> (b) violent or threatening behaviour;
> (c) controlling or coercive behaviour;
> (d) economic abuse (see subsection (4));
> (e) psychological, emotional or other abuse.
>
> and it does not matter whether the behaviour consists of a single incident or a course of conduct.
>
> (4) "Economic abuse" means any behaviour that has a substantial adverse effect on B's ability to—

(a) acquire, use or maintain money or other property, or
(b) obtain goods or services.

(5) For the purposes of this Act A's behaviour may be behaviour "towards" B despite the fact that it consists of conduct directed at another person (for example, B's child).

(6) References in this Act to being abusive towards another person are to be read in accordance with this section.

(7) For the meaning of "personally connected", see section 2.'

1.11 Section 3 of the Bill provides a further definition designed to protect children. The section provides that:

'(1) This section applies where behaviour of a person ("A") towards another person ("B") is domestic abuse.

(2) Any reference in this Act to a victim of domestic abuse includes a reference to a child who—
(a) sees or hears, or experiences the effects of, the abuse, and
(b) is related to A or B.

(3) A child is related to a person for the purposes of subsection (2) if—
(a) the person is a parent of, or has parental responsibility for, the child, or
(b) the child and the person are relatives.

(4) In this section—

"child" means a person under the age of 18 years;

"parental responsibility" has the same meaning as in the Children Act 1989;

"relative" has the meaning given by section 63(1) of the Family Law Act 1996.'

1.12 A number of definitions in this section need to be examined more closely. It may be convenient to consider s 1(7) first, since that leads in s 2 to a definition of who is intended to be protected by the Bill and who can apply for such protection.

Section 2 provides as follows:

'Definition of "personally connected"—

(1) . . . two people are "personally connected" if any of the following applies—
(a) they are, or have been, married to each other;
(b) they are, or have been, civil partners of each other;
(c) they have agreed to marry one another (whether or not the agreement has been terminated);
(d) they have entered into a civil partnership agreement (whether or not the agreement has been terminated);
(e) they are, or have been, in an intimate personal relationship with each other;
(f) they each have, or there has been a time when they each have had, a parental relationship in relation to the same child (see subsection (2));
(g) they are relatives.'

1.13 Sub-sections (2) and (3) then tidy up the meanings of various terms contained in s 2(1) as follows:

> 'For the purposes of subsection (1)(f) a person has a parental relationship in relation to a child if:
>
> (a) the person is a parent of the child, or
>
> (b) the person has parental responsibility for the child.
>
> In this section—
>
> "child" means a person under the age of 18 years;
>
> "civil partnership agreement" has the meaning given by section 73 of the Civil Partnership Act 2004;
>
> "parental responsibility" has the same meaning as in the Children Act 1989;
>
> "relative" has the meaning given by section 63(1) of the Family Law Act 1996.'

The structure of the Bill is therefore clear. It envisages two protagonists, a victim (B) and a perpetrator (A). A and B must either have been married or civil partners or have agreed to be so, been in an 'intimate relationship' with each other, have been the parents of a child or be relatives. Some sort of family relationship is therefore essential.

Intimate relationship

1.14 These definitions are clear and need little explanation. The only term which is not defined and might in theory give rise to some argument is 'intimate relationship'. Section 62(3)(ea) of the FLA 1996 included in its list of associated persons (ie those entitled to apply for protection) persons who 'have or have had an intimate personal relationship with each other which was of significant duration'. In this Bill there is no reference to the duration of the relationship. One can only presume that this definition is intended to be less potentially restrictive.

Agreed to marry

1.15 Although the sense of what is intended here is clear, there is, at present, room for doubt about this category. When a similar definition appeared in s 62(3)(e) FLA 1996 it was thought necessary to include another section of the Act, s 44, to make provision about evidence of agreement to marry. It was provided, in effect, that such agreement to marry must be evidenced by either written evidence, the giving of a ring, or a ceremony. There are no such provisions in this Bill, so the issue may arise for challenge at some future date.

New Domestic Abuse Protection Notice and Order

1.16 The previous provisions for a Domestic Violence Protection Notice and a Domestic Violence Protection Order have been replaced by the Domestic Abuse Protection Notice and Domestic Abuse Protection Order, without any significant change in their effect. The changes are dealt with in more detail at Chapter 4 and Chapter 5.

Domestic Abuse Commissioner

1.17 The Act creates the post of Domestic Abuse Commissioner whose role will be to encourage good practice in the prevention of domestic abuse and detection of perpetrators of abuse. This will be considered in more detail at CHAPTER **11**.

Restrictions on cross-examination of victims

1.18 Section 63 of the Bill inserts Part 4B into the Matrimonial and Family Proceedings Act 1984, which introduces restrictions on the cross-examination of a victim of domestic abuse by the alleged perpetrator. These changes are dealt with in more detail in CHAPTER 8 (Procedure for Personal Protection orders).

Miscellaneous changes

1.19 There are various other changes in the Bill such as the establishment of Domestic Abuse Local Partnership Boards and provisions relating to offences committed abroad which are outlined in CHAPTER **11** (Miscellaneous Provisions).

Chapter 2

WHO MAY APPLY FOR PROTECTION FROM ABUSE?

2.1 The purpose of this book is to provide a quick and reliable guide to practitioners and others relating to the various forms of personal protection available through the court process. The remedies which will be described are those which are designed to protect the individual from some wrong which has been committed against them or which is threatened. These wrongs include assault, molestation, harassment and interference with occupation of a home. The general description of such events is now 'domestic abuse' and this is the term which will be used throughout this book. A detailed account of which this term comprises will be found in Chapter 1. The common element in all these remedies under the existing law is normally that the victim and the perpetrator have, at some stage, been 'associated' in a family or quasi-family sense although, as will be seen, even this is not always the case where 'stalking' is alleged under the Protection from Harassment Act 1997 (PHA 1997).

2.2 The legal position has become complicated by the passing into law of the Domestic Abuse Bill 2020. On the one hand, this Bill provides a new procedure and set of remedies in domestic abuse cases which appear to be a self-contained code. One would normally have expected that the existing law and procedure would be repealed in favour of the new code. However, that is not to be the case, at least for the time being, and it appears that the new procedure will, at least for some while, exist side by side with the previous procedure. As a result of this the two systems will have to be explained in this book and guidance given, where it is available, of when the whole of the new system is likely to be in effect.

2.3 The remedies available under the existing law are provided partly by statute and partly by the general law. Part IV of the Family Law Act 1996 (FLA 1996) as amended by the Domestic Violence, Crime and Victims Act 2004 (DVCVA 2004) provides a comprehensive code for applications for personal protection from molestation by a member of the family or other associated person, and also for occupation of a family home. A person who is not associated cannot apply under FLA 1996. However, there remain cases of harassment and violence between persons who are not included in the class of associated persons eligible under FLA 1996. Here, the position may be remedied by injunctions, made in actions under the PHA 1997 or founded on common law torts. The remedies available under the Domestic Abuse Bill 2020 will have to be considered side by side with the existing remedies.

2.4 *Who may apply for protection from abuse?*

2.4 The various sections of this book are designed to deal with each of the separate possibilities which may arise. In many cases, of course, there may be overlapping remedies (not to mention the overlapping provided by the Domestic Abuse Bill 2020) but it is hoped that this approach will provide the quickest solution for the reader.

THE EXISTING LAW: STEP ONE – IS THE VICTIM 'ASSOCIATED'?

2.5 It has already been shown that victims and potential applicants for relief are divided into those who are associated and those who are not. This is the first question the adviser has to deal with. This division into associated and non-associated persons is one of the key concepts of FLA 1996. Section 62(3) of FLA 1996 provides that a person is associated with another person if:

> '(3) For the purposes of this Part[1], a person is associated with another person if—
> (a) they are or have been married to each other;
> (aa) they are or have been civil partners of each other;
> (b) they are cohabitants or former cohabitants;
> (c) they live or have lived in the same household, otherwise than merely by reason of one of them being the other's employee, tenant, lodger or boarder;
> (d) they are relatives;
> (e) they have agreed to marry one another (whether or not that agreement has been terminated);
> (eza) they have entered into a civil partnership agreement (as defined by section 73 of the Civil Partnership Act 2004) (whether or not that agreement has been terminated);
> (ea) they have or have had an intimate personal relationship with each other which is or was of significant duration;
> (f) in relation to any child, they are both persons falling within subsection (4)[2]; or
> (g) they are parties to the same family proceedings (other than proceedings under this Part).'

This definition introduces further terms, some of which must themselves be defined.

1 Ie Pt IV of the FLA 1996.
2 Subsection (4) provides that a person falls within its scope if:
(a) he is a parent of the child; or
(b) he has or has had parental responsibility for the child.

Cohabitation

2.6 Section 62(3)(a) presents no problems. The first term requiring definition is 'cohabitant'. Section 62(1) defines 'cohabitants' thus:

> '(a) Cohabitants are two persons who, although not married to each other, are living together as husband and wife or (if of the same sex) in an equivalent relationship; and
> (b) "former cohabitants" is to be read accordingly, but does not include cohabitants who have subsequently married each other.'

2.7 Before the amendments made by the DVCVA 2004, s 62(1) of the FLA 1996 required cohabitants to be 'a man and a woman'. The amended section extends the definition to include same sex couples. With that difference in mind, the position is clear; the parties must have lived together as if husband and wife or the same sex equivalent. This would involve a shared life and living arrangements and, normally, a sexual element in the relationship. In most cases, the meaning of cohabitant will be clear enough, although it has to be said that, given the almost infinite variety of conditions of married life, there may be room for interesting arguments about what does and does not come within 'living together as husband and wife'.

2.8 Same sex couples who have married can of course take advantage of s 62(3)(a).

2.9 The question of what constitutes cohabitation is not only relevant in the field of family law; there is a body of jurisprudence on the subject in social security law, which is frequently overlooked by family practitioners. The issue to be determined in those cases is normally whether an applicant for income support is disqualified because of cohabitation.

2.10 In *Crake v Supplementary Benefits Commission*[1], Woolf J approved six factors as 'admirable signposts' for the existence of cohabitation. These are membership of the same household, stability, financial support, sexual relationship, children and public acknowledgment. However, in *Re J (Income Support: Cohabitation)*[2], a Social Security Commissioner held that to consider only these factors placed a wholly inadequate emphasis on the parties' 'general relationship'. The parties' sexual and financial relationship was relevant only for the light it cast on this general relationship. Where there had never been a sexual relationship, there must be strong alternative grounds for holding that there existed a relationship akin to that of husband and wife.

1 [1982] 1 All ER 498.
2 [1995] 1 FLR 660.

2.11 In *G v G (Non-molestation Order: Jurisdiction)*[1], justices found that the applicant and respondent were not associated because they had never lived in the same household, were not cohabitants and there was insufficient evidence of agreement to marry. Wall J allowed the appeal and directed a rehearing, saying that the court should adopt a purposive construction of the FLA 1996 and jurisdiction should not be declined unless the facts of the case were plainly incapable of being brought within the statute. In this case, three of the 'signposts' set out in *Crake* (see above) were present.

1 [2000] 2 FLR 533.

2.12 Section 62(3)(c) introduces a new class of applicants into the law. The previous law, taken as a whole, recognised present or former spouses and cohabitants as potential applicants; this provision broadens the range of applicants. The essential characteristic of this class of person is that they have lived in the same household as the other person.

2.13 *Who may apply for protection from abuse?*

Household

2.13 'Household' had been considered by the Law Commission, which, when defining the relationships to be protected in addition to spouses and cohabitants, began with[1]:

> 'The phrase "living in the same household" may be expected to retain the usual meaning which it has acquired in matrimonial proceedings. Thus, it is possible for people to live in different households, although they are actually living in the same house. The crucial test is the degree of community life which goes on. If the parties shut themselves up in separate rooms and cease to have anything to do with each other, they live in separate households. But if they share domestic chores and shopping, eat meals together or share the same living room, they are living in the same household, however strained their relations may be.'

1 Law Com, para 3.21.

2.14 The term implies some shared living arrangements; people living under the same roof, for example by occupying flats or bedsits in the same building, would not be living in the same household. The class clearly could overlap with cohabitants, in the sense that someone could qualify under this classification and as a cohabitant; however, one could not qualify as a cohabitant without being of the opposite sex to the other party, and without the relationship being similar to that of husband and wife.

2.15 In the same way, the class would overlap with that of relatives, so it must be taken that, in attempting to define those intended to qualify here, relatives should be excluded. Section 62(3)(c) specifically excludes people who live in the same household 'merely by reason' of their being employer and employee, landlord and tenant (although it is difficult to see how a landlord and tenant, properly so called, could live in the same household), and 'landlord' and lodger or boarder. It would be possible for someone to argue that, although he or she was an employee or boarder, that was not the only reason for living in the same household as someone else; for example, it might be argued that there was some sexual relationship which made it convenient for them to be close at hand.

2.16 It seems, therefore, that people who might be associated with each other would include people who share a home for reasons of friendship, convenience or some other reason.

'Relative'

2.17 'Relative' is defined in s 63(1). In relation to a person, 'relative' means:

> '(a) the father, mother, stepfather, stepmother, son, daughter, stepson, stepdaughter, grandmother, grandfather, grandson or granddaughter of that person or of that person's spouse or former spouse, or
>
> (b) the brother, sister, uncle, aunt, niece or nephew (whether of the full blood or of the half blood or by affinity) of that person or of that person's spouse or former spouse,
>
> and includes, in relation to a person who is living or has lived with another person as husband and wife, any person who would fall within paragraph (a) or (b) above if the parties were married to each other.'

The significance of this last provision is, therefore, that the word 'cohabitant' or 'former cohabitant' can be substituted for 'spouse' in the definition. Apart from this, the definition needs little further elaboration, save for a consideration of the effect of s 62(4) and (5).

2.18 Section 62(4) begins 'A person falls within this subsection in relation to a child . . . '. Pausing there, it will be remembered that the purpose of the section is to define 'associated persons', relatives are associated persons, and, of course, parents are relatives of their children. It is unsurprising, therefore, to find that sub-s (4) continues:

> 'if—
> (a) he is a parent of the child; or
> (b) he has or has had parental responsibility for the child.'

By s 63(1), 'parental responsibility' has the same meaning as in the Children Act 1989.

2.19 In *Re A (Non-Molestation Application by a Child)*[1] it was held that, absent adequate evidence of the child's understanding, and of the other parent commencing family proceedings or applying for a non-molestation order in respect of the child, then except in the most exceptional circumstances leave should not be given for a child to commence non-molestation proceedings against a parent. This was a decision of the High Court of Northern Ireland but it may be relevant in England and Wales because of the provision entitling a child to commence proceedings.

1 [2010] 1 FLR 1363.

2.20 Section 62(5) deals with the position where a child has been adopted or freed for adoption by virtue of any of the enactments mentioned in s 16(1) of the Adoption Act 1976. In such circumstances, two persons may be associated for the purposes of this Act if:

> '(a) one is a natural parent of the child or a parent of such a natural parent; and
> (b) the other is the child or any person—
> (i) who has become a parent of the child by virtue of an adoption order or has applied for an adoption order, or
> (ii) with whom the child has at any time been placed for adoption.'

Engaged couples

2.21 Section 62(3)(e) introduces another class of associated persons, namely the former engaged couple.

2.22 Section 44, the marginal note to which is 'Evidence of agreement to marry', provides, in sub-s (1), that the court shall not make an order under s 33 (an occupation order in favour of an entitled person) or s 42 (a non-molestation order) by virtue of s 62(3)(e) unless there is produced to it evidence in writing of the existence of an agreement to marry. However, this is subject to sub-s (2), which provides as follows:

> 'Subsection (1) above does not apply if the court is satisfied that the agreement to marry was evidenced by—

(a) the gift of an engagement ring by one party to the agreement to the other in contemplation of their marriage, or
(b) a ceremony entered into by the parties in the presence of one or more other persons assembled for the purpose of witnessing the ceremony.'

2.23 The practical circumstances under which these provisions are likely to have to be considered are, therefore, either where an applicant entitled by some freehold, leasehold or contractual interest in a property is seeking an occupation order against a person to whom he was engaged, or where someone seeks a non-molestation order against someone to whom he was engaged; the latter is likely to be the more common. In either case, the court will have to be satisfied of the agreement to marry, and s 44 establishes that there are only three ways to do this.

2.24 First, the applicant may produce written evidence of the agreement; this does not mean a written agreement as such, but some written evidence of the fact that there was an agreement to marry. This could take the form of letters passing between the parties referring to their engagement, press announcements, wedding invitations or such other evidence as might satisfy the court; it would be for the court in each case to find as a fact that the written evidence put before it tended to prove the existence of the agreement, and this would have to be considered together with the oral evidence of the parties. The written evidence would be necessary but not, of itself, sufficient.

2.25 Secondly, where no such written evidence existed, the applicant could seek to prove that an engagement ring had changed hands, by way of gift. This would be a matter of evidence, no doubt oral in most cases. It would be helpful if the ring still existed. There might be room for argument as to whether a ring was an engagement ring, a mere gift, or a demonstration of affection and intent falling short of a commitment to marry.

2.26 Thirdly, the applicant could seek to prove that there had been a ceremony in the presence of others at which the agreement to marry had been made. This would be most likely to have happened where the parties belonged to one of the minority ethnic communities. The important element is that the agreement to marry itself is made at a formal ceremony; this would distinguish it from, say, an engagement party.

2.27 Where none of these three possibilities exists, the court may not entertain an application under s 33 or s 42. There could be an army of witnesses to prove an agreement to marry, but without proof in one of the three specified ways the court would be precluded from acting. What would happen if there was no such evidence but the respondent appeared before the court and admitted the engagement is unclear. At the very least, his verbal admission would be of no effect if he did not commit it to writing. If he did so, could it be argued that the court should not have allowed the matter to proceed so far in the absence of the pleading of one of the three specified grounds, and that the application should have been refused ad limine? This has not been adjudicated upon since the coming into force of the FLA 1996 and may be a matter for future debate.

Non-cohabiting couples

2.28 The class of associated persons was extended by s 4 of the DVCVA 2004 so that s 62(3) of the FLA 1996 reads as follows:

> 'For the purposes of this Part, a person is associated with another person if—
> (ea) they have or have had an intimate personal relationship with each other which is or was of significant duration.'

2.29 When explaining the possible meaning of this clause in debates on the Bill leading to the 2004 Act in Standing Committee[1], the Parliamentary Under-Secretary of State Mr Goggins said that it was the government's intention to close a significant loophole in the protection afforded by the FLA 1996 by including within it non-cohabiting couples. The Bill defined the meaning of this in the broadest terms and it would be for the court in individual circumstances to determine whether it applied. It was not the government's intention to include platonic friendships or brief sexual encounters such as one-night stands. Intimacy and duration were the key elements. For short or non-intimate relationships the Protection from Harassment Act 1997 (PHA 1997) was available.

1 Official Report (HC) Standing Committee 22 June 2004 cols 54 and 55.

2.30 It seems, therefore, that the intention of the legislation is to include the boyfriend and girlfriend who had not actually lived together. It is easy to see the problems of definition which might be encountered, and it has to be said that the court may be faced with significant difficulties in certain cases. While it may not have been the government's intention to include platonic relationships, the word 'intimate' has a variety of meanings and cannot be taken always to import a sexual connotation. Again, what is 'significant duration'? Would one month, or one week, suffice?

2.31 Mr Goggins' view was clearly that the judges would recognise a suitable candidate for this description when they saw one, and this may well be true in the majority of cases, but there is certainly room for argument in peripheral cases. When a similar provision under the Domestic Abuse Bill 2020 is considered (see **1.14**) it will be seen that a further complication may arise in that there is now no reference to 'duration'.

Family proceedings

2.32 'Family proceedings' are defined by s 63(2) as any proceedings under the inherent jurisdiction of the High Court in relation to children, and any under the following enactments:

(a) Part II of the FLA 1996;
(b) Part IV of the FLA 1996;
(c) the Matrimonial Causes Act 1973 (MCA 1973);
(d) the Adoption Act 1976;
(e) the Domestic Proceedings and Magistrates' Courts Act 1978;
(f) Part III of the Matrimonial and Family Proceedings Act 1984;
(g) Parts I, II, and IV of the Children Act 1989;
(h) section 30 of the Human Fertilisation and Embryology Act 1990.

2.33 'Family proceedings' also includes proceedings in which the court has made an emergency protection order under s 44 of the Children Act 1989 which includes an exclusion requirement as defined in s 44A(3) of that Act.

2.34 By s 62(2), 'relevant child' means:

'(a) any child who is living with or might reasonably be expected to live with either party to the proceedings;
(b) any child in relation to whom an order under the Adoption Act 1976 or the Children Act 1989 is in question in the proceedings; and
(c) any other child whose interests the court considers relevant.'

2.35 The Law Commission had concluded that it was unnecessary for the court to have to have regard to the interests of every child of every party; it was clearly desirable for the court to have a discretion to make orders in relation to as wide a range of children as possible, without necessarily being required to consider the position of children whose interests might be completely unaffected by the matters before the court; hence the somewhat broad definition[1].

1 Law Com, para 3.27.

Checklist

2.36 It may be helpful to set out in summary form the classes of persons with whom an applicant may be related. Such application may be made if the respondent is in one of the following categories:

(a) in relation to the applicant:
- spouse;
- former spouse;
- cohabitant;
- former cohabitant.

(b) in relation to the applicant or to any class of person in (a):
- father;
- mother;
- stepfather;
- stepmother;
- son;
- daughter;
- stepson;
- stepdaughter;
- grandmother;
- grandfather;
- grandson;
- granddaughter;
- brother;
- sister;
- half- or step-brother or sister;
- uncle;
- aunt;
- niece;
- nephew.

(c) in relation to any of the persons in (b):
- spouse;
- former spouse;
- cohabitant;
- former cohabitant.

(d) someone who lives, or has lived, in the same household (for detail see **1.12** onwards);

(e) someone whom the applicant has agreed to marry (for detail see **1.20** onwards); where agreement terminated, only within three years of termination;

(f) a person with whom the applicant has had an intimate personal relationship of significant duration;

(g) where the applicant is the parent of a child or has parental responsibility for a child, any other parent or person having parental responsibility;

(h) where a child has been adopted or freed for adoption:
  (i) a natural parent, or the parent of such a natural parent, is associated with
  (ii) the child, or
  - a parent of the child by virtue of an adoption order, or
  - a person who has applied for an adoption order, or
  - any person with whom the child has at any time been placed for adoption.

  anyone in class (i) may apply for an order against anyone in class (ii);

(i) the other party to any family proceedings.

Procedure under the Domestic Abuse Bill 2020

2.37 Under s 1(2)(a) of the Domestic Abuse Bill 2020 an applicant for protection and a perpetrator have both to be over 16 and 'personally connected' with each other. Section 2 defines 'personally connected' and is set in detail at **1.12.**

2.38 That deals with the question of who is eligible to make an application for protection under the Domestic Abuse Bill 2020. Under the existing law a further requirement is that the applicant is 'entitled'. This requirement does not exist under the new law since the Bill does not deal with issues of occupation of property (except in emergency situations).

THE EXISTING LAW: STEP TWO – IS THE VICTIM 'ENTITLED'?

2.39 The other preliminary classification, which relates to occupation orders made under FLA 1996 only, is whether or not the applicant is, in the terms of FLA 1996, 'entitled'. A person who is entitled makes her application for an occupation order under a different section of FLA 1996 from one who is not entitled; entitled applicants are then subdivided further according to whether or not they are or have been married. The reason for this complication is that Parliament was anxious not to confer on someone who had been in a casual relationship the same rights as a person who was or had been married, and it was thought necessary to take account of the various gradations of permanence of relationship.

2.40 The simple distinction between entitled and non-entitled applicants is that an entitled applicant is someone who has a legal right to occupy the property in question by reason of being the freehold owner, the tenant or a contractual licensee, or by reason of some statutory provision (this is rare). Section 33(1) of FLA 1996 therefore defines a 'person entitled' as one who:

(a) is entitled to occupy a dwelling house by virtue of a beneficial estate or interest or contract or by virtue of any enactment giving him the right to remain in occupation; or
(b) has matrimonial home rights in relation to a dwelling house.

2.41 A non-entitled person has no such legal right and is therefore in the position of asking the court to give her such a right. However, a person who would not otherwise be regarded as entitled may be so regarded because she has 'matrimonial home rights'. Such rights arise by virtue of a marriage and are lost on the grant of decree absolute unless an order is made before decree absolute to the effect that they survive[1].

1 FLA 1996, ss 31(8) and 33(5).

2.42 By FLA 1996, s 30(1), matrimonial home rights are conferred where:

> '(a) one spouse is entitled to occupy a dwelling-house by virtue of—
> (i) a beneficial estate or interest or contract; or
> (ii) any enactment giving that spouse the right to remain in occupation; and
> (b) the other spouse is not so entitled.'

2.43 These rights are conferred on the spouse 'not so entitled', and consist of the following:

> '(a) if in occupation, a right not to be evicted or excluded from the dwelling-house or any part of it by the other spouse except with the leave of the court given by an order under section 33;
> (b) if not in occupation, a right with the leave of the court so given to enter into and occupy the dwelling-house.'

2.44 Certain other consequential provisions are contained in the section, and these will be considered at more appropriate places in this book. For the moment, it is necessary only to mention s 30(7), which provides that the section does not apply to:

> 'a dwelling-house which has at no time been, and which was at no time intended by the spouses to be, a matrimonial home of the spouses in question.'

2.45 The words 'and which was at no time intended by the spouses to be' represent a change in the law effected by the FLA 1996. Under the Matrimonial Homes Act 1983 (MHA 1983), there was no power to regulate the occupation of a property which the parties intended to be their home, but in which they had never actually lived together. The Law Commission gave the example of a couple who had sold their existing house and were living in temporary rented accommodation while renovating a new house bought in the sole name of the husband. In such a case, the wife would have had no occupation rights over the new property if the relationship broke down in the meantime, since they had never lived in it together[1]. Section 30(7) of FLA 1996 corrects this gap in the law, so that matrimonial home rights may be acquired in respect of such a property.

1 Law Com, para 4.4.

2.46 The effect of matrimonial home rights is, therefore, that a spouse who occupies a dwelling-house which is, has been, or was intended to be the matrimonial home, and which is vested in the sole name of the other spouse, whether as beneficial owner or tenant, has a right of occupation and a right not to be evicted by the other spouse; where she is not in occupation, for example if the other spouse had evicted her, she is entitled to apply to the court for an order under s 33 of FLA 1996.

2.47 In summary therefore, if the victim is associated but not entitled she may apply under the FLA 1996 for a non-molestation order and for an occupation order; the exact kind of occupation order will depend on the section under which she is able to apply.

2.48 If the victim is not associated she can make no application under the FLA 1996. She may be able to apply for personal protection though not for any kind of occupation order. In practical terms, such protection is likely to be limited to that available under the PHA 1997.

Quick checklist

2.49 The following might be an instant checklist for use in conjunction with the information given above:

Non-molestation order

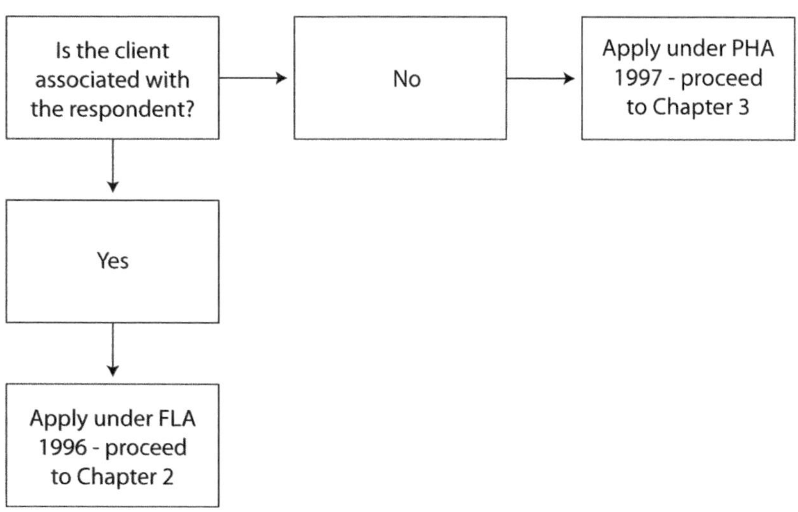

2.49 *Who may apply for protection from abuse?*

Occupation orders

Question 1: Preliminaries

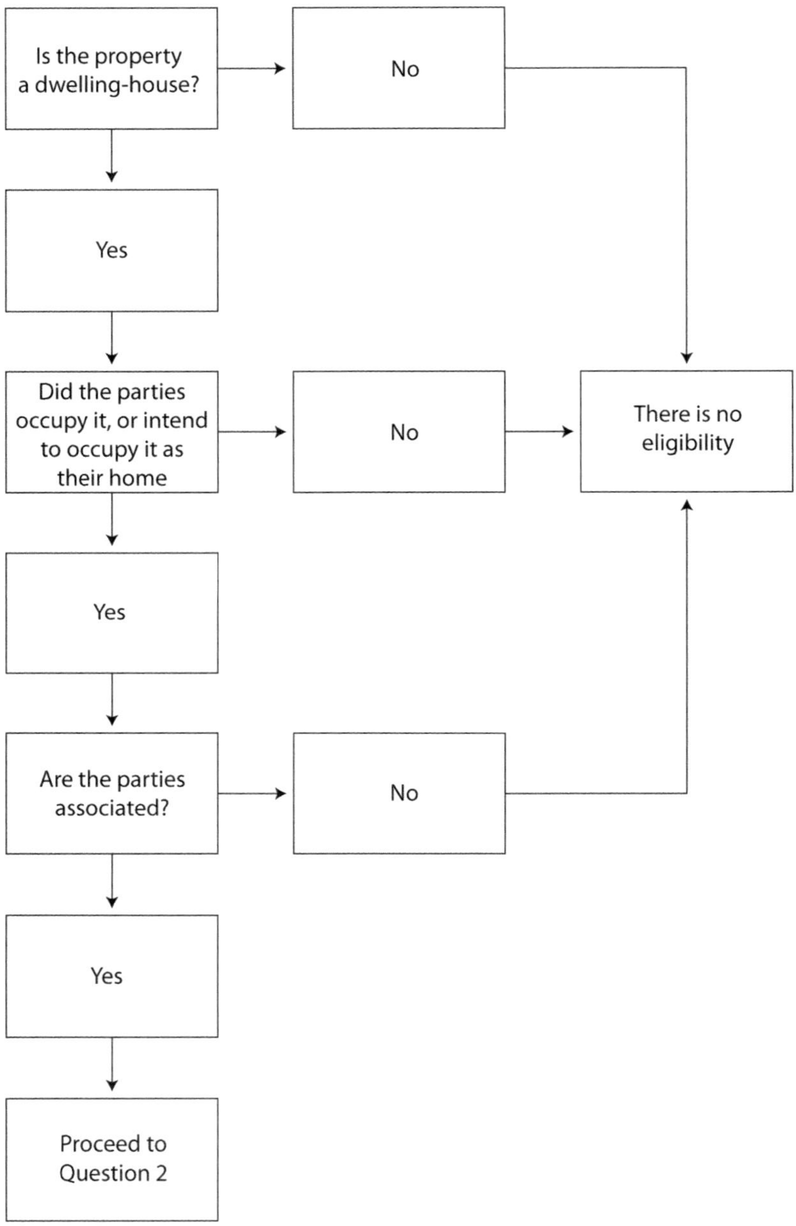

Question 2: Section 33 orders

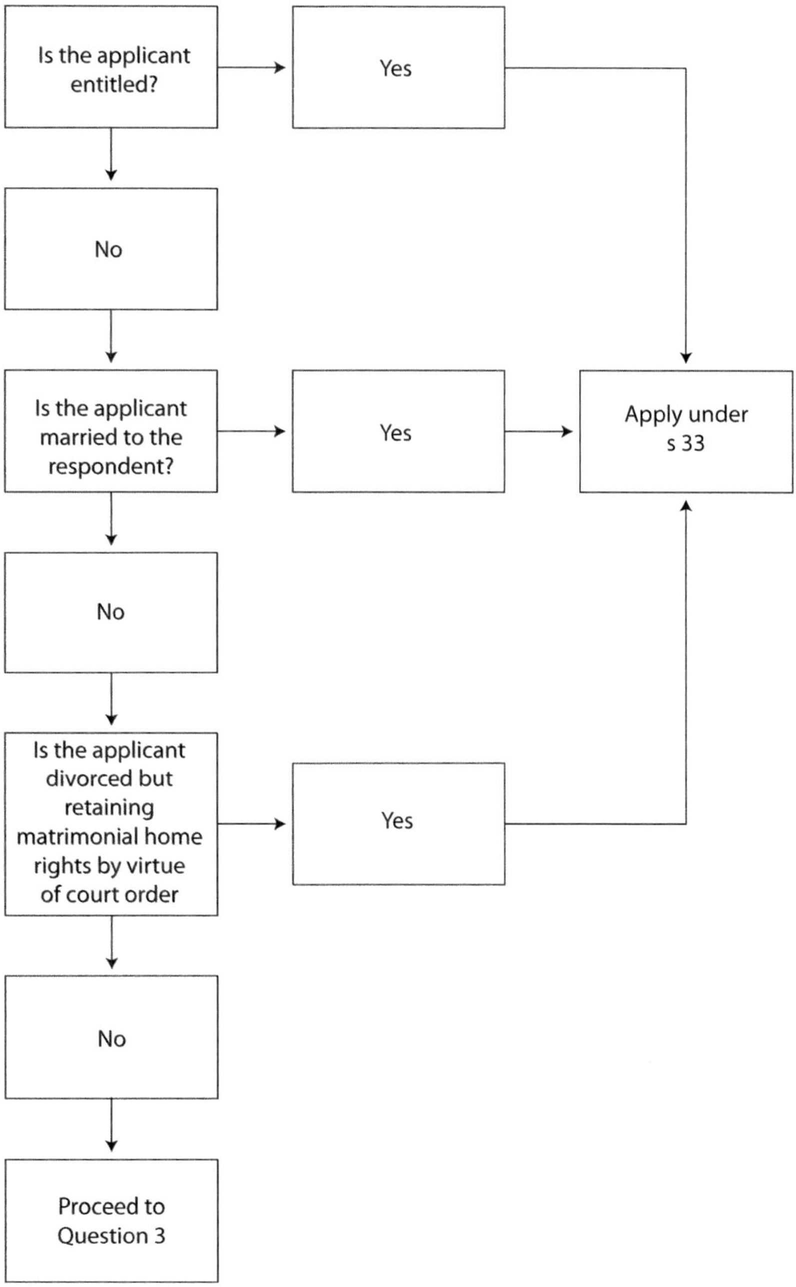

2.49 *Who may apply for protection from abuse?*

Question 3: Section 35 and 36 orders

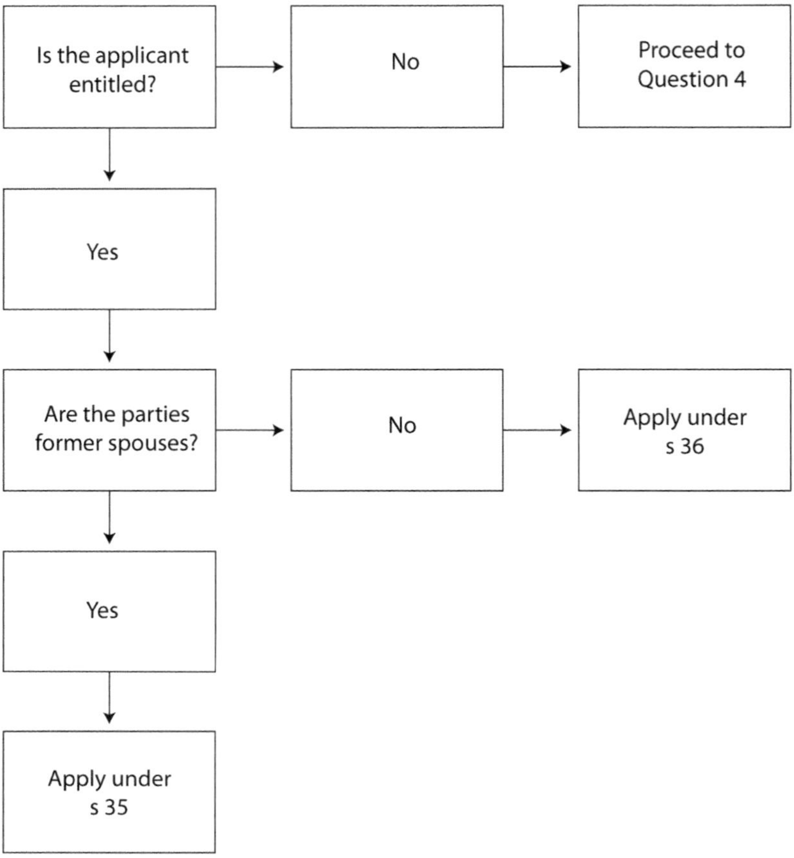

Question 4: Section 37 and 38 orders

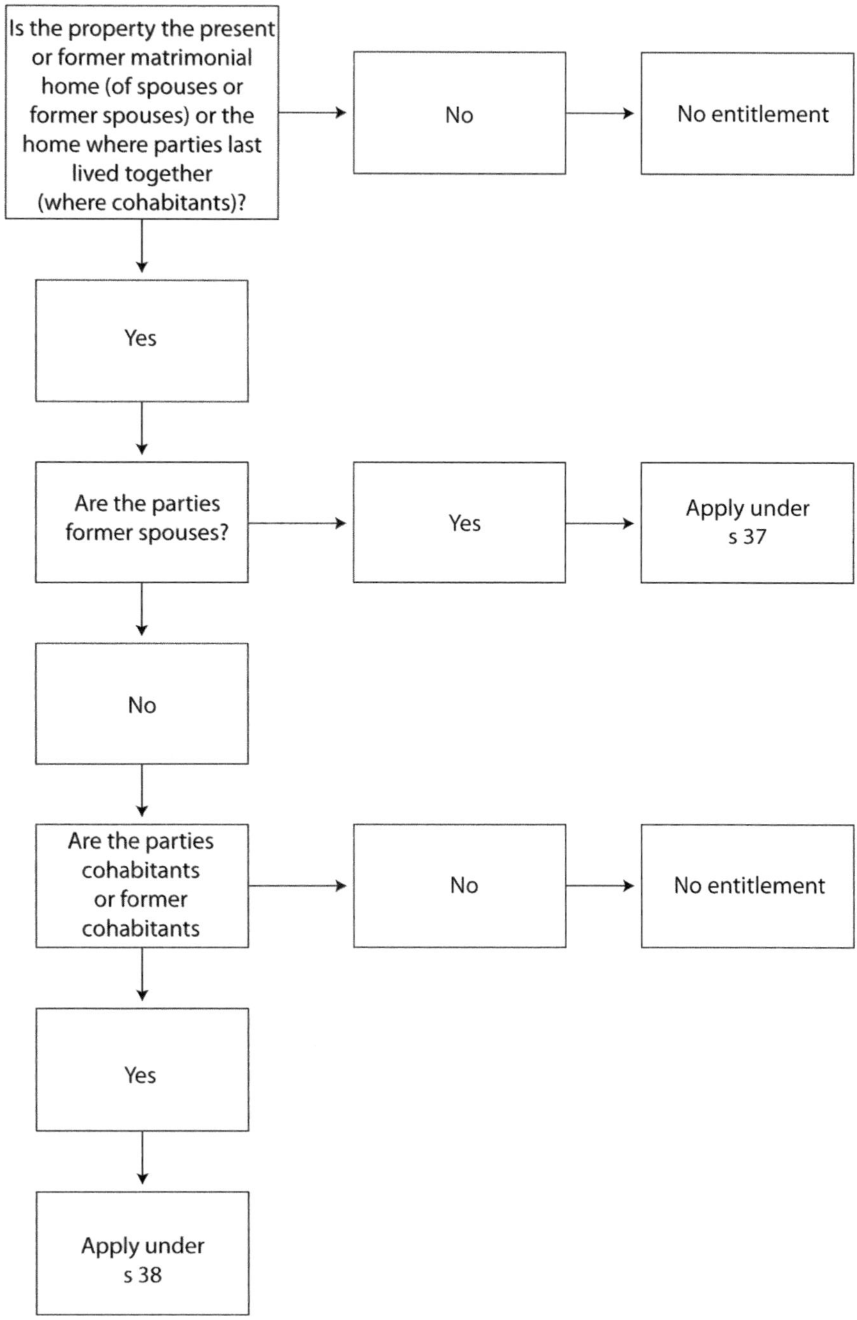

GENERAL NOTE AS TO PROCEDURE AND JURISDICTION

Applications under Part IV of FLA 1996 may be 'free-standing' or made within family proceedings

2.50 Most applications for personal protection or regulation of occupation of the family home under the FLA 1996 will be 'free-standing', but protection under the Act is also available on applications made within other family proceedings. In particular, sometimes an order under the powers in the FLA 1996 for protection of children is appropriate within proceedings under the Children Act 1989 (ChA 1989). The court may make a non-molestation order in other family proceedings whether or not a formal application has been made and, in appropriate cases, of its own motion[1].

1 FLA 1996, s 42(2).

Concurrent jurisdiction

2.51 FLA 1996, Pt IV, follows the approach of ChA 1989 in creating, with small exceptions, a structure of unified remedies and procedures available in the High Court, county courts and family proceedings courts. Parliament has chosen to achieve concurrent jurisdiction in different tiers of our historical court structure as the best way to create a flexible system of family law remedies in respect of personal protection and the welfare of children, dealt with at the appropriate level of court according to the importance and difficulties of each case.

Orders under the FLA 1996 and injunctions are granted to protect a legal right

2.52 This is not at the whim of the court or on 'palm-tree' justice. The general law is that an injunction can be granted only in support of a legal or equitable right. This was reaffirmed in the context of family law by the House of Lords in *Richards v Richards*[1].

1 [1984] AC 174, [1984] FLR 11 at 16H–17C, 17F, 23B, 29H, 32A and 35H.

Jurisdiction of the Family Court (previously county courts and family proceedings courts)

2.53 The County Court and the Family Court have jurisdiction given to them by statute. They have no inherent jurisdiction over any substantive matters beyond their statutory jurisdiction. They have inherent power to regulate their own proceedings[1], subject to statute and rules made by statutory instrument. Both tiers of courts have jurisdiction over rights and causes of action only where it is given to them expressly by statute, such as by the ChA 1989 and the FLA 1996 and, in the county court in relation to torts, by the County Courts Act 1984, s 15(1).

1 *Langley v North West Water Authority* [1991] 3 All ER 610.

2.54 As far as family proceedings courts are concerned, there is no inherent jurisdiction or provision within rules to enable magistrates to exercise any general form of supervisory control over their own final orders or over the parties' arrangements. They are left with orders for taking charge and delivering a child under FLA 1986, s 34 and enforcement penalties under the Magistrates' Courts Act 1980, s 63(3). Unlike a judge in the High Court or a county court, magistrates in a family proceedings court may not make a final order with 'liberty to restore' nor adjourn proceedings which have been concluded for review at a later date. Proceedings are pending only for such time as it takes for the court to make a final order. Upon the making of a final order, the original proceedings cease and the magistrates become functus officio. Any subsequent orders sought in the context of those proceedings, including an application for committal or for taking charge and delivery of a child, must be sought by a fresh application being lodged and new proceedings issued.

2.55 Family proceedings courts remain unable to decide contested matters of title to property and the Lord Chancellor has power to restrict the level of court to which an application may be made[1]. However, in general, whether an application is made in a family proceedings court, a county court or the High Court, the remedies and procedures are essentially the same. Thus, magistrates now have the same power to accept an undertaking in proceedings under Pt IV of FLA 1996 as the High Court and county courts[2], and magistrates are provided with penal enforcement procedures similar to the High Court and county courts, for example penal or warning notices[3], Notice to Show Good Reason[4], order or committal[5] and purging contempt[6].

1 FLA 1996, s 57(3).
2 FLA 1996, s 46(1).
3 Form FL404.
4 Form FL418.
5 Form FL419.
6 Form FL421.

2.56 Similarly, statutory provisions, designed to ensure that enforcement powers are the same for each tier of courts, include new powers for the High Court and county courts (and re-enactment of existing family proceedings courts' powers) to issue a warrant of arrest, where no power of arrest had been attached to the provision of the order alleged to have been breached[1], also to remand an alleged contemnor until a full hearing can be conducted[2] and to remand a contemnor who appears to be mentally unbalanced for the purpose of obtaining a medical report[3].

1 FLA 1996, s 47(8).
2 FLA 1996, s 47(7), (10), Sch 5, bail notice (Form FL412).
3 FLA 1996, s 48.

2.57 The 'parens patriae' inherent jurisdiction for the protection of minors and mentally incompetent adults is vested in the High Court alone.

2.58 *Who may apply for protection from abuse?*

Injunction powers of the High Court under the Senior Courts Act 1981 and of county courts under the County Courts Act 1984

2.58 The High Court has general powers, under s 37(1) of the Senior Courts Act 1981, to grant an injunction where it is 'just and convenient to do so'. These general powers are also available in a county court, under the County Courts Act 1984, s 38(1), provided that the county court has jurisdiction over the rights and obligations in support of which an injunction may be just and convenient. Where such rights and obligations are not within the jurisdiction conferred on county courts, a county court cannot assume or draw down the inherent jurisdiction of the High Court.

Injunctions for protection under the PHA 1997 and under the general law of torts

2.59 There remain some situations where a person seeks a remedy against harassment by someone who is not within the scope of the FLA 1996, for example a former lover who has not lived with the applicant and they have not produced any children. Such victims of harassment may be able to obtain a remedy under the PHA 1997 or under the general law of torts.

2.60 Because the county court has jurisdiction in cases founded in torts, it can grant an injunction to prevent a threatened tort or repetition of a tortious harm.

Chapter 3

PERSONAL PROTECTION UNDER THE EXISTING LAW

3.1 The existing law, based on the FLA 1996, bases its code for personal protection on the prohibition of molestation, and establishes a system of application for non-molestation orders. The wrong which the law was designed to prevent was commonly known as 'domestic violence'. Since a Practice Direction of 2011 (see **3.8** below) the term 'domestic abuse' has been preferred. However, the orders which the court could make have continued to be called non-molestation orders.

3.2 The Domestic Abuse Bill 2020 provides for the first time a statutory definition of 'abuse' and provides a new set of remedies which, in many ways, are not significantly different from the effect of the existing orders. Nevertheless there are significant improvements. Given the fact that the new law will, for some time at least, exist side by side with the existing law, the two systems must both be considered and any differences highlighted. The existing law will therefore be set out in full.

3.3 The difference between 'domestic violence' and 'molestation' under the existing law and 'domestic abuse' under the Domestic Abuse Bill 2020 will be explained here, but the new provision for personal protection under the Bill will be explained in more detail in CHAPTER 4 and CHAPTER 5.

THE LAW REGARDING NON-MOLESTATION ORDERS UNDER THE FAMILY LAW ACT 1996

What is 'molestation'?

3.4 The FLA 1996 does not define 'molestation'. In *C v C (Non-molestation Order: Jurisdiction)*[1], Sir Stephen Brown P held that molestation:

> 'implies some quite deliberate conduct which is aimed at a high degree of harassment of the other party, so as to justify the intervention of the court . . . It does not include enforcing an invasion of privacy per se; there has to be some conduct which clearly harasses and affects the applicant to such a degree that the intervention of the court is called for.'

This is consistent with the case law in force before the FLA 1996, which established that 'molestation' means deliberate conduct which interferes with the victim, whether by violence, intimidation, harassment, pestering or interference that is sufficiently serious to warrant the intervention of the court[2].

[1] [1998] 1 FLR 554.
[2] See *Davis v Johnson* [1979] AC 264 at 334A; *Vaughan v Vaughan* [1973] 3 All ER 449 at 452E; *Horner v Horner* (1983) 4 FLR 50 at 51G.

3.5 The Family Proceedings Rules Committee decided to adopt as part of Prescribed Form FL404 language similar to precedents in common use which avoided using the word 'molestation'. However, under s 47(2) of FLA 1996, there is a presumption in favour of a power of arrest where there has been actual or threatened violence, which is why threats of violence have been included in orders 38 and 40, rather than in orders 39 and 41, in Form FL404. A power of arrest may no longer be attached to a non-molestation order (see **3.20–3.23** below).

3.6 The words of the non-molestation menu of orders 38–41 in Prescribed Form FL404 give the convenient definition of 'molestation'.

> '38. The respondent [name] is forbidden to use or threaten violence against the applicant [name] [and must not instruct, encourage or in any way suggest that any other person should do so]. AND/OR
>
> 39. The respondent [name] is forbidden to intimidate, harass or pester [or [specify]] the applicant [name] [and must not instruct, encourage or in any way suggest that any other person should do so]. AND/OR
>
> 40. The respondent [name] is forbidden to use or threaten violence against the relevant child(ren) [name(s) and date(s) of birth] [and must not instruct, encourage or in any way suggest that any other person should do so]. AND/OR
>
> 41. The respondent [name] is forbidden to intimidate, harass or pester [or [specify]] [the relevant child(ren) [name(s) and date(s) of birth]] [and must not instruct, encourage or in any way suggest that any other person should do so].'

3.7 Note that psychological harm can amount to actual bodily harm[1], and silent phone calls can amount to an assault under s 47 of the Offences Against the Person Act 1861[2].

[1] *Kendrick v Kendrick* [1990] 2 FLR 107.
[2] *R v Ireland; R v Burstow* [1998] 1 FLR 105, HL.

3.8 The terms 'molestation', 'domestic violence' and 'harassment' are sometimes regarded as interchangeable but of course attitudes and definitions do change and develop. In his *Practice Direction: Residence and Contact Orders: Domestic Violence and Harm* the President of the Family Division directed that:

> '"domestic violence" includes physical violence, threatening or intimidating behaviour and any other form of abuse which, directly or indirectly, may have caused harm to the other party or to the child or which may give rise to the risk of harm.'

These matters were conclusively defined by the Practice Direction FPR PD12J (as to which see **Chapter 12**). Here it is provided that:

> '"domestic abuse" includes any incident or pattern of incidents of controlling, coercive or threatening behaviour, violence or abuse between those aged 16 or over who are or have been intimate partners or family members regardless of gender or

sexuality. This can encompass, but is not limited to, psychological, physical, sexual, financial, or emotional abuse. Domestic abuse also includes culturally specific forms of abuse including, but not limited to, forced marriage, honour-based violence, dowry-related abuse and transnational marriage abandonment;

"abandonment" refers to the practice whereby a husband, in England and Wales, deliberately abandons or "strands" his foreign national wife abroad, usually without financial resources, in order to prevent her from asserting matrimonial and/or residence rights in England and Wales. It may involve children who are either abandoned with, or separated from, their mother;

"coercive behaviour" means an act or a pattern of acts of assault, threats, humiliation and intimidation or other abuse that is used to harm, punish, or frighten the victim;

"controlling behaviour" means an act or pattern of acts designed to make a person subordinate and/or dependent by isolating them from sources of support, exploiting their resources and capacities for personal gain, depriving them of the means needed for independence, resistance and escape and regulating their everyday behaviour;

"development" means physical, intellectual, emotional, social or behavioural development;

"harm" means ill-treatment or the impairment of health or development including, for example, impairment suffered from seeing or hearing the ill-treatment of another, by domestic abuse or otherwise;

"health" means physical or mental health;

"ill-treatment" includes sexual abuse and forms of ill-treatment which are not physical.'

Abuse defined by the Domestic Abuse Bill 2020

3.9 As has been explained above, there has previously been no statutory definition of domestic abuse, or domestic violence as it used to be called. There have been various attempts, by judges and others, to provide a satisfactory definition but there has never been one form of words designed to be all-embracing. The Domestic Abuse Bill 2020 clearly wished to put this beyond any doubt and the new statutory definition will be found in **Chapter 1** at **1.10**.

Who may apply for non-molestation orders?

3.10 The FLA 1996 extended substantially the class of persons eligible to apply for non-molestation orders. The Act was designed as a family law statute and to protect persons with a family connection. Any person, including a child if he obtains leave of the High Court can apply for a non-molestation order[1]. 'Associated persons' are defined in s 62(3) and the concept of family connection is not restricted to a nuclear family or to relatives. More details are given in **Chapter 2** at **2.5**.

[1] FLA 1996, s 42(1).

Is the applicant eligible (being associated with the proposed respondent) for a non-molestation order?

3.11 The class of associated persons is considerably wider than the class eligible under the previous law, which was for practical purposes restricted to married persons and cohabitants of different sex[1]. Under the previous law, after decree absolute of divorce, the family law remedies in relation to occupation of the family home ceased unless an order had been made extending a right to occupy the matrimonial home, and all the family law remedies between cohabitants ceased when cohabitation ended or after a limited period of about three months thereafter.

1 See **2.5**.

3.12 In *G v G (Non-molestation Order: Jurisdiction)*[1], Wall J urged courts to adopt a purposive construction of Pt IV of FLA 1996. In that case, justices had found that the applicant and respondent were not associated because they had never lived in the same household, they were not cohabitants and there was insufficient evidence of agreement to marry. Wall J said that jurisdiction should not be declined unless the facts of the case were clearly not capable of being brought within the statute. In the instant case, three of the six 'signposts' set out by Woolf J in *Crake v Supplementary Benefits Commission*[2] (membership of the same household, stability, financial support, sexual relationship, children and public acknowledgement) were present.

1 [2000] 2 FLR 533.
2 [1982] 1 All ER 498.

Exclusion orders in respect of a defined area around a home or place of work

3.13 An occupation order (or, arguably, a non-molestation order) can include provision to 'exclude the respondent from a defined area in which the dwelling-house (the subject of the occupation order) is included'[1].

1 FLA 1996, ss 33(3)(g), 35(5)(d), 36(5)(d), 37(3)(d), 38(3)(d).

3.14 In *Burris v Azadani*[1], it was held that where a personal protection injunction is granted against torts, in order to make it effective the order can be supplemented by an order that the defendant shall not be within a defined area around the home of the plaintiff. This power should also enable the High Court or a county court to add to a non-molestation injunction an order excluding the respondent from a defined area around the home or place of work of the applicant, even if an occupation order is not available. There seems to be no reason in principle why a non-molestation order granted under Pt IV of FLA 1996 should not include an order to exclude the respondent from a defined area around the applicant's place of work if such order is necessary to prevent molestation.

1 [1996] 1 FLR 266.

3.15 Care should be taken when drafting orders excluding a respondent from a defined area around a home. The distance should never be such as might lead to unintentional breach by the respondent. In any event, the distance must not exceed that which is necessary for the protection of the applicant. When the respondent has contact with a child residing in the house, consideration must be given to how this would be affected by a restriction as to radius.

Own motion non-molestation orders

3.16 Section 42(2)(b) of FLA 1996 enables the court when dealing with other family proceedings to make a non-molestation order in favour of one party, or a relevant child, against another party even though no application for such an order has been made.

Duration of non-molestation orders

3.17 Section 42(7) of FLA 1996 provides:

> 'A non-molestation order may be made for a specified period or until further order.'

3.18 The courts are likely to make initial orders of up to six months, following the practice before the FLA 1996[1]. A longer order may be appropriate where the respondent persists in molesting the applicant after the initial injunctive order. In *M v W (Non-Molestation Order: Duration)*[2], Cazalet J held that justices had erred in making an open-ended non-molestation order. Unless there are exceptional circumstances, such an order should be for a fixed period; in the instant case, 18 months was reasonable. However, this decision was expressly disapproved by the Court of Appeal in *Re B-J (Power of Arrest)*[3], where it was held that it was not helpful to seek to limit the making of indefinite non-molestation orders to circumstances which were exceptional or unusual; there were a great variety of cases where non-molestation orders might be required, and the statute clearly provided for indefinite orders if appropriate in the circumstances.

1 See *Practice Note* [1978] 2 All ER 1056, [1978] 1 WLR 1123; *Practice Direction* [1981] 1 All ER 224, [1981] 1 WLR 27.
2 [2000] 1 FLR 107.
3 [2000] 2 FLR 443.

3.19 An (interim) without notice order need not last only until the precise time of the return day. Indeed, to avoid problems of service, it would be wise for the order to last at least several hours after the time listed for the hearing on the return day. The procedures concerning without notice orders are considered in detail in Chapter 8.

POWER OF ARREST UNDER THE FAMILY LAW ACT 1996

3.20 Section 47(2) of FLA 1996 provided that a power of arrest must be attached to one or more provisions of a non-molestation order if it appeared to the court that the respondent had used or threatened violence against the applicant or a relevant child, unless the court was satisfied that in all the circumstances of the case the applicant or child would be adequately protected without such a power of arrest. This provision enabled a constable to arrest without warrant a person whom he reasonably suspected had disobeyed the non-molestation order, and was regarded as a most important weapon for the protection of victims of domestic violence.

3.21 However, this changed in July 2007 with the bringing into effect of DVCVA 2004, Sch 10, para 38 which amends FLA 1996, s 47 so that as from that date the power to attach a power of arrest to a non-molestation order is removed, while allowing it to remain for occupation orders.

3.22 The reason for this is that breach of a non-molestation order has become a criminal arrestable offence (see **10.14** below) and it was thought that it would be unduly confusing for police officers to have to decide whether a person arrested by them should be dealt with under the previous procedure of bringing before the Family Court within 24 hours, or as a criminal defendant to be dealt with in the magistrates' court[1].

1 For an interesting analysis of the results of this change see '*The Domestic Violence, Crime and Victims Act 2004 Part 1 – Is it working?*' by His Honour Judge John Platt [2008] Fam Law (Jul).

3.23 The result is that the Family Court may no longer be able to attach a power of arrest to a non-molestation order. Methods of enforcement will be considered below, and the position relating to occupation orders is considered at **8.48** et seq.

PROCEDURE REGARDING NON-MOLESTATION ORDERS UNDER THE FAMILY LAW ACT 1996

3.24 Having established that the client is eligible under FLA 1996 and determined the kind of order to be sought, how does the practitioner go about obtaining such an order? The following quick procedural guide will explain, though it should be noted that there is a detailed chapter on procedure at CHAPTER **8**.

Which court?	The Family Court (Any county court or FPC) (see **2.53**ff).
Documents to be filed at court.	Form FL401
	Written statement (FPC) or affidavit (county court).
	Draft order
Fees.	None in FPC. £ in county court.
Without notice hearing (where appropriate).	Applicant attends court with solicitor. NB statement must state why the application is being made without notice.

	Court will either make order, abridge time for service or decline to make order.
	The without notice order must provide for an on notice hearing.
Service.	The documents listed above, plus any without notice order, must be served personally on respondent allowing two clear days' notice (unless time for service has been abridged).
	A statement of service in Form FL415 must be filed at court.
	Where a power of arrest has been attached to a without notice order the applicant must file notice in Form FL406 at the applicant's local police station forthwith after service.
On notice hearing.	Applicant, witnesses and solicitor or counsel attend court.
	Court either makes order, accepts undertaking, or dismisses application. (See **8.55** et seq as to undertakings.)
	Where undertaking accepted, respondent should be served with a sealed copy of the undertaking before leaving court.
Service.	As before, except where undertaking accepted and served at court.

Chapter 4

DOMESTIC ABUSE PROTECTION NOTICES

4.1 Sections 24–31 of the Crime and Security Act 2010 (CASA 2010) provided for the Domestic Violence Protection Notice (DVPN) and Domestic Violence Protection Orders (DVPN) which, after a piloting period, have been in use nationally since March 2014. Section 52 of the Domestic Abuse Bill 2020 repeals these provisions and presumably this will have effect from an early date after the Bill receives Royal Assent. The DAPN is replaced by the Domestic Abuse Protection Notice (DAPN) and the Domestic Abuse Protection Order (DAPN) created by Pt 3 of the Act. The DAPO will be considered in detail in CHAPTER 5.

4.2 The DAPN is initiated and effected by the police, so is not the direct responsibility of legal practitioners; moreover, as will be seen in CHAPTER 5, any order arising out of the giving of a notice may be of limited duration. However, the DAPN is clearly designed to be an emergency remedy to protect a victim and to allow her, perhaps in consultation with solicitors, to consider the options open to her. The service of the notice is therefore the first step in a process which will lead to a hearing in a magistrates' court.

4.3 Section 20(1) of the Domestic Abuse Bill 2020 provides that 'a senior police officer may give a [DAPN] to a person ('P') if conditions A and B are met'. The DAPN is 'a notice prohibiting P from being abusive towards a person aged 16 or over to whom P is personally connected'[1]. 'P' is defined[2] as the person to whom the notice is given, which may seem somewhat circular but the intention is clear. 'Personally connected' is defined in s 2 (see CHAPTER 1).

1 Domestic Abuse Bill, s 20(2).
2 Domestic Abuse Bill, s 21(1).

CONDITIONS FOR GIVING A DAPN

4.4 The DAPN may not be given unless two conditions are met. These are:

(a) Condition A – 'that the senior police officer has reasonable grounds for believing that P has been abusive towards a person aged 16 or over to whom P is personally connected'[1], and
(b) Condition B – 'that the senior police officer has reasonable grounds for believing that it is necessary to give the notice to protect that person from domestic abuse, or the risk of domestic abuse, carried out by P'[2].

> "Senior police officer" means a member of a relevant police force (which includes British Transport and Ministry of Defence police) who is a constable of at least the rank of inspector'[3].

1 Domestic Abuse Bill, s 20(3).
2 Domestic Abuse Bill, s 20(4).
3 Domestic Abuse Bill, s 20(8). Under the CASA 2010 the senior officer had to be at least a Superintendent.

4.5 A DAPN may not be given to a person who is under the age of 18[1]. The abuse or suspected abuse need not have occurred within the United Kingdom[2] and the notice has effect in all parts of the United Kingdom[3].

1 Domestic Abuse Bill, s 20(6).
2 Domestic Abuse Bill, s 20(5).
3 Domestic Abuse Bill, s 20(7).

CONTENTS OF DAPN

4.6 Section 21 deals with some of the provisions which may be contained in the notice. The notice may provide that P 'may not contact the person for whose protection the notice is given'[1], and may not come within a specified distance of any premises in England or Wales in which that person lives[2]. 'Specified' means in effect such distance as the notice may specify. Where P and the person for whose benefit the notice is given live in the same premises the notice may also contain provision:

(a) prohibiting P from evicting or excluding that person from the premises;
(b) prohibiting P from entering the premises;
(c) requiring P to leave the premises[3].

1 Domestic Abuse Bill, s 21(1)(a).
2 Domestic Abuse Bill, s 21(1)(b).
3 Domestic Abuse Bill, s 21(2).

4.7 The provisions which may be contained in the notice will therefore be similar to the kind of orders which have been routinely made by courts under Pt IV FLA and virtually the same as those contained in the previous Domestic Violence Protection Notices.

4.8 Section 23 provides further requirements. The notice must be in writing[1] and must give the grounds upon which it has been given[2]. It must also state:

(a) that a constable may arrest P without warrant if the constable has reasonable grounds for believing that P is in breach of the notice,
(b) that an application for a domestic abuse protection order under s 25 will be heard by a magistrates' court within 48 hours of the time of giving the notice (disregarding any days mentioned in s 26(3)) and a notice of the hearing will be given to P,
(c) that the notice continues in effect until that application has been determined or withdrawn, and
(d) the provision that a magistrates' court may include in a domestic abuse protection order[3].

1 Domestic Abuse Bill, s 23(1).
2 Domestic Abuse Bill, s 23(2).

3 Domestic Abuse Bill, s 23(2)(b)–(e).

MATTERS TO BE CONSIDERED BEFORE GIVING THE NOTICE

4.9 Section 22(1) provides that before giving a DAPN the senior police officer must, among other things, consider the following matters:

(a) the welfare of any person under the age of 18 whose interests the officer considers relevant to the giving of the notice (whether or not that person and P are personally connected);
(b) the opinion of the person for whose protection the notice would be given as to the giving of the notice;
(c) any representations made by P about the giving of the notice;
(d) in a case where the notice includes provision relating to premises lived in by the person for whose protection the notice would be given, the opinion of any relevant occupant as to the giving of the notice.

> '"relevant occupant" means a person other than P or the person for whose protection the notice would be give who lives in the premises, and who is personally connected to the person for whose protection the notice would be given. Further, if P also lives in the premises, the opinion of P must also be sought.[1]'

1 Domestic Abuse Bill, s 22(2).

4.10 In other words, before deciding to give the notice the senior officer must consider the views of the alleged abused person, the views of the P and the views of anyone personally connected to the abused person who lives in the property. He must also consider the welfare of any person under 18 who may be affected by the giving of the notice. It is further provided that the senior officer must take reasonable steps to discover these opinions[1]. However, significantly, it is also provided that it is not necessary for the person for whose protection a notice is given to consent to the giving of the notice[2]. Victims of domestic abuse are frequently ambivalent or indecisive about action being taken on their behalf, for a variety of reasons which may include pressure from the abuser, and this makes clear that the senior police officer may use his own judgement as to whether protection is necessary.

1 Domestic Abuse Bill, s 22(3).
2 Domestic Abuse Bill, s 22(4).

SERVICE OF NOTICE

4.11 Section 23(3) provides that the notice must be served on P personally by a constable. It is further provided[1] that, on serving the notice on P, the constable must ask P for an address at which P may be given the notice of the hearing of the application for the domestic abuse protection order. There are further provisions about service on a member of the armed forces, where the notice includes provision prohibiting P from entering premises, or requiring P to leave premises, and the officer believes that the premises are relevant[2] service accommodation. In such cases the officer must make reasonable efforts to inform P's commanding officer of the giving of the notice[3].

1 Domestic Abuse Bill, s 23(4).

2 'Relevant service accommodation' means premises which fall within para (a) of the definition of 'service living accommodation' in s 96(1) of the Armed Forces Act 2006.
3 Domestic Abuse Bill, s 23(5)–(7).

BREACH OF NOTICE

4.12 As has been seen, the next stage of the procedure is that, once a DAPN has been given, the matter must be listed for hearing by a magistrates' court when the court will consider whether or not to make a Domestic Abuse Protection Order; this is considered in more detail in CHAPTER 5. However, it is always possible that in the intervening period P may breach the terms of the notice and s 24 contains provisions to deal with this.

4.13 Where a constable has reasonable grounds for believing that a person is in breach of a domestic abuse protection notice, he may arrest the person without warrant[1]. A person so arrested must be held in custody and brought before the appropriate magistrates' court before the end of the period of 24 hours beginning with the time of the arrest, or, if earlier, at the hearing of the application for a domestic abuse protection order against the person[2].

1 Domestic Abuse Bill, s 24(1).
2 Domestic Abuse Bill, s 24(2).

4.14 When the person is brought before the court the court may remand that person[1]. When remanding a person on bail, the court may require that person to comply, before release on bail or later, with any requirements that appear to the court to be necessary to secure that the person does not interfere with witnesses or otherwise obstruct the course of justice[2].

1 Domestic Abuse Bill, s 27(8).
2 Domestic Abuse Bill, s 24(7).

Chapter 5

PERSONAL PROTECTION UNDER THE DOMESTIC ABUSE BILL 2020

DOMESTIC ABUSE PROTECTION ORDERS

5.1 Section 26 of the Domestic Abuse Bill 2020 provides the power for the court to make a Domestic Abuse Protection Order (DAPO)[1]. This order duplicates and one presumes will eventually replace the orders which could be made under Pt IV FLA 1996, notably non-molestation orders and occupation orders. In one sense, therefore, the Act will bring about a complete transformation of the role of the court (though it seems that the existing system will continue to exist for a time at least).

1 Domestic Abuse Bill, s 26(1).

Definition of DAPO

5.2 Section 25(1) defines a DAPO as:

> 'an order which, for the purpose of preventing a person ("P") from being abusive towards a person aged 16 or over to whom P is personally connected—
> (a) prohibits P from doing things described in the order, or
> (b) requires P to do things described in the order.'

5.3 This chapter will consider how applications for a DAPO are made, and matters which the court must consider when making an order.

Two principal routes for applications

5.4 In effect, there are two methods of application for a DAPO, depending on who is making the application. The first route is an application by the police[1], which must be heard in the magistrates' court[2]. The second is an application by the person for whose benefit the order is sought, and this must be heard in the Family Court[3]. These two routes to an order will be considered separately.

1 Domestic Abuse Bill, s 26(2)(b).
2 Domestic Abuse Bill, s 26(6).
3 Domestic Abuse Bill, s 26(5).

5.5 However, for the sake of completeness, two other situations in which a DAPO can be made should be mentioned here. First, s 26 provides that applications may be made by 'a person specified in regulations made by the

Secretary of State'[1] and 'any other person with the leave of the court to which the application is to be made'[2]. It is expected that the applicants envisaged by this provision will be, for example, Women's Aid organisations or refuges. However, regulations for this class of applicant have not yet been made. Secondly, a DAPO may be made in the course of certain other proceedings without a formal application having been made. This class of cases will be considered below at **5.12**.

1 Domestic Abuse Bill, s 26(2)(c).
2 Domestic Abuse Bill, s 26(2)(d).

5.6 The principles on which an order may be made and the contents of such an order are common to all hearings where a DAPO is being considered and will be considered in detail at **5.17** *et seq*. First, the routes which may be taken to arrive at such a situation will be considered.

Applications by the police

5.7 Applications by the police may come about in two ways. First, where a DAPN has been given by a member of a relevant police force 'the chief officer of police in relation to that force must apply for a domestic abuse protection order against P'[1]. (The definition of appropriate chief officer of police will be found in s 26(4) and is fairly obvious.) It will be remembered[2] that s 23(2)(c) provides that the DAPN must state that:

> 'an application for a domestic abuse protection order under section 26 will be heard by a magistrates' court within 48 hours of the time of giving the notice (disregarding any days mentioned in section 27(3)) and a notice of the hearing will be given to P'.

This set of circumstances is therefore an emergency remedy and will result in a hearing at short notice. However, the Chief Officer of Police is under an obligation to apply for the order once a DAPN is given.

1 Domestic Abuse Bill, s 26(3).
2 See Chapter 4 at 4.8.

5.8 It may happen that P will breach the DAPN and will be arrested in consequence of the breach. Breaches of the DAPN are dealt with in Chapter 4 at **4.12–4.14**. Here it should merely be noted that when an arrested person is brought before the court and the hearing is adjourned he may be remanded[1]. Remand in such circumstance is considered in detail at **4.14** above.

1 Domestic Abuse Bill, s 27(8).

5.9 P must have been given notice of the hearing[1]. It is sufficient for the notice to have been left at the address which he gave when served with the notice[2]. Where he gave no address the court may nevertheless proceed to hear the application if the court is satisfied that the chief officer of police has made reasonable efforts to give him the notice[3].

1 Domestic Abuse Bill, s 27(4).
2 Domestic Abuse Bill, s 27(5).
3 Domestic Abuse Bill, s 27(6).

5.10 Where no DAPN has been given, a chief officer of police may make an application for an order[1]. Any such application must made by complaint to a magistrates' court[2].

1 Domestic Abuse Bill, s 26(2)(b).
2 Domestic Abuse Bill, s 26(6).

Application by 'victim'

5.11 Any application by the person in need of protection[1] must be made to the Family Court[2]. The method of and procedure for such an application will be prescribed by regulation.

1 Domestic Abuse Bill, s 26(2)(a) describes this class of applicant as 'person for whose benefit the order is sought' but 'victim' seems a more user-friendly description.
2 Domestic Abuse Bill, s 26(5).

Orders made otherwise than on application

5.12 Section 29 provides as follows:

> '(1) A court may make a domestic abuse protection order under this section in any of the cases set out below.
>
> **Family proceedings**
>
> (2) The High Court or the family court may make a domestic abuse protection order against a person ("P") in any family proceedings to which both P and the person for whose protection the order would be made are parties.
>
> **Criminal proceedings**
>
> (3) Where a person ("P") has been convicted of an offence, the court dealing with P for that offence may (as well as sentencing P or dealing with P in any other way) make a domestic abuse protection order against P.
>
> (4) But subsection (3) does not apply where the Court of Appeal is dealing with a person for an offence.
>
> (5) A court by or before which a person is acquitted of an offence may make a domestic abuse protection order against the person.
>
> (6) Where the Crown Court allows a person's appeal against a conviction for an offence, the Crown Court may make a domestic abuse protection order against the person.
>
> **Civil proceedings**
>
> (7) The county court may make a domestic abuse protection order against a person ("P") in any relevant proceedings to which both P and the person for whose protection the order would be made are parties.
>
> (8) In subsection (7) "relevant proceedings" means proceedings of a description specified in regulations made by the Secretary of State.'

Conditions for making an order

5.13 Having considered the methods by which a court may be in a position to make a DAPO, we must now consider the conditions for making such an order, or, to put it another way, what has to be established to justify the court in making such an order.

5.14 By s 30(1) two conditions, A and B, must be met.

Condition A is that the court is satisfied on the balance of probabilities that P has been abusive towards a person aged 16 or over to whom P is personally connected[1].

Condition B is that the order is necessary and proportionate to protect that person from domestic abuse, or the risk of domestic abuse, carried out by P[2].

1 Domestic Abuse Bill, s 30(2).
2 Domestic Abuse Bill, s 30(3).

5.15 It will be seen that the standard of proof and the conditions for making an order are the same whether the application is made by the police by complaint in a magistrates' court or by application in the Family Court. It might also be thought that the definition of the conditions for making an order is clearer and less convoluted than the conditions set out in Pt IV FLA 1996 for making equivalent orders.

5.16 By s 30(4) it does not matter whether the abusive behaviour took place in England and Wales or elsewhere, or whether it took place before or after the coming into force of this section. A DAPO may not be made against a person aged under 18[1].

1 Domestic Abuse Bill, s 30(5).

Matters to be considered by the court

5.17 Section 31 sets out the matters which the court must consider before making a DAPO. The court must, among other things, consider:

(a) The welfare of any person under the age of 18 whose interests the court considers relevant to the making of the order (whether or not that person and P are personally connected)[1].
This provision clearly envisages a child of either the victim or P who may or may not be residing in the same premises as either of them. The court must only have regard to such a child or young person if it considers his or her interests relevant to the making of the order:

(b) Any opinion of the person for whose protection the order would be made which relates to the making of the order, and of which the court is made aware[2].
Where the victim is the applicant this would seem to be self-evident. The application will then have been based on the opinion of the victim and, if those opinions were not being taken into account presumably the application could have been withdrawn.

1 Domestic Abuse Bill, s 31(1)(a).
2 Domestic Abuse Bill, s 31(1)(b).

5.18 The provision has more significance, however, where the application is made by the police. It is not unknown for victims of domestic abuse to vacillate in their pursuit of an order; this may occur because of pressure from P or others on his behalf or simply from lack of self-confidence. The significance of this provision is that, while the court must have regard to any possible lack of enthusiasm on the part of the victim it is not bound by the victim's opinion and it may make an order if it seems right to do so. This is reinforced by s 31(3) which provides that it is not necessary for the person for whose protection a domestic abuse protection order is made to consent to the making of the order:

> '(a) in a case where the order includes provision relating to premises lived in by the person for whose protection the order would be made, any opinion of a relevant occupant:
> (i) which relates to the making of the order, and
> (ii) of which the court is made aware[1].'

'Relevant occupant' is defined as a person other than P or the person for whose protection the order would be made:

> '(a) who lives in the premises, and
> (b) who is personally connected to:
> (i) the person for whose protection the order would be made, or
> (ii) if P also lives in the premises, P[2].'

1 Domestic Abuse Bill, s 31(1)(c).
2 Domestic Abuse Bill, s 31(2).

5.19 An order including provision relating to premises would necessarily be an order under s 33(4) or s 33(5) regulating or terminating P's occupation of premises including premises in which he lived or restricting his ability to visit such premises. Here it is provided that the court must have regard to the opinion of any other person living in the premises who is personally connected to the victim or to P.

Provision that may be made by orders

5.20 Section 33 contains details of what may be included in a DAPO. Section 25 defined a DAPO as an order which prohibited P from doing things described in the order, or required P to do things described in the order. Section 33 goes into more detail about the provisions which may be included to achieve the aims of s 25.

5.21 Section 33(1) gives a general overview. A court may by a domestic abuse protection order impose any requirements that the court considers necessary to protect the person for whose protection the order is made from domestic abuse or the risk of domestic abuse. 'Requirement' includes any prohibition or restriction[1]. This is a very far-reaching grant of power to the court. Section 33(2) is an equally broad-brush approach. The court must, in particular, consider what requirements (if any) may be necessary to protect the person for whose protection the order is made from different kinds of abusive behaviour.

1 Domestic Abuse Bill, s 33(1).

5.22 The remainder of the section goes on to give example of provisions which may be included in the order, while making the point that these do not limit the provision which may be made. The two classes of provision with which practitioners will be most familiar from the law previously in effect are set out in sub-s (4) and (5). By s 33(4):

> 'A domestic abuse protection order may provide that P—
> (a) may not contact the person for whose protection it is made;
> (b) may not come within a specified distance of any premises in England or Wales in which that person lives'.
>
> "Specified" means specified in the order. This is a comprehensive power to prevent P from coming into contact with the victim.'

5.23 Section 33(5) provides authority to protect the victim's occupation of a home and also for what used to be called an 'ouster injunction'. If P lives in premises in England or Wales in which the person for whose protection the order is made also lives, the order may contain provision:

(a) prohibiting P from evicting or excluding that person from the premises;
(b) prohibiting P from entering the premises;
(c) requiring P to leave the premises.

5.24 Section 34(1) provides for protection for P in certain cases. Requirements imposed on a person by a DAPO must, so far as practicable, be such as to avoid:

(a) conflict with the person's religious beliefs;
(b) interference with any times at which the person normally works or attends an educational establishment;
(c) conflict with the requirements of any other court order or injunction to which the person may be subject.

Electronic monitoring

5.25 A new form of protection for the victim is provided by s 33(6). A DAPO may require P to submit to electronic monitoring in England and Wales of P's compliance with other requirements imposed by the order. This is referred to as an 'electronic monitoring requirement'. This is sometimes known as 'tagging'. However, there are certain limitations on the ability of the court to make such an order. The requirement may not be imposed in P's absence[1]. Furthermore, if there is a person (other than P) without whose co-operation it would be impracticable to secure the monitoring in question, the requirement may not be imposed without that person's consent[2].

1 Domestic Abuse Bill, s 35(2).
2 Domestic Abuse Bill, s 35(3).

5.26 Section 35(4) imposes a more significant restriction. The court may only make an electronic monitoring order where it has been notified by the Secretary of State that electronic monitoring arrangements are available in the relevant area, and it is satisfied that the necessary provision can be made under the arrangements currently available. 'Relevant area' is the local justice area where P resides. Where it is proposed to include in the order a requirement that P must remain, for specified periods, at a specified place, or a provision prohibiting P from entering a specified place or area, 'relevant area' means the local justice area in which the place or area proposed to be specified is situated[1].

1 Domestic Abuse Bill, s 35(5)(b).

5.27 Sections 35(6)–(8) contain detailed provisions about the mechanics for making an electronic monitoring order. The person who is to be responsible for the monitoring must be specified[1]. P must obey that person's instructions and must not interfere with the equipment[2].

1 Domestic Abuse Bill, s 35(6).
2 Domestic Abuse Bill, s 35(8).

Orders without notice

5.28 Section 32(1) provides that a court may, in any case where it is just and convenient to do so, make a DAPO against a person ('P') even though P has not been given such notice of the proceedings as would otherwise be required by rules of court. However, this does not apply in relation to the making of an order under s 26(3) (application by police after DAPN given).

5.29 By s 32(3), in deciding whether or not to make such a without notice order that court must have regard to all the circumstances including:

(a) any risk that, if the order is not made immediately, P will cause significant harm to the person for whose protection the order would be made,
(b) in a case where an application for the order has been made, whether it is likely that the person making the application will be deterred or prevented from pursuing the application if an order is not made immediately, and
(c) whether there is reason to believe that:
    (i) P is aware of the proceedings but is deliberately evading service, and
    (ii) the delay involved in effecting substituted service will cause serious prejudice to the person for whose protection the order would be made.

5.30 If a court makes a without notice order against a person, it must give the person an opportunity to make representations about the order as soon as just and convenient, and at a hearing of which notice has been given to all the parties in accordance with rules of court[1].

1 Domestic Abuse Bill, s 32(4).

Duration etc of orders

5.31 A DAPO takes effect on the day on which it is made[1]. However, if, on the day on which that order is made P is subject to another DAPO, the new order may be made so as to take effect on the previous order ceasing to have effect[2].

1 Domestic Abuse Bill, s 36(1).
2 Domestic Abuse Bill, s 36(2).

5.32 A DAPO has effect:

(a) for a specified period,
(b) until the occurrence of a specified event, or
(c) until further order.

'Specified' means specified in the order[1]. The order may also specify periods for which particular requirements imposed by the order have effect. However, the order may not provide for an electronic monitoring requirement to have effect for more than 12 months[2].

1 Domestic Abuse Bill, s 36(3).
2 Domestic Abuse Bill, s 36(4) and (5).

Breach of order

5.33 A person who is subject to a DAPO commits an offence if without reasonable excuse he or she fails to comply with any requirement imposed by the order[1]. However, where the order was made against the person without that person being given notice of the proceedings, they commit an offence under this section only in respect of behaviour engaged in at a time when they were aware of the existence of the order[2]. Accordingly, a person cannot be held to have committed an offence in respect of an order made without notice and of which notice has not been given to him.

1 Domestic Abuse Bill, s 37(1).
2 Domestic Abuse Bill, s 37(2).

5.34 Where a person is convicted of an offence under this section in respect of any behaviour, that behaviour is not punishable as a contempt of court[1]. A person may not be convicted of an offence under this section in respect of any behaviour which has been punished as a contempt of court[2]. These provisions are obviously intended to prevent double jeopardy in cases where enforcement action may have been taken elsewhere.

1 Domestic Abuse Bill, s 37(3).
2 Domestic Abuse Bill, s 37(4).

5.35 On summary conviction an offender is liable to a fine or not more than 12 months imprisonment or both, and on indictment to not more than 5 years imprisonment or a fine or both[1]. It is not open to the court to grant a conditional discharge[2].

1 Domestic Abuse Bill, s 37(5).
2 Domestic Abuse Bill, s 37(6) and (7).

Arrest for breach of order

5.36 This will be considered in more detail in CHAPTER 10 (Enforcement).

Notification requirements

5.37 A person subject to a DAPO must, within 3 days of the making of the order, notify the police of his name (including all names used by him) and his home address. Any change of name or address must be notified within 3 days of such change[1]. Notification must be given by the person attending a police station in the area where his home is situated and giving the information orally[2]. Such notification must be acknowledged in writing[3]. When notification is given the person must allow the person to whom notification is given to take his fingerprints and a photograph of him[4].

1 Domestic Abuse Bill, s 39(1)–(6).
2 Domestic Abuse Bill, s 40(1) and s 40(2).
3 Domestic Abuse Bill, s 40(4).
4 Domestic Abuse Bill, s 40(5).

5.38 A person commits an offence if he fails, without reasonable excuse, to comply with a requirement imposed by or under s 39, or notifies the police, in purported compliance with such a requirement, of any information which he knows to be false[1]. A person who fails, without reasonable excuse, to comply with s 40(5) commits an offence[2].

1 Domestic Abuse Bill, s 41(1).
2 Domestic Abuse Bill, s 41(2).

Variation and discharge of DAPO

5.39 Sections 42 and 43 deal with variation and discharge of orders. By s 42(1) 'A court may vary or discharge a domestic abuse protection order made by that or any other court'. The practical issues arising are as follows.

Which court?

5.40 The basic rule is that any application to vary or discharge a DAPO under s 42 must be made to the court that made the order[1]. However, where the order was made by a magistrates' court, any other magistrates' court in the same local justice area may make the order[2]. Furthermore, where the order was made under s 29 on an appeal in relation to a person's conviction or sentence for an offence, or the order was made by a court under that section against a person committed or remitted to that court for sentencing for an offence, any application to vary or discharge the order must be made to the court by or before which the person was convicted[3].

1 Domestic Abuse Bill, s 43(1).
2 Domestic Abuse Bill, s 43(2).
3 Domestic Abuse Bill, s 43(3).

Who may apply?

5.41 A court may vary or discharge an order in any case where it could make an order under s 29[1] (see **5.4** above). In any other case[2], the persons who may apply to vary or discharge are:

- the person for whose protection the order was made;

- the person against whom the order was made ('P');
- where the order was made under s 26, the person who applied for the order;
- the chief officer of police of the force maintained for any police area in which P resides;
- the chief officer of police of any other force maintained for a police area who believes that P is in that police area or is intending to come to it[3].

The court must hear from any relevant chief officer of police who wishes to be heard and, where the application is made by the person for whose protection the order was made it must hear from that person[4].

1 Domestic Abuse Bill, s 42(2)(b).
2 Domestic Abuse Bill, s 42(2)(a).
3 Domestic Abuse Bill, s 42(3).
4 Domestic Abuse Bill, s 42(4).

Matters to be taken into account

5.42 The court must take into account all the matters contained in the Domestic Abuse Bill 2020, ss 31 and 32 which it would take into account when making an order[1].

1 Domestic Abuse Bill, s 42(6) and (7).

Orders which may be made on variation application

5.43 The court may make any order varying or discharging a domestic abuse protection order that it considers appropriate[1]. However, this is subject to certain qualifications; most importantly, the court may only discharge the order if satisfied that the order is no longer necessary to protect the person for whose protection it was made from domestic abuse, or the risk of domestic abuse, carried out by the same perpetrator[2].

1 Domestic Abuse Bill, s 42(8).
2 Domestic Abuse Bill, s 42(13).

5.44 The court may include an additional requirement in the order, or extend the period for which the order, or a requirement imposed by the order, has effect, but only if it is satisfied that it is necessary to do so in order to protect the person for whose protection the order was made from domestic abuse, or the risk of domestic abuse, carried out by the perpetrator[1]. Similarly, the court may only remove any requirement imposed by the order, or make such a requirement less onerous, if satisfied that the requirement as imposed is no longer necessary to protect the person for whose protection the order was made from domestic abuse, or the risk of domestic abuse, carried out by the perpetrator[2].

1 Domestic Abuse Bill, s 42(9).
2 Domestic Abuse Bill, s 42(11).

Appeals

5.45 Section 44 and s 45 of the Domestic Abuse Bill 2020 deal with appeals from any decision or order relating to a DAPO and should be consulted for the detail. Essentially, an appeal from a magistrates' court lies to the Crown Court and from the Crown Court to the Court of Appeal[1]. Where the DAPO was made by the Family Court, the appeal will be governed by s 31K Matrimonial and Family Proceedings Act 1984.

1 Domestic Abuse Bill, s 44(7).

Chapter 6

OCCUPATION ORDERS

INTRODUCTION TO OCCUPATION ORDERS

If the client is an associated person with proposed respondent, is the client eligible for an occupation order (or for a non-molestation order under s 42)?

6.1 As was seen at CHAPTER 2, the structure of classification of rights of occupation in the FLA 1996, vested or contingent on grant of an order of the court, is governed first by property rights and, secondly, by the personal relationship between the parties. The appropriate category for the client can be found as follows[1].

1 Note that occupation orders under the FLA 1996 are not affected by the Domestic Abuse Bill 2020. It remains to be seen (probably in rule change or by Practice Direction) how practitioners will be directed towards using the DAA rather than the FLA 1996.

6.2 The applicant can apply for an occupation order in respect of the family home if he or she is:

- the person in occupation who has a legal right of occupation, against any associated person (s 33, see **6.20**);
- the spouse who is in occupation but has no legal right of occupation against the spouse who has a right of occupation (ss 30(2)(a), 33(3), (4), see **6.20–6.33**);
- the spouse who is not in occupation and has no legal right of occupation against the spouse in occupation who has a right of occupation (ss 30(2)(b), 33(3), (4), see **6.8–6.33**);
- the spouse in occupation against the other spouse also in occupation where neither spouse has a right of occupation (s 37, see **6.64–6.69**);
- the previous spouse, whether or not in occupation against the previous spouse in occupation who has a right of occupation (s 35; see **6.34–6.45**);
- a cohabitant or former cohabitant where either party has a right of occupation (s 36, see **6.46–6.63**);
- a cohabitant or former cohabitant where both parties in occupation but neither party has a right of occupation (s 38, see **6.70–6.77**).

Expiration of s 30 matrimonial home rights on death or divorce

6.3 Where a spouse, who has no legal title, has matrimonial home rights under FLA 1996, s 30(1) and (2)(a), or is granted such rights under s 30(2)(b), under s 33(8) the rights expire on divorce or death of the other party unless:

(a) an order is made to charge the rights on an estate or interest in the home under s 31; or
(b) an order is made before the divorce or death, under s 33(5), extending the rights beyond the divorce or death.

Therefore, if divorce or death of the respondent who has the legal title is anticipated, it may be wise to seek an order under s 31 or s 33(5).

What criteria apply for the grant of an occupation order?

6.4 The criteria vary between s 33 and ss 35–38. They vary according to who has legal title (if either party does) and according to a 'balance of harm' test.

6.5 It will be necessary in each case to be clear which criteria are required by the applicable section to be taken into account by the court.

6.6 The criteria common to all applications are:

> '(a) the housing needs and housing resources of each of the parties and of any relevant child;
> (b) the financial resources of each of the parties;
> (c) the likely effect of any order, or any decision by the court not to exercise its powers [to make an occupation order], on the health, safety or well-being of the parties and of any relevant child; and
> (d) the conduct of the parties in relation to each other and otherwise.'

The 'balance of harm' test

> 'In considering whether to make an occupation order, the court will have to apply a "balance of harm" test. Under this test, in the case of spouses [where at least one has a legal right of occupation (ss 33(7), 35(8)), or neither has such right (s 37(4))], and others who have a right to occupy the home [s 33(7)], the court has a duty to make an occupation order where the applicant or a relevant child is likely to suffer significant harm attributable to conduct of the respondent if the order is not made, greater than the respondent or a relevant child is likely to suffer if the order is made. This power is discretionary in the case of cohabitants who do not have existing property rights [ss 36(7), (8), 38(5)] so that the court has additional flexibility in dealing with these situations[1].'

1 Consultation Paper on Part IV, Draft Rules and Forms, LCD, March 1997 at p 43, para 133.

6.7 In its report, the Law Commission explained the reasoning behind its recommendation, and how this would work in practice[1]:

> 'In cases where the question of significant harm does not arise, the court would have power to make an order taking into account the three factors set out above; but, in cases where there is a likelihood of significant harm, this power becomes a duty and the court must make an order after balancing the degree of harm likely to be suffered by both parties and any children concerned. This approach would still work in the case of cross applications, where the court would firstly consider who would suffer

the greatest risk of harm if the order were not made. In the event of the balance of harm being equal, the court would retain power to make an order, but would have no duty to do so, and so would still be able to reach the right result. Harm has a narrower meaning than hardship. It is defined as "ill-treatment or impairment of physical or mental health". In relation to children, the term will attract the definition used in s 31 of the Children Act 1989. It is likely that a respondent threatened with ouster on account of his violence would be able to establish a degree of hardship (perhaps in terms of difficulty in finding or unsuitability of alternative accommodation or problems in getting to work). But he is unlikely to suffer significant harm, whereas his wife and children who are being subjected to his violence or abuse may very easily suffer harm if he remains in the house. In this way the court will be treating violence or other forms of abuse as deserving immediate relief, and will be directed to make an order where a risk of significant harm exists. However, by placing an emphasis on the need for a remedy rather than on the conduct which gave rise to that need, the criteria will not actually put a premium on allegations of violence and thus may avoid the problems which would be generated by a scheme which focuses upon it. The proposed test also has the advantage that it will avoid giving rise to a situation in which the court is put in the undesirable position of having to choose between the interests of a child and those of an adult, as, in cases where there is a risk of significant harm to a child, the duty to make an order will come into operation and the child's welfare will effectively become the paramount consideration.'

1 Law Com, para 4.34.

6.8 It will be seen, therefore, that the first decision which the court has to make is whether or not to make any order at all; having decided to make an order, it must then decide which of the menu of orders contained in s 33(3) it should make. If the decision-making process anticipated by the Law Commission were adopted, the chain of reasoning would be as follows.

(a) The first consideration will be the direction contained in sub-s (7), namely to decide whether the applicant has established that she, or a relevant child, is likely to suffer significant harm attributable to conduct of the respondent if an order is not made (the meaning of 'significant harm' is considered below). The harm which may be taken into account is limited to harm which is attributable to the conduct of the respondent; other harm is not to be taken into consideration.
(b) Next, the court would have to consider whether the respondent had established that he or any relevant child would suffer significant harm if the order were made. Here, there is no requirement that the harm to be considered be attributable to the conduct of the applicant; the court may consider harm in the widest sense, for example, the harm which might be suffered as a result of being evicted.
(c) Finally, the court would have to decide which party would suffer the greater harm; the applicant or a child if the order were not made, or the respondent or child if the order were made.

6.9 The process therefore has a cumulative effect; if the applicant fails to clear the first hurdle, sub-s (7) does not apply at all, and sub-s (6) alone would govern the decision. If the applicant passed that stage, but the respondent failed to satisfy the court as to the second test, the court would have to find in favour of the applicant. It would only be if both hurdles were crossed that the court would be faced with the 'balance of harm' test.

6.10 With those principles in mind, the cases decided since the implementation of the Act can be considered.

6.11 In *B v B (Occupation Order)*[1], the wife and daughter of the marriage had left the home because of the husband's severe violence; he remained in occupation with his son from a previous marriage. It was held that the harm which he and his son would suffer if an order were made outweighed that which the wife and daughter would suffer if an order were not made, because they, being unintentionally homeless, would be rehoused by the local authority, whereas he would not be rehoused.

1 [1999] 1 FLR 715, CA.

6.12 In *Chalmers v Johns*[1], Mr Johns had been ordered to leave the home after a series of relatively minor incidents which were the culmination of a long and stormy relationship. His appeal was allowed. The Court of Appeal stated that this was not 'in any ordinary forensic language a domestic violence case' and that a less drastic order would have dealt with the problem.

1 [1999] 1 FLR 392, CA.

6.13 Thorpe LJ observed that the wider provisions of Pt IV did not obliterate the previous authorities to the effect that to require someone to vacate a family home was a Draconian order which should be restricted to exceptional cases. 'It remains an order which overrides proprietary rights and it seems to me that it is an order that is only justified in exceptional circumstances[1]'.

1 [1999] 1 FLR 392, CA at 397.

6.14 The various authorities were considered, and helpful guidance as to approach of the court given, in *G v G (Occupation Order: Conduct)*[1]. The significant aspects may be summarised as follows:

(a) An exclusion order is Draconian and should be made only in exceptional circumstances.
(b) When considering an application under s 33, the court must first consider s 33(7). Then, if the precondition of significant harm is found not to be satisfied, the court may move to s 33(6)[2].
(c) Under s 33(7), significant harm must be attributed to the respondent's conduct. However, it does not have to be intentional conduct.
(d) The 'balance of harm' test involves comparison of the harm which would be suffered by the applicant and the relevant child if the order were not made with that which would be suffered by the respondent and any relevant child if the order were made. In the instant case, the judge had erroneously compared both situations from the applicant's perception.

1 [2000] 2 FLR 36, CA.
2 See also *Chalmers v Johns* [1999] 1 FLR 392, CA.

6.15 The discretionary exercise under s 33(6) is a precise one, which is strictly governed by the specific factors in the checklist. The court must make express reference to those factors; a generalised consideration of all the circumstances will not suffice.

6.16 One of the most recent cases in which the Court of Appeal gives helpful guidance is *Re L (Occupation Order)*[1]. Here, the trial judge found that, although there were no recent examples of violence, the relationship between the parents was extremely acrimonious and the children were suffering as a result. He made a shared residence order and excluded the father from the home for three months. The father appealed, but the appeal was dismissed. The court held that in line with the authority of *Chalmers v Johns* (above) a judge considering an occupation order had, first, to consider whether there was evidence that the applicant or any relevant child was likely to suffer significant harm attributable to the conduct of the respondent if an order were not made. If the answer was 'yes' then by virtue of s 33(7) he would have to make an occupation order unless the respondent was likely to suffer significant harm if the order was made and that harm would be as great as or greater than the harm attributable to the conduct of the respondent which was likely to be suffered by the applicant if the order was not made.

1 [2012] 2 FLR 1417, CA.

6.17 There was nothing in s 33(6) to limit the discretion to make an occupation order to cases in which there had been physical violence. There was equally no authority for the proposition that a spouse could only be excluded from the home if reprehensible conduct on his behalf were found. Section 33(6) required consideration of all the circumstances.

6.18 In the instant case the judge found that the children were likely to suffer significant harm if the parents were not separated and that the harm was attributable to both parents' conduct and their presence together in the home.

TYPES OF OCCUPATION ORDERS IN DETAIL

6.19 The ingredients of an occupation order in respect of the family home, the criteria for an order, and the duration of an order all depend on the relationship between the parties and whether and what legal rights either of them have to occupy the home. See **6.4–6.18** for the general criteria which apply upon an application for an occupation order.

Section 33 orders

6.20 Occupation orders under s 33 are available to:

(a) a party in occupation who has a legal right of occupation, against any associated person (s 33); this includes cases where both parties are in occupation and both have a legal right of occupation;
(b) a spouse who is in occupation but has no legal right of occupation against the spouse who has a right of occupation (s 33(3), (4)); such an applicant has vested 'matrimonial home rights' under s 30(2)(a);
(c) a spouse who is not in occupation and has no legal right of occupation against the spouse in occupation who has a right of occupation (s 33(3), (4)); such an applicant has a right to apply for leave to enter and occupy, ie contingent 'matrimonial home rights' under s 30(2)(b).

6.21 The menu of possible orders under s 33(3) is set out in Form FL404, as follows:

> '1. The court declares that the applicant [name] is entitled to occupy [address of home or intended home] as [his/her] home. OR
>
> 2. The court declares that the applicant [name] has matrimonial home rights in [address of home or intended home]. AND/OR
>
> 3. The court declares that the applicant [name's matrimonial home rights shall not end when the respondent [name] dies or their marriage is dissolved and shall continue until . . . or further order.
>
> **It is ordered that:**
>
> 4. The respondent [name] shall allow the applicant [name] to occupy [address of home or intended home] OR
>
> 5. The respondent [name] shall allow the applicant [name] to occupy part of [address of home or intended home] namely: [specify part]
>
> 6. The respondent [name] shall not obstruct, harass or interfere with the applicant [name]'s peaceful occupation of [address of home or intended home]
>
> 7. The respondent [name] shall not occupy [address of home or intended home] OR
>
> 8. The respondent [name] shall not occupy [address of home or intended home] from [specify date] until [specify date] OR
>
> 9. The respondent [name] shall not occupy [specify part of address of home or intended home] AND/OR
>
> 10. The respondent [name] shall not occupy [address or part of address] between [specify dates or times]
>
> 11. The respondent [name] shall leave [address or part of address] [forthwith] [within ______ [hours/days] of service on [him/her] of this order] AND/OR
>
> 12. Having left [address or part of address], the respondent [name] shall not return to, enter or attempt to enter [or go within [specify distance] of] it.'

The detailed effect of these provisions will be considered in turn.

(a) Enforce the applicant's entitlement to remain in occupation

6.22 An order in these terms would be required where the respondent had interfered, or threatened to interfere with the applicant's right to occupy the dwelling-house. The order would, where necessary, declare the applicant's right of occupation, and take the form of an injunction restraining the respondent from interfering with that right. It would be for the court to decide whether any of the other classes of order contained in sub-s (3) should also be made.

(b) Require respondent to permit applicant to enter and remain in dwelling-house or part

6.23 This would apply where the applicant had been excluded from the home, or where the respondent threatened to exclude her. It would take the form of a mandatory order requiring the respondent to allow the applicant back into possession, and/or a restraining order requiring him not to exclude her.

6.24 Such an order could direct that the applicant be permitted to occupy part only of the house; this might be appropriate where, for example, the house was large enough for the respective quarters of the parties to be defined, and it was in their best interests to be kept apart.

(c) Regulate the occupation of dwelling-house by either party

6.25 This overlaps, to some extent, with the final comments in para (b) above. In theory, to 'regulate' the occupation of a house could involve excluding one party from it. However, the fact that there is specific provision in this section for exclusion suggests that this provision is designed to enable the court to dictate which parts of a house may be used by one or other party, and to prescribe areas which one party may not enter.

(d) If respondent entitled, prohibit, suspend or restrict the exercise of his right to occupy

6.26 This applies where the respondent is 'entitled' under s 33(1)(a)(i); that is to say, he is entitled to occupy because he is a freehold or beneficial owner, or tenant, or contractual licensee. He does not need the protection of the FLA 1996 in order to occupy; he occupies as of right.

6.27 This provision, therefore, enables the court to override his legal property rights, and to deny him the right to occupy the house. This can be a complete denial ('prohibit'), a temporary denial ('suspend'), or a partial denial ('restrict').

(e) If respondent has matrimonial home rights, restrict or terminate those rights

6.28 To some extent, this is a mirror image of the previous provision. Whether or not a person has matrimonial home rights is a matter of law, not discretion. Where the parties are spouses, and one of them is 'entitled' because of general legal rights, the other automatically acquires matrimonial home rights by virtue of s 30(2). If these rights could not be interfered with, there would be the absurd position that such a person would be in a stronger position than the spouse who was 'entitled'.

6.29 Accordingly, this provision permits the court to order that a person with matrimonial home rights may be excluded from the home either partially, temporarily or permanently.

(f) Require respondent to leave the dwelling-house or part thereof

6.30 This is self-explanatory, and clearly fits in with the general array of powers conferred on the court. This provision would be the specific authority for making an ouster order.

(g) Exclude respondent from a defined area in which the dwelling-house is included

6.31 This is a power which derives from the DVMPA 1976, there being no corresponding provision in the MHA 1983; it is clearly sensible that it is to be included in the unified powers of the court. The tendency has been for courts to approach such orders with caution. On the one hand, it may obviously be wise to prevent a potential molester from lurking in the vicinity of the home and intimidating by his very presence. However, it is necessary to have regard to and protect the liberty of the subject, and also to avoid the possibility of unintentional breaches of orders. Accordingly, it is submitted that any order of this kind should be made only where a clear need for it, in order to protect the applicant and family, has been demonstrated, and then only in the most limited terms consistent with the safety of the applicant. Having said that, it must also be said that the specimen orders attached to Form FL404 include, at numbers 12, 19 and 23, an appropriate order for use in such cases.

6.32 By s 33(7), the 'balance of harm' test applies. For the effect of this, and the matters contained in s 33(6), see **6.4–6.18**.

(b) Duration of s 33 orders

6.33 An order under s 33(3) may be indefinite or for a defined period[1]. However, where a spouse, who has no legal title, has matrimonial home rights under s 30(1) and (2)(a), or is granted such rights under s 30(2)(b), under s 33(8) the rights expire on divorce or death of a party unless:

(a) an order is made to charge the rights on an estate or interest in the home under s 31; or
(b) an order is made before the divorce or death, under s 33(5), extending the rights beyond the divorce or death.

Therefore, if divorce or death of the respondent who has the legal title is anticipated, it will be wise to seek an order under s 31 or s 33(5).

[1] FLA 1996, s 33(10).

Section 35 orders

6.34 Section 35 orders are available to a former spouse, whether or not in occupation, who has no right of occupation against the former spouse who has a right of occupation of a dwelling-house in which they lived or intended to live (s 35(1), (2)).

6.35 Section 35 deals with cases where the applicant is non-entitled, the respondent is entitled and the applicant is a former spouse. Section 35(1) applies where:

> '(a) one former spouse is entitled to occupy a dwelling-house by virtue of a beneficial estate or interest or contract, or by virtue of any enactment giving him the right to remain in occupation; and
> (b) the other former spouse is not so entitled; and
> (c) the dwelling-house was at any time their matrimonial home or was at any time intended by them to be their matrimonial home.'

Section 35(2) then provides that, in such cases, the former spouse, not so entitled, may apply for an order under this section against the entitled former spouse.

6.36 The section will never apply to spouses, since they have matrimonial home rights. Applicants under this section will therefore always be former spouses; the respondent will always be 'entitled'.

6.37 The menu of possible orders under s 35(3), (4) and (5) is set out in Form FL404.

6.38 If the court grants an order, it must (s 35(3), (4)) include menu orders 13 and 14:

> '13. The applicant [name] has the right to occupy [address of home or intended home] and the respondent [name] shall allow the applicant [name] to do so.
>
> 14. The respondent [name] shall not evict or exclude the applicant [name] from [address of home or intended home] or any part of it namely [specify part].'

6.39 These orders are mandatory. If the court makes any order at all under s 35, it must include these orders. In addition, the possible supplementary orders under s 35(5) are set out in menu orders 15–19:

> '15. The respondent [name] shall not occupy [*address of home or intended home*]. OR
>
> 16. The respondent [name] shall not occupy [*address of home or intended home*] from [*specify date*] until [*specify date*] OR
>
> 17. The respondent [name] shall not occupy [*specify part of address of home or intended home*] OR
>
> 18. The respondent [name] shall leave [*address or part of address*] [forthwith] [within ______ [*hours/days*] of service on [*him/her*] of this order.] AND/OR
>
> 19. Having left [*address or part of address*], the respondent [name] shall not return to, enter or attempt to enter [or go within [*specify distance*] of] it.'

6.40 It will be seen that the provisions of s 5(3) and (4) are similar to, but not identical with, matrimonial home rights. The similarities are obvious, and may be demonstrated by comparing these subsections with s 30(2).

6.41 The differences are as follows. First, there is no mention of 'leave of the court'. The reason for this is that matrimonial home rights are an entitlement conferred by statute, whereas the protection under a s 35 order is always contained in an order of the court.

6.42 Secondly, whereas matrimonial home rights are a general protection, with no time-limit (save that they disappear on decree absolute), the rights under a s 35 order will subsist only for 'the period specified in the order'. Courts will, therefore, have to ensure that every order under s 35 specifies a period for the duration of the rights conferred.

6.43 The criteria applicable in deciding whether to make a s 35 order are set out in s 35(6) and are:

> 'all the circumstances including?—
> (a) the housing needs and housing resources of each of the parties and of any relevant child;
> (b) the financial resources of each of the parties;

(c) the likely effect of any order, or of any decision by the court not to exercise its powers under subsection (3) or (4), on the health, safety or well-being of the parties and of any relevant child;
(d) the conduct of the parties in relation to each other and otherwise;
(e) the length of time that has elapsed since the parties ceased to live together;
(f) the length of time that has elapsed since the marriage was dissolved or annulled; and
(g) the existence of any pending proceedings between the parties?—
  (i) for an order under section 23A or 24 of MCA 1973 (property adjustment orders in connection with divorce proceedings etc.);
  (ii) for an order under para 1(2)(d) or (e) of Schedule 1 to the Children Act 1989 (orders for financial relief against parents); or
  (iii) relating to the legal or beneficial ownership of the dwelling-house.'

6.44 If the court decides to grant a s 35 order, then the 'balance of harm' test is applied by s 35(8) in relation to whether the court includes in the order a supplementary order under s 35(5):

'(8) If the court decides to make an order under this section and it appears to it that, if the order does not include a subsection (5) provision, the applicant or any relevant child is likely to suffer significant harm attributable to conduct of the respondent, the court shall include the subsection (5) provision in the order unless it appears to the court that?—
  (a) the respondent or any relevant child is likely to suffer significant harm if the provision is included in the order; and
  (b) the harm likely to be suffered by the respondent or child in that event is as great as or greater than the harm attributable to conduct of the respondent which is likely to be suffered by the applicant or child if the provision is not included.'

Further criteria apply for deciding whether, if the 'balance of harm' test does not apply, to make a supplementary order under s 35(5). The further criteria are items (a) to (e) in the list from s 35(6) set out above.

Duration of s 35 orders

6.45 By s 35(10), a s 35 order 'must be limited so as to have effect for a specified period not exceeding six months, but may be extended on one or more occasions for a further specified period not exceeding six months. Further, an order under s 35:

'(a) may not be made after the death of either of the former spouses; and
(b) ceases to have effect on the death of either of them.'

Where an occupation order is granted without notice, and is renewed at a hearing on notice, the period it may remain effective is calculated from the date on which the initial without notice order is granted[1].

1 FLA 1996, s 45(4).

Section 36 orders

6.46 Section 36 orders are available, at the discretion of the court, to a person who is a cohabitant or former cohabitant where one of them only has a right of occupation in the home where they live or intended to live together as man and wife[1]. If both cohabitants have a right of occupation, the application should be made under s 33.

1 FLA 1996, s 36(1).

6.47 It may be remembered that FLA 1996, s 41 provided that where the parties were cohabitants or former cohabitants, in considering the nature of the parties' relationship the court 'is to have regard to the fact that they have not given each other the commitment involved in marriage'. This always was a meaningless provision, and it will come as no surprise to learn that this was not part of the government's original draft Bill but was accepted as a backbencher's amendment when the progress of the Bill was in difficulty.

6.48 Section 2(1) of DVCVA 2004 has repealed FLA 1996, s 41 so this will no longer be an issue to trouble the court.

6.49 The menu of possible orders under s 36(3), (4) and (5) is set out in Form FL404, orders 13–19.

6.50 If the court grants an order, it must (s 36(3), (4)) include menu orders 13 and 14. Orders 13 and 14, made under s 36(3) or (4) give the applicant the right to live in and not to be excluded from the home:

> '13. The applicant [name] has the right to occupy [*address of home or intended home*] and the respondent [name] shall allow the applicant [name] to do so. OR
>
> 14. The respondent [name] shall not evict or exclude the applicant [name] from [*address of home or intended home*] or any part of it namely [specify part].'

6.51 The court can add orders 15–19 under s 36(5), to regulate the occupation of the home by the respondent. Orders 15–19 are:

> '15. The respondent [name] shall not occupy [*address of home or intended home*] OR
>
> 16. The respondent [name] shall not occupy [*address of home or intended home*] from [*specify date*] until [*specify date*] OR
>
> 17. The respondent [name] shall not occupy [*specify part of address of home or intended home*] OR
>
> 18. The respondent [name] shall leave [*address or part of address*] [forthwith] [within ______ [*hours/days*] of service on [*him/her*] of this order] AND/OR
>
> 19. Having left [*address or part of address*], the respondent [name] shall not return to, enter or attempt to enter [or go within [*specify distance*] of] it.'

6.52 Orders under s 36 are discretionary. The criteria applicable in deciding whether to make a s 36(3) or (4) order in orders 13 and 14 are set out in s 35(6). The matters to be considered under s 36(6) are:

> 'all the circumstances including?—
> (a) the housing needs and housing resources of each of the parties and of any relevant child;
> (b) the financial resources of each of the parties;

(c) the likely effect of any order, or of any decision by the court not to exercise its powers under subsection (3) or (4), on the health, safety or well-being of the parties and of any relevant child;
(d) the conduct of the parties in relation to each other and otherwise;
(e) the nature of the parties' relationship and in particular the level of commitment attached to it;
(f) the length of time during which they have lived together as husband and wife;
(g) whether there are or have been any children who are children of both parties or for whom both parties have or have had parental responsibility;
(h) the length of time that has elapsed since the parties ceased to live together; and
(i) the existence of any pending proceedings between the parties?—
   (i) for an order under paragraph 1(2)(d) or (e) of Schedule 1 to the Children Act 1989 (orders for financial relief against parents); or
   (ii) relating to the legal or beneficial ownership of the dwelling-house.'

If the court decides to grant orders 13 or 14 under s 36(4), then further criteria apply as to whether the court should add orders 15–19 under s 36(5). The further criteria are set out in s 36(6) and (8).

6.53 The considerations in s 36(6) are:

'(a) the housing needs and housing resources of each of the parties and of any relevant child;
(b) the financial resources of each of the parties;
(c) the likely effect of any order, or of any decision by the court not to exercise its powers under subsection (3) or (4), on the health, safety or well-being of the parties and of any relevant child;
(d) the conduct of the parties in relation to each other and otherwise.'

6.54 If the court decides to grant a s 36 order then the 'balance of harm' test is applied by s 36(7) and (8) in relation to whether the court includes in the order a supplementary order under s 36(5) to regulate the occupation of the home by the respondent. The court must consider:

'(a) whether the applicant or any relevant child is likely to suffer significant harm attributable to conduct of the respondent if the subsection (5) provision is not included in the order; and
(b) whether the harm likely to be suffered by the respondent or child if the provision is included is as great as or greater than the harm attributable to conduct of the respondent which is likely to be suffered by the applicant or child if the provision is not included.'

6.55 Comparison with s 35(6) shows that s 36(6)(h) has its counterpart in sub-s 6(e) of that section. The real differences are therefore contained in s 36(6)(e), (f) and (g). Given that the parties have never married, the court has, in effect, to make a value judgment on the nature of the relationship; cohabitants may vary from those who have entered into a fleeting relationship to those who have lived together in a stable relationship for many years and have brought up children together. In deciding who is to occupy the home, and for how long, the court will have to take these matters into account.

6.56 A potentially more significant difference from the s 35 provisions is contained in s 36(7), which deals with whether or not to include any of the sub-s (5) provisions in an order which the court has decided to make which contains the matters mentioned in sub-s (3) or (4); this is, essentially, the significant harm test. By sub-s (7), the court is directed to have regard to:

> '. . . all the circumstances including?—
> (a) the matters mentioned in subsection (6)(a) to (d); and
> (b) the questions mentioned in subsection (8).'

6.57 By sub-s (8), the questions are:

> '(a) whether the applicant or any relevant child is likely to suffer significant harm attributable to conduct of the respondent if the subsection (5) provision is not included in the order; and
> (b) whether the harm likely to be suffered by the respondent or child if the provision is included is as great as or greater than the harm attributable to conduct of the respondent which is likely to be suffered by the applicant or child if the provision is not included.'

6.58 This is similar in some respects to the 'greater harm' test contained in s 35. However, there is one obvious difference. Under s 35(8), which applies the 'greater harm' test to former spouses, the court must include a sub-s (5) provision where the first limb of the 'greater harm' test is satisfied, unless satisfied as to the second limb; once significant harm is established, the onus passes to the respondent to show why a sub-s (5) provision should not be included.

6.59 Under s 36(8), applicable to cohabitants or former cohabitants, there is no such requirement on the court. The issue of the balance of significant harm is a 'question' for the consideration of the court; the court must consider it, but there is no obligation on the court to exercise its discretion in any particular direction once it has made a finding.

6.60 It might be argued that the court would be acting unreasonably, or unjudicially, if it did not include a sub-s (5) provision after making a finding in favour of one party as to one of the sub-s (8) questions. However, the difference in wording between the two provisions is deliberate and it might be thought, therefore, that the intention of Parliament was that the protection to be afforded to a cohabitant is less than that which the court is obliged to afford to a former spouse.

Duration of s 36 orders

6.61 Section 36(9) contains provisions identical with those in s 35(9). Subsection (10) provides that an order under s 36 must be limited so as to have effect for a specified period not exceeding six months, but may be extended on one further occasion for a further specified period not exceeding six months. This is the second principal difference between these provisions and the s 35 provisions. A cohabitant or former cohabitant is limited to an occupation order for one year; then she must leave.

6.62 The intention is clearly that, if the applicant is unable to justify occupation on other grounds in other proceedings (eg under the Children Act

1989, or by proving a beneficial or equitable interest), an occupation order should not in the long term displace the interest in the property of the entitled party.

6.63 Finally, s 36(13) provides that, so long as the order remains in force, sub-ss (3)–(6) of s 30 apply in relation to the applicant as if he were a spouse entitled to occupy the dwelling-house by virtue of that section and the respondent were the other spouse. These provisions relate to payment of rent, mortgage, etc.

Section 37 orders

6.64 Section 37 orders are available to a spouse in occupation against other spouse also in occupation where neither have a right of occupation[1].

1 FLA 1996, s 37(1), (2).

6.65 The menu of possible orders under s 37(3) is set out in Form FL404 orders 20–23:

> '20. The respondent [name] shall allow the applicant [name] to occupy [*address of home or intended home*] or part of it namely: [*specify*]. AND/OR
>
> 21. [One or both of the provisions in paragraphs 6 and 10 above may be inserted] AND/OR
>
> 22. The respondent [name] shall leave [*address or part of address*] [forthwith] [within ______ [*hours/days*] of service on [*him/her*] of this order] AND/OR
>
> 23. Having left [*address or part of address*], the respondent [name] may not return to, enter or attempt to enter [or go within [*specify distance*] of] it.'

6.66 The criteria applicable in deciding whether to make a s 37 order are the same as in s 33(6).

> '(a) the housing needs and housing resources of each of the parties and of any relevant child;
> (b) the financial resources of each of the parties;
> (c) the likely effect of any order, or of any decision by the court not to exercise its powers under subsection (3) or (4), on the health, safety or well-being of the parties and of any relevant child;
> (d) the conduct of the parties in relation to each other and otherwise.'

6.67 By s 37(4) and s 33(7), the 'balance of harm' test applies to create a presumption that a s 37(3) order should be made 'if it appears to the court that the applicant or any relevant child is likely to suffer significant harm attributable to conduct of the respondent if an order containing one or more of the provisions mentioned in sub-s (3) is not made'. If this appears to the court, the court must make an order:

> 'unless it appears to the court that?—
> (a) the respondent or any relevant child is likely to suffer significant harm if the order is made; and
> (b) the harm likely to be suffered by the respondent or child in that event is as great as, or greater than, the harm attributable to conduct of the respondent

which is likely to be suffered by the applicant or child if the order is not made.'

Duration of s 37 orders

6.68 By s 37(5), a s 37 order 'must be limited so as to have effect for a specified period not exceeding six months, but may be extended on one or more occasions for a further specified period not exceeding six months'.

6.69 Where an occupation order is granted without notice and is renewed at a hearing on notice, the period it may remain effective is calculated from the date on which the initial without notice order is granted (s 45(4)).

Section 38 orders

6.70 Section 38 orders are available where the client is cohabitant or former cohabitant and where both parties in occupation but neither has a right of occupation[1].

1 FLA 1996, s 38.

6.71 The menu of possible orders under s 38(3) is set out in Form FL404 orders 20–23.

6.72 The criteria applicable in deciding whether to make a s 38 order are set out in s 38(4) and (5).

6.73 By s 38(4), the court must 'have regard to all the circumstances' including:

'(a) the housing needs and housing resources of each of the parties and of any relevant child;
(b) the financial resources of each of the parties;
(c) the likely effect of any order, or of any decision by the court not to exercise its powers under subsection (3), on the health, safety or well-being of the parties and of any relevant child;
(d) the conduct of the parties in relation to each other and otherwise; and
(e) the questions mentioned in subsection (5).'

6.74 By s 38(5), the 'balance of harm' test applies when the court is considering whether to grant a s 38 order. The court must 'have regard to':

'(a) whether the applicant or any relevant child is likely to suffer significant harm attributable to conduct of the respondent if the subsection (3) provision is not included in the order; and
(b) whether the harm likely to be suffered by the respondent or child if the provision is included is as great as or greater than the harm attributable to conduct of the respondent which is likely to be suffered by the applicant or child if the provision is not included.'

6.75 Section 38(4) provides that in the exercise of its discretion the court must have regard to all the circumstances including the matters which it goes on to set out. These are, in fact, identical to those contained in s 36(7) and (8) (see **6.55**), with five exceptions.

6.76 There is no reference to:

(a) children;
(b) the nature of the relationship;
(c) the length of the relationship;
(d) the length of time since they ceased to live together;
(e) other proceedings.

This, in effect, leaves needs, resources, effect of order and conduct as the relevant factors. Significant harm is dealt with as a 'question' the court must consider but, as in s 36, there is no requirement on the court to make any particular order as a result of that inquiry.

Duration of s 38 orders

6.77 By s 38(6):

> 'An order under this section shall be limited so as to have effect for a specified period not exceeding six months, but may be extended on one occasion for a further specified period not exceeding six months.'

Where an occupation order is granted without notice, and is renewed at a hearing on notice, the period it may remain effective is calculated from the date on which the initial without notice order is granted[1].

1 FLA 1996, s 45(4).

Penal notice incorporated in an occupation order

6.78 Where no non-molestation order is included in an occupation order, the court has a discretion as to whether to attach a penal notice, but where a non-molestation order is included a penal notice is to be incorporated[1].

1 Form FL404, Notices A and B.

Power of arrest attached to occupation order

6.79 As was seen in CHAPTER 2, breach of a non-molestation order is now a criminal offence and the power to attach a power of arrest to such an order has been removed. To that end, s 46 of FLA 1996 has been amended.

6.80 It should be made clear, however, that the court retains the power to attach a power of arrest to an occupation order, so that the procedure for arrest and bringing a contemnor before the county court remains the same. One of the several difficulties this might bring is where the court chose to make both a non-molestation order and an occupation order (these would be drawn up by the court as two separate orders). In the event of a breach, a person could be arrested under the power of arrest for breach of the occupation order but not the non-molestation order. A further difficulty might be where the court had made an occupation order with a radius clause, eg not to attempt to enter the former home nor to come within 100 metres of it. Breach of such an order might well involve violence but, in the absence of a non-molestation order, would be dealt with under the power of arrest, which is normally attached to such a provision.

6.81 What was previously an interesting issue of whether such a radius clause should be classed as an occupation order or a non-molestation order will now become much more relevant, not to say vital, and will have important practical effects. The following guidance is offered somewhat tentatively. If the order is, for example, to leave the property and then not to return within 100 metres of it, it will certainly be an occupation order. However, what about an order where the parties do not live together and there is no ouster involved? Here, the radius clause would be imposed as an adjunct to the non-molestation order and would therefore be a non-molestation order itself. The way in which such orders are drafted will therefore be of great practical significance.

FORMS OF ORDER

6.82 As a result of the changes effected by DVCVA 2004, the forms of order (formerly Form FL404) have had to be changed. For a full explanation see **8.48** et seq below. A form of occupation order approved by Sir James Munby P will be found in Appendix 3.

Supplementary orders providing for maintenance, repair, mortgage or rent payments and care and use of furniture, available for orders under s 33, s 35 or s 36

6.83 FLA 1996, s 40 provides for certain supplementary orders to be available when an occupation order is made under s 33, s 35 or s 36. These are to be found in the menu of orders in Form FL404, orders 24–31.

> '24. The [applicant [name]] [respondent [name]] shall maintain and repair [address of home or intended home] AND/OR
>
> 25. The [applicant [name]] [respondent [name]] shall pay the rent for [address of home or intended home]. OR
>
> 26. The [applicant [name]] [respondent [name]] shall pay the mortgage payments on [address of home or intended home]. OR
>
> 27. The [applicant [name]] [respondent [name]] shall pay the following for [address of home or intended home]: [specify outgoings as bullet points].
>
> 28. The [party in occupation] shall pay to the [other party] £ each [week, month, etc] for [address of home etc].
>
> 29. The [party in occupation] shall keep and use the [furniture] [contents] [specify if necessary] of [address of home or intended home] and the [applicant [name]] [respondent [name]] shall return to the [party in occupation] the [furniture] [contents] [specify if necessary] [no later than [date/time]].
>
> 30. The [party in occupation] shall take reasonable care of the [furniture] [contents] [specify if necessary] of [address of home or intended home].

31. The [party in occupation] shall take all reasonable steps to keep secure [address of home or intended home] and the furniture or other contents [specify if necessary].'

6.84 In *Nwogbe v Nwogbe*[1], it was held that an order made under FLA 1996, s 40 cannot be enforced by committal and that, indeed, it seems that there is no obvious way to enforce such an order.

1 [2000] 2 FLR 744, CA.

6.85 It will be noted that these provisions do not apply to s 37 or s 38 orders; the reason is that in those cases neither party has any legal right of occupation, and therefore the question of liability for outgoings does not arise.

6.86 Section 40(2) contains guidelines to govern the exercise of the court's discretion. It is provided that in deciding whether and, if so, how to exercise its powers, the court shall have regard to all the circumstances of the case, including:

'(a) the financial needs and financial resources of the parties; and
'(b) the financial obligations which they have, or are likely to have in the foreseeable future, including financial obligations to each other and to any relevant child.'

No particular comment is needed on these provisions.

6.87 By sub-s (3), any order under this section ceases to have effect when the occupation order to which it relates ceases to have effect.

SUGGESTED DRAFT ORDER/CHECKLIST IN PT IV OF THE FAMILY LAW ACT 1996

6.88 As has been seen, in applications for injunctions, it is the duty of the applicant to supply the court with a draft order. Part IV of the Family Law Act 1996 provides a somewhat bewildering menu of possible orders, and in many county courts the practice has arisen of handing up a checklist with the appropriate orders ticked. This is entirely acceptable to most county courts because the orders themselves are available on a computer programme used by the court service. The form is also useful for the judge and for court staff to ensure that all necessary matters have been considered.

6.89 The tick box form which is set out below was originally the work of District Justice Gordon Ashton of the Preston County Court and was first published in the *Bulletin of the Association of District Judges*. This form is reprinted here in case it is still of practical use, but it must be remembered that Sir James Munby P has approved a form of occupation order which will be found in APPENDIX 3 and all orders must comply with that form.

Draft order/checklist

Applicant		Case No and	Respondent	
Date	....	CJ/DJ	....	[name]
Ex parte	Yes/No			

Applicant	counsel	solicitor	in person	no attendance	Present	Yes/No
Respondent	counsel	solicitor	in person	no attendance	Present	Yes/No
Statements						[name/date]
Evidence						[name/date]
NOTICE	Type A – *non-molestation order (includes penal notice)*				OR	
	Type B – *no non-molestation order*			Delete penal notice		Yes/No
DURATION *of non-molestation orders*				the order shall continue until		

NON-MOLESTATION ORDERS

It is ordered that:

1. The Respondent is *forbidden* to use or threaten violence against the *Applicant* [and must not instruct, encourage or in any way suggest that any other person should do so] AND/OR
2. The *Respondent* is forbidden to intimidate, harass or pester [*or specify*] the *Applicant* [and must not instruct, encourage or in any way suggest that any other person should do so] AND/OR
3. The *Respondent* is forbidden to use or threaten violence against the children [*specify name(s) and date(s) of birth of relevant children*] [and must not instruct, encourage or in any way suggest that any other person should do so] AND/OR
4. The *Respondent* is forbidden to intimidate, harass or pester [*or specify*] the children [*specify name(s) and date(s) of birth of relevant children*] [and must not instruct, encourage or in any way suggest that any other person should do so]
5. The *respondent* is forbidden to approach within metres of

COSTS

Respondent/Applicant to pay assessed costs of £

Respondent/Applicant to pay costs to be determined by detailed assessment

Public funding detailed assessment *Applicant/Respondent/both parties*Certificate for counsel — Certificate for counsel

Costs reserved — No Order as to costs

HEARING – *for ex parte orders*

Next available date after . . . . days, Time estimate . . . . hours/minutes

Service abridged to *days/hours*

OCCUPATION ORDERS

ARREST — The power of arrest applies to paragraphs below and remains in force until [date]

Home: [address]

Section 33 – *Applicant has estate or interest or matrimonial home rights*

6. The court declares that the *Applicant* is entitled to occupy [*home*] as *his/her* home OR
7. The court declares that the *Applicant* has matrimonial home rights in [*home*] AND/OR
8. The court declares that the *Applicant's* matrimonial home rights shall not end when the *Respondent* dies or their marriage is dissolved and shall continue until . . . . [*date*] or further order

It is ordered that:

9. The *Respondent* shall allow the *Applicant* to occupy [*home*] OR
10. The *Respondent* shall allow the *Applicant* to occupy part of [*home*] namely:

. . . . [specify part]

11. The *Respondent* shall not obstruct, harass or interfere with the *Applicant's* peaceful occupation of [*home*]

13. The *Respondent* shall not occupy [*home*] from . . . . [*date*] until . . . . [*date*] OR

14. The *Respondent* shall not occupy . . . . [specify part] AND/OR

15. The *Respondent* shall not occupy [*home*] between . . . . [*date*] and . . . . [*date*]

16. The *Respondent* shall leave [*home*] [forthwith] [within . . . . [hours/days]] of service on *him/her* of this order AND/OR

17. Having left [*home*] the *Respondent* shall not return to, enter or attempt to enter [or go within . . . . [specify distance] of] it

Sections 35 – *former spouse* – 36 *(former) cohabitant* – *No existing right to occupy*

It is ordered that:

18. The *Applicant* has the right to occupy [*home*] and the *Respondent* shall allow the *Applicant* to do so OR

19. The *Respondent* shall not evict or exclude the *Applicant* from [*home*] or any part of it namely:
. . . . [specify part] AND/OR

20. The *Respondent* shall not occupy [*home*] OR

21. The *Respondent* shall not occupy [*home*] from . . . . [date] until . . . . [date] OR

22. The *Respondent* shall not occupy . . . . [specify part] OR

23. The *Respondent* shall leave [*home*] [forthwith] [within . . . . [hours/days]] of service on *him/her* of this order AND/OR

24. Having left [*home*] the *Respondent* shall not return to, enter or attempt to enter [or go within . . . . [specify distance] of] it

Sections 37 & 38 – *No rights to occupy – refer to* Family Law Act 1996 *when required*

ADDITIONAL PROVISIONS – *for ss 33, 35 & 36 Orders only*

It is ordered that:

25. The *Applicant/Respondent* shall maintain and repair [*home*] AND/OR

26. The *Applicant/Respondent* shall pay the rent for [*home*] OR

27. The *Applicant/Respondent* shall pay the mortgage payments on [*home*] OR

28. The *Applicant/Respondent* shall pay the following for [*home*]:
. . . . [specify outgoings]

29. The *Applicant/Respondent in occupation* shall pay to the *other party* £ . . . . each [*week/month*] for [*home*]

30. The *Applicant/Respondent in occupation* shall keep and use the [*furniture/contents*] of [*home*] and the *Applicant/Respondent* shall return to the *Applicant/Respondent in occupation* the [furniture/contents/specify] no later than [date/time]

31. The Applicant/Respondent in occupation shall take reasonable care of the [*furniture/contents/specify*] of [*home*]

32. The *Applicant/Respondent in occupation* shall take all reasonable steps to keep secure [*home*] and the furniture or other contents [*specify if necessary*]

DURATION – *of occupation Orders*

Under s 33

33. This Order shall last until . . . . [date or event] OR

34. This Order shall last until a further Order is made

Under ss 35 & 37

35. This Order shall last until . . . . [date up to 6 months hence]

36. The occupation Order made on . . . . [date] is extended until . . . . [extension of up to 6 months]

Under ss 36 & 38

37. This Order shall last until . . . . [date up to 6 months hence]

38. The occupation Order made on [date] is extended until . . . . [extension of up to 6 months] and must end on that date

PROCEDURE FOR OBTAINING AN OCCUPATION ORDER

6.90 The basic procedural steps for obtaining an occupation order under any of the sections set out above are identical to those for applying for a non-molestation order (see **3.24**). However, there are certain additional provisions which must be observed, arising out of the fact that, as a property is always involved in an occupation order, the rights of third parties may have to be observed. These provisions are contained in FPR 10.3(3), which provides that a copy of an application for an occupation order under s 33, s 35 or s 36 must be served by the applicant by first class post on the mortgagee or, as the case may be, the landlord of the dwelling house in question with a notice in Form FL416 informing him of his right to make representations in writing or at any hearing. For a more detailed account of procedure, see CHAPTER 8.

Chapter 7

PROTECTION FROM HARASSMENT ACT 1997

INTRODUCTION TO THE PROTECTION FROM HARASSMENT ACT 1997

7.1 The protection available under Pt IV of FLA 1996 is not the only remedy for the victim of domestic violence. Soon after the FLA 1996 was enacted, the PHA 1997 was also enacted.

7.2 It is open to doubt whether the PHA 1997 was drafted with domestic violence in mind, but this seems to be its result.

7.3 The PHA 1997 was introduced after widespread public concern over the apparent inability of the law to control the practice known as 'stalking'. The essential characteristics of this phenomenon are the obsessive harassment of a victim, usually female, by someone who pursues her by following her movements, telephoning and so on. Any relationship between the parties has ended, if, indeed, it ever existed outside the imagination of the perpetrator. Several well-publicised cases led to a pledge by the government of the day to legislate to provide protection from this form of harassment. Unfortunately, whether or not the Act succeeded in achieving the aims of its proponents, it provides a system of law and procedure which is overlapping and parallel with Pt IV of the Family Law Act 1996, which may result in some confusion. Whether Parliament ignored the scope for confusion, or was unaware of the fact that it had recently debated at some length a measure providing very similar remedies is a matter for speculation.

7.4 The operation of the PHA 1997 is further complicated by the fact that it creates an offence of harassment which is the subject of the criminal law, and also provides civil remedies for the restraining of and damages for such offences, so that an unusual hybrid has come into being.

OFFENCES UNDER PHA 1997

7.5 The foundation of the PHA 1997 is laid in s 1, which provides that[1]:

> 'A person must not pursue a course of conduct—
> (a) which amounts to harassment of another, and

(b) which he knows or ought to know amounts to harassment of the other.'

1 PHA 1997, s 1(1).

7.6 Section 1(1A) then goes on to set out more detail. It provides that a person must not pursue a course of conduct:

(a) which involves harassment of two or more persons, and
(b) which he knows or ought to know involves harassment of those persons, and
(c) by which he intends to persuade any person (whether or not one of those mentioned above):
  (i) not to do something that he is entitled or required to do, or
  (ii) to do something that he is not under any obligation to do.

Section 1(2) clarifies the matter further. It provides that:

> 'For the purposes of this section [or section 2A(2)(c), the person whose course of conduct is in question ought to know that it amounts to [or involves] harassment of another if a reasonable person in possession of the same information would think the course of conduct amounted to harassment of the other.'

Section 1(3) provides an important safeguard by providing that:

> 'Subsection (1) [or (1A)] does not apply to a course of conduct if the person who pursued it shows—
> (a) that it was pursued for the purpose of preventing or detecting crime,
> (b) that it was pursued under any enactment or rule of law or to comply with any condition or requirement imposed by any person under any enactment, or
> (c) that in the particular circumstances the pursuit of the course of conduct was reasonable.'

7.7 By section 2(1) a person who pursues a course of conduct in breach of section 1(1) or (1A) is guilty of an offence and is liable on summary conviction to imprisonment for a term not exceeding six months, or a fine not exceeding level 5 on the standard scale, or both[1].

1 PFHA 1997, s 2(2).

7.8 The provisions set out so far constitute and define the offence of harassment. The PHA 1997 now goes on to create and define the offence of stalking. Section 2A(1) provides that a person is guilty of an offence if:

(a) the person pursues a course of conduct in breach of s 1(1), and
(b) the course of conduct amounts to stalking.

Stalking, for the purposes of s 2A(1)(b) (and s 4A(1)(a)) a person's course of conduct amounts to stalking of another person if:

(a) it amounts to harassment of that person,
(b) the acts or omissions involved are ones associated with stalking, and
(c) the person whose course of conduct it is knows or ought to know that the course of conduct amounts to harassment of the other person.

7.9 Section 2A(3) provides examples of acts or omission which in particular circumstances, are ones associated with stalking, as follows:

(a) following a person,
(b) contacting, or attempting to contact, a person by any means,
(c) publishing any statement or other material:
  (i) relating or purporting to relate to a person, or
  (ii) purporting to originate from a person,
(d) monitoring the use by a person of the internet, email or any other form of electronic communication,
(e) loitering in any place (whether public or private),
(f) interfering with any property in the possession of a person,
(g) watching or spying on a person.

7.10 By s 2A(4) a person guilty of an offence under this section is liable on summary conviction to imprisonment for a term not exceeding 51 weeks, or a fine not exceeding level 5 on the standard scale, or both.

7.11 Section 2B creates an important power of entry in relation to the offence of stalking. It provides that:

> (1) A justice of the peace may, on an application by a constable, issue a warrant authorising a constable to enter and search premises if the justice of the peace is satisfied that there are reasonable grounds for believing that—
>
> (a) an offence under section 2A has been, or is being, committed,
> (b) there is material on the premises which is likely to be of substantial value (whether by itself or together with other material) to the investigation of the offence,
> (c) the material—
>   (i) is likely to be admissible in evidence at a trial for the offence, and
>   (ii) does not consist of, or include, items subject to legal privilege, excluded material or special procedure material (within the meanings given by sections 10, 11 and 14 of the Police and Criminal Evidence Act 1984), and
> (d) either—
>   (i) entry to the premises will not be granted unless a warrant is produced, or
>   (ii) the purpose of a search may be frustrated or seriously prejudiced unless a constable arriving at the premises can secure immediate entry to them.
>
> (2) A constable may seize and retain anything for which a search has been authorised under subsection (1).
> (3) A constable may use reasonable force, if necessary, in the exercise of any power conferred by virtue of this section.
> (4) In this section "premises" has the same meaning as in section 23 of the Police and Criminal Evidence Act 1984.'

7.12 Section 4 provides protection against being put in fear of violence. It provides that:

> (1) A person whose course of conduct causes another to fear, on at least two occasions, that violence will be used against him is guilty of an offence if he knows or ought to know that his course of conduct will cause the other so to fear on each of those occasions.

(2) For the purposes of this section, the person whose course of conduct is in question ought to know that it will cause another to fear that violence will be used against him on any occasion if a reasonable person in possession of the same information would think the course of conduct would cause the other so to fear on that occasion.

(3) It is a defence for a person charged with an offence under this section to show that—

(a) his course of conduct was pursued for the purpose of preventing or detecting crime,

(b) this course of conduct was pursued under any enactment or rule of law or to comply with any condition or requirement imposed by any person under any enactment, or

(c the pursuit of his course of conduct was reasonable for the protection of himself or another or for the protection of his or another's property.

(4) A person guilty of an offence under this section is liable—

(a) on conviction on indictment, to imprisonment for a term not exceeding ten years, or a fine, or both, or,

(b) on summary conviction, to imprisonment for a term not exceeding six months, or a fine not exceeding the statutory maximum, or both.

(5) If on the trial on indictment of a person charged with an offence under this section the jury find him not guilty of the offence charged, they may find him guilty of an offence under section 2 or 2A.

(6) The Crown Court has the same powers and duties in relation to a person who is by virtue of subsection (5) convicted before it of an offence under section 2 or 2A as a magistrates' court would have on convicting him of the offence.'

CIVIL REMEDIES

7.13 The provisions considered far relate to criminal liabilities and will not be considered further here.

7.14 Civil remedies properly so-called arise under s 3, which provides as follows.

(a) An actual or apprehended breach of s 1 may be the subject of a claim in civil proceedings by the person who is or may be the victim of the course of conduct in question.

(b) On such a claim, damages may be awarded for (among other things) any anxiety caused by the harassment and any financial loss resulting from the harassment.

7.15 The PHA 1997 therefore provides a cause of action in damages. The right to apply for an injunction, which will probably be the most common civil remedy to be sought, is not specifically mentioned in the PHA 1997, but the general law as to interlocutory and final injunction orders applies.

7.16 Harassment therefore became a statutory tort on 16 June 1997, when most of the civil remedy provisions of the PHA 1997 were implemented. The scope of protection afforded by the law of torts has substantially been expanded by the PHA 1997. The remedy available under the Act may be supplemented by the general law of torts, in particular the torts of harassment amounting to nuisance, harassment at work amounting to interference with a contract of employment, personal injury by molestation, assault, battery and trespass. Before considering the detailed provisions of PHA 1997, some essential principles of the law of tort must be considered.

7.17 Personal injury by molestation, which became fully established in *Khorasandjian v Bush*[1], is wider than, but includes conduct amounting to assault and battery.

1 [1993] QB 727, [1993] 2 FLR 66.

No general remedy for invasion of privacy

7.18 There is 'no general remedy for invasion of privacy'[1]. 'It is well known that in English law there is no right to privacy, and accordingly there is no right of action for breach of a person's privacy'[2]. The practical effects of this are substantially mitigated by the new statutory tort of harassment, which provides a remedy against a 'course of conduct'[3] which amounts to harassment. However, the new tort does not cover a single act of invasion of privacy[4]. The courts might be ready to infer an intended course of conduct where a person, having once perpetrated a serious invasion of the privacy of another, threatens to repeat the invasion, in which case injunctive relief might be granted after only one actual invasion. However, the case-law which establishes that there is no tort of invasion of privacy in general is still good law.

1 Lord Denning MR in *Re X (A Minor) (Wardship: Restriction on Publication)* [1975] 1 All ER 697 at 704E.
2 Glidewell LJ in *Kaye v Robertson & Sport Newspapers Ltd* [1991] FSR 62.
3 PHA 1997, s 1(1).
4 PHA 1997, s 7(3).

Factual basis of an actual or threatened tort needed for grant of an injunction

7.19 An application based in tort must be supported by evidence that a tort has been committed or threatened[1]. Further, in general, no court can either grant an injunction against a person who is not a party to the proceedings[2] or join as a party someone against whom the plaintiff has no justiciable claim or lis[3].

1 *South Carolina Insurance Co v Assurantie Maatschappij 'De Zeven Provincien' NV* [1987] AC 24, [1986] 3 All ER 487; *Khorasandjian v Bush* [1993] QB 727, [1993] 2 FLR 66.
2 *Marengo v Daily Sketch and Sunday Graphic Ltd* [1948] 1 All ER 406.
3 See *Kalsi v Kalsi* [1992] 1 FLR 511 at 502A.

7.20 As to the standard of proof to be applied, see *Hipgrave and Hipgrave v Jones*[1], where it was held that in an action under s 3 of the Protection from Harassment Act 1997, the civil standard of proof applied. For a recent decision as to 'course of conduct' see *R v Patel*[2].

1 [2004] EWHC 290 (Fam).
2 [2004] EWCA Crim 3284.

Orders to exclude the defendant from an area surrounding the plaintiff's home and place of work

7.21 An injunction can be granted to forbid the defendant from entering a defined area within which the home of the plaintiff is situated. Such an injunction can be based on the plaintiff's right not to suffer harassment or, if she has a legal title to the home, any other relevant tortious acts which interfere with her peaceful enjoyment of her home.

7.22 In *Burris v Azadani*[1], the Court of Appeal held that an order prohibiting the defendant from being in a defined area in which the plaintiff's home was situated was possible, in support of an injunction forbidding tortious harassment. The court determined that the deletion of such an order in *Patel v Patel*[2] was not conclusive in principle, and that a person's right to exercise a public right of way can be over-ridden by an injunction prohibiting him from being within a specified area around the home of the applicant if his presence there is likely to lead to him committing some tortious harassment of the applicant. The court held that the general powers of the High Court in s 37(1) of the Senior Courts Act 1981 enable the court, where it appears necessary to ensure that an injunction forbidding tortious conduct shall be effective, to forbid coming within an exclusion zone around the home of the plaintiff. Sir Thomas Bingham MR said that such an order should not be made at all readily or without good reason, however, if the plaintiff has a legal right not to be harmed by the defendant, the court can grant such injunction as may be needed to protect the plaintiff from that harm.

1 [1996] 1 FLR 266, [1995] 4 All ER 802.
2 [1988] 2 FLR 179.

7.23 Although in *Hunter v Canary Wharf Ltd*[1], it was held that a licensee cannot sue in nuisance, a licensee such as the daughter of the tenants in *Khorasandjian v Bush* (above)[2], who can persuade the court that harassment is being perpetrated outside the home where she lives, may be able to obtain an injunction which forbids such harassment.

1 [1997] 2 All ER 426.
2 [1993] QB 727, [1993] 2 FLR 66.

7.24 The powers of the court to prohibit harassment can extend to prohibition of the exercise of a general public right in specified circumstances and may extend to forbidding any behaviour which may be likely to result in the person enjoined harassing or tortiously harming the applicant. Thus an exclusion zone could be imposed around the plaintiff's place of work as well as her home, provided that the court is satisfied that this is needed to protect the plaintiff from tortious harm.

HARASSMENT UNDER PHA 1997

The ingredients of and civil remedies against the statutory tort of harassment

7.25 The statutory tort of harassment, introduced by the PHA 1997, is a 'course of conduct' pursued by a person[1] 'which amounts to harassment of another'[2] and 'which he knows or ought to know amounts to harassment of the other [person]'[3]. Thus it must be a deliberate course of behaviour, which the perpetrator knew or should have known would amount to harassment, and which in fact harasses the other person.

1 PHA 1997, s 1(1).
2 PHA 1997, s 1(1)(a).
3 PHA 1997, s 1(1)(b).

7.26 The test for whether the perpetrator of conduct, which in fact amounts to harassment of the victim, knows or ought to know that the conduct amounts to harassment is objective[1]:

> ' . . . the person whose course of conduct is in question ought to know that it amounts to harassment of another if a reasonable person in possession of the same information would think the course of conduct amounted to harassment of the other.'

1 PHA 1997, s 1(2).

7.27 PHA 1997 provides a civil remedy for the victim of harassment[1], in which damages may be awarded[2] for 'any anxiety caused by the harassment and any financial loss resulting from the harassment'. An injunction may be granted[3]. The Act also enables a restraining order to be granted by a criminal court sentencing or dealing with a person convicted of a criminal offence of harassment under s 2, or convicted under s 4 of putting another in fear of violence on at least two occasions.

1 PHA 1997, s 3(1).
2 PHA 1997, s 3(2).
3 PHA 1997, s 3(3).

Definition of 'harassment'

7.28 Harassment includes, but is not restricted to 'alarming the person' or 'causing the person distress'[1]. 'Harassment . . . includes within it an element of intent, intent to cause distress or harm'[2]. Harassment is a 'course of conduct'[3]. '"Conduct" includes speech'[4].

1 PHA 1997, s 7(2).
2 Per Lord Donaldson MR in *Johnson v Walton* [1990] 1 FLR 350 at 352H.
3 PHA 1997, s 1(1).
4 PHA 1997, s 7(4).

7.29 In *Huntingdon Life Sciences Ltd v Curtin and Others*[1], Eady J said that the courts would resist any wide interpretation of the PHA 1997, and held that it could not be used to restrain public discussion and demonstration about matters of public interest.

1 [1997] TLR 646, (1997) The Times, December 11.

7.30 The tort of harassment is not complete unless the conduct amounting to harassment happened 'on at least two occasions'[1]. However, an 'apprehended' harassment 'may be the subject of a claim in civil proceedings by the person who is or may be the victim of the course of conduct in question'[2]. Therefore, where the evidence enables the court to conclude that the perpetrator is likely to conduct a course of harassing conduct, the court may restrain such anticipated conduct. However, the evidence would have to justify such a conclusion.

1 PHA 1997, s 7(3).
2 PHA 1997, s 3(1).

7.31 Two cases on the criminal aspects of harassment cast some further light on the meaning of the term. In *R v Hills*[1], the indictment was based on two assaults some six months apart, between which times the couple had frequently come back together and sexual intercourse had taken place. It was held that the necessary cogent link between the assaults had not been made out and there was not the requisite 'course of conduct'.

1 [2001] 1 FLR 580, CA.

7.32 In *R v Colohan*[1], it was held that (to justify a criminal conviction) it was necessary for the jury to answer the question of whether the defendant ought to have known that what he was doing amounted to harassment by the objective test of what a reasonable person would think. Section 1(3) of PHA 1997 posed an even more objective test, namely whether the conduct was reasonable.

1 [2001] 2 FLR 757, CA.

7.33 In *Singh v Bhakar and Bhakar*[1] (not a binding authority but one which carries considerable persuasive authority) a young woman of Sikh origin sued her mother in law under the PHA 1997 alleging that during her marriage the defendant conducted a campaign of harassment which had the effect of bringing the marriage to an end and caused her depression, and claiming general damages for injury and aggravated damages for the way in which the case had been conducted by the defendant. The judge found that the defendant had coerced the claimant into having her hair cut contrary to her religious obligations and traditions, forced her to wear a locket with Hindu symbols, restricted her use of the telephone and movements outside the home and her access to television and newspapers in order to isolate her, and made her do housework which was not only excessive but pointless and demeaning. The claimant's depression had been caused by the maltreatment she had suffered at the hands of the defendant. The provisions of the 1997 Act applied to the facts of this case. The defendant's treatment of the claimant was serious conduct and more than enough to amount to harassment for the purposes of the Act. General damages were assessed at £27,500 (plus an award for aggravated damages because of the way the defence had been pursued).

1 [2007] 1 FLR 880, Nottingham County Court.

Threatened repetition of a single harassing act

7.34 Although the tort is incomplete until the conduct complained of has happened 'on at least two occasions'[1], the courts have power to restrain a threatened tort. This is consistent with the availability of the civil remedy, provided under s 3(1), for an apprehended harassment.

1 PHA 1997, s 7(3).

7.35 By s 6 of PHA 1997, the standard limitation period of three years for bringing an action for personal injuries is disapplied. Therefore, where an act of harassment happened more than three years, and not more than six years, before civil proceedings are begun for harassment, that earlier act may be relied on as part of the conduct amounting to a course of conduct.

Justifiable harassment

7.36 By s 1(3) of PHA 1997, a person who pursues a course of conduct which might otherwise amount to harassment, is excused from liability, civil and criminal, if the person who pursued it shows:

> '(a) that it was pursued for the purpose of preventing or detecting crime,
> (b) that it was pursued under any enactment or rule of law or to comply with any condition or requirement imposed by any person under any enactment, or
> (c) that in the particular circumstances the pursuit of the course of conduct was reasonable.'

HARASSMENT AMOUNTING TO NUISANCE

7.37 Nuisance is based on infringement of a right to peaceful occupation of real property or exercise of an easement. Therefore, nuisance cannot provide the legal basis for personal protection against conduct which does not interfere with a legal right of occupation of property or exercise of an easement. In *Hunter v Canary Wharf Ltd*[1], overruling *Khorasandjian v Bush*[2] on this point, it was confirmed that a licensee (a daughter of the parents with legal title in *Khorasandjian v Bush*) has insufficient legal interest in occupation of a house to found the tort.

1 [1997] 2 All ER 426, HL.
2 [1993] QB 727, [1993] 2 FLR 66.

7.38 Loitering near a person's home, where the plaintiff has legal title to the home, also can be forbidden if the court considers that the loitering seriously interferes with the plaintiff's enjoyment of her home[1].

1 See *J Lyons & Sons Ltd v Wilkins* [1989] 1 Ch 255; *Ward Lock & Co Ltd v Operative Printer's Assistants' Society* (1906) 22 TLR 327; *Hubbard v Pitt* [1976] QB 142, [1975] 3 All ER 1; *Pidduck v Molloy* [1992] 2 FLR 202 at 205H–206A.

7.39 Noise can amount to nuisance. In *Soltau v De Held*[1], it was held that excessive bell-ringing could amount to nuisance.

1 (1851) 1 Sim (NS) 133.

7.40 Persistent or abusive telephone calls can amount to nuisance[1]. Professor Flemming in the leading Australian book *The Law of Torts* (7th edn) says (at p 575):

> 'Clearly, no liability is warranted unless the intrusion is substantial and of a kind that a reasonable person of normal sensitivity would regard as offensive and intolerable. Merely knocking at another's door or telephoning on one or two occasions is not actionable, even when designed to cause annoyance; but if the calls

are repeated with persistence, and in the midst of night, so as to interfere unreasonably with comfort or sleep, liability will ensue.'

1 *Khorasandjian v Bush* [1993] QB 727, [1993] 2 FLR 66; *Stoakes v Brydges* [1958] QWN 5, (1958) 32 Austral LJ 205; *Motherwell v Motherwell* (1977) 73 DLR (3d) 62 at 74.

7.41 Persistent 'silent telephone calls' causing psychiatric injury can amount to an assault[1].

1 *R v Ireland; R v Burstow* [1998] 1 FLR 105, [1997] 4 All ER 225, HL.

7.42 Persistent or abusive, harassing telephone calls which amount to interference with the peaceful occupation of the plaintiff's home could be held to be a nuisance, whether made by night or by day[1].

1 *Khorasandjian v Bush* [1993] QB 727, [1993] 2 FLR 66.

HARASSMENT AT THE PLAINTIFF'S PLACE OF WORK: INTERFERENCE WITH A CONTRACT OF EMPLOYMENT

7.43 Sometimes, pestering a victim at or near his or her place of work can amount to harassment. Sometimes, the pestering is done to re-establish communication with the victim, sometimes to denigrate the victim in the eyes of his or her employer. Such conduct is susceptible of relief against the tort of harassment.

7.44 Following *Burris v Azadani*[1], it would appear that where the court concludes that an injunction should be granted to forbid harassment, the injunction could include forbidding the defendant from harassing the plaintiff near his or her place of work, and from entering a specified area around the plaintiff's place of work.

1 [1996] 1 FLR 266, [1995] 4 All ER 802; see also **4.8**.

7.45 Interference with a contract of employment by unlawful conduct intended to induce an employer to dismiss an employee is an actionable tort[1]. 'Molestation' and 'obstruction' can amount to unlawful interference with a contract of employment[2]. However, aggressive trade competition by a rival business, not amounting to unlawful interference with a contract, is neither actionable nor restrainable[3].

1 *Read v The Friendly Society of Operative Stonemasons of England, Ireland and Wales and Others* [1902] 1 KB 732; *Conway v Wade* [1909] AC 506.
2 *Mogul Steamship Co Ltd v McGregor, Gow & Co* (1889) 23 QBD 598 at 607, 614, 622 and 626; *National Phonographic Co Ltd v Edison-Bell Consolidated Phonograph Co Ltd* [1908] 1 Ch 355 at 355, 361 and 369.
3 See *Mogul Steamship Co Ltd v McGregor, Gow & Co* (1889) 23 QBD 598 at 614 and 620.

7.46 No reported cases are known in which the court has given a remedy on the basis that a tortious interference with a contract has been committed by acts primarily motivated by a malignant personal relationship between the defendant and the plaintiff[1]. However, it may be that where the defendant harasses or molests the plaintiff by oppressive and injurious visits, letters or telephone calls to the premises of the plaintiff's employer, and the defendant's acts are of a character that enables the court to infer that the defendant must have known and intended that the employer will be driven to dismiss the plaintiff, such molestation could amount to a restrainable tort. In such a case, an appropriate formulation of an injunction might be:

> 'The defendant is forbidden to communicate with the employers of the plaintiff whether by visits, letters or telephone calls to their premises in any way calculated to cause the said employers to dismiss the plaintiff.'

1 See *Glamorgan Coal Co Ltd and Others v South Wales Miners' Federation and Others* [1903] 2 KB 545 at 577; *Crofter Hand Woven Harris Tweed Co Ltd and Another v Veitch and Another* [1942] AC 435 at 442–443.

PERSONAL INJURY BY MOLESTATION

7.47 In *Burnett v George*[1], and *Khorasandjian v Bush*[2], the tort of personal injury by molestation was recognised. Actual or threatened probable injury to physical or mental health must be proved or reasonably foreseeable. Psychological harm can amount to actual bodily harm[3]. The perpetrator must have intended or realised that his conduct was likely to cause impairment to the health of the victim.

1 [1992] 1 FLR 525, CA.
2 [1993] 2 FLR 66, CA.
3 *R v Ireland; R v Burstow* [1998] 1 FLR 105, [1997] 4 All ER 225, HL; *Kendrick v Kendrick* [1990] 2 FLR 107.

7.48 The new statutory tort of harassment diminishes the circumstances in which it might be useful to resort to the tort of personal injury by molestation. However, where the victim of threatened further harassment, following a single severe act of harassment which caused harm to the mental health of the victim, seeks injunctive relief, the separate tort may provide a peg on which to hang an injunction if the court is reluctant to discern a 'course of conduct' within s 7(3) of PHA 1997.

7.49 Intentional bad behaviour, calculated to cause distress or harm, must be proved in support of the allegation of personal injury by molestation[1].

1 See Lord Donaldson MR in *Johnson v Walton* [1990] 1 FLR 350 at 352H.

TRESPASS

Removal of an obstreperous adult from the family home

7.50 The most convenient remedy for removal of an obstreperous adult from the home is an occupation order under s 33 of the FLA 1996 (see **6.54**).

7.51 An adult child, relative or friend living in the family home with the plaintiff can be ordered to leave and not to return on the basis of the tort of trespass, provided that the person has no legal right to stay there other than a revocable licence and that licence has been terminated[1].

1 See *Egan v Egan* [1975] Ch 218, [1975] 2 All ER 167; *Waterhouse v Waterhouse* (1905) 94 LT 133; *Stevens v Stevens* (1907) 24 TLR 20.

7.52 Provided that a licensee shares accommodation with the family, and the premises are the principal home of the licensor or another member of his family, the licence will be an 'excluded licence' within the meaning of the Protection from Eviction Act 1977, s 3A, and the licensee will not be entitled to protection under that Act.

WARRANT FOR ARREST FOR BREACH OF INJUNCTION FORBIDDING HARASSMENT

Availability of warrant

7.53 Under PHA 1997, s 3(3), (4) and (5) where, following the grant of an injunction forbidding harassment, a judge, including a district judge, 'has reasonable grounds for believing that the defendant has done anything which he is prohibited from doing by the injunction', which must be substantiated on oath, a warrant for the arrest of the defendant may be issued by the judge. A warrant of arrest cannot be granted for breach of an undertaking in respect of tortious harassment, as s 3(3), (4) applies only in respect of breach of an injunction.

7.54 A person who disobeys an injunction granted under s 3 of the 1997 Act cannot be both convicted of an offence under s 3(6) and punished for contempt in respect of the same conduct[1].

1 PHA 1997, s 3(7), (8).

7.55 The remedy of power of arrest is not available at the time when the injunction is granted.

SPECIMEN CLAUSES FOR FORBIDDING TORTIOUS PERSONAL MOLESTATION

7.56 In the discussion above, it is demonstrated that the variety of relief available in the law of torts is more extensive than the conventional injunctions against assault and trespass. As the variety of possible injunctive clauses which may be helpful for an injunction where personal molestation or harassment by a relative or former cohabitant is complained of is so extensive, a menu of specimen clauses is offered at **7.57**. Some of the language in the menu, which appeared in the first edition of *Emergency Remedies* (Jordan Publishing), was adopted in *Pidduck v Molloy*[1] and *Khorasandjian v Bush*[2], and was not criticised in the Court of Appeal.

1 [1992] 2 FLR 202.
2 [1993] QB 727, [1993] 2 FLR 66.

Menu of specimen clauses for molestation injunctions in torts

7.57 An example of a clause for a molestation injunction order is set out below:

> *The claimant applies to the court for an injunction order in the following terms:*
>
> *That the Defendant (name) . . . be forbidden whether by himself or by instructing any other person to do any unlawful act of the kind listed below.*

(1) harassing or harming the claimant, whether by actual or threatened violence, or any other conduct likely to cause her alarm, distress, physical or mental harm, and whether she is at home, at work, in any public place or anywhere else;
(2) wrongful damage to or interference with the personal possessions of the claimant (including any motor vehicle which belongs to or is being used by the claimant);
(3) coming or being within [200] metres of the home of the claimant.
[Additional possible detailed clauses]
(4 and 5 are available only to a claimant who has a legal title to the property)
(4) disturbing the peaceful occupation by the claimant of her home and property at . . . (whether by [loitering outside or] [being within 200 metres thereof or] [making (abusive) telephone calls (persistently or) (late at night)] or in any other way]);
(5) trespassing on the home of the claimant;
(6) interfering with the employment of the claimant whereby the employers of the plaintiff may be induced to dismiss the claimant: the defendant is forbidden to harass or pester . . . , the employers of the claimant, and is forbidden to harass or pester the claimant at or entering or leaving . . . , her place of work.

Duration of injunction against, or undertaking about, torts

7.58 An injunction granted to forbid tortious harassment should be tailored in length to suit the circumstances of the case. Three and six months are common upon a first application.

7.59 Undertakings may be given for as long as the giver accepts; three months is common.

PROCEDURE FOR APPLICATIONS UNDER THE PHA 1997

7.60 There are no new rules relating to applications under PHA 1997, s 3(1), and the general rules of procedure apply. Proceedings may be issued in the High Court, but this is likely to be unusual and the procedure to be considered here will be that of the county courts, to which the great majority of applications are likely to be made. The former Principal Registry of the Family Division does not have jurisdiction since its jurisdiction is limited to family business.

7.61 Proceedings may be issued as follows:

(a) Liquidated claim where no injunction sought.
Default summons (Form N1).
(b) Unliquidated claim, or liquidated claim with an injunction application.
Fixed date summons (Form N2 or N3).
(c) Free-standing injunction (not linked to damages claim).
Form N16a (as amended).

The requirements for applications for injunctions will be the same as those for any other injunction.

7.62 Where the damages sought are limited to £3,000, and a defence is filed, the action will be dealt with as a small claim. Where damages are limited to £5,000 (or such sum as is the district judge's current trial jurisdiction), or no damages are sought, the district judge will have jurisdiction.

7.63 The following quick guide may assist as a procedural check.

Which court?	Any county court. Where damages are sought, district judge has jurisdiction up to £15,000 and a circuit judge above that figure.
Documents to issue.	Claim form N1 (including particulars of claim and statement of truth where possible). Particulars of claim (where not endorsed on N1). Any medical report to be relied on. Draft order. Form N16A (where interim order sought). Affidavit in support of any interim order.
Interim orders.	Application without notice is made to district judge in chambers. If order made, this must be served with the documents listed above. A return day giving at least two days' notice will be fixed.
Interim orders.	Application without notice is made to district judge in chambers. If order made, this must be served with the documents listed above. A return day giving at least two days' notice will be fixed.
Service.	Where no interim order made, court office serves documents on defendant. Where interim order made and return date fixed, claimant must serve all documents above plus the interim order. NB personal service of interim order is required. Claimant must file affidavit of service.
Hearing.	Where interim order made, hearing on return day. Order either continued, dismissed or varied. Where case continues, directions given as to filing of defence and evidence. Where no interim order, full hearing fixed (probably about 6 weeks ahead). Before that date defendant intending to oppose should have filed defence and evidence. Where final order made, claimant must serve on defendant.

ENFORCEMENT UNDER THE PHA 1997

7.64 Enforcement is dealt with in s 3(3)–(6). There is no provision for the attachment of a power of arrest to the order itself, and the procedure is very similar to that prescribed for the issue of a warrant of arrest under s 47 of FLA 1996.

7.65 Where the court grants an injunction for the purpose of restraining a defendant from pursuing any course of conduct which amounts to harassment, and the plaintiff considers that the defendant has done anything which he is prohibited from doing by the injunction, the plaintiff may apply for a warrant for the arrest of the defendant[1]. Where the injunction is granted by a county court, application may be made to a judge or district judge of that or any other county court[2].

1 PHA 1997, s 3(3).
2 PHA 1997, s 3(4).

7.66 The judge or district judge may only issue a warrant if the application is substantiated on oath, and he has reasonable grounds for believing that the defendant has done anything which he is prohibited from doing by the injunction[1].

1 PHA 1997, s 3(5).

7.67 The procedure set out above is of course in addition to what was the usual method of dealing with contempt, namely a notice to show cause as to why the offender should not be committed.

CRIMINAL PENALTY FOR BREACH OF INJUNCTION

7.68 As an alternative to the civil contempt procedure, the PHA 1997 provides that when the High Court or a county court has granted an injunction for the purpose of restraining a defendant from pursuing any course of conduct which amounts to harassment, and, without reasonable excuse, the defendant does anything which he is prohibited from doing by the injunction, he is guilty of an offence[1]. Such an offence attracts a penalty of up to five years' imprisonment or a fine or both, on conviction on indictment, or, on summary conviction, up to six months' imprisonment or a fine not exceeding the statutory maximum or both[2].

1 PHA 1997, s 3(6).
2 PHA 1997, s 3(9).

7.69 However, a person cannot be convicted of an offence under sub-s (6) in respect of any conduct which has been punished as a contempt of court[1]. Similarly, where a person is convicted of an offence under sub-s (6), that conduct is not punishable as a contempt of court[2].

1 PHA 1997, s 3(8).
2 PHA 1997, s 3(7).

7.70 A person seeking to punish breach of an injunction will therefore have to elect as to whether to deal with the matter by civil committal or to seek to bring about a criminal prosecution.

LIMITATION OF ACTION UNDER THE PHA 1997

7.71 A claim for harassment is, in effect, a claim for personal injuries, and would normally be subject to a limitation period of three years. To avoid any problems which this might cause, s 6 of PHA 1997 amends s 11 of the Limitation Act 1980 by inserting a new sub-s (1A) which provides that s 11 (which contains the respective periods of limitation) does not apply to any action brought for damages under s 3 of PHA 1997.

7.72 It will therefore be possible to rely on events forming a course of conduct going back in time without limit.

COMPARISON OF THE PHA 1997 AND PT IV OF THE FLA 1996

7.73 As has been seen, the PHA 1997 overlaps with Pt IV of FLA 1996, and a victim of domestic violence may have to decide under which statute proceedings should be brought. The following considerations may be among those to be considered.

Availability of remedy

7.74 An applicant for an occupation order would not choose to bring proceedings under the PHA 1997 because it provides no remedy comparable with those in Pt IV of the FLA 1996. The comparison is therefore limited to non-molestation orders.

7.75 Both statutes provide protection against harassment, the legal definition of which must be identical in both cases. Although the PHA 1997 is intended to provide for conduct falling short of physical assault, there can be little doubt that physical assault amounts to harassment. There is nothing in the PHA 1997 which makes it more difficult to establish harassment, save that it requires proof of a course of conduct, defined as conduct on at least two occasions.

Entitlement to apply

7.76 As was seen at **2.5** et seq, in order to apply for a non-molestation order under Pt IV of FLA 1996, the applicant must be 'associated' with the other party, and there is a complicated list of who may be associated. There is no such requirement in respect of the PHA 1997, s 1 merely refers to 'a person' and 'another'. In this respect, therefore, there may be some advantage in the PHA 1997. Anyone may apply for an order against anyone else.

Nature of remedy

7.77 The first and most obvious advantage of the PHA 1997 is that, if a victim could persuade the police to become involved, there might be a prosecution under either s 2 or s 4, which would relieve the victim of the responsibility of taking civil action. However, it may be open to doubt that the police would wish to be involved in most domestic disputes where a civil remedy would be available.

7.78 Apart from this, the civil orders which could be obtained under the two statutes would seem to be identical; in neither case is there any limitation on the time during which the order will remain in force.

7.79 Section 42(5) of FLA 1996 sets out guidelines which the court must observe when deciding whether or not to grant a non-molestation injunction. The PHA 1997 contains no such guidelines so that, in theory, the court would be unconstrained.

Undertakings

7.80 As can be seen at **8.55** et seq, Pt IV of FLA 1996 contains provision for an application to be resolved by one party giving an undertaking, which is then as enforceable as an order of the court. This is, in fact, how the great majority of domestic violence applications have always been resolved. There is nothing in the PHA 1997 which permits the court to accept an undertaking, and certainly nothing regarding its enforceability. It may be argued that there was nothing in the DVMPA 1976 to permit undertakings to be given; the court has an inherent jurisdiction to accept an undertaking, and the practice of the court evolved over a period of time and now reflected in, for example prescribed forms in the county court, clearly gives the court a discretion.

7.81 On the other hand, it may be said that there is nothing in the Act to support this, and it might be argued that, Parliament having gone to some lengths to prescribe the availability and enforceability of undertakings in Pt IV of FLA 1996, it would not intentionally have left the question in doubt in the PHA 1997 so soon afterwards.

7.82 If the latter argument were to be accepted (which is probably unlikely, but possible in theory), the court would have the choice of either granting or refusing an application, with no room for 'settlement' or compromise.

Enforcement

7.83 One advantage of a Pt IV order was that a power of arrest could be attached. This is no longer the case now that the DCVCA 2004 is implemented. Of course the system of applying for a warrant of arrest is common to both statutes.

Choice of court

7.84 Applications under FLA 1996, Pt IV may be brought in magistrates' courts or in a county court (now the Family Court) or the High Court, whereas protection under the PHA 1997 is only available in a county court or in the High Court.

Combined applications

7.85 There would seem to be no reason in principle why the provisions of both statutes should not be relied on in the same application, and why, except in matters proceeding in the PRFD, the court should not make an order, or orders, drawing on its jurisdiction under both statutes (provided, of course, that the orders did not duplicate each other).

Chapter 8

PROCEDURES FOR PERSONAL PROTECTION ORDERS

APPLICATIONS FOR PERSONAL PROTECTION ORDERS AND INJUNCTIONS

Preliminary note

8.1 The procedural rules governing the Domestic Abuse Bill 2020 have not yet been promulgated or introduced, so little can be said about it. This chapter will therefore deal only with the procedures for dealing with applications under Pt IVFLA 1996. however, particulars of the new procedures for the protection of witnesses are included here since they are significant changes which may well be introduced generally before the rules governing the Bill.

Venue when starting proceedings under FLA 1996, Pt IV

8.2 Part IV of FLA 1996 followed the ChA 1989 in conferring concurrent jurisdiction to hear most applications on the High Court, specified county courts and family proceedings courts[1]. The Lord Chancellor has power to make rules about where proceedings should start or be transferred, and with the introduction of the Family Court in April 2104, proceedings must now be issued in the Family Court[2]. The case will be allocated to a judge under the Family Court (Composition and Distribution of Business) Rules 2014.

1 FLA 1996, s 57(8).
2 FPR 5.4

8.3 With regard to occupation orders, s 59 placed a limitation on the family proceedings courts' powers to the extent that magistrates are not competent to hear any application or to make an order involving a disputed question as to any party's entitlement to occupy any property unless it is unnecessary to determine the question in order to deal with the application or make the order. In practice, this provision is not likely to apply very often as such issues rarely arise in personal protection applications. Furthermore, as an emergency measure, a family proceedings court could always decide that it is unnecessary to determine a dispute as to title to property prior to making an initial occupation order for the protection of the applicant or a relevant child, allowing the dispute as to title to be dealt with later in a county court or the High Court, following transfer of the proceedings. With the advent of the

Family Court, and the allocation of proceedings within the court, these issues should no longer be of practical importance.

8.4 Actions for injunctions under the law of torts have no place in the Family Court and should be conducted in county courts. Similarly, claims under the PHA 1997 may not be issued in the Family Court and should be issued in either the High Court or a county court.

Transfer of proceedings between courts

8.5 Before the advent of the Family Court there was specific statutory provision to allow a family proceedings court to decline jurisdiction when it considered the case could be more conveniently dealt with in another court[1]. In addition, the Family Law Act 1986 (Pt IV) Allocation of Proceedings Order 1997 permitted transfer of proceedings under Pt IV. The arrival of the Family Court from April 2014 should mean that these somewhat complicated provisions are no longer necessary.

1 FLA 1996, s 59(2).

Standard form of application for non-molestation or occupation order

8.6 The standard Prescribed Form of application, Form FL401, for an order under Pt IV of FLA 1996, is designed to elicit from the applicant the details which make him or her eligible to apply for an order and the details of what orders are sought. Form FL401 will be found in **Appendix 3**. While this entails more careful preparation than was the case under the previous law, the form really requires no more attention than would be necessary in any event to find the right pigeonhole for applications, given the complexity of the law in the Act. The form operates as a checklist and, in practice, facilitates applications being made appropriately. The separate menus of possible orders, in Prescribed Form FL404 et seq, specify which detailed occupation orders are available according to which section of the Act is applicable. See **8.48** below for further details. These menus enable someone advising a client, and preparing an application, to be clear about what is available for the client. They also operate as useful checklists for courts to see readily what they can order in each particular case. See **6.19–6.77**.

Evidence in support required for application for FLA 1996, Pt IV order or injunction against torts

8.7 FPR 10.2 requires a witness statement in support of an application to a county court, which is required by FPR 10.3(1)(a) to be served with the application in Form FL401. An affidavit in support is required for an application for an injunction forbidding torts[1].

1 CCR Ord 13, r 6(3).

General requirements appropriate for evidence in support of application

8.8 The evidence of the applicant and any corroborative witness, submitted in support of an application, should set out succinctly the essential facts relied on.

Special requirement where application begun without notice

8.9 No additional form is required in addition to the standard Form FL401 to begin an application without notice. However, the grounds why an order without notice is needed are required to be set out in the statement in support[1].

1 CCR Ord 13, r 6(3A).

Special requirement for permission for child under the age of 16 to apply for a non-molestation or occupation order

8.10 A child under the age of 16 can make an application for a non-molestation order or an occupation order, but requires permission[1] of the High Court. The circumstances relied on for obtaining permission must be set out adequately in support of the application. (See discussion in Chapter **2** at **2.50**.)

1 FLA 1996, s 43(1).

Special requirement where applicant relies on agreement to marry

8.11 An applicant who is eligible to apply for a non-molestation order[1] or occupation order[2] by reason of an agreement to marry the respondent made within three years preceding the application, will need to assert the evidence required by s 44.

1 FLA 1996, s 42(4).
2 FLA 1996, s 33(2).

8.12 Under s 44(1), an agreement in writing to marry suffices. Under s 44(2), an agreement to marry may be proved by the gift of an engagement ring or a ceremony of betrothal witnessed by other persons.

APPLICATIONS WITHOUT NOTICE, INFORMAL NOTICE, AND ABRIDGED AND SUBSTITUTED SERVICE

The power to grant an initial order without notice

8.13 Section 45(1) of FLA 1996, reflecting the general law, allows a court 'in any case where it considers it just and convenient to do so, [to] make an occupation order or a non-molestation order even though the respondent has not been given such notice of the proceedings . . . '. The power is subject to criteria in s 45(2) (see **8.18**).

8.14 In county court actions founded in torts, an application can be begun without notice[1].

1 CCR Ord 13, r 6(3A), CPR 25.3(3) and PD 25 (interim injunctions), para 4.

8.15 Before proceeding without notice, the applicant and the court should consider whether it would be better to give 'informal notice' (ie short notice), or abridge the time for service or provide for substituted service[1].

1 See *Wookey v Wookey; Re S (A Minor)* [1991] 2 FLR 319 at 323G, quoted at **8.12**.

8.16 For the situation of a respondent who objects to an order without notice, see Chapter 10.

8.17 The statement in support of an application for an order without notice must contain reasons as to why the application is being made without notice to the respondent.

Criteria for applications without notice

8.18 Orders without notice should be the exception, not the norm. The criteria applicable when an application is begun without notice under FLA 1996, Pt IV are set out in s 45(2). Section 45(2) reflects the policy in previous case-law in civil as well as family proceedings.

8.19 FLA 1996, s 45(2) states:

> 'In determining whether to exercise its powers under subsection (1) [to grant an occupation or non-molestation order without notice] the court shall have regard to all the circumstances including—
> (a) any risk of significant harm to the applicant or a relevant child, attributable to the conduct of the respondent, if the order is not made immediately;
> (b) whether it is likely that the applicant will be deterred or prevented from pursuing the application if an order is not made immediately; and
> (c) whether there is reason to believe that the respondent is aware of the proceedings but is deliberately evading service and that the applicant or a relevant child will be seriously prejudiced by the delay involved—
> (i) where the court is a magistrates' court, in effecting service of proceedings; or
> (ii) in any other case, in effecting substituted service.'

8.20 The policy that orders without notice should be the exception, not the norm, has not always been respected in some courts. An order granted without notice inherently carries a risk of inflaming the situation, whereas at a hearing on notice the respondent frequently accepts that the applicant needs protection and is willing to submit to an injunction or give a binding undertaking. Most respondents do not know that an order without notice is only provisional and subject to early review as if nothing had been proved. Upon receiving service of an order without notice, it is likely that it will appear to most respondents that the court has assumed that the allegations made against him were accepted as true by the court without question.

8.21 A hearing on notice is an opportunity to address outstanding issues. For example, allegations of molestation are often answered by a respondent claiming that the applicant has frustrated contact with a child: if the first hearing is held urgently and on notice, mutually acceptable arrangements for contact with a child may be achieved and the problem defused. Orders which interfere with civil liberties ought not to be made without notice unless they are clearly warranted; audi alterem partem is a fundamental legal principle of great importance.

8.22 CPR 25.3(1) enables the court to grant an order without notice 'if it appears to the court that there are good reasons for not giving notice', and the reasons for not giving notice must be set out in the applicant's evidence in support[1]. CPR PD 25 (interim injunctions), para 4.3 prescribes further requirements of the applicant, and para 4.5 provides for urgent, out-of-hours telephone applications.

1 CPR 25.3(3).

Case-law on the policy

8.23 In *Loseby v Newman* Hoffman LJ said:

> 'An ex parte order should be made only when either there is no time to give the defendant notice to appear, or when there is reason to believe that the defendant, if given notice, would take action which would defeat the purpose of the order[1].'

In *Wookey v Wookey; Re S (A Minor)* Butler-Sloss LJ said:

> 'Ex parte applications for injunctions should, in general, only be made where there are strong grounds to justify such an application, where there is real urgency and impossibility of giving notice. It will often be preferable to abridge time, and the respondent may attend on short notice. In cases such as application for a non-molestation order, the presence of both sides may well lead to agreed undertakings and the opportunity for the judge to try to reduce the tension in family disputes and to underline the importance of compliance with the undertaking accepted or the order granted[2].

1 [1995] 2 FLR 754 at 758C.
2 [1991] 2 FLR 319 at 323G.

8.24 These words of Butler-Sloss LJ remain appropriate as a statement of the policy in relation to applications without notice.

8.25 *Loseby v Newman*[1] followed a clear line of case law. An application for an injunction should not be made, or granted, without notice unless there is real immediate danger of serious injury or irreparable damage[2]. The principle that both sides must be heard can be displaced only where it appears to the court that giving the other party an opportunity to be heard 'appears likely to cause injustice to the applicant, by reason either of the delay involved or the action which it appears likely that the respondent or others would take before the order can be made[3]'.

1 [1995] 2 FLR 754.
2 *Beese (Managers of Kimpton Church of England Primary School) v Woodhouse* [1970] 1 All ER 769; *Practice Note (Matrimonial Cause: Injunction)* [1978] 2 All ER 919.
3 *Re First Express Ltd* [1991] BCC 782 at 785.

8.26 An application for an injunction without notice, including one for personal protection should not be made, or granted, unless either it is not reasonably practicable to give notice, even informal notice (see below), or giving notice would give the defendant time to defeat the purpose of the application and it is likely that he would do so[1].

1 *Ansah v Ansah* [1977] Fam 138, CA, [1977] 2 All ER 638; *G v G (Ouster: Ex Parte Application)* [1990] 1 FLR 395, CA; *Wookey v Wookey; Re S (A Minor)* [1991] 2 FLR 319, CA; *Practice Note (Matrimonial Cause: Injunction)* [1978] 2 All ER 919; *Re First Express Ltd* [1991] BCC 782; *Bates v Lord Hailsham of St Marylebone* [1972] 3 All ER 1019.

8.27 A good statement of principle on these issues is contained in the judgments of Munby J in *Re W (Ex Parte Orders)*[1] and *Re S (Ex Parte Orders)*[2]. The following guidelines were set out.

(a) Those who obtained injunctive relief without notice were under a duty to make the fullest disclosure of all the relevant circumstances known to them.
(b) The applicant is also under a duty to bring to the attention of the respondent at the earliest practicable opportunity the evidential and other persuasive materials on the basis of which the injunction had been granted.
(c) Generally, the court would require the applicant to give an undertaking to serve proceedings on the respondent at the earliest opportunity, such proceedings to include copies of all evidence and orders including a return date; where the order had been made otherwise than on the basis of sworn evidence, a statement or affidavit must be sworn and served. Where no such undertaking was obtained, the applicant and her solicitor still had an obligation to act in these terms.
(d) Any order without notice should set out on its face, whether by way of recital or in a schedule, a list of all affidavits, statements and other evidential materials read by the judge.

1 [2000] 2 FLR 927.
2 [2001] 1 FLR 308.

8.28 The most recent example is *R v R (Family Court: Procedural Fairness)*[1] where Peter Jackson J set out a number of principles to govern orders without notice, as follows:

(1) The default position of a judge faced with a without notice application should always be 'why?' not 'why not?' Without notice applications can only be made in exceptional circumstances with proper consideration for the rights of the absent party.
(2) The court should use its sweeping powers under the FLA 1996 with caution, particularly at a one-sided hearing.
(3) When an order is made it is the responsibility of the court and any lawyers involved to ensure that it is accurately drafted.
(4) Extra injunctive powers such as exclusion orders and orders prohibiting direct communication should not be routinely included in non-molestation orders. They are serious infringements of freedom of action and required specific evidence to justify them.

1 [2014] EWFC 48, [2015] 1 WlR 2743, [2015] 2 FLR 1005.

8.29 The question of the duration of a without notice order has recently been the subject of Practice Guidance[1] by Sir James Munby P who stated that the law was to be found in the following decisions:

- *Horgan v Horgan*[2];
- *R (Casey) v Restormel Borough Council*[3];
- *In re C (A Child) (Family Proceedings: Practice)*[4]; and
- *JM v CZ*[5].

1 *Practice Guidance: Family Court – Duration of Ex Parte (Without Notice) Orders* dated 13 October 2014.
2 [2002] EWCA Civ 1371, paras 5–6 (Ward LJ).
3 [2007] EWHC 2554 (Admin), paras 37–41 (Munby J).
4 [2013] EWCA Civ 1412, [2014] 1 WLR 2182, [2014] 1 FLR 1239, para 15 (Ryder LJ).
5 [2014] EWHC 1125 (Fam), paras 5–13 (Mostyn J).

8.30 His Lordship went on to summarise the principles, compliance with which is essential in all cases, as follows:

(a) An ex parte (without notice) injunctive order must never be made without limit of time. There must be a fixed end date.
(b) It is not sufficient merely to specify a return day. The order must specify on its face and in clear terms precisely when it expires (eg, 4.30pm on 19 November 2014).
(c) The duration of the order should not normally exceed 14 days.
(d) The order must also specify the date, time and place of the hearing on the return day. It is usually convenient for this date to coincide with the expiry date of the order (eg, list the return day for 10.30am on 19 November 2014 and specify that the order expires at 4.30pm on 19 November 2014).
(e) The order (see FPR 18.10(3)) 'must contain a statement of the right to make an application to set aside or vary the order under r 18.11'. The phrase 'liberty to apply on 24 hours' notice' is not sufficient for this purpose. The order must spell out that the respondent is entitled, without waiting for the return day, to apply on notice (the details of which and the need for which must be set out on the face of the order) to set aside or vary the order.
(f) If the respondent does apply to set aside or vary the order the court must list the application as a matter of urgency, within a matter of days at most.

8.31 His Lordship was aware of the practical difficulties which might arise and added the following:

> 'Experience suggests that in certain types of case, for example, non-molestation injunctions granted in accordance with Pt IV of the Family Law Act 1996, the respondent frequently neither applies to set aside or vary the order nor attends the hearing on the return day. In such cases the court may decide to proceed in the way suggested by Mostyn J in *JM v CZ* [2014] EWHC 1125 (Fam), para 13:
>
> > "the return date should be listed, say, 14 days after the initial ex parte order had been made but that the respondent ought to confirm in writing, seven days before the return date, both to the applicant and to the court, whether he in fact wished to attend on the return date and to argue for variation or discharge of the order; and that if the respondent failed to write to the court within that period, it would

be open to the applicant to notify the court that the return date should be vacated and to invite the court to extend the injunction as a matter of box work."'

8.32 To ensure compliance with these principles, his Lordship suggested that the following form of order be used:

'1 Paragraph(s) [*insert*] of this order shall be effective against the respondent [*insert* names] once it is personally served on [him]/[her] [and/or] once [he]/[she] is made aware of the terms of this order whether by personal service or otherwise.

2 Paragraph(s) [*insert*] of this order shall last until [*insert* date and time] unless it is set aside or varied before then by an order of the court.

3 The case is listed for a further hearing in the Family Court sitting at [*insert* place] on [*insert* date] ('the return date'), time estimate: [*insert* time]. At the hearing on the return date the court will reconsider the application and decide whether the order should continue. If the respondent does not attend on the date and at the time shown the court may make an order in [his]/[her] absence.

4 The respondent has the right to apply to the court at any time, and without waiting until the return date, to set aside or vary this order. [*Insert if appropriate*: The respondent must give [*insert* hours/days] [written] notice of the application to the [applicant]/[applicant's solicitors].]

5 If the respondent intends to rely on any evidence in support of [his]/[her] application to set aside or vary this order, or intends to rely on any evidence to oppose the continuation of the order at the hearing on the return date, the substance of the evidence must be provided in writing to the [applicant]/[applicant's solicitors] in advance.

[*Add if appropriate*]

6 If the respondent intends to oppose the continuation of the order on the return day [he]/[she] must notify the court [in writing or by email] no later than [*insert* date and time] that [he]/[she] intends to attend the hearing on the return day and to oppose the continuation of the order. If the respondent does not notify the court then the court may, if appropriate, make an order dispensing with the need for any attendance by the [applicant]/[applicant's solicitors] on the return day and may, if appropriate, on the return day make an order extending the injunction.'

When may an occupation order which ousts the respondent from his home be made without notice?

8.33 The case law under the MHA 1983 and the DVMPA 1976 was that removal of a party from his home was 'Draconian' and should rarely be granted without notice[1]. It can confidently be predicted that the Court of Appeal will continue to regard removal of a person from his home without notice as something which is so serious as to be seldom justifiable.

1 *G v G (Ouster: Ex Parte Application)* [1990] 1 FLR 395; *Masich v Masich* (1977) Fam Law 245.

Mode of application begun without notice

8.34 It is not necessary to file a separate form of application to achieve an initial hearing without notice. The standard form of application FL401, or

N16A in a tort action, will suffice, provided that the reasons for starting without notice are set out in the statement or evidence in support, unless leave is given for oral evidence to be given.

Grounds for application without notice required to be set out in statement in support

8.35 The grounds for starting without notice are required by FPR 10.2(4) to be stated in the sworn statement or evidence in support of the application.

Ensuring issue and service of correct forms after grant of order without notice

8.36 Where a non-molestation order or occupation order is granted without notice under the FLA 1996, the application in Form FL401 and statement in support must be served with the order without notice, in order to comply with FPR 10.3(1). Where a power of arrest is granted without notice, the court is required to announce the order in open court at the earliest opportunity[1].

[1] *President's Direction (Children Act 1989: Exclusion Requirement)* [1998] 1 FLR 495 and *President's Direction (Family Law Act 1996, Pt IV)* [1998] 1 FLR 496.

8.37 In a tort action in a county court, if an order is granted without notice in Form N16, it is important to ensure that the court issues for service the application Form N16A with the correct return date entered, as well as the order without notice, or else the defendant will not receive notice of any additional clauses required in the order on notice, the client may not get the additional order at the first hearing on notice and the solicitor may be ordered to pay wasted costs.

'Informal' notice

8.38 In *G v G (Ouster: Ex Parte Application)*[1], it was said at 402B that informal notice, ie notice which is too late to comply with the requirements of the rules for notice, is better than no notice at all. Such notice could be, for example, a telephone call, text or email to the respondent or his solicitor. Where a respondent attends having received informal notice, and does not object, or the court is satisfied that the matter can fairly be dealt with as a hearing on notice, the court can abridge time for service retrospectively.

[1] [1990] 1 FLR 395.

Return date for hearing on notice where order granted without notice

8.39 Section 45(3) of FLA 1996 provides that where the court does grant an order without notice, it 'must afford the respondent an opportunity to make representations relating to the order as soon as just and convenient at a full hearing'. This reflects the general case-law about without notice orders in civil and family proceedings. The more drastic or invasive the order without notice, the greater the urgency for providing a hearing on notice.

Abridged time for service

8.40 The period required for notice to be given to the respondent of a hearing may be abridged by order under FPR 4.1 or, in a torts action in a county court, CPR 6.9 enables the court to dispense with service. (CPR 6.7 deals with the dates upon which documents served by the various means permitted by the rules are deemed served.)

Substituted service

8.41 The standard requirement for personal service of an application for a non-molestation or occupation order can be modified by an order under FPR 6.23.

8.42 In an action based in torts, personal service is not required by the Rules, but judges are reluctant to grant an order without being satisfied that the respondent has been effectively served, whether personally or in some substituted way approved by the court.

8.43 CPR 6.8 enables the court to provide for service by an alternative method where the court considers that 'there is a good reason to authorise service by a method not permitted by these Rules'. An application must be supported by evidence, but may be made without notice. If granted, the order will state the method of service and the date on which service is to be deemed.

Evidence in support of without notice (ex parte) applications

8.44 An applicant for a without notice order must make full disclosure of all matters known to him which may be material for the judge to know, both for and against the application[1]:

> 'It is perfectly well settled that a person who makes an ex parte application to the court . . . is under an obligation to the court to make the fullest possible disclosure of all the material facts within his knowledge, and if he does not make the fullest possible disclosure, then he cannot obtain any advantage from the proceedings.'

1 *R v Kensington Income Tax Commissioners ex p Princess Edmond de Polignac* [1917] 1 KB 486, CA; and see, eg, *Rochdale Borough Council v A* [1991] 2 FLR 192, Douglas Brown J.

8.45 Thus, disclosure extends to, and includes, any weaknesses in the applicant's case and points which it might be thought that the defendant would raise were the application being heard on notice. This is because an injunction is an equitable remedy: there is a duty on the applicant to come to the court with clean hands, in this instance by giving full disclosure to the court of all relevant facts. Further, advocates have a duty not to mislead the court, ie they must provide to the court all relevant information known to them. An injunction which has been made without full disclosure is likely to be set aside with costs, perhaps on the indemnity basis[1].

1 See, eg, *Burgess v Burgess* [1996] 2 FLR 34, CA.

CONDUCT OF HEARING FOR PERSONAL PROTECTION ORDERS

Procedure: evidence

8.46 The court may act on the witness statement in support of the application, if it is unopposed or made without notice and sufficient facts are given. However, the applicant and any supporting witness should be ready to give oral evidence.

Announcement of a power of arrest granted without notice

8.47 Where a power of arrest is granted without notice, the court is required to announce the order in open court at the earliest opportunity[1].

1 *President's Direction (Children Act 1989: Exclusion Requirement)* [1998] 1 FLR 495 and *President's Direction (Family Law Act 1996, Pt IV)* [1998] 1 FLR 496.

Forms of orders

8.48 Before DVCVA 2004, the standard form for a non-molestation order or an occupation order was Prescribed Form, FL404, which was required to be used by FPR 1991, r 3.9(6)(b) and FPC (MP etc) R 1991, r 12A(1)(b).

8.49 The fact that powers of arrest may no longer be attached to non-molestation orders has meant that this form had to be amended and in fact from July 2007, the date of implementation of the DVCVA 2004, there have been three relevant forms:

- FL404 – (Occupation order)
- FL404a – (Non-molestation order)
- FL406a – (Record of non-molestation order)

A drafting committee under Mostyn J has recently issued further draft orders for consultation; these are set out in Appendix **3**. These forms have been issued for consultation and it is possible that they may be amended. However, they are a useful guide to what will be acceptable to the court and it is probably unlikely that they will be greatly changed. In addition, the form of application for a non-molestation order or occupation order has been changed (see **8.6**).

8.50 Form FL406 is the form which contains details of the power of arrest. Where the court makes an occupation order and a power of arrest is attached to one or more of the provisions ('the relevant provisions') of the order, the relevant provisions shall be set out in Form FL406 and the form shall not contain any provisions of the order to which the power of arrest was not attached.

8.51 Where the court makes a non-molestation order, all the provisions of the order must be set out in Form FL406a. FPR 10.10 provides that where an occupation order containing a power of arrest or a non-molestation order have been made, a copy of Form FL406 or FL406a must be delivered to the police station for the applicant's address or any other police station which the court may specify, together with a statement showing service on the respondent or stating that he has been informed of its terms (whether by being present when the order was made or by telephone or otherwise).

8.52 The menu of forms of non-molestation order (see **3.4**) may be supplemented by specific directive orders, for example forbidding particular acts of molestation as permitted by s 42(6) of FLA 1996, Pt IV, but should not otherwise be varied. Any variations must not exceed the powers of the court.

8.53 County court Form N16 remains the appropriate prescribed form for issue of an injunction in proceedings founded in torts. See **7.57** for menu of specimen clauses for molestation injunctions in torts.

Service or notification of orders required to make orders enforceable

8.54 An order which is capable of enforcement by committal must, in general, and subject to the court's powers to provide otherwise, be served personally on the respondent to make it enforceable[1]. This is dealt with substantively at **8.61**.

1 FPR 37.5.

Undertakings: availability

8.55 By s 46(1) of FLA 1996 the court had power to accept an undertaking from any party where it has power to make an occupation order or non-molestation order. The only restriction on this power was that the court had to attach a power of arrest where violence had been used and a power of arrest cannot be attached to an undertaking. In those circumstances an order was mandatory.

8.56 Because the ability to attach a power of arrest to a non-molestation order has been removed, the restriction on the right of the court to accept an undertaking was redefined. First, s 46(3) now reads as follows:

> 'The court shall not accept an undertaking under subsection (1) instead of making an occupation order in any case where apart from this section a power of arrest would be attached to the order.'

This recognises that a power of arrest may still be attached to an occupation order.

8.57 Secondly, a new sub-s (3A) is inserted[1], which reads as follows:

> '(3A) The court shall not accept an undertaking under subsection (1) instead of making a non-molestation order in any case where it appears to the court that—
> (a) the respondent has used or threatened violence against the applicant or a relevant child; and
> (b) for the protection of the applicant or child it is necessary to make a non-molestation order so that any breach may be punishable under section 42A.'

1 By DVCVA 2004, Sch 10, para 37(3).

8.58 It will be seen that the restrictions on the court's powers and the standard to be applied by the court have not changed insofar as the principal matter is whether the respondent has used or threatened violence. The test is whether the court considers that it is necessary to make a non-molestation order, breach of which is an arrestable offence, for the protection of the applicant.

Undertakings: practice and the prescribed forms

8.59 Form FL422 for undertakings in family proceedings courts has been adapted from county court Form N117.

8.60 It is important that the court ensures that the giver of an undertaking understands both the ingredients of his promises to the court and the possible consequences of breach. See **8.54**, where the implications of committal proceedings are discussed.

Delivery of a form of undertaking

8.61 The record of the undertaking in county court Form N117 or FL422 should usually be delivered to the giver by the court. This is dealt with substantively in **Chapter 10**.

RESTRICTIONS ON CROSS-EXAMINATION

8.62 One of the most heralded and publicised parts of the Domestic Abuse Bill 2020 has been the introduction of restrictions on cross-examination of victims of domestic abuse by the alleged perpetrator of the abuse. The evidence that permitting such cross-examination caused undue hardship and new traumas for victims was very strong and has resulted in the changes now implemented by the Act.

8.63 These changes are contained in a new Pt 4B of the Matrimonial and Family Proceedings Act 1984 (MFPA 1984) which is inserted by Domestic Abuse Bill 2020, s 60. An overview is that the Act prevents cross-examination of a witness[1] in four specified sets of circumstances in family proceedings[2] and provides for the representation of a party who is thereby deprived of his right to cross-examine. The four sets of circumstances will now be examined in turn.

1 'Witness', in relation to any proceedings, includes a party to the proceedings (MFPA 1984, s 31Q).
2 Any proceedings in the Family Court or designated proceedings in the Family Division (MFPA 1984, s 31Q).

Cross-examination of victim of offence

8.64 MFPA 1984, s 31R(1) provides that:

> '(1) In family proceedings, no party to the proceedings who has been convicted of or given a caution for, or is charged with, a specified offence may cross-examine in person a witness who is the victim, or alleged victim, of that offence.

(2) In family proceedings, no party to the proceedings who is the victim, or alleged victim, of a specified offence may cross-examine in person a witness who has been convicted of or given a caution for, or is charged with, that offence.'

8.65 Section 31R(1) is clear; where a person has been convicted of or cautioned for a specified offence he may not cross-examine the victim. 'Conviction' and 'caution' are defined in s 31R(5) as is 'specified offence' which means an offence to be specified in regulations. Presumably it will be defined as meaning an offence in relation to the victim, not just any offence.

As a reciprocal measure, the victim may not cross-examination the convicted or cautioned person.

Cross-examination of person protected by injunction

8.66 MFPA 1984, s 31S provides that:

'(1) In family proceedings, no party to the proceedings against whom an on-notice protective injunction is in force may cross-examine in person a witness who is protected by the injunction.

(2) In family proceedings, no party to the proceedings who is protected by an on-notice protective injunction may cross-examine in person a witness against whom the injunction is in force.'

8.67 The second set of circumstances in which cross-examination is forbidden is therefore where an injunction has been granted in favour of the witness. Note however that the injunction must have been on notice; an order made without notice will not trigger this subsection. Section 31S(5) defines an 'on-notice' injunction as where

'(a) the court is satisfied that there has been a hearing at which the person against whom the protective injunction is in force asked, or could have asked, for the injunction to be set aside or varied, or

(b) the protective injunction was made at a hearing of which theâ€¨court is satisfied that both the person who applied for it and the person against whom it is in force had notice.'

However, it may be that a restriction could be imposed under the third category.

Cross examination where specified evidence of domestic abuse

8.68 TMFPA 1984, s 31 provides that:

'(1) In family proceedings, where specified evidence is adduced that a person who is a witness has been the victim of domestic abuse carried out by a party to the proceedings, that party to the proceedings may not cross-examine the witness in person.

(2) In family proceedings, where specified evidence is adduced that a person who is a party to the proceedings has been the victim of domestic abuse carried out by a witness, that party may not cross- examine the witness in person.'

In order for this provision to apply the evidence has to be 'adduced', presumably by the victim in support of her application. The evidence must be of a specified nature; s 31T(3) defines 'specified' as specified in regulations by the Lord Chancellor. Some help is derived from s 31T(4) which provides that:

> 'Regulations under subsection (3) may provide that any evidence which satisfies the court that domestic abuse, or domestic abuse of a specified description, has occurred is specified evidence for the purposes of this section.'

'Domestic abuse' is of course defined by the Domestic Abuse Bill 2020, s 1.

Other cases

8.69 It is important to note that, in the cases described above, the court has no discretion. Once the factors contained in the Act are satisfied the court must not allow cross-examination. In the case which now follows, some discretion is allowed.

8.70 MFPA 1984 contains provisions giving the court a fairly broad discretion to prevent cross-examination. Section 31U applies in any family proceedings where none of ss 31R to 31T apply and:

> '(b) it appears to the court that—
>   (i) the quality condition or the significant distress condition is met, and
>   (ii) it would not be contrary to the interests of justice to give the direction.'

The court may give such a direction either on the application of a party to the proceedings or on its own motion[1].

1 Section 31U(4).

8.71 There are therefore two conditions to be met. The first is the 'quality condition' which s 31U(2) provides is met if:

> 'the quality of evidence given by the witness on cross-examination—
> (a) is likely to be diminished if the cross-examination (or continued cross-examination) is conducted by the party in person, and
> (b) would be likely to be improved if a direction were given under this section.'

Reference to the quality of a witness's evidence is to 'its quality in terms of completeness, coherence and accuracy'[1].

1 Section 31U(6).

8.72 This is obviously a broad definition which will be open to a variety of interpretations. However, if the court is satisfied about that it must address the 'distress condition'. This is defined by s 31U(3) as follows:

> '(3) The "significant distress condition" is met if—
>   (a) the cross-examination (or continued cross-examination) of the witness by the party in person would be likely to cause significant distress to the witness or the party, and
>   (b) that distress is likely to be more significant than would be the case if the witness were cross-examined other than by the party in person.'

8.73 The intention of this provision is clear. It would be unfair to call it a 'catch-all' provision but it is intended to achieve the aim of the legislation to prevent distressing cross-examination in cases which are not covered by the strict wording of the other provisions. To avoid any excessively subjective application of these rules, s 31U(5) sets out detailed matters to which the court must have regard. It is provided that:

> 'In determining whether the quality condition or the significant distress condition is met in the case of a witness or party, the court must have regard to, among other things—
>
> (a) any views expressed by the witness as to whether or not the witness is content to be cross-examined by the party in person;
>
> (b) any views expressed by the party as to whether or not the party is content to cross-examine the witness in person;
>
> (c) the nature of the questions likely to be asked, having regard to the issues in the proceedings;
>
> (d) any behaviour by the party in relation to the witness in respect of which the court is aware that a finding of fact has been made in the proceedings or any other family proceedings;
>
> (e) any behaviour by the witness in relation to the party in respect of which the court is aware that a finding of fact has been made in the proceedings or any other family proceedings;
>
> (f) any behaviour by the party at any stage of the proceedings, both generally and in relation to the witness;
>
> (g) any behaviour by the witness at any stage of the proceedings, both generally and in relation to the party;
>
> (h) any relationship (of whatever nature) between the witness and the party.'

By s 31U(7) 'coherence' refers to a witness's ability in giving evidence to give answers which—

> '(a) address the questions put to the witness, and
>
> (b) can be understood, both individually and collectively.'

8.74 Section 31V contains supplementary matters concerning a direction under this section. A direction is binding until revoked but may be revoked at any time. The court must give reasons for either making, refusing to make or revoking a direction.

Alternatives to cross-examination in person

8.75 The principal objection to provisions such as these has always been the potential unfairness to the alleged perpetrator. To remedy this, s 31W applies wherever a party is prevented from cross-examining under any of ss 31R to 31U. The court must first consider whether there is a satisfactory alternative means for the witness to be cross-examined in the proceedings, or of obtaining evidence that the witness might have given under cross-examination in the proceedings[1]. If the court decides that there is not, the court must invite the party to the proceedings thereby prevented to arrange for a qualified legal representative to act for him for the purpose of cross- examining the witness[2], and require him to notify the court, by the end of a period specified by the court, of whether a qualified legal representative is to act for him for that purpose[3].

1 Section 31W(2).
2 Section 31W(3)(a).
3 Section 31W(3)(b).

8.76 If no such notification is received by the court within the specified period, the court must consider whether it is necessary in the interests of justice for the witness to be cross-examined by a qualified legal representative appointed by the court to represent the interests of the party[1]. If the court decides that it is, then the court must appoint a qualified legal representative (chosen by the court) to cross-examine the witness in the interests of the party[2].

1 Section 31W(5).
2 Section 31W(6).

8.77 A legal representative appointed by the court is not responsible to the party[1]. This presumably means that he or she has no contractual relationship with that party and could not be liable to him in contract or tort While he or she will clearly have to interview the party on whose behalf they are cross-examining, their duty is to the court to ask such questions as are necessary in the interests of justice. The role of this representative will be limited to cross-examination; they will play no further part in the proceedings, such as addressing the court or adducing evidence. The Lord Chancellor may issue guidance concerning the role which a representative appointed by the court may play and the representative must have regard to such guidance[2].

1 Section 31W(7).
2 Section 31Y.

8.78 A representative appointed by the court will be paid out of public funds[1].

1 Section 31X.

Special arrangements for witnesses

8.79 By s 17 of the Youth Justice and Criminal Evidence Act 1999 provision already exists for the protection of vulnerable witnesses (for example, by permitting them to give evidence by video link or from behind a screen). Section 59 Domestic Abuse Bill 2020 amends s 17 of the 1999 Act by a new sub-s 4A extending this statutory presumption of protection to witnesses in fear and need of protection when giving evidence regarding:

> '(a) a sexual offence;
> (b) an offence under section 1 or 2 of the Modern Slavery Act 2015;
> (c) any other offence where it is alleged that the behaviour of the accused amounted to domestic abuse within the meaning of the Domestic Abuse Act 2020 (see section 15 of that Act).'

INTERLOCUTORY INJUNCTIONS, FREE-STANDING INJUNCTIONS AND DECLARATORY ORDERS, IN COUNTY COURT ACTIONS

8.80 An interlocutory injunction can, by reason of the County Courts Act 1984, s 38, be granted in any proceedings pending in the court. This includes proceedings in the family jurisdiction and other civil proceedings. CCR Ord 13, r 6(1) provides that:

> '. . . an application for the grant of an injunction may be made by any party to an action or matter before or after trial or hearing, whether or not a claim for the injunction was included in that party's particulars of claim, originating application, petition, counterclaim or third party notice, as the case may be.'

8.81 CPR 25.1(1) provides that the court may grant interim remedies, including injunctions and declarations, and such injunctions can be granted:

(a) whether or not there is a claim in the proceedings in question for a final remedy of the kind covered by the injunction[1];
(b) before the proceedings have been started[2], but only where the matter is urgent or the interests of justice require it[3];
(c) after judgment has been given in the case[4].

1 CPR 25.1(4).
2 CPR 25.2(1)(a).
3 CPR 25.2(2)(b).
4 CPR 25.2(1)(b).

8.82 A free-standing injunction (ie in proceedings in which no other relief such as damages is claimed) can be granted in a county court since a new s 38 of the County Courts Act 1984 was substituted by the Courts and Legal Services Act 1990.

8.83 Although such a situation is unlikely in the context of personal protection, upon a claim for declaratory relief, such as who is legally entitled to occupy a house, the court can grant an interlocutory injunction in support of the claim for declaratory relief[1].

1 *Newport Association Football Club Ltd v Football Association of Wales* [1995] 2 All ER 87.

8.84 In order for any court to have power to grant a free-standing injunction, there must be a lis, a legal right or basis for starting proceedings, which is within the jurisdiction of the court and which can be protected by an injunction[1]. The person against whom the injunction is sought must be someone who can properly be made a party in proceedings based on the lis, except where there is a specific statutory jurisdiction to grant an injunctive direction against a non-party.

1 *Richards v Richards* [1984] AC 174, [1984] FLR 11 at pp 17F, 23C, 29G, 32A and 35H; *Khorasandjian v Bush* [1993] QB 727, [1993] 2 FLR 66; *Chief Constable of Kent v V* [1983] QB 34, [1982] 3 All ER 36 at 40G, 42J, 45G and 46C–H; *Chief Constable of Hampshire v A* [1985] QB 132, [1984] 2 All ER 385 at 387E–H, 388C and 390A.

Power to grant and enforce an injunction against a person aged at least 18 and less than 21

8.85 Anti-molestation injunctions sometimes are sought against people who are aged under 21, usually by parents or neighbours. An injunction can be granted against a person aged under 21 to protect a parent as well as in favour of any other person[1].

1 *Egan v Egan* [1975] Ch 218, [1975] 2 All ER 167.

8.86 There is power, where a person aged at least 18 and less than 21 is guilty of contempt of court, to commit him to detention under s 9(1) of the Criminal Justice Act 1981 as amended by the Criminal Justice Act 1991, s 63(1), (5).

Power to grant and enforce an injunction against a person aged less than 18

8.87 There is jurisdiction to grant an injunction against a person under the age of 18, whether to restrain molestation in a family case[1] or to restrain tortious behaviour[2]. In *Re L*, an injunction had been granted against a 17-year-old molester of a ward, and in *Shea v Shea*, an injunction against the plaintiff's 17-year-old son.

1 *Re L (A Minor) (Injunction and Committal: Guardian ad Litem)* [1997] Fam Law 91 (1993) CAT No 0952.

2 *Shea v Shea* (1982) CAT No 387.

8.88 A person aged less than 18 cannot be committed to any form of detention for contempt of court: s 1(1) of the Criminal Justice Act 1981[1].

1 See *R v Selby Justices ex parte Frame* [1991] 2 All ER 344; *Mason v Lawton* [1991] 2 FLR 50.

Power to enforce an injunction against a person who is mentally disordered

8.89 In *Wookey v Wookey; Re S (A Minor)*[1], the Court of Appeal said that a person who was incapable of understanding an injunction could not be guilty of contempt by disobeying it.

1 [1991] Fam 121, [1991] 2 FLR 319.

Suitability of injunction as remedy against person aged less than 18 or mentally disordered

8.90 In *Wookey v Wookey; Re S (A Minor)*[1], the Court of Appeal said that it is not appropriate to grant an injunction against a person who, because he is aged less than 18, cannot be detained, if he has no income or money. Butler-Sloss LJ said[2]:

> '. . . in the vast majority of cases where the minor is still of school age, or unemployed, recourse to the civil courts is not the appropriate procedure . . .
>
> Barristers and solicitors consulted by relatives of violent or unmanageable teenagers ought to think very carefully before advising the institution of civil proceedings to regulate their unacceptable behaviour.'

1 [1991] 2 FLR 319.

2 [1991] 2 FLR 319 at 328D–E.

8.91 A mentally disordered person, against whom an injunction could be granted because his condition is not so serious as to render him 'incapable of managing and administering his property and affairs', may, nevertheless, be unlikely to respond appropriately to an injunction, and so careful consideration should be given before seeking one.

Procedure where the defendant is a minor or mental patient

8.92 Where the defendant is a minor, or is by reason of mental disorder incapable of managing and administering his property and affairs[1], unless the defendant already has a litigation friend, the applicant must, after the time for delivering a defence or admission has expired and before taking any further step in the proceedings, apply to the court for a litigation friend to be appointed for the defendant[2]. FPR 15 and 16 deal with service of proceedings on a minor or patient.

1 [1991] 2 FLR 319 at 328D–E.
2 [1991] 2 FLR 319 at 328D–E.

8.93 In *Wookey v Wookey; Re S (A Minor)*, Butler-Sloss LJ discussed[1] the considerations which apply, and the procedure to be followed, when it appears that a person who is molesting the plaintiff may be suffering from a mental disorder. In particular, it was stated that the Official Solicitor should be notified as soon as possible if an application is to be made to a court for an injunction, and the possible need for a litigation friend must be addressed.

1 [1991] 2 FLR 319 at 325, 326.

8.94 In *Gull v Gull*[1], which was an appeal against a committal order by a man with limited understanding, the court clearly thought that an approach whereby the parties' advisers worked with social services would have been preferable to the court enforcement route, even though the applicant had been entitled to an order.

1 [2007] EWCA Civ 900.

8.95 In *Shea v Shea*[1], the Court of Appeal directed that the 17-year-old son of the plaintiff should be served personally with the injunction and that the Official Solicitor should be invited to consider whether he should represent the child.

1 (1982) CAT No 387.

8.96 In *Re L (A Minor) (Injunction and Committal: Guardian ad Litem)*[1], the Court of Appeal allowed the appeal against committal of the 17-year-old for breach of an injunction on procedural grounds, of which the failure to appoint a guardian was treated as the most significant. Neill LJ, with whom Russell and Rose LJJ agreed, indicated that a child against whom an injunction has been granted should have the benefit of a guardian following the grant of the injunction, to ensure that the child understands the consequences of disobedience.

1 [1997] Fam Law 91.

Chapter 9

TRANSFER OF TENANCIES

INTRODUCTION TO TRANSFER OF TENANCIES

9.1 The bulk of the provisions in Pt IV of the FLA 1996 were concerned with the regulation of the occupation of a dwelling-house which is, or has been a family home, and with the behaviour of the parties towards each other; longer-term issues, such as transfers of title to property are not dealt with, because they are normally the subject of proceedings under the MCA 1973.

9.2 The exception to this, namely the provisions dealing with transfer of tenancies, concerned the position of cohabitants or former cohabitants, and, in effect, adapts the existing law which had previously applied only to spouses. This reflects the fact that the previous law relating to the position of cohabitants was unsatisfactory and, in some cases, unfair. The Domestic Abuse Bill 2020 does not amend or substantially change any of the provisions regarding transfer of tenancies and so this chapter deals entirely with the existing law established by Part IV FLA.

9.3 As will be seen, the provisions as to transfer of tenancies repeat, and are designed to improve, the existing law relating to former spouses, and extend that law to cohabitants and former cohabitants. In each case, the rights previously enjoyed by spouses are extended to unmarried people. These will be considered in turn.

9.4 The power to transfer a tenancy from one party to another has existed for some time in the case of former spouses whose marriage has been dissolved or annulled, or spouses to whom a decree of judicial separation has been granted. It was arguable that this power existed by virtue of s 24(1) of the MCA 1973, although a potential difficulty was that the court could not compel an unwilling landlord to accept a transfer of tenant where there was a covenant against assignment. However, there was no doubt that by virtue of s 7 of and Sch 1 to MHA 1983 the court did have the power to transfer tenancies between spouses or former spouses.

9.5 This power did not exist in the case of cohabitants, and the Law Commission considered that this anomaly should be rectified. Although the Family Law Reform Act 1987 gave the court jurisdiction to order the transfer or settlement of property between unmarried parents for the benefit of their children, this was thought to be unduly restrictive and unsatisfactory for a number of reasons[1].

[1] See Law Com, para 6.5.

9.6 Such considerations led the Law Commission to[1]:

> '. . . the firm conclusion that the power to transfer tenancies at present contained in the Matrimonial Homes Act 1983 should be extended to cohabitants, whether they are joint tenants or whether one party is a sole tenant and the other is non-entitled. We therefore recommend accordingly. There would, of course, be no entitlement to such a transfer in any particular situation. The court would simply have power to make such an order if the merits of the case justified it. If they did not, it would not be done.'

This change was, therefore, brought about by s 53 of FLA 1996, which provides that Sch 7 to the Act shall have effect.

[1] See Law Com, para 6.6.

9.7 It should be noted that, by virtue of para 15(1) of Sch 7, the court's powers under this Schedule are in addition to the court's powers to make occupation orders under whatever section is appropriate. These powers are therefore additional to those arising under the remainder of the Act. It is interesting to note that unmarried couples are, in this respect, placed in a more favourable position with respect to rented property than to property which one of them might have owned.

APPLICANTS FOR TRANSFER OF TENANCY

9.8 The MHA 1983 is abolished in its entirety by the FLA 1996. As a result, the FLA 1996 has to confer on spouses and former spouses the rights which they enjoyed under the earlier legislation, as well as extending those rights to others. This part of the legislation is, therefore, of considerable significance to divorced couples whose matrimonial home has been tenanted property, within the classes of tenancy covered by Sch 7.

9.9 Schedule 7 begins by defining some terms. 'Cohabitant', except in one limited case which will be considered later, includes a 'former cohabitant'. 'Landlord' includes any person deriving title under the original landlord. 'Relevant tenancy' means:

> '(a) a protected tenancy or statutory tenancy within the meaning of the Rent Act 1977;
> (b) a statutory tenancy within the meaning of the Rent (Agriculture) Act 1976;
> (c) a secure tenancy within the meaning of section 79 of the Housing Act 1985; or
> (d) an assured tenancy or assured agricultural occupancy within the meaning of Pt I of the Housing Act 1988.'

9.10 'Tenancy' includes a sub-tenancy, and 'spouse', except in one case, includes a former spouse[1]. It will be noted that this list does not include assured shorthold tenancies, or long leases. The orders for transfer which the court may make are collectively referred to as 'Pt II orders'[2]. Paragraph 2 of Pt I of

Sch 7 goes on to define the cases in which the court may make an order. These are as follows.

1 FLA 1996, Sch 7, Pt I, para 1.
2 Ie orders made under FLA 1996, Sch 7, Pt II.

Spouses

9.11 Paragraph 2(1) applies if:

> ' . . . one spouse is entitled, either in his own right or jointly with the other spouse, to occupy a dwelling-house by virtue of a relevant tenancy.'

9.12 Paragraph 2(2) goes on to provide that, at any time where it has power to make a property adjustment order under s 23A (divorce or separation) or s 24 (nullity) of MCA 1973 with respect to the marriage, the court may make a Pt II order.

9.13 It follows from this that a spouse may apply for a transfer of tenancy under Pt II only when she is in a position to apply for a property adjustment order; when the whole of the FLA 1996 comes into force, this will be, in the case of divorce or separation, at any time after the filing of a statement of marital breakdown. Until then, and in any event in the case of nullity, the appropriate time is on or after the grant of a decree. The applicant does not have to apply for a property adjustment order; the requirement is merely that she should be entitled to do so.

9.14 Paragraph 4 provides that the court shall not make such an order unless the dwelling-house is or was, in the case of spouses, a matrimonial home or, in the case of cohabitants, a home in which they lived together as husband and wife. A tenancy must therefore be contrasted with the much wider class of property which may be transferred under s 24 of MCA 1973.

9.15 The 1995 Bill provided that only the court which granted the decree may make the order under Pt II; that is no longer the case, so that the application may be brought in any county court.

9.16 Finally, it should be noted that para 13 of Sch 7 provides that a spouse who remarries cannot thereafter apply for an order under Pt II. This has exactly the same effect as s 28(3) of MCA 1973, which prevents a spouse who has remarried from applying for a capital order under s 24 of that Act; however, as will be seen, this restriction does not apply to cohabitants, who may marry with impunity and not lose the right to apply.

Cohabitants

9.17 Paragraph 3(1) of Pt I of Sch 7 applies if:

> ' . . . one cohabitant is entitled, either in his own right or jointly with the other cohabitant, to occupy a dwelling-house by virtue of a relevant tenancy.'

9.18 Paragraph 3(2) provides that:

> 'If the cohabitants cease to live together as husband and wife, the court may make a Pt II order.'

As was seen above, by para 4, the court may not make an order unless the dwelling-house is or was a home in which the cohabitants lived together as husband and wife.

9.19 The meaning of 'cohabitant' has already been considered in CHAPTER **3** and need not be considered further here. There is, in the FLA 1996, no restriction on the time within which such an application may be made by a former cohabitant.

PRINCIPLES TO BE APPLIED

9.20 The orders which the court may make are set out at **9.31** et seq. Paragraph 5 of Pt I of Sch 7 sets out the matters to which the court shall have regard; these are:

> ' . . . all the circumstances of the case including—
> (a) the circumstances in which the tenancy was granted to either or both of the spouses or cohabitants or, as the case requires, the circumstances in which either or both of them became tenant under the tenancy;
> (b) the matters mentioned in section 33(6)(a), (b) and (c) and, where the parties are cohabitants and only one of them is entitled to occupy the dwelling-house by virtue of the relevant tenancy, the further matters mentioned in section 36(6)(e), (f), (g) and (h); and
> (c) the suitability of the parties as tenants.'

9.21 'All the circumstances of the case' gives the court a wide discretion to admit any evidence which may be relevant.

9.22 FLA 1996, Sch 7, para 5(a) directs the court to have regard to how the tenancy came into being, and to whom it was granted. It will, therefore, be relevant to consider which party is the tenant and how it was that he or she became the tenant.

9.23 Section 33(6)(a), (b) and (c) of FLA 1996 contains the matters to which the court is directed to have regard when deciding whether, and, if so, how, to exercise its powers to make an occupation order in favour of a person who is entitled or has matrimonial home rights; this is considered in more detail, in the context of occupation orders, in CHAPTER **6**. It will be remembered that s 36 contains sub-s (7), which sets out the 'greater harm' test, but it might be thought that, if Parliament had intended subs (7) to apply, it would have said so, and the wording of para 5(b) of this Schedule seems to incorporate only s 33(6)(a), (b) and (c). It might seem, therefore, that the 'greater harm' test is not applicable.

9.24 In all cases, therefore, the court will have to have regard to the respective housing needs of the parties and of any relevant child, and the respective financial resources of the parties. By s 33(6)(c), the court must also have regard to:

> '. . . the likely effect of any order, or of any decision by the court not to exercise its powers under subsection (3) above, on the health, safety or well-being of the parties and of any relevant child.'

9.25 Subsection (3) of s 33 sets out the different kinds of occupation orders which a court may make. If the wording is read literally, it would seem that the court is directed to have regard to the consequences of making, or not making, an occupation order, which might broaden the scope of the court's enquiry. It may be that this difficulty is more apparent than real, since the consequences of an order for transfer of tenancy would be that the 'unsuccessful' party would have to leave, which would have the same effect as an occupation order; this provision would then be interpreted as meaning that the court must consider the effect on both parties of an order that one of them leave.

9.26 It is worth noting that s 33(6)(d), which directs the court to have regard to the conduct of the parties, is not applicable to Sch 7. Conduct, therefore, is irrelevant.

9.27 Paragraph 5(b) of Pt I of Sch 7 then sets out further matters to which the court must have regard when the parties are cohabitants and only one of them is the tenant (it would not, therefore, apply when both were tenants); 'cohabitant' includes 'former cohabitant'.

9.28 These matters are those contained in s 36(6)(e), (f), (g) and (h), which are the factors to be considered by the court when deciding whether, and, if so, in what manner, to make an occupation order where the applicant was non-entitled; they are set out and considered in detail in **CHAPTER 6**. They are, where the parties are cohabitants or former cohabitants: the nature of their relationship; the duration of the cohabitation; whether there are children for whom they are responsible; and the length of time since they ceased to live together. Once again, the conduct of the parties, which is relevant to an issue of an occupation order, is not included as a relevant factor here.

9.29 These provisions are clearly designed to give the court wide discretion to make orders in accordance with the justice of the case.

9.30 The final matter to which the court must have regard is the suitability of the parties as tenants. It will be seen below that landlords will be entitled to be heard on applications for transfer of tenancies, and this provision enables the court to take account of the landlord's interests as well as those of the parties. It would also have some relevance as between the parties, since there would be little point, for example, in transferring a tenancy to someone who was incapable of paying the rent or who had proved to be a nuisance or annoyance to his neighbours.

ORDERS WHICH MAY BE MADE

9.31 By para 1 of Pt I of Sch 7, 'the court' does not include a magistrates' court. Applications will therefore have to be brought in a county court.

9.32 The orders which the court may make will depend on the nature of the tenancy; these orders are, therefore, set out by reference to the type of tenancy which is involved. Pt II of Sch 7 begins with one clarification of terms; whenever this part of the Schedule refers to a cohabitant or spouse being entitled to occupy a dwelling-house by virtue of a relevant tenancy, this applies whether the tenancy is sole or joint[1].

1 FLA 1996, Sch 7, para 6.

9.33 It is, perhaps, also worth noting here the restrictions which apply in respect of some former spouses. As has already been noted above, a spouse who has remarried is not entitled to apply for an order under Sch 7[1]. If this is interpreted in the same way as other claims under the pre-1996 law for ancillary relief, it will mean that a petitioner who has applied for a transfer of a tenancy in the prayer to her petition will be taken to have applied, and her claim will not be defeated by her remarriage. However, a respondent who had not filed an answer claiming relief would be barred from applying after remarriage.

1 FLA 1996, Sch 7, para 13.

9.34 By para 12 of Sch 7, it is provided that the date on which an order for transfer of tenancy is to take effect may not be earlier than decree absolute.

9.35 Neither of these restrictions applies, of course, to cohabitants. A spouse whose marriage has not been dissolved, or to whom a decree of judicial separation has not been granted, has no right to apply under Sch 7.

9.36 The orders which the court may make are classified by reference to the nature of the tenancy to be transferred. This is not a textbook on the law of landlord and tenant; accordingly, no explanation is provided of the meaning of the various terms used, for example 'assured agricultural occupancy'. The reader who requires further information as to the rights and obligations attaching to such terms should therefore consult a more specialised publication.

9.37 In all cases, the interest to be transferred is the tenancy to which the transferor is entitled. They are as follows: protected tenancy, secure tenancy, assured tenancy, assured agricultural occupancy.

9.38 These terms are defined by reference to their meaning in the Rent Act 1977, the Housing Act 1985, and Pt I of the Housing Act 1988 respectively. It will be noted that an assured shorthold tenancy is not one which may be transferred, but a 'council tenancy' is. (The most common form of tenancy in the private sector is therefore excluded.) What is to be transferred is the estate or interest which the entitled spouse had in the dwelling-house immediately before the order for transfer[1]:

> ' . . . by virtue of the lease or agreement creating the tenancy and any assignment of that lease of agreement, with all rights, privileges and appurtenances attaching to that estate or interest but subject to all covenants, obligations, liabilities and incumbrances to which it is subject . . . '

The transfer is effected by the order, and no further assurance or document in writing is needed[2].

1 FLA 1996, Sch 7, para 7(1)(a).
2 FLA 1996, Sch 7, para 7(1).

9.39 Paragraph 7(1)(b) provides that where the entitled party is an assignee, his liability under any covenant of indemnity, whether express or implied, may also be transferred.

9.40 Paragraph 7(2) provides, in effect, that when an order for transfer is made, any liability or obligation to which the party whose tenancy has been transferred was liable shall no longer be enforceable against that party; this is only in respect of liabilities or obligations falling due to be discharged after the date of the transfer.

9.41 By para 7(3), (3A) and (4), where the entitled party is a successor within the meaning of Pt IV of the Housing Act 1985, s 17 of the Housing Act 1988, or s 132 of the Housing Act 1996, his former spouse or cohabitant is also deemed to be a successor.

9.42 Paragraph 7(5) deals with the position where the transfer is of an assured agricultural occupancy. For the purposes of Chapter III of Pt I of the Housing Act 1988, the agricultural worker condition shall be fulfilled with respect to the dwelling-house while the spouse or cohabitant to whom the occupancy is transferred continues to be the occupier under that occupancy, and that condition shall be treated as so fulfilled by virtue of the same paragraph of Sch 3 to the Housing Act 1988 as was applicable before the transfer.

Statutory tenancy within the meaning of the Rent Act 1977

9.43 The court may order that, as from the date specified in the order, the entitled party shall cease to be entitled to occupy the dwelling-house, and that the other party shall be deemed to be the tenant, or, as the case may be, the sole tenant, under the statutory tenancy[1].

1 FLA 1996, Sch 7, para 8(2).

9.44 Paragraph 8(3) deals with the question of whether the provisions of paras 1–3, or, as the case may be, paras 5–7 of Sch 1 to the Rent Act 1977, as to the succession by the surviving spouse of a deceased tenant, or by a member of the deceased tenant's family, to the right to retain possession, are capable of having effect in the event of the death of a person deemed by an order under these provisions to be the tenant or sole tenant under the statutory tenancy. It is provided that this question shall be determined according as those provisions have or have not already had effect in relation to the statutory tenancy.

Statutory tenancy within the meaning of the Rent (Agriculture) Act 1976

9.45 The court may order that, as from such date as may be specified in the order, the entitled party shall cease to be entitled to occupy the dwelling-house and that the other party shall be deemed to be the tenant, or, as the case may be, the sole tenant under the statutory tenancy[1]. A spouse or cohabitant who is deemed under this provision to be the tenant under a statutory tenancy shall be (within the meaning of the Rent (Agriculture) Act 1976) a statutory tenant in his own right, or a statutory tenant by succession, according to whether the other spouse or cohabitant was a statutory tenant in his own right or a statutory tenant by succession.

1 FLA 1996, Sch 7, para 9.

SUPPLEMENTARY PROVISIONS

9.46 Part III of Sch 7 to the FLA 1996 contains what are described as 'supplementary provisions'. These are orders which may be made supplementary to the order for transfer of tenancy in any case. They are, in fact, potentially more important than their description might indicate.

9.47 The first of these relates to payment in return for transfer. By para 10(1), the court may order a party to whom a tenancy is transferred to make a payment to the other party. In deciding whether to exercise this power, and, if so, in what manner, the court is directed by para 10(4) to have regard to all the circumstances including:

> '(a) the financial loss that would otherwise be suffered by the transferor as a result of the order;
> (b) the financial needs and financial resources of the parties; and
> (c) the financial obligations which the parties have, or are likely to have in the foreseeable future, including financial obligations to each other and to any relevant child.'

A wide discretion is therefore conferred on the court.

9.48 By para 10(2), the court may, in effect, order that the payment need not be made immediately. Instead, it may direct that payment of the sum, or part thereof, be deferred, or be paid by instalments. Further, by para 10(3), the court may vary any order for payment, or exercise its powers under para 10(2) at any time before payment in full has been made.

9.49 In deciding how to exercise its powers as to the method of payment, the court must have regard to the factors set out in para 10(4) above. However, this is subject to the overriding provision, contained in para 10(5), that the court shall not give any direction under para 10(2) unless it appears to the court that immediate payment of the sum required by the order would cause the transferee financial hardship which is greater than any hardship that would be caused to the transferor if the direction were given.

9.50 The second type of supplementary order relates to liabilities and obligations in respect of the dwelling-house. By para 11, the court may direct that both parties shall be jointly and severally liable to discharge and perform any obligation or liability in respect of the dwelling-house (whether arising under the tenancy or otherwise) which, before the order for transfer, may have fallen to be discharged or performed by only one of them, and which were due as at the date of the transfer. Where such a direction is given, the court may also direct that either party shall be liable to indemnify the other in whole or in part against any payment made or expenses incurred by the other in discharging or performing any such liability or obligation.

RIGHTS OF LANDLORDS REGARDING TRANSFER OF TENANCIES

9.51 FLA 1996, Sch 7, para 14(1) provides that rules of court shall be made requiring the court to give the landlord of any dwelling-house, to which any order for transfer of tenancy will relate, an opportunity to be heard. The principal provision in Sch 7 which protects a landlord is para 5(c), which directs the court to have regard to the suitability of the parties as tenants when deciding how to exercise its powers. For procedure, see **9.53**.

DATE WHEN ORDER TAKES EFFECT

9.52 There is no special provision as to when an order between cohabitants or former cohabitants is to take effect. However, provision has had to be made for orders made between spouses because of the provisions of the MCA 1973 introduced by the FLA 1996 as to the date on which a property adjustment order may take effect. Paragraph 12 of Sch 7 provides that, in the cause of nullity, the order may not take effect before decree absolute, and, in the case of divorce or separation, the date on which it may take effect is to be determined as if the court were making a property adjustment order under s 23A of MCA 1973, regard being had to the restrictions imposed by s 23B of that Act.

PROCEDURE REGARDING TRANSFER OF TENANCIES

9.53 The procedure for applications for transfer of tenancies is different from the other applications under FLA 1996, Pt IV and is governed by FPR 8.29–8.34.

Issue and application

9.54 Application is made to the Family Court or the same court as existing family proceedings[1]. There are no prescribed forms for this application in Pt IV and applications are made in accordance with the Pt 19 procedure.

1 PD 8A, para 1.1(a).

9.55 The court will serve the application on the respondent and the landlord[1]. The landlord may be made a party to the application[2].

1 FPR 8.31.
2 FPR 8.32.

Interlocutory orders

9.56 The court may make orders for disclosure or order a production appointment[1]. It may also grant an interlocutory injunction[2] though the application for the injunction must be made in accordance with FPR 20.4.

1 FPR 8.33.
2 FPR 8.34.

9.57 The court has jurisdiction to order, for example discovery, further particulars etc as if the application were for financial provision.

Service on landlords

9.58 An application for transfer of tenancy must be served on the other cohabitant or spouse and on the landlord. Any person so served is entitled to be heard on the application. This is, therefore, a different requirement from that relating to third parties in applications for occupation orders where a landlord or mortgagee must be served with notice of an application rather than the application itself.

Chapter 10

ENFORCEMENT

INTRODUCTION TO ENFORCEMENT IN RELATION TO DOMESTIC ABUSE

10.1 Many if not most orders of the court (or undertakings in lieu of orders) designed to protect against domestic abuse are broken at some stage. When the breach is trivial the victim may well think it not worth pursuing, particularly if it is not part of a regular pattern. However, when the breach is significant urgent consideration must usually be given to the best way of enforcing the order. The Domestic Abuse Bill 2020 makes no specific changes to enforcement procedures so this chapter is concerned entirely with enforcement of orders made under FLA 1996, Pt IV.

10.2 One of the first questions to be asked is whether the order which has been broken was endorsed with a power of arrest. As has been seen, by virtue of the DVCVA 2004, a power of arrest may no longer be attached to a non-molestation order, so different considerations will apply to non-molestation orders, occupation orders and undertakings. These will be considered in turn. First however, the general principle of enforcement must be considered.

GENERAL PRINCIPLE RELATING TO ENFORCEMENT FOR DOMESTIC ABUSE

Disobedience of an order as a contempt of court

10.3 Disobedience of a directive order capable of enforcement by committal, or an undertaking to like effect, is a civil contempt of court.

10.4 Disobedience of a magistrates' order capable of enforcement under s 63(3) is a civil contempt[1].

1 See *B (BPM) v B (MM)* [1969] P 103, [1969] 1 All ER 891 at 899H and the heading of the Contempt of Court Act 1981, Sch 3.

10.5 Directive orders made under FLA 1996, Pt IV, in particular non-molestation orders and those parts of occupation orders which provide personal protection and the right to enjoy occupation of the family home, are in principle enforceable by committal. Committal is available for breach of an injunction forbidding a common law tort or harassment within the PHA 1997, but if the contemnor has already been convicted of an offence of harassment, he cannot be punished for contempt in respect of the same conduct[1].

1 PHA 1997, s 3(7).

10.6 Contempt consists of 'actus reus' and 'mens rea'. This means a deliberate act or neglect to act by the respondent who knew what the order was. It is *not* necessary to prove that the respondent's purpose was to breach the order or undertaking.

Orders not capable of enforcement by committal

10.7 Some orders are not capable of enforcement by committal (eg orders to attend court as witness). In the High Court or a county court, family financial support orders are enforceable only by judgment summons or enforcement as civil debts. Orders for payment of money also cannot be enforced as civil contempts under s 63(3) of the Magistrates' Courts Act 1980. Some parts of occupation orders, such as responsibility for maintaining the home cannot be enforced by committal.

10.8 In *Nwogbe v Nwogbe*[1] it was held that there was no power to commit a respondent who had failed to obey an order to pay the monthly rent on a property pursuant to s 40 of FLA 1996. It was observed that this revealed a statutory lacuna of real significance.

1 [2000] 2 FLR 744, CA.

SUMMARY OF REMEDIES FOR ENFORCEMENT

10.9 In the light of what has been said in earlier paragraphs the position will now be summarised before detailed consideration is given to each method of enforcement.

Non-molestation orders

10.10 A person entitled to the benefit of a non-molestation order may enforce by means of:

(a) Complaint to the police, leading to prosecution for the offence of breach of order.
(b) Application for committal to the Family Court.

When complaint is made to the police, the police may issue a domestic violence protection notice (see Chapter 8).

Occupation orders

10.11 A person with the benefit of an occupation order may enforce by application for committal to the Family Court. In addition, where the order is endorsed with a power of arrest, the complainant may ask the police to enforce the order by arresting the respondent and bringing him before the court.

Undertakings

10.12 An undertaking may only be enforced by application for committal to the Family Court. The detail of these provisions will now be examined.

BREACH OF NON-MOLESTATION ORDERS AS AN OFFENCE

10.13 This section is primarily concerned with the fact that, since 2005, breach of a non-molestation order has been an offence and what flows from that. The detail of what happens when an application is made to the Family Court is dealt with later, as those procedures are the same as those for breach of an occupation order.

10.14 Section 1 of DVCVA 2004 inserts a new s 42A into the FLA 1996. This provides as follows:

> '(1) A person who without reasonable excuse does anything that he is prohibited from doing by a non-molestation order is guilty of an offence.
> (2) In the case of a non-molestation order made by virtue of section 45(1), a person can be guilty of an offence under this section only in respect of conduct engaged in at a time when he was aware of the existence of the order.
> (3) Where a person is convicted of an offence under this section in respect of any conduct, that conduct is not punishable as a contempt of court.
> (4) A person cannot be convicted of an offence under this section in respect of any conduct which has been punished as a contempt of court.'

10.15 Section 42A(1) therefore contains the ingredients of the offence. The act complained of must be forbidden by the non-molestation order, and there must be no reasonable excuse for the breach; put another way, reasonable excuse is a defence to the charge.

10.16 Breach of anything forbidden by the order may constitute a criminal offence and so render the offender liable to arrest and prosecution. Under the previous law, care was always taken to distinguish between those matters involving violence or the threat of violence, to which a power of arrest could be attached, and other matters not involving violence, to which a power of arrest was not attached. For example, an order not to use or threaten violence would carry a power of arrest; this would not routinely be the case with an order prohibiting harassment, intimidation or pestering.

10.17 There is no such distinction in the amended FLA, and this is deliberate. Speaking in the Grand Committee debate, the government spokesperson Baroness Scotland said[1]:

> 'The police may be unclear to which part of the order any power of arrest may be attached . . . Our aim is to ensure the immediate safety of the applicant and any children, and we want to underline the seriousness of any breach. That is why [section] 1 makes a breach of the order a criminal offence.'

The position is therefore that breach of any provision of the order, however comparatively insignificant, may constitute an offence.

1 Official Report (HL), 19 January 2004, col GC238.

10.18 Section 42A(2) refers to orders made under s 45(1) of FLA 1996, namely without notice orders. The significance of this is, therefore, that the respondent must be aware of the order before an offence can be committed. He will normally have been made aware by means of personal service of the order. However, the subsection merely says that he must be aware of the existence of the order and it is arguable that if, for example, he had learnt of the order in some other way, such as a telephone conversation with someone, he would be liable. Subsections (3) and (4) deal with the overlapping of criminal proceedings and contempt proceedings.

10.19 The position with relation to this was clearly set out by the government spokesman in the parliamentary debates as follows[1]:

> 'I was asked what action could be taken in relation to the breach with regard to the person who is protected by the order. Broadly speaking, there are two options. First, the police could be called and, because of the maximum five year imprisonment on conviction, the police will have automatically have the power of arrest for any breach of the terms of a non-molestation order . . . The decision on whether to prosecute for the breach will be for the police and the Crown Prosecution Service – always of course in consultation with the victim herself. If the decision is not to prosecute for a criminal offence, the victim can still pursue an action through the civil court and breach remains contempt with the same penalties available as now.
>
> The second option is to pursue the civil route. The victim may decide that they do not want to involve the police at all. in those circumstances the victim will still be able to apply to the civil court for a warrant of arrest if the molestation (sic) order is breached, and to have the perpetrator arrested and brought back to the civil court for the judge to decide what should happen.'

1 Mr Paul Goggins, Official Report, HC Standing Committee E, 22 June 2004, col 45.

10.20 Even though the power of arrest is to be removed, therefore, there is no reason why a complainant should not seek to punish breach of an order by means of the issue of a warrant of arrest under FLA 1996, s 47(10) or by the issue and service of a notice to show good reason why the respondent should not be committed to prison (Form N78 in the county court, Form FL418 in magistrates' courts). The Act imposes no restrictions or time limits on either a prosecutor or a complainant wishing to enforce by a contempt application. Mr Goggins referred above to the warrant of arrest procedure only but it has to be said that this procedure has been little used and it is most likely that the notice to show good reason procedure would be more widely used.

10.21 Section 42A(3) and (4) provide, in effect, that a person who has been punished for contempt in the family proceedings may not be convicted of an offence and vice versa. This is obviously fair and sensible as far as it goes but it still leaves an unfortunate lacuna. There is nothing to prevent a complainant beginning contempt proceedings where the respondent has been arrested, and there is nothing to prevent prosecution of an alleged offender where contempt proceedings are pending.

10.22 However, the position is potentially even worse than that. There is nothing to prevent a complainant who is dissatisfied by the acquittal of a respondent, or the dismissal of contempt proceedings against him, making a second attempt to punish him in the other court, perhaps armed with better evidence. The Act only prohibits duplicate proceedings in the event of a favourable outcome for the applicant; it does not contemplate the result of unsuccessful proceedings. For further guidance, see **10.40** et seq which deals with principles of sentencing for contempt.

10.23 Section 42A(5) deals with the penalties for the offence. On indictment, an offender is liable to up to five years' imprisonment or a fine or both. On summary conviction, an offender is liable to up to 12 months' imprisonment or a fine not exceeding the statutory maximum of both. This contrasts with the maximum of two years' imprisonment or a fine in civil contempt proceedings.

10.24 Section 10 of DVCVA 2004 amends the Police and Criminal Evidence Act 1984 by inserting a new s 14A. This inserts common assault into the list of arrestable offences. This removes any doubt about whether a constable who would previously have had a power of arrest may arrest an alleged offender for breach of a non-molestation order, even though such doubt should have been removed by the new s 42A.

ENFORCEMENT BY APPLICATION TO COMMIT

Introduction – the importance of abiding by correct procedure

10.25 The Court of Appeal has stressed in several cases that, because committal for contempt of court is concerned with offences of a quasi-criminal nature and the liberty of the subject is at stake, the relevant rules of court must be complied with and the prescribed forms must be used. However[1]:

> 'Any procedural defect in the commencement or conduct by the applicant of a committal application may be waived by the court if satisfied that no injustice has been caused to the respondent by the defect.'

1 CPR PD Committal, para 10, supplemental to RSC Ord 52 and CCR Ord 29.

10.26 In *Nicholls v Nicholls*[1], Lord Woolf MR, giving the judgment of the Court of Appeal, stated (at 655D) that: 'While the . . . requirements of Ord 29, r 1 [County Court Rules] are there to be observed, in the absence of authority to the contrary, even though the liberty of the subject is involved, we would not expect the requirements to be mandatory, in the sense that any non-compliance with the rule means that a committal for contempt is irredeemably invalid'. Lord Woolf gave the following guidance[2]:

> '(1) As committal orders involve the liberty of the subject it is particularly important that the relevant rules are duly complied with. It remains the responsibility of the judge when signing the committal order to ensure that it is properly drawn and that it adequately particularises the breaches which have been proved and for which the sentence has been imposed.
>
> (2) As long as the contemnor has had a fair trial and the order has been made on valid grounds the existence of a defect either in the application to commit or in the committal order served will not result in the order being set aside except insofar as the interests of justice require this to be done.
>
> (3) Interests of justice will not require an order to be set aside where there is no prejudice caused as the result of errors in the application to commit or in the order to commit. When necessary the order can be amended.

(4) When considering whether to set aside the order, the court should have regard to the interests of any other party and the need to uphold the reputation of the justice system.

(5) If there has been a procedural irregularity or some other defect in the conduct of the proceedings which has occasioned injustice, the court will consider exercising its power to order a new trial unless there are circumstances which indicate that it would not be just to do so.'

1 [1997] 1 FLR 649.
2 [1997] 1 FLR 649 at 661E.

10.27 The checklists set out at **10.73** are designed to cover the practical points which most often arise, and need to be considered, in preparation for, and in the course of, committal hearings. They are not comprehensive of every point which has reached the Court of Appeal.

Penal or warning notice on orders capable of enforcement by committal

10.28 Any order which is capable of enforcement by committal may be thus enforced, subject to due service, if it has on it a penal notice[1], warning the respondent of the consequences of breach.

1 FPR 10.12.

10.29 Prescribed Form FL404, for non-molestation and directive occupation orders, and county court injunction Form N138 (harassment) have a penal notice incorporated in the text. Prescribed Forms for undertakings, Form N117 in a county court and Form FL422 in a family proceedings court, also incorporate a penal notice.

10.30 The person who has the benefit of a non-molestation order or an injunction order against torts is entitled to have the order issued with a penal notice incorporated[1].

1 FPR 10.12.

10.31 Where an occupation order is made, which does not have a non-molestation order included, the court has a discretion as to whether to authorise a penal notice[1].

1 Form FL404, Notice B.

Forms, rules and Practice Directions

10.32 The forms to be used and procedure followed in committal proceedings are to be found in FPR Pt 18 and Pt 37 and Practice Directions 5A and 37A. The content of these provisions may be summarised as follows.

Requirement for penal notice

10.33 A judgment or order which restrains a party from doing an act or requires an act to be done must have a penal notice endorsed on it as follows (or in words to substantially the same effect)[1]:

> 'If you the within-named [ ] do not comply with this order you may be held to be in contempt of court and imprisoned or fined, or your assets may be seized.'

1 FPR 37.9.

10.34 In the case of an undertaking, except where the undertaking is contained in an order or judgment, the form of an undertaking to do or abstain from doing any act must be endorsed with a notice setting out the consequences of disobedience as follows (or in words to substantially the same effect)[1]:

> 'You may be held to be in contempt of court and imprisoned or fined, or your assets may be seized, if you break the promises that you have given to the court.'

1 FPR 37.9.

10.35 The court may decline to accept an undertaking; and deal with disobedience in respect of an undertaking by contempt of court proceedings, unless the party giving the undertaking has made a signed statement to the effect that he or she understands the terms of the undertaking and the consequences of failure to comply with it, as follows (or in words to substantially the same effect):

> 'I understand the undertaking that I have given and that if I break any of my promises to the court I may be sent to prison, or fined, or my assets may be seized, for contempt of court.'

This statement need not be given before the court in person, but may be endorsed on the court copy of the undertaking or may be filed in a separate document such as a letter.

Forms for committal applications

10.36 CPR Practice Direction *RSC 52 and CCR 29 – Committal Applications* applies with necessary modifications to the enforcement of an order in family proceedings[1]. The form to be used for a committal application is set out in that Practice Direction.

1 FPR 33.1(2).

10.37 FPR 37.10(1) (How to make a committal application) provides that a committal application is made by an application notice using the Pt 18 procedure. PD5A provides that that the application notice under Pt 18 is Form FP2. Additionally, the Annex to PD37A prescribes a form of notice to be included on a committal application.

10.38 Accordingly, where a committal application is made in existing proceedings, it must be commenced by filing an application notice under FPR Pt 18 in those proceedings[1]. Otherwise a committal application must be commenced by the issue of a Pt 19 application notice (Form FP1)[2].

1 FPR 37.10.
2 FPR PD 5A.

10.39 The application notice must set out full details of the alleged breaches of the orders, giving as much information as possible about dates, times etc and must be supported by one or more affidavits. It must be personally served on the respondent[1]. However, the court may dispense with service where it considers it just or direct some alternative method of service.

1 FPR PD 5A.

Contempt proceedings where criminal prosecution under way

10.40 Where criminal proceedings are pending in respect of the conduct alleged to be contempt, the court has a discretion as to whether to proceed with an application for committal. The principles were set out in *M v M (Contempt: Committal)*[1] by Lord Bingham of Cornhill CJ, giving the judgment of the court.

> 'It would appear that (the) authorities establish three principles. The first is that there is no absolute rule that civil proceedings (including contempt proceedings) should not proceed when criminal proceedings are pending. The second is that there is a general rule that contempt proceedings should be dealt with "swiftly and decisively" . . . The third principle is that the test as to whether or not contempt proceedings should proceed in advance of criminal proceedings is whether there is a risk of serious prejudice leading to injustice if the contempt proceedings go ahead . . . If the answer is that there is no real risk of serious prejudice leading to injustice, then in the ordinary way the contempt proceedings should go ahead. If, on the other hand, there is judged to be a real risk of serious prejudice leading to injustice if the contempt proceedings go ahead, the court may properly stay the contempt proceedings and would ordinarily do so.'

1 [1997] 1 FLR 762, CA at 764B.

10.41 If the court does proceed upon a contempt where criminal charges are pending in relation to the same conduct, any sentence for the contempt must be based on the disobedience of the court rather than punishment for the crime[1]. However, in *Wilson v Webster*[2], a sentence of two weeks for a violent assault was increased to three months on appeal and the court did not seek to discourage pursuit of criminal proceedings[3].

1 *Smith v Smith* [1991] 2 FLR 55.
2 [1998] 1 FLR 1097.
3 [1998] 1 FLR 1097 at 1100G and 1101B.

Contempt proceedings for harassment where criminal charges pending or contemnor convicted

10.42 A person who disobeys an injunction forbidding harassment cannot be both convicted of a criminal offence and punished for contempt for the same disobedience[1]. A plaintiff victim of harassment who applies for a warrant of arrest for breach of an injunction forbidding harassment must disclose whether he has informed the police of the defendant's conduct and whether, to his knowledge, criminal proceedings are being pursued[2], and at the hearing of committal proceedings, the court must be told if the contemnor has been convicted of an offence in respect of the same matters.

1 PHA 1997, s 3(7), (8).
2 CCR Ord 49, r 15A(5)(c), (d).

Arrest under power of arrest attached to an occupation order under FLA 1996, s 47

10.43 Availability of power of arrest is dealt with at **6.79** and **6.80**. There is no power to attach a power of arrest to an injunction granted under the PHA 1997.

10.44 It is the occupation order which is required to be served on the respondent, and the order should include the provision of attachment of the power of arrest.

10.45 The power of arrest in Form FL406 is for delivery to the police, although it is sensible for the applicant to have a copy in case the police ask to see it when called to her assistance. The Form FL406 should recite the particular clauses of the order to which the power was attached and no others.

Arrest under warrant of arrest for breach of an occupation order or an undertaking to like effect

10.46 There is doubt as to whether, where the court has accepted an undertaking to like effect as a non-molestation or occupation order, a warrant of arrest can be granted under s 47(8), (9) where the respondent has failed to comply with the undertaking: because although under s 46(4) an undertaking 'is enforceable as if it were an order', the court has not 'made a relevant order'[1].

1 FLA 1996, s 47(8).

10.47 An application for a warrant of arrest is made in Form FL407 and must be substantiated on oath[1], usually by affidavit in a county court, but oral evidence can be sufficient. The warrant is issued in Form FL408.

1 FLA 1996, s 47(9).

10.48 A warrant of arrest is exercised by the Tipstaff in the High Court, usually assisted by the police, a bailiff of the court or the police upon a county court warrant, and the police where the warrant was granted by a family proceedings court.

10.49 Following the grant of a warrant of arrest by a family proceedings court, responsibility for delivery to the police rests with the justices' chief executive who must cause the warrant to be delivered to the officer for the time being in charge of any police station for the respondent's address or such other police station as the court may specify. Section 47(10) of the FLA 1996, which provides the power for issue of a warrant of arrest, unlike s 47(7), does not require a person arrested under a warrant to be brought before the court at any particular time. Form FL408, for warrants, authorises the person(s) who arrest the respondent 'to bring him before this court immediately'. The FPR do not further regulate this, so the wording of Form FL408 is the operative requirement. In practice, as attendance of the applicant will almost always be needed to enable the court to deal with the alleged breach, arrangements for her presence will have to be made urgently or, if she is not available within a reasonable time, the court should adjourn the matter and remand the respondent under s 47(10).

POWER OF THE COURT RELATING TO ENFORCEMENT PROCEDURES

Procedural powers of court when arrested person brought before court under FLA 1996, s 47

10.50 When the respondent is brought before the court upon arrest under s 47 of FLA 1996, whether under a power of arrest or a warrant, the court may hear and deal with the alleged breach, or adjourn the hearing. The court may adjourn without having determined whether a breach has been proved, or after finding a breach proved. If the hearing is adjourned, the arrested person may be remanded under s 47(7)(b) or s 47(10), (11), or granted bail under s 47(12), or remanded for the purpose of enabling a medical examination to be made under s 48(1) or for a report on his mental condition under s 48(4).

Bail under the FLA 1996

10.51 An application for bail by an arrested person may be with or without a surety. The prescribed forms for a recognisance of the person making an application (Form FL411), recognisance of a surety (Form FL411), and bail notice (Form FL412) should be referred to for the requirements for bail.

10.52 The penalty for non-attendance of the respondent in answer to bail is forfeiture of his recognisance and that of any surety. If the respondent fails to attend, it is submitted that the court may revert to the exercise of a power of arrest where one had been attached to a term of the order alleged to have been breached, otherwise it may grant a warrant of arrest if there are provisions of the original order to which no power of arrest was attached.

Warrant of arrest for breach of an injunction under the PHA 1997

10.53 The claimant victim of a breach of an injunction against harassment, granted under the PHA 1997, may apply for a warrant of arrest[1]. The application is made to the High Court if the injunction was granted there, or any county court if the injunction was granted in a county court[2]. A warrant is not available for breach of an undertaking as s 3(3), (4) refers only to injunctions.

1 PHA 1997, s 3(3).
2 PHA 1997, s 3(4).

10.54 A warrant under the PHA 1997 is appropriate:

(a) if the court considers that the breach needs to be dealt with promptly, for example where the court believes that the plaintiff is at risk of a further breach;
(b) where the defendant has avoided service of a Notice to Show Good Reason; or

(c) where the defendant fails to appear for an adjourned hearing.

10.55 No special form is prescribed for the application[1], so the general from of notice, Form N244, should be used in a county court. The application must set out the grounds for making the application, and state whether the plaintiff has informed the police of the conduct complained of and whether, to the plaintiff's knowledge, criminal proceedings are being pursued[2]. The evidence should normally be by affidavit, but in an emergency the court can act on oral evidence. The affidavit should state the believed address of the defendant, which is required to be entered in the warrant.

1 CCR Ord 49, r 15A(5)(a).
2 CCR Ord 49, r 15A(5); the application must be supported by affidavit or evidence on oath (s 3(5)(a) of the 1997 Act and CCR Ord 49, r 15(5)(b)).

10.56 The warrant is issued in county court Form N140. It directs 'all police constables, [and] the district judge and bailiffs . . . to arrest the defendant . . . and bring him before this court immediately'. The defendant must be brought before the court the same day, if it can be reached while still sitting, or the next sitting day. Where no judge is sitting at the same courthouse, one nearby should be arranged. There is power to deal with the breach immediately, without issue and service of an application in Form N78[1], or to adjourn for up to 14 days[2]. There is no power to remand under the PHA 1997.

1 CCR Ord 49, r 15A(7)(a).
2 CCR Ord 49, r 15A(7)(b).

10.57 As the PHA 1997 makes no provision for remand of a defendant, and the presence of the victim is usually needed to enable the court to deal with the breach then and there, the court before which the defendant is brought must either deal with him for the alleged breach or adjourn and release the defendant.

Further arrest where the respondent fails to appear at an adjourned hearing after being released following arrest under a power of arrest

10.58 Where a person has been arrested under a power of arrest under the FLA 1996 and the case has been adjourned and the respondent remanded or released, but the respondent fails to appear for the adjourned hearing, the court cannot grant a warrant of arrest under s 47(8) of the FLA 1996, unless the power of arrest was attached only to some of the terms of the non-molestation order. However, it is arguable that the respondent can be re-arrested under the original power of arrest, provided that he is again brought before a judge within 24 hours of the second arrest. In *Wheeldon v Wheeldon*[1], the Court of Appeal held that where a person had been arrested for a criminal offence of assault and released on bail, he was validly re-arrested under a power of arrest for domestic violence and brought before a judge within 24 hours of the second arrest, although the 'spirit (of the statutory power of arrest) requires that he be brought before the judge within 24 hours of the initial arrest where the circumstances clearly indicate two reasons for the arrest prevail' (per Ward LJ); thus a power of arrest is a procedural device which can be used for detaining the respondent and bringing him before the court even though the breach of the injunction is not continuing.

1 [1998] 1 FLR 463.

Warrant of arrest where the respondent fails to appear at an adjourned hearing, having appeared at the first hearing of a Notice to Show Good Reason, under FLA 1996, Pt IV

10.59 Where a person appeared in answer to a Notice to Show Good Reason, and the case was adjourned and/or the respondent bailed, and he fails to appear at the adjourned hearing, and no power of arrest had been attached to the non-molestation order, a warrant for arrest under FLA 1996 can be granted in respect of the order[1]. If a power of arrest was attached to all of the terms of the order, and a warrant of arrest cannot be granted because there are no terms of the injunction to which it was not attached, it is arguable that the respondent can be arrested under the original power of arrest (see the reasoning at **10.53**).

1 FLA 1996, s 47(8), (9).

Application by contemnor or respondent who objects to an injunctive order

10.60 An injunction order must be obeyed even if the person to whom the order is directed considers that the order is irregular in law or onerous on the merits[1]. Likewise, an undertaking must be complied with even if the court would not have had jurisdiction to grant an injunction to the same effect. Want of jurisdiction in the making of an injunction or accepting an undertaking is no answer to an application for committal for a breach.

1 *Chuck v Cremer* (1846) 1 Coop temp Cott 338; *Hadkinson v Hadkinson* [1952] P 285, [1952] 2 All ER 567; *Isaacs v Robertson* [1985] AC 97, [1984] 3 All ER 140; *Johnson v Walton* [1990] 1 FLR 350.

10.61 The court has a discretion not to entertain any application by a contemnor in the same proceedings in relation to which the contempt has been or is being committed, until the contemnor has purged his contempt[1]. The court which granted an injunction will generally entertain an application by a contemnor where:

(a) the application is founded on argument that, on the true construction of the original injunction or undertaking, the conduct said to be a contempt did not amount to a contempt[2];
(b) the application is grounded on an alleged lack of jurisdiction to have made the order[3];
(c) the application is to purge or in mitigation of the contempt[4].

1 *X Ltd v Morgan-Grampian (Publishers) Ltd and Others* [1991] 1 AC 1, [1990] 2 All ER 1; see also *Hadkinson v Hadkinson* [1952] P 285, [1952] 2 All ER 567.
2 *Hadkinson v Hadkinson* [1952] P 285, [1952] 2 All ER 567.
3 *X Ltd v Morgan-Grampian (Publishers) Ltd and Others* [1991] 1 AC 1, [1990] 2 All ER 1.
4 *Hadkinson v Hadkinson* [1952] P 285, [1952] 2 All ER 567.

10.62 An order made without notice is a provisional order and every judge who makes an order without notice expects that the merits will be reviewed by the court on the return day or upon application[1]. A person against whom an injunction has been granted without notice is entitled to a review by the court as a matter of urgency[2]. Where it is contended that an injunction order granted on notice is irregular or oppressive, the proper course is to appeal.

1 *WEA Records Ltd v Visions Channel 4 Ltd* [1983] 2 All ER 589 at 593F–G; and see *R v R (Contempt of Court)* [1988] Fam Law 388.
2 *G v G (Ouster: Ex Parte Application)* [1990] 1 FLR 395.

Committal hearings

10.63 In general terms, hearings of committal proceedings are in many respects similar to hearings of criminal charges. Thus, the burden of proof rests on the person making the allegation of contempt; the standard of proof is the criminal standard; the respondent must be allowed to cross-examine witnesses and to call evidence; the respondent is entitled to submit that there is no case to answer; if a contempt is found proved, the contemnor must be allowed to address the court by way of mitigation or seeking to purge his contempt; and autrefois acquit and autrefois convict apply.

10.64 Since the coming into force of Pt IV of the FLA 1996, the Court of Appeal has given guidance as to the proper approach when dealing with breaches of orders. Not all of these decisions are consistent and some cases, clearly, turn on their own facts. It has been held that:

(a) imprisonment is only appropriate in the most serious cases involving repeated breaches[1];
(b) there is no principle that a first breach of an injunction is not to be visited with imprisonment, and the length of the sentence must reflect the fact that orders of the court must be obeyed[2];
(c) courts must take incidents of domestic violence very seriously and it is important as a matter of public policy that the court's jurisdiction be upheld (three months substituted for 'wholly inadequate' 14 days after violent assault breaching undertaking)[3].

1 *G v C (Residence Order: Committal)* [1998] 1 FLR 43, CA.
2 *Thorpe v Thorpe* [1998] 2 FLR 127, CA.
3 *Wilson v Webster* [1998] 1 FLR 1097, CA.

10.65 In *Rafiq v Muse*[1], a son who had been in care terrorised his mother and ignored several non-molestation orders. The court took account of the terrifying effect on the mother, the gross interference with her way of life, the resolute defiance of court orders and the absence of remorse and upheld a sentence of six months' imprisonment.

1 [2000] 1 FLR 820, CA.

10.66 It was no doubt in an effort to remove some ambiguities that the Court of Appeal set out some detailed guidelines in *Hale v Tanner*[1]. Without wishing to suggest that there was a general rule that the principles of sentencing in criminal cases applied in contempt proceedings, the court said that the following principles were applicable in family cases only.

(a) Contempt of court cases had to come before the court on an application to commit. That was the procedure available. It was not surprising, therefore, that the court had to direct itself as to whether committal to prison was appropriate. However, it did not follow that prison was the automatic consequence of breach of an order, nor was there any principle that prison should not be imposed at the first occasion[2].

(b) Although the full range of sentencing options available in criminal cases was not available in contempt proceedings, there was a range of things the court might consider. It could make no order; it might adjourn, and in a case where the alleged contemnor had not attended court, depending on the reason for not doing so, that might be appropriate; it might fine or sequester assets, or a mental health order might be appropriate. Such alternatives might need to be considered, in particular, where no act of violence was proved.

(c) If prison was appropriate, the length of committal should be determined without reference to whether it was to be suspended. A longer custodial period was not justified because it was suspended.

(d) The length of committal had to depend on the court's objectives. In contempt proceedings there were always two objectives. One was to mark the court's disapproval of disobedience to its order; the other was to secure future compliance with the order. Thus, the seriousness of what had taken place had to be viewed in that light as well.

(e) The period of imprisonment had to bear some reasonable relationship to the maximum two years' imprisonment available.

(f) Suspension was available in a wider range of circumstances than in criminal cases. It was the first way of securing compliance.

(g) The length of suspension required separate consideration, although it was linked to the period of the underlying order.

(h) The court had to bear in mind the context, which might be aggravating or mitigating.

(i) In many cases, the court would have to bear in mind that there were concurrent proceedings in another court based on the same or some of the same facts. The court could not ignore those proceedings and might have to take the outcome into account in practical terms. Contempt proceedings had a different purpose and often the overlap was not exact, but the court would not want a contemnor to suffer the same punishment twice for the same events.

(j) It would usually be desirable for the court to explain briefly why it had made the choices it had made in a particular case. It was appropriate in most cases for a contemnor to know why he was being sent to prison, why for so long, and why the period was being suspended. It was an important part of the exercise that a contemnor understood the importance of keeping court orders and not breaking them and the consequences of breach.

1 [2000] 2 FLR 879.
2 See *Thorpe v Thorpe* [1998] 2 FLR 127, CA.

10.67 Important guidance, bearing in mind the Human Rights Act 1998, was given by the Court of Appeal in *Hammerton v Hammerton*[1]. An order had been made that the father was forbidden to use or threaten violence against, or to intimidate, harass or pester the mother, or to encourage anyone else to do so. The mother alleged that the father had breached the undertaking and the order in a variety of ways and sought his committal to prison. The father was unrepresented. The judge chose to hear the mother's committal application at the same time as the father's contact application.

[1] [2007] EWCA Civ 248.

10.68 The judge found that the father was in breach of the order and committed him to prison for three months. The father appealed on the basis of grave procedural errors in the committal process, in that he had been unrepresented and that the judge had decided to hear the committal application together with the contact application. The appeal was allowed. The court gave the following guidance.

(a) The principles applicable to committal proceedings were contained within the Human Rights Act 1998, the European Convention for the Protection of Human Rights and Fundamental Freedoms 1950 (the Convention), *Practice Direction (Family Proceedings: Committal)* sub nom *President's Direction (Committal Applications and Proceedings in which a Committal Order may be made)* and various authorities; none of these had been drawn to the attention of the judge at any stage. Every family tribunal must take the greatest possible care, when hearing committal proceedings, to ensure that the applicable evidential and procedural rules were properly obeyed, redoubling their vigilance in the case of a litigant in person.

(b) It would rarely be open to anyone opposing an appeal based on Art 6 of the Convention to contend that Art 6 rights, such as legal assistance when defending criminal charges, would have made no difference in the particular case. The liberty of the subject was at stake in contempt proceedings; no family court should send a litigant in person to prison for contempt without first making arrangements for that litigant to be represented. The judge, having noted that the father was unrepresented, ought to have gone on to ask appropriate questions as to the reasons for the lack of legal representation and to consider whether it would be appropriate to adjourn to enable the father to obtain representation. Had the judge asked the relevant questions he would have discovered that the withdrawal of the father's legal aid was to be reviewed by the Legal Services review panel in two weeks' time. Once that information had been forthcoming, there was no reason why the committal hearing should not have been adjourned until the legal representation issue had been resolved.

(c) In this case, the decision to hear both applications at the same time had led to grave procedural errors, concerning burden and standard of proof and particularly an unresolved conflict between the father's right not to give evidence in his own defence and his need to give evidence to establish his claim for some form of contact. The court had to warn a defendant in a committal case that he was not obliged to give evidence at all in his own defence (no such warning was given), but in this case evidence about the alleged breaches was clearly relevant to the issue as to whether contact was appropriate; accordingly, if the father exercised his right not to give evidence in the committal proceedings, he would almost inevitably fail in his claim for some form of contact.

(d) A sense of urgency often impeded the fair conduct of committal proceedings; it was important to ensure that there was time for reflection. In the instant case the contact application may have been urgent, but that was no basis whatever for the conclusion that the committal proceedings were similarly urgent. The judge should have adjourned the committal proceedings to be heard by a different judge, or even, if there were no alternative, by himself, although the better course would have been for another judge to hear the committal.

(e) It might be that applications for contact and for committal could be heard at the same time, but it was difficult to envisage circumstances that would compel such a procedure. It did not follow that because allegations of breaches of an undertaking were relevant to contact proceedings it was necessary to hear the proceedings for committal at the same time as the contact proceedings. A judge hearing an application in proceedings under Pt II of the Children Act 1989 and related committal proceedings arising out of the same facts would have to make it clear that he acknowledged, despite any adverse findings in the contact proceedings, that the burden and standard of proof were different (see paras [18], [19], [31]).

(f) Further, since the father was unrepresented and had never been given an opportunity to mitigate, the process of sentencing had been fatally flawed. The findings and the sentence would be quashed (see para [22]).

The hearing

10.69 Since 26 March 2015 the procedure governing what is to happen at the hearing has been set out in the Lord Chief Justice's *Practice Direction 'Committal for Contempt of Court – Open Court'* of that date. This Practice Direction applies to all committal applications in any court or under any statutory jurisdiction and supersedes any existing Practice Direction, rule or other guidance.

10.70 The general principle is clearly stated as follows:

> '**Open Justice**
>
> 3. Open justice is a fundamental principle. The general rule is that hearings are carried out in, and judgments and orders are made in, public. This rule applies to all hearings, whether on application or otherwise, for committal for contempt irrespective of the court in which they are heard or of the proceedings in which they arise.
> 4. Derogations from the general principle can only be justified in exceptional circumstances, when they are strictly necessary as measures to secure the proper administration of justice. Derogations shall, where justified, be no more than strictly necessary to achieve their purpose.'

10.71 The Practice Direction is set out in full at **Appendix 2** and readers should refer to it for details. Its content may be briefly summarised as saying that all hearings must be in public and details of the hearing must be posted outside the court. There are certain exceptions to this and there is provision for private hearings in limited circumstances.

Application to purge contempt

10.72 A person committed to prison for disobedience of an injunction or breach of an undertaking is entitled to apply to purge his contempt and to be discharged from prison[1].

1 CPR 81.31; FPR 37.30; and see Forms N79 and FL419.

10.73 Whenever a person is committed immediately to prison in judge courts, the court sends copies of the committal order in Form N79 and the application in Form N78 to the Official Solicitor, who reviews all cases where imprisonment is imposed[1].

1 *Notes for Guidance and Completion of N79 and LCD Court Business*, November 1996, B 3288.

Warrant of possession for enforcing an occupation order requiring the respondent to vacate the family home

10.74 Where a respondent fails to obey an order that he shall vacate the family home, in a county court a warrant of possession is an appropriate means for procuring the removal of the respondent[1].

1 *Danchevsky v Danchevsky* [1975] Fam 17, [1974] 3 All ER 934; *Larkman v Lindsell* [1989] Fam Law 229; *C v C (Contempt: Committal)* [1989] Fam Law 477.

10.75 Issue of a warrant of possession may be requested without notice under CCR Ord 26, r 17(2); the applicant is entitled to apply without giving notice[1]. However, it may be less likely to cause resentment if the respondent is warned by letter that an application for a warrant is being made.

1 *Leicester City Council v Aldwinkle* (1991) 24 HLR 40.

APPLICATIONS FOR COMMITTAL ORDERS: CHECKLIST

10.76

Preliminary matters	An injunctive order must be served personally on the person to whom it is directed, unless there has been an order for substituted service or dispensing with service	CPR 81.5 (civil); FPR 37.5 (family)
	However, pending service, if the respondent disobeys an injunctive order which requires him to abstain from doing an act, the court can impose a penalty if it is satisfied that he knew about the terms of the order	CPR 81.8 (civil); FPR 37.8 (family)
	Proof of service of the order is required. In all courts this is usually by Form FL415. Service should be effected in accordance with the Protocol	Family Justice Council *Protocol for Process Servers*, November 2011

	A mandatory injunctive order directing a person to do an act cannot be enforced unless it was served before the time at or by which the act was directed to be done	CPR 81.5 (civil); FPR 37.5 (family)
	An undertaking becomes enforceable on being given to and accepted by the court; however, the court can require the giver to sign a statement to the effect that he understands the terms of his undertaking and the consequences of failure to comply with it	*Hussain v Hussain* [1986] 2 FLR 271; CPR PD81, para 2.2
	A copy of the undertaking in Form N117 in the county court, D787 in the Principal Registry or FL422 in a family proceedings court, is required to be delivered to the giver of the undertaking, but the giver is bound even if he does not receive a copy	CPR 81.7 (civil); FPR 37.7 (family)
Who may apply for committal or enforcement?	Person in whose favour the injunctive order was granted or the undertaking was given	CPR 81.3 (civil); FPR 37.3 (family)
Which court?	The court which granted the injunctive order or accepted the undertaking	CPR PD81, para 10 (civil); FPR 37.10 (family)
	The powers of the county court to deal with disobedience or breach are the same as the High Court	CCA 1981; CCA 1984, s 38
	Lay justices' statutory powers to deal with disobedience or breach are limited to imposing immediate or suspended committal, fine or adjourning consideration of penalty	Family Court (Contempt of Court) (Powers) Regulations 2014
Application (family proceedings)	Application is made using the Pt 18 procedure	FPR 37.10
	In every case, the summons or notice must 'identify, separately and numerically, each alleged act of contempt'	FPR 37.10(3)
Committal applications (civil proceedings)	Application under CPR 1998 Pt 23, supported by affidavit	CPR 81.10

Committal applications (general)	The affidavit or statement in support should narrate the facts relied on, but the list of alleged breaches must be given in the application notice	CPR 81.10 (civil); FPR 37.10 (family); *Harmsworth v Harmsworth* [1988] 1 FLR 349 at [354D]–[355B]
Fee	Fee on application in the Family Court: £155	FPFO 2008, fee 5.3
Application for warrant of arrest under FLA 1996, s 47(8) or s 63J	Application is made, without notice to the respondent, in Form FL408, to 'the relevant judicial authority', ie the convenient hearing centre in whichever tier of court the injunctive order was granted	FLA 1996, ss 47(8), 63(1) and 63J
	The application must be substantiated on oath and the court must have reasonable grounds for believing that the respondent has failed to comply with an order, or part of an order to which no power of arrest had been attached	FLA 1996, s 47(9), 63J
	The application must be substantiated on oath and the court must have reasonable grounds for believing that the respondent has failed to comply with an order, or part of an order to which no power of arrest had been attached	FLA 1996, s 47(9), 63J
	Breach of a non-molestation order is a criminal offence. However, the respondent cannot be both punished for a criminal offence and a contempt of court for the same breach. An application for a warrant of arrest to a civil court should confirm that there is no conviction	FLA 1996, s 42A(3),(4)
	The warrant is executed in the High Court by the Tipstaff, in the county court by the bailiffs (or, in each case, by the police on request), and in the magistrates' court by the police	Form FL408
	In the magistrates' court the justices' clerk is responsible for delivering the warrant to the police	
Application for warrant of arrest under PHA 1997, s 3(3)	Application must be made in accordance with CPR Pt 23 and may be made without notice	PHA 1997, s 3(4); CPR 65.29

	The application must be supported by affidavit evidence setting out the grounds for the application and state whether the claimant has informed the police and whether criminal proceedings are being pursued	PHA 1997, s 3(5); CPR 65.29
Production in court following arrest under FLA 1996, s 47 or s 63I	A person arrested under a power of arrest must be brought before the relevant judicial authority within 24 hours not including Sunday, Christmas Day or Good Friday	FLA 1996, ss 47(7), 63I
	Neither FLA 1996 nor the rules prescribe how soon a person arrested under a warrant of arrest must be brought before the court. Nevertheless it must be as soon as practicable	FLA 1996, ss 47(8)–(10), 63J
Procedures open to court under FLA 1996, ss 47, 48 when arrested person produced in court and under ss 63I–63M	The court may hear the facts upon which the arrest was based, and decide penalty or adjourn, in which case the respondent must be given not less than two days' notice of the adjourned hearing, or	FLA 1996, s 47(7)(b), (10); FPR 10.11(3)
	remand in custody for a period not exceeding eight days or	FLA 1996, ss 47(11), 63K, Sch 5 para 2(5)
	remand on bail on conditions and/or recognisances	FLA 1996, s 47(11),(12), Sch 5 para 2(5)
	where the court has reason to suspect mental illness or severe mental impairment, the court may remand, to enable a medical examination and report, for not more than three weeks if in custody or four weeks if on bail	FLA 1996, ss 48, 63L
Powers of court under PHA 1997, s 3(5) when arrested person produced in court	The court may hear the facts upon which the arrest was based, and decide penalty, or adjourn for not more than 28 days, in which case the defendant must be given not less than two days' notice of the adjourned hearing	CPR 65.30
Hearing without notice to the respondent	In exceptional circumstances, the court may, without notice having been given to the respondent, deal with an application begun by notice to show good reason, by dispensing with service of the summons or notice	CPR 1998, rr 39.3, 81.28 (civil); FPR 37.27 (family)

	It is not appropriate for a court to proceed without notice where arrest under a power or warrant can be achieved under FLA 1996, s 47, or under PHA 1997, s 3(5). However, where a power or warrant of arrest is not available, proceeding without notice may exceptionally be appropriate. When the court takes this exceptional step and imposes imprisonment, the court should fix a date and time for the contemnor to be brought before the court	CPR 81.28 (civil), FPR 37.27 (family)
Service of application to commit	Personal service of the application is required	FPR 37.27
	In both family and civil proceedings, a period of 14 clear days after service is required unless the court directs otherwise by using its powers to abridge time for service in exceptional cases, the court can dispense with service	CPR PD81, para 15.2 (civil); FPR PD37A, para 12.1 (family)
		see Hearing without notice to the respondent (above)
Service of notice of adjourned hearing	Where a hearing is adjourned, personal service of notice of the adjourned hearing is required, unless the respondent was present in court and was told when and where the adjourned hearing would resume and/or was remanded under FLA 1996, s 47(7),(10), Sch 5	*Chiltern DC v Keane* [1985] 1 WLR 619 at [622H]–[623C]
Case management	The court can make directions at any time as to service of evidence and conduct of the proceedings, or strike out an inappropriate application	CPR PD81, paras 15, 16 (civil); FPR PD37A, para 12.3 (family)
The hearing	District judges as well as High Court and circuit judges have power to hear committal proceedings under FLA 1996, Pts 4 and 4A	FLA 1996, ss 58, 63(1), 63O, 63S; Family Court (Contempt of Court) (Powers) Regulations 2014
	However district judges do not have power to hear committal proceedings under PHA 1997	PHA 1997, s 3(3), (4) only gives power to issue a warrant; CPR PD Committal, para 11

	Normally held in open court	CPR 1998, rr 39.2, 81.28 (civil); *President's Guidance of 3 May 2013* (family)
	If it is just to do so, the court can proceed if the respondent, having been duly served, fails to attend	*Begum v Anam* [2004] EWCA Civ 578; CPR 39.3
	Committal proceedings, although technically civil proceedings, are treated as criminal proceedings for the purposes of ECHR, Art 6. Consequently, persons in danger of losing their liberty are, subject to means, eligible for legal aid. (Contempt in the face of the court is separately dealt with in LASPOA 2012, s 14(g))	LASPOA 2012, Schs 1 and 3; Lord Chancellor's Guidance under s 4; *Chelmsford County Court v Ramet* [2014] EWHC 56 (Fam)
	Procedure is akin to criminal trial. The criminal standard of proof ('beyond reasonable doubt') applies	*Dean v Dean* [1987] 1 FLR 517
	An application notice can be amended with the permission of the court but not otherwise	CPR PD81, paras 12(2), 13.2(2), (civil); FPR 37.27 (family)
	An alleged contemnor cannot be directed or compelled to give information	CPR 81.28 (civil); FPR 37.27(3)
	A deliberate act or failure to act (actus reus) with knowledge of the terms of the order (mens rea) must be proved	*DG of Fair Trading v Smiths Concrete* [1992] QB 213
Powers of court	The disposal must be proportionate to the seriousness of the contempt, reflect the court's disapproval and be designed to secure compliance in future. The principles of sentencing in the CJA 2003 apply. The judge cannot sentence again for matters already dealt with by the criminal court. The court should briefly explain its reasons for the choice of disposal	*Murray v Robinson* [2006] 1 FLR 365; *Hale v Tanner* [2000] 2 FLR 879; *Lomas v Parle* [2004] 1 FLR 812; *Slade v Slade* [2010] 1 FLR 160
	Committal to prison is appropriate only where no reasonable alternative exists	*Hale v Tanner* (above)

	Imprisonment is restricted to total of two years in the High Court and the County Court, two months in a magistrates' court, and must be for a fixed term	CCA 1981, s 14; MCA 1980, s 63(3); Family Court (Contempt of Court) (Powers) Regulations 2014
	Sentence can be suspended or adjourned on terms	CPR 81.29 (civil); FPR 37.28 (family)
	Any time spent on remand in custody must be taken into account in the sentence	*Kerai v Patel* [2008] 2 FLR 2137
	Person under the age of 21 can be detained under Powers of Criminal Courts (Sentencing) Act 2000, s 96	*R v Selby Justices ex parte Frame* [1992] 1 QB 72
	Person under the age of 18 cannot be committed to any form of detention for contempt of court (but could be prosecuted for breach of a non-molestation order)	R v Selby Justices (above); FLA 1996, s 42A
	MHA powers are available	CCA 1981, s 14; MHA 1983, ss 35, 37, 38
	Fine can be imposed	*Hale v Tanner* [2000] 2 FLR 879
	A fresh injunction can be granted	*Coats v Chadwick* [1894] 1 Ch 347
	A power of arrest can be attached, if available, to the injunctive order	*Ansah v Ansah* (1976) FLR Rep 9; FLA 1996, s 47
	Sequestration is available only in the High Court	CPR 1998, rr 81.19–81.27, CPR PD81, paras 6, 7 (civil); FPR 37.25 (family)
Form of order	The order must specify 'exact details' of each contempt found proved and specify the disposal ordered	*Nguyen v Phung* [1984] FLR 773 at [778C]; *Re C (A Minor) (Contempt)* [1986] 1 FLR 578 at [585A]

	Where sentence is suspended or adjourned, the period of suspension or adjournment and the precise terms for activation must be specified	*Pidduck v Molloy* [1992] 2 FLR 202; CPR 81.29 (civil), FPR 37.28 (family)
	In the High Court, the order is issued in Form A85 and warrant in Form PF303. In the county court, Form N79 and warrant in Form N80. In a magistrates' court, Form FL419 and warrant in Form FL420	
Service of order	Where immediate imprisonment or detention is imposed, the court serves the order	CPR 1998, rr 6.21(2), 81.30 (civil); FPR 37.29 (family); *Clarke v Clarke* [1990] 2 FLR 115
	Where sentence is suspended, the applicant must serve the order, unless the court directs otherwise	CPR 81.29(2) (civil); FPR 37.28 (family)
Review by Official Solicitor	The court sends a copy of every committal order and relevant details to the Official Solicitor, who reviews the case and may apply or appeal of his own motion or at the contemnor's request	*Lord Chancellor's Direction of 29 May 1963; Secretary's Circular of 28 September 1981*
Discharge of contemnor	A contemnor is entitled to apply to purge his contempt and be discharged from prison	CPR 81.31 (civil); FPR 37.30 (family)
	The application should be made in accordance with CPR 1998 Pt 23 or FPR Pt 18 but in practice a letter from the contemnor usually suffices	*CJ v Flintshire Borough Council* [2010] 2 FLR 1224
	If the committal was made in civil proceedings, the application notice must be served as soon as practicable after it is filed and at least three days before the hearing. If made in family proceedings, the application must be served at least seven days before the hearing	CPR 23.7(1) (civil); FPR 18.8
	The contemnor should be in court	*PD of 25 July 1983*
	On an application to purge, the court can say 'yes', 'no' or 'not yet' but may not suspend the remainder of the sentence	*Harris v Harris* [2002] 1 FLR 248

Chapter 11

THE DOMESTIC ABUSE COMMISSIONER, AND MISCELLANEOUS MATTERS

11.1 Part 2 of the Domestic Abuse Bill 2020 is concerned with the creation and the new role of Domestic Abuse Commissioner, and the detail of this part extends to several pages of the Act. While this is undoubtedly an important development, the finer details are not the everyday concern of those directly involved with the protection of the victims of domestic abuse and so will be dealt with in outline only.

11.2 Sections 4–6 of the Domestic Abuse Bill 2020 require the Secretary of State to appoint a Domestic Abuse Commissioner (hereafter 'the Commissioner') and to provide the Commissioner with a staff and funding; in fact, a Commissioner designate had already been appointed some time before the Act became law. The Commissioner is not to be regarded as the servant or agent of the Crown or as enjoying any status, immunity or privilege of the Crown[1].

1 Domestic Abuse Bill, s 4(3).

FUNCTIONS OF THE COMMISSIONER

11.3 Section 7(1) of the Bill requires the Commissioner to encourage good practice in:

> '(a) the prevention of domestic abuse;
> (b) the prevention, detection, investigation and prosecution of offences involving domestic abuse;
> (c) the identification of—
>   (i) people who carry out domestic abuse;
>   (ii) victims of domestic abuse;
>   (iii) children affected by domestic abuse;
> (d) the provision of protection and support to people affected by domestic abuse.'

POWERS OF COMMISSIONER

11.4 Section 7(2) provides that in exercise of his functions as set out above the things that Commissioner may do include:

'(a) assessing, monitoring, and publishing information about, the provision of services to people affected by domestic abuse;
(b) making recommendations to any public authority about the exercise of its functions;
(c) undertaking or supporting (financially or otherwise) the carrying out of research;
(d) providing information, education or training;
(e) taking other steps to increase public awareness of domestic abuse;
(f) consulting public authorities, voluntary organisations and other persons;
(g) co-operating with, or working jointly with, public authorities, voluntary organisations and other persons, whether in England and Wales or outside the United Kingdom.'

11.5 Section 7(3)–(6) contains restrictions on the Commissioner's powers relating to Wales which seem to be concerned with preventing overlap between the Commissioner's role and that of the Welsh authority.

11.6 Section 8 deals with the ability of the Commissioner to report to the Secretary of State and to publish reports, and s 9 enables the Commissioner to advise the Secretary of State on matters relating to domestic abuse.

FRAMEWORK DOCUMENT

11.7 By s 11(1) the Secretary of State must issue a document (a 'framework document') that deals with matters relating to the Commissioner. The matters that may be dealt with by a framework document include (among other things):

(a) matters relating to governance, funding and staffing;
(b) matters relating to the exercise of functions of the Commissioner;
(c) matters relating to scrutiny of the Commissioner's activities by Parliament or by Senedd Cymru[1];

and both the Commissioner and the Secretary of State must have regard to the framework document[2].

1 Domestic Abuse Bill, s 11(2).
2 Domestic Abuse Bill, s 11(3) and s 11(4).

ADVISORY BOARD

11.8 Section 12 deals with the establishment and role of an Advisory Board.

DUTY TO CO-OPERATE

11.9 Section 15 contains the obligation of specified public authorities to co-operate with the Commissioner. The list of specified authorities appears exhaustive.

DUTY TO RESPOND

11.10 Where the Commissioner publishes a report concerning any public body or a government department, that body or government minister must within 56 days make and publish comments on each part of the report[1].

[1] Domestic Abuse Bill, s 16.

POWER OF SECRETARY OF STATE TO ISSUE GUIDANCE

11.11 By s 48(1) the Secretary of State must issue guidance relating to the exercise by relevant persons of functions under Pt 3 of the Act (powers for dealing with domestic abuse). 'Relevant persons' are defined[1] as a constable and 'a person specified in regulations under s 26(2)(c) for the purpose of making applications for orders under that section' (ie any person specified as being able to make an application for a DAPO). A relevant person must have regard to any guidance issued under this section when exercising a function to which the guidance relates[2].

[1] Domestic Abuse Bill, s 48(2).
[2] Domestic Abuse Bill, s 48(3).

11.12 The Secretary of State must consult the Commissioner and any other appropriate person before issuing the guidance[1], which may be revised from time to time. Any guidance or revision must be published[2].

[1] Domestic Abuse Bill, s 48(5).
[2] Domestic Abuse Bill, s 48(7).

11.13 In a separate provision, s 73 provides that the Secretary of State may issue guidance about the effect of any provision made under specified parts of the Act (virtually the whole of it) and other matters relating to domestic abuse in England and Wales. In particular, the Secretary of State must issue guidance about the effect of s 1 and s 2, including guidance as to particular kinds of behaviour that amount to domestic abuse[1] and the effect of domestic abuse on children[2]. It is further provided that any guidance issued under this section must, so far as relevant, take account of the fact that the majority of victims of domestic abuse in England and Wales are female[3].

[1] Domestic Abuse Bill, s 73(2)(a).
[2] Domestic Abuse Bill, s 73(2)(b).
[3] Domestic Abuse Bill, s 73(3).

11.14 The difference between this guidance and guidance under s 48(1) is that the latter is specifically addressed to those making applications for a DAPO whereas this guidance is addressed to any person exercising public functions to whom guidance issued under this section relates; such person must have regard to it in the exercise of those functions[1].

[1] Domestic Abuse Bill, s 69(4).

11.15 Those exercising a judicial function may be relieved to see that ' . . . nothing in this section permits the Secretary of State to issue guidance to a court or tribunal'[1].

[1] Domestic Abuse Bill, s 73(4).

LOCAL AUTHORITY SUPPORT

11.16 By s 55(1) each relevant local authority in England must:

(a) assess, or make arrangements for the assessment of, the need for domestic abuse support in its area,
(b) prepare and publish a strategy for the provision of such support in its area, and
(c) monitor and evaluate the effectiveness of the strategy.

Further details of the obligations placed on local authorities are contained in s 55.

11.17 By s 56(1) a relevant local authority must appoint a domestic abuse local partnership board for the purposes of providing advice to the authority about the exercise of the authority's functions under s 55. The section contains further detail about the duties and the composition of such a Board.

PROHIBITION OF 'ROUGH SEX' DEFENCE

11.18 Section 65 of the Bill introduces the principle that consent to serious harm for sexual gratification cannot be a defence to criminal proceedings. It is provided that, when an alleged perpetrator is prosecuted for offences against a victim, it is not a defence that the victim consented to the infliction of the serious harm for the purposes of obtaining sexual gratification.

SECURE TENANCIES FOR VICTIMS OF DOMESTIC ABUSE

11.19 The Domestic Abuse Bill 2020 requires local authorities, when re-housing an existing lifetime social tenant, or offering them a new sole tenancy in their own home, to grant a new lifetime tenancy if the local authority is satisfied that the tenant or a member of their household has been a victim of domestic abuse and the new tenancy is granted in connection with that abuse. Section 72 amends Pt 4 of the Housing Act 1985 by inserting a new s 81ZA of that Act. Since this is not a book on housing law readers should refer to the Act for further detail.

Chapter 12

THE EFFECT OF DOMESTIC ABUSE ON RELATED PROCEEDINGS

12.1 The importance of changed attitudes to domestic violence is not confined to applications for non-molestation and exclusion orders. Domestic violence has a significant effect on all family relationships, and can have a particularly malign effect on children. The importance of this factor has gradually come to be recognised and, in relation to cases involving children, is now governed by a Practice Direction of the President, a revised Practice Direction annexed to the Family Procedure Rules 2010 and various cases in which judges give guidance as to the interpretation of these provisions. it may well be that some of these Practice directions will be replaced once the Domestic Abuse Bill 2020 is fully in effect. Some of the provisions of the Domestic Abuse Bill 2020 will undoubtedly have an effect on other proceedings; the reader's attention is drawn to s 3 (see **1.11**) and to the new protection for witnesses contained in Part 5 (see **8.62** onwards).

12.2 In this chapter an outline will be given of these provisions in the hope that this will provide an introduction to this increasingly important area of the law. The two Practice Directions referred to above overlap in several instances so a summary of the combined effect of both will be attempted.

PRESIDENT'S PRACTICE DIRECTION

12.3 The starting point in any consideration of these matters was the *Practice Direction: Residence and Contact Orders: Domestic Violence and Harm*[1], given by the President in 2009. This replaced an earlier Direction[2] in the light of a decision of the House of Lords in *Re B (Care Proceedings: Standard of Proof)*[3]. The background to this development was the practice, which had evolved over several years, of ordering fact-finding hearings in child-related cases involving allegations of domestic violence. The rationale for this, which is now generally accepted, was that, where domestic violence is alleged, and appears to have a potential effect on the outcome of the case, the court should as a first step hear and adjudicate on evidence relating to those allegations, and should only then proceed to consider the issues directly relating to the children once those findings of fact had been made.

1 [2009] 2 FLR 1400.
2 [2008] 2 FLR 103.
3 [2008] 2 FLR 141.

12.4 The Practice Direction applied to any family proceedings in the High Court, or the Family Court in which an application is made for a residence order or a contact order (now known as child arrangements orders) in respect of a child under the Children Act 1989 or the Adoption and Children Act 2002 or in which any question arises about residence or about contact (child arrangements) between a child and a parent or other family member[1]. The practice set out in this direction was to be followed in any case in which it is alleged, or there is otherwise reason to suppose, that the subject child or a party has experienced domestic violence perpetrated by another party or that there is a risk of such violence.

1 *Practice Direction: Residence and Contact Orders: Domestic Violence and Harm* [2009] 2 FLR 1400 at [1].

12.5 The general principle was that the court must, at all stages of the proceedings, consider whether domestic violence is raised as an issue, either by the parties or otherwise, and if so must:

- identify at the earliest opportunity the factual and welfare issues involved;
- consider the nature of any allegation or admission of **domestic violence** and the extent to which any **domestic violence** which is admitted, or which may be proved, would be relevant in deciding whether to make an order about residence or contact and, if so, in what terms; and
- give directions to enable the relevant factual and welfare issues to be determined expeditiously and fairly[1].

1 *Practice Direction: Residence and Contact Orders: Domestic Violence and Harm* [2009] 2 FLR 1400 at [3].

12.6 Events have overtaken this Practice Direction and while its general principles are still relevant for the up to date position reference should be made to FPR PD12J referred to in subsequent paragraphs.

PRACTICE DIRECTION 12J

12.7 The directions contained in previous Practice Directions, together with those contained in the President's Practice Direction on Split Hearings[1] were incorporated into a Practice Direction to the FPR PD12J. With the passage of time, it became clear that the principles in PD12J were not being universally observed and that some further refinement of the Practice Direction was required. Women's Aid published a report on the topic[2] and launched a campaign to avoid child deaths arising out of unsafe child contact. This led to parliamentary activity and recommendations. As a result of this the President appointed Cobb J to review the operation of PD12J, and this review, and subsequent consideration by the Family Justice Council, has led to the new revisions of PD12J.The mandatory effect of PD12J is reinforced and care has obviously been taken to ensure that courts will no longer be able to overlook its provisions, whether inadvertently or deliberately. PD12J is set out in full at APPENDIX 3 and should be referred to for its full effect. What follows is a summary of the most important points.

1 [2010] 2 FLR 1897.
2 Women's Aid, *Nineteen Child Homicides* (Women's Aid, 2016).

12.8 The purpose of PD12J is to set out what the court is required to do in any case where it is alleged or admitted or there is reason to believe that a child or party has experienced domestic abuse perpetrated by the other party. It is provided by the Children Act 1989, s 1(2A) that there is a presumption that involvement of a parent in a child's life will further the welfare of the child, unless there is evidence to the contrary. Paragraph 7 of PD12J requires the court, in every case to which it applies, to 'consider carefully whether the statutory presumption applies, having particular regard to any allegation or admission of harm by domestic abuse to the child or parent or any evidence indicating such harm or risk of harm'. Where domestic abuse is raised as an issue the court must at the earliest opportunity identify the factual and welfare issues involved and consider the extent to which such abuse is likely to be relevant in deciding whether and in what terms to make a child arrangements order[1]. Provision is made to protect parties or children attending a hearing[2] and for the recording by the court of any admission made[3].

1 PD12J, para 7.
2 PD12J, para 10
3 PD12J, para 15.

12.9 Care must be taken when making consent orders. The court has a duty to decide whether any order is for the child's welfare; proposed orders must be carefully scrutinised and the court must not make a child arrangements order by consent unless the parties are present in court, all initial safeguarding checks have been obtained, and a Cafcass officer has spoken to the parties separately except where the court is satisfied that there is no risk of harm to the child or other parent in making an order[1]. In making that decision the court must consider all the evidence and information available and may direct a s 7 report. Where the report is not in writing the court must record on the court file and set out in a schedule to the order the substance of the report.

1 PD12J, paras 6 and 8.

12.10 Subsequent to its initial perusal of the papers, the first involvement of the court will be at the first hearing dispute resolution appointment (FHDRA). It is provided[1] that the court must, at all stages of the proceedings, and specifically at the FHDRA, consider whether domestic violence is raised as an issue, either by the parties or by Cafcass or CAFCASS Cymru or otherwise, and if so must:

- identify at the earliest opportunity (usually at the FHDRA) the factual and welfare issues involved;
- consider the nature of any allegation, admission or evidence of domestic violence or abuse, and the extent to which it would be likely to be relevant in deciding whether to make a child arrangements order and, if so, in what terms;
- give directions to enable contested relevant factual and welfare issues to be tried as soon as possible and fairly;
- ensure that where violence or abuse is admitted or proven, that any child arrangements order in place protects the safety and wellbeing of the child and the parent with whom the child is living, and does not expose them to the risk of further harm. In particular, the court must be satisfied that any contact ordered with a parent who has perpetrated violence or abuse is safe and in the best interests of the child; and

- ensure that any interim child arrangements order (ie considered by the court before determination of the facts, and in the absence of admission) is only made having followed the guidance in paras 25–27 (this relates to possible interim arrangements and the protection for the parties and the child which must be ensured).

1 PD12J, para 6.

12.11 Paragraph 16 of PD12J provides that the court must determine as soon as possible whether or not a fact-finding hearing is required, and paras 16 and 17 give directions as to how this should be approached. It is necessary to take into account, inter alia, the views of the parties and of Cafcass and the evidence which is available. Para 19 sets out the directions which may or must be given, including statements from the parties, schedules of allegations and whether any admissions have been made. The requirements of para 19 are detailed and must be carefully considered. By para 20 a further Dispute Resolution Hearing must be timetabled to follow the fact-finding hearing so that no time is lost in pursuing the case.

12.12 Paragraph 36 of PD12J then considers what must follow where the fact-finding hearing has established that there has been domestic violence. The court must apply the individual matters in the welfare checklist with reference to any findings; in particular, where relevant findings of domestic violence or abuse have been made, the court must in every case consider any harm which the child and the parent with whom the child is living has suffered as a consequence of that violence or abuse, and any harm which the child and the parent with whom the child is living, is at risk of suffering if a child arrangements order is made. The court should only make an order for contact if it can be satisfied that the physical and emotional safety of the child and the parent with whom the child is living can, as far as possible, be secured before during and after contact, and that the parent with whom the child is living will not be subjected to further controlling or coercive behaviour by the other parent.

12.13 Paragraph 37 provides that, in every case where a finding of domestic violence or abuse is made, the court should consider the conduct of both parents towards each other and towards the child; in particular, the court should consider:

(a) the effect of the domestic violence or abuse on the child and on the arrangements for where the child is living;
(b) the effect of the domestic violence or abuse on the child and its effect on the child's relationship with the parents;
(c) whether the applicant parent is motivated by a desire to promote the best interests of the child or is using the process to continue a process of violence, abuse, intimidation or harassment or controlling or coercive behaviour against the other parent;
(d) the likely behaviour during contact of the parent against whom findings are made and its effect on the child; and
(e) the capacity of the parents to appreciate the effect of past violence or abuse and the potential for future violence or abuse.

JUDICIAL GUIDANCE ON THE INTERPRETATION OF PRACTICE DIRECTIONS RELATING TO DOMESTIC ABUSE

12.14 Guidance has been given by the judiciary in certain cases as to the proper approach to the various practice directions. It must be emphasised, of course, that the practice directions themselves are the primary authorities, but some of the cases are useful as indications of how the issues must be kept in proper proportion.

12.15 In *Re C (Domestic Violence: Fact-Finding Hearing)*[1] the Court of Appeal made clear that it is within the trial judge's discretion to decline to order a fact-finding hearing provided reasons are given for this decision.

1 [2010] 1 FLR 1728, CA.

12.16 In *AA v NA and KAB (Fact-Finding Hearing)*[1] Mostyn J held that a fact-finding hearing should only be ordered if the court considering setting one up can discern a real purpose for such a hearing. If the inquiry would not be purposeful then one should not be ordered. In the instant case, and with the benefit of hindsight, there was a strong case for arguing that the whole exercise had been completely futile. All that had been achieved was that the mother now had in her hands a series of damning findings against the father which might well come to haunt their future dealings as the children's parents. The seriousness of allegations of domestic violence for the alleged perpetrator in a private law case mean that they must be carefully pleaded and be the subject of clear evidence. In making factual findings the court must examine carefully any inconsistencies made by the complainant, and where inconsistencies are exposed these must be clearly analysed and rationalised in the verdict. If someone is to be found guilty of domestic violence then fairness demands that it is clearly explained to him why his defence has been rejected and why the case advanced by the complainant accepted. In this case, given the significant inconsistencies in the mother's various accounts of her seven allegations of assault against the father, the judge's findings in her favour were all untenable had he correctly applied the burden and standard of proof.

1 [2010] 2 FLR 1173.

12.17 In *Re H (Interim Contact: Domestic Violence Allegations)*[1] the Court of Appeal held that para 15 of PD12J contemplated a two-stage process of fact-finding hearing and welfare hearing, but it did not require two separate hearings. Such would have been inconsistent with the *President's Guidance in Relation to Split Hearing* and associated authorities which sought to limit the proliferation of split hearings. PD12J should be read as imposing an obligation on the court to determine whether findings needed to be made about factual issues at all and whether, if so, that should be done in a separate fact-finding hearing or as part of a composite fact-finding and welfare hearing.

1 [2014] 1 FLR 41, CA.

12.18 In *Re J (Costs of Fact-Finding Hearing)*[1] the Court of Appeal ordered a father to pay the mother's costs of a fact-finding hearing. The nature of the fact-finding hearing in this case had contained a feature, the allegations of domestic violence, which was relevant to costs and which differentiated the hearing from a conventional hearing under ChA 1989, in which both parties were submitting rival proposals for the optimum arrangements for a child. The effect of the direction for a separate fact-finding hearing was that the costs incurred by the mother in relation to that hearing were wholly referable to the mother's allegations against the father, unrelated to the paradigm situation to which the general proposition in favour of no order as to costs applied.

1 [2010] 1 FLR 1893, CA.

12.19 In *Re A (Supervised Contact Order: Assessment of Impact of Domestic Violence)*[1] the Court of Appeal held that where domestic violence had been established the court was bound to accord appropriate weight to those findings in accordance with *Re L (A Child)(Contact: Domestic Violence)*[2] and to conduct a risk assessment in accordance with PD12J, paras 35–37. It was always wise for some reference to PD12J to be made in the judgment. Unproven allegations were not established facts and could not therefore be relied upon in forming further conclusions.

1 [2015] EWCA Civ 486.
2 [2001] Fam 260, [2000] 4 All ER 609.

12.20 In *Re K (Contact)*[1] the judge at first instance found that the children had witnessed aggressive and controlling behaviour by the father and ordered no direct contact. On appeal it was reaffirmed that contact is almost always in the interests of the child. The judge should have been directed to PD12J and should have considered the available options by way of direct work with the father.

1 [2016] EWCA Civ 99.

12.21 In *MN v MN (Contact)*[1] the judge found as fact that the father had perpetrated acts of violence against the mother and had made threats to kill her. The Cafcass officer said that it was not safe for the father to spend time with the child. However, the judge ordered a short period of indirect contact followed by direct contact. On appeal, Moor J said that direct contact could not be ordered without a further risk assessment and directed the local authority to provide such an assessment. He observed that the judge had apparently not considered PD12J.

1 [2017] EWHC 324 (Fam).

12.22 In *Re V (a child) (Inadequate Reasons for Findings of Fact)*[1] the Court of Appeal emphasised that in a fact-finding hearing the court must state reasons for conclusions in the form of a basic, short description of the matters considered and the factors which gave rise to the conclusions. The law required that a losing party should know why he had lost on a particular point. The court also said that it is erroneous to assume that each and every allegation must be thoroughly examined. The enquiry must be focussed on the relevance of alleged domestic violence to the issue of contact before the court. For a similar result see *Re T (A Child)*[2].

1 [2015] EWCA Civ 274.
2 [2016] EWCA Civ 1210.

12.23 In *Re LG (Re-Opening of Fact-Finding)*[1] Baker J had to consider a case where a circuit judge had dismissed a mother's appeal against a magistrates' order for contact after a fact-finding hearing had concluded that the mother's allegations of violence were not proved. Baker J allowed the appeal and ordered a new hearing. He observed that there is a three-stage process to be applied when determining whether to order a fact-finding hearing. At the first hearing the court considers whether it will allow any reconsideration of the earlier finding. The second stage relates to the extent of the investigations and evidence in the review. The third stage is the review itself. In directing a party to identify and rely on a few allegations as specimen allegations the court must ensure that significant issues are not overlooked.

1 [2017] EWHC 2626 (Fam)

12.24 Baker J pointed out that the Practice Direction stresses that the court must consider at all stages whether domestic violence or abuse is raised as an issue and he the court is under an obligation to scrutinise carefully orders made by consent. The fact that a child arrangements order was made by consent does not absolve the court from the ongoing responsibility of considering whether domestic abuse was an issue or, where it was established, that the order did not expose the mother or child to further abuse.

12.25 The need for strict observance of PD12J was stressed by McFarlane LJ in *Re J (Contact Orders: Procedure)*[1].

1 [2018] EWCA Civ 115.

Appendix 1

STATUTES

CHILDREN ACT 1989

A1.1

38A Power to include exclusion requirement in interim care order

(1) Where—

- (a) on being satisfied that there are reasonable grounds for believing that the circumstances with respect to a child are as mentioned in section 31(2)(a) and (b)(i), the court makes an interim care order with respect to a child, and
- (b) the conditions mentioned in subsection (2) are satisfied,

the court may include an exclusion requirement in the interim care order.

(2) The conditions are—

- (a) that there is reasonable cause to believe that, if a person ("the relevant person") is excluded from a dwelling-house in which the child lives, the child will cease to suffer, or cease to be likely to suffer, significant harm, and
- (b) that another person living in the dwelling-house (whether a parent of the child or some other person)—
  - (i) is able and willing to give to the child the care which it would be reasonable to expect a parent to give him, and
  - (ii) consents to the inclusion of the exclusion requirement.

(3) For the purposes of this section an exclusion requirement is any one or more of the following—

- (a) a provision requiring the relevant person to leave a dwelling-house in which he is living with the child,
- (b) a provision prohibiting the relevant person from entering a dwelling-house in which the child lives, and
- (c) a provision excluding the relevant person from a defined area in which a dwelling-house in which the child lives is situated.

(4) The court may provide that the exclusion requirement is to have effect for a shorter period than the other provisions of the interim care order.

(5) Where the court makes an interim care order containing an exclusion requirement, the court may attach a power of arrest to the exclusion requirement.

(6) Where the court attaches a power of arrest to an exclusion requirement of an interim care order, it may provide that the power of arrest is to have effect for a shorter period than the exclusion requirement.

(7) Any period specified for the purposes of subsection (4) or (6) may be extended by the court (on one or more occasions) on an application to vary or discharge the interim care order.

(8) Where a power of arrest is attached to an exclusion requirement of an interim care order by virtue of subsection (5), a constable may arrest without warrant any person whom he has reasonable cause to believe to be in breach of the requirement.

(9) Sections 47(7), (11) and (12) and 48 of, and Schedule 5 to, the Family Law Act 1996 shall have effect in relation to a person arrested under subsection (8) of this section as they have effect in relation to a person arrested under section 47(6) of that Act.

(10) If, while an interim care order containing an exclusion requirement is in force, the local authority have removed the child from the dwelling-house from which the relevant person is excluded to other accommodation for a continuous period of more than 24 hours, the interim care order shall cease to have effect in so far as it imposes the exclusion requirement.

38B Undertakings relating to interim care orders

(1) In any case where the court has power to include an exclusion requirement in an interim care order, the court may accept an undertaking from the relevant person.

(2) No power of arrest may be attached to any undertaking given under subsection (1).

(3) An undertaking given to a court under subsection (1)—

(a) shall be enforceable as if it were an order of the court, and

(b) shall cease to have effect if, while it is in force, the local authority have removed the child from the dwelling-house from which the relevant person is excluded to other accommodation for a continuous period of more than 24 hours.

(4) This section has effect without prejudice to the powers of the High Court and family court apart from this section.

(5) In this section "exclusion requirement" and "relevant person" have the same meaning as in section 38A.

39 Discharge and variation etc of care orders and supervision orders

(1) A care order may be discharged by the court on the application of—

(a) any person who has parental responsibility for the child;

(b) the child himself; or

(c) the local authority designated by the order.

(2) A supervision order may be varied or discharged by the court on the application of —

(a) any person who has parental responsibility for the child;

(b) the child himself; or

(c) the supervisor.

(3) On the application of a person who is not entitled to apply for the order to be discharged, but who is a person with whom the child is living, a supervision order may be varied by the court in so far as it imposes a requirement which affects that person.

(3A) On the application of a person who is not entitled to apply for the order to be discharged, but who is a person to whom an exclusion requirement contained in the order applies, an interim care order may be varied or discharged by the court in so far as it imposes the exclusion requirement.

(3B) Where a power of arrest has been attached to an exclusion requirement of an interim care order, the court may, on the application of any person entitled to apply for the discharge of the order so far as it imposes the exclusion requirement, vary or discharge the order in so far as it confers a power of arrest (whether or not any application has been made to vary or discharge any other provision of the order).

(4) Where a care order is in force with respect to a child the court may, on the application of any person entitled to apply for the order to be discharged, substitute a supervision order for the care order.

(5) When a court is considering whether to substitute one order for another under subsection (4) any provision of this Act which would otherwise require section 31(2) to be satisfied at the time when the proposed order is substituted or made shall be disregarded.

. . .

44A Power to include exclusion requirement in emergency protection order

(1) Where—

(a) on being satisfied as mentioned in section 44(1)(a), (b) or (c), the court makes an emergency protection order with respect to a child, and

(b) the conditions mentioned in subsection (2) are satisfied,

the court may include an exclusion requirement in the emergency protection order.

(2) The conditions are—

(a) that there is reasonable cause to believe that, if a person ("the relevant person") is excluded from a dwelling-house in which the child lives, then—

(i) in the case of an order made on the ground mentioned in section 44(1)(a), the child will not be likely to suffer significant harm, even though the child is not removed as mentioned in section 44(1)(a)(i) or does not remain as mentioned in section 44(1)(a)(ii), or

(ii) in the case of an order made on the ground mentioned in paragraph (b) or (c) of section 44(1), the enquiries referred to in that paragraph will cease to be frustrated, and

(b) that another person living in the dwelling-house (whether a parent of the child or some other person)—

(i) is able and willing to give to the child the care which it would be reasonable to expect a parent to give him, and

(ii) consents to the inclusion of the exclusion requirement.

(3) For the purposes of this section an exclusion requirement is any one or more of the following—

(a) a provision requiring the relevant person to leave a dwelling-house in which he is living with the child,

(b) a provision prohibiting the relevant person from entering a dwelling-house in which the child lives, and

(c) a provision excluding the relevant person from a defined area in which a dwelling-house in which the child lives is situated.

(4) The court may provide that the exclusion requirement is to have effect for a shorter period than the other provisions of the order.

(5) Where the court makes an emergency protection order containing an exclusion requirement, the court may attach a power of arrest to the exclusion requirement.

(6) Where the court attaches a power of arrest to an exclusion requirement of an emergency protection order, it may provide that the power of arrest is to have effect for a shorter period than the exclusion requirement.

(7) Any period specified for the purposes of subsection (4) or (6) may be extended by the court (on one or more occasions) on an application to vary or discharge the emergency protection order.

(8) Where a power of arrest is attached to an exclusion requirement of an emergency protection order by virtue of subsection (5), a constable may arrest without warrant any person whom he has reasonable cause to believe to be in breach of the requirement.

(9) Sections 47(7), (11) and (12) and 48 of, and Schedule 5 to, the Family Law Act 1996 shall have effect in relation to a person arrested under subsection (8) of this section as they have effect in relation to a person arrested under section 47(6) of that Act.

(10) If, while an emergency protection order containing an exclusion requirement is in force, the applicant has removed the child from the dwelling-house from which the

relevant person is excluded to other accommodation for a continuous period of more than 24 hours, the order shall cease to have effect in so far as it imposes the exclusion requirement.

44B Undertakings relating to emergency protection orders

(1) In any case where the court has power to include an exclusion requirement in an emergency protection order, the court may accept an undertaking from the relevant person.

(2) No power of arrest may be attached to any undertaking given under subsection (1).

(3) An undertaking given to a court under subsection (1)—

- (a) shall be enforceable as if it were an order of the court, and
- (b) shall cease to have effect if, while it is in force, the applicant has removed the child from the dwelling-house from which the relevant person is excluded to other accommodation for a continuous period of more than 24 hours.

(4) This section has effect without prejudice to the powers of the High Court and family court apart from this section.

(5) In this section "exclusion requirement" and "relevant person" have the same meaning as in section 44A.

45 Duration of emergency protection orders and other supplemental provisions

(1) An emergency protection order shall have effect for such period, not exceeding eight days, as may be specified in the order.

(2) Where—

- (a) the court making an emergency protection order would, but for this subsection, specify a period of eight days as the period for which the order is to have effect; but
- (b) the last of those eight days is a public holiday (that is to say, Christmas Day, Good Friday, a bank holiday or a Sunday),

the court may specify a period which ends at noon on the first later day which is not such a holiday.

(3) Where an emergency protection order is made on an application under section 46(7), the period of eight days mentioned in subsection (1) shall begin with the first day on which the child was taken into police protection under section 46.

(4) Any person who—

- (a) has parental responsibility for a child as the result of an emergency protection order; and
- (b) is entitled to apply for a care order with respect to the child, may apply to the court for the period during which the emergency protection order is to have effect to be extended.

(5) On an application under subsection (4) the court may extend the period during which the order is to have effect by such period, not exceeding seven days, as it thinks fit, but may do so only if it has reasonable cause to believe that the child concerned is likely to suffer significant harm if the order is not extended.

(6) An emergency protection order may only be extended once.

(7) Regardless of any enactment or rule of law which would otherwise prevent it from doing so, a court hearing an application for, or with respect to, an emergency protection order may take account of—

- (a) any statement contained in any report made to the court in the course of, or in connection with, the hearing; or
- (b) any evidence given during the hearing,

which is, in the opinion of the court, relevant to the application.

(8) Any of the following may apply to the court for an emergency protection order to be discharged—

(a) the child;

(b) a parent of his;

(c) any person who is not a parent of his but who has parental responsibility for him; or

(d) any person with whom he was living immediately before the making of the order.

(8A) On the application of a person who is not entitled to apply for the order to be discharged, but who is a person to whom an exclusion requirement contained in the order applies, an emergency protection order may be varied or discharged by the court in so far as it imposes the exclusion requirement.

(8B) Where a power of arrest has been attached to an exclusion requirement of an emergency protection order, the court may, on the application of any person entitled to apply for the discharge of the order so far as it imposes the exclusion requirement, vary or discharge the order in so far as it confers a power of arrest (whether or not any application has been made to vary or discharge any other provision of the order).

(9) (*repealed*)

(10) No appeal may be made against—

(a) the making of, or refusal to make, an emergency protection order;

(b) the extension of, or refusal to extend, the period during which such an order is to have effect;

(c) the discharge of, or refusal to discharge, such an order; or

(d) the giving of, or refusal to give, any direction in connection with such an order.

(11) Subsection (8) does not apply—

(a) where the person who would otherwise be entitled to apply for the emergency protection order to be discharged—

(i) was given notice (in accordance with rules of court) of the hearing at which the order was made; and

(ii) was present at that hearing; or

(b) to any emergency protection order the effective period of which has been extended under subsection (5).

(12) A court making an emergency protection order may direct that the applicant may, in exercising any powers which he has by virtue of the order, be accompanied by a registered medical practitioner, registered nurse or registered midwife, if he so chooses.

(13) The reference in subsection (12) to a registered midwife is to such a midwife who is also registered in the Specialist Community Public Health Nurses' Part of the register maintained under article 5 of the Nursing and Midwifery Order 2001.

FAMILY LAW ACT 1996

PART IV
FAMILY HOMES AND DOMESTIC VIOLENCE

Rights to occupy matrimonial home

A1.2

30 Rights concerning matrimonial home where one spouse or civil partner has no estate etc

(1) This section applies if—

(a) one spouse or civil partner ("A") is entitled to occupy a dwelling-house by virtue of—

(i) a beneficial estate or interest or contract; or

(ii) any enactment giving A the right to remain in occupation; and

(b) the other spouse or civil partner ("'B") is not so entitled.

(2) Subject to the provisions of this Part, B has the following rights ("home rights")—

(a) if in occupation, a right not to be evicted or excluded from the dwelling-house or any part of it by A except with the leave of the court given by an order under section 33;

(a) if in occupation, a right not to be evicted or excluded from the dwelling-house or any part of it by A except with the leave of the court given by an order under section 33;

(b) if not in occupation, a right with the leave of the court so given to enter into and occupy the dwelling-house.

(3) If B is entitled under this section to occupy a dwelling-house or any part of a dwelling-house, any payment or tender made or other thing done by "B" in or towards satisfaction of any liability of A in respect of rent, mortgage payments or other outgoings affecting the dwelling-house shall, whether or not it is made or done in pursuance of an order under section 40, be as good as if made or done by A.

(4) "B's" occupation by virtue of this section—

(a) is to be treated, for the purposes of the Rent (Agriculture) Act 1976 and the Rent Act 1977 (other than Part V and sections 103 to 106 of that Act), as occupation by A as A's residence, and

(b) if B occupies the dwelling-house as B's only or principal home, is to be treated, for the purposes of the Housing Act 1985, Part I of the Housing Act 1988, Chapter 1 of Part 5 of the Housing Act 1996 and the Prevention of Social Housing Fraud Act 2013, as occupation by A as A's only or principal home.

(5) If B—

(a) is entitled under this section to occupy a dwelling-house or any part of a dwelling-house, and

(b) makes any payment in or towards satisfaction of any liability of A in respect of mortgage payments affecting the dwelling-house,

the person to whom the payment is made may treat it as having been made by A, but the fact that that person has treated any such payment as having been so made does not affect any claim of B against A to an interest in the dwelling-house by virtue of the payment.

(6) If B is entitled under this section to occupy a dwelling-house or part of a dwelling-house by reason of an interest of A under a trust, all the provisions of subsections (3) to (5) apply in relation to the trustees as they apply in relation to A.

(7) This section does not apply to a dwelling-house which—

(a) in the case of spouses, has at no time been, and was at no time intended by them to be, a matrimonial home of theirs; and

(b) in the case of civil partners, has at no time been, and was at no time intended by them to be, a civil partnership home of theirs.

(8) B's home rights continue—

(a) only so long as the marriage or civil partnership subsists, except to the extent that an order under section 33(5) otherwise provides; and

(b) only so long as A is entitled as mentioned in subsection (1) to occupy the dwelling-house, except where provision is made by section 31 for those rights to be a charge on an estate or interest in the dwelling-house.

(9) It is hereby declared that a person—

(a) who has an equitable interest in a dwelling-house or in its proceeds of sale, but

(b) is not a person in whom there is vested (whether solely or as joint tenant) a legal estate in fee simple or a legal term of years absolute in the dwelling-house,

is to be treated, only for the purpose of determining whether he has home rights, as not being entitled to occupy the dwelling-house by virtue of that interest.

31 Effect of home rights as charge on dwelling-house

(1) Subsections (2) and (3) apply if, at any time during a marriage or civil partnership, A is entitled to occupy a dwelling-house by virtue of a beneficial estate or interest.

(2) B's home rights are a charge on the estate or interest.

(3) The charge created by subsection (2) has the same priority as if it were an equitable interest created at whichever is the latest of the following dates—

(a) the date on which A acquires the estate or interest;

(b) the date of the marriage or of the formation of the civil partnership; and

(c) 1 January 1968 (the commencement date of the Matrimonial Homes Act 1967).

(4) Subsections (5) and (6) apply if, at any time when B's home rights are a charge on an interest of A under a trust, there are, apart from A or B, no persons, living or unborn, who are or could become beneficiaries under the trust.

(5) The rights are a charge also on the estate or interest of the trustees for A.

(6) The charge created by subsection (5) has the same priority as if it were an equitable interest created (under powers overriding the trusts) on the date when it arises.

(7) In determining for the purposes of subsection (4) whether there are any persons who are not, but could become, beneficiaries under the trust, there is to be disregarded any potential exercise of a general power of appointment exercisable by either or both of A and B alone (whether or not the exercise of it requires the consent of another person).

(8) Even though B's home rights are a charge on an estate or interest in the dwelling-house, those rights are brought to an end by—

(a) the death of A, or

(b) the termination (otherwise than by death) of the marriage or civil partnership,

unless the court directs otherwise by an order made under section 33(5).

(9) If—

(a) B's home rights are a charge on an estate or interest in the dwelling-house, and

(b) that estate or interest is surrendered to merge in some other estate or interest expectant on it in such circumstances that, but for the merger, the person taking the estate or interest would be bound by the charge,

the surrender has effect subject to the charge and the persons thereafter entitled to the other estate or interest are, for so long as the estate or interest surrendered would have endured if not so surrendered, to be treated for all purposes of this Part as deriving title to the other estate or interest under A or, as the case may be, under the trustees for A, by virtue of the surrender.

(10) If the title to the legal estate by virtue of which A is entitled to occupy a dwelling-house (including any legal estate held by trustees for A) is registered under the Land Registration Act 2002 or any enactment replaced by that Act—

(a) registration of a land charge affecting the dwelling-house by virtue of this Part is to be effected by registering a notice under that Act; and

(b) B's home rights are not to be capable of falling within paragraph 2 of Schedule 1 or 3 to that Act.

(11) (*repealed*)

(12) If—

(a) B's home rights are a charge on the estate of A or of trustees of A, and

(b) that estate is the subject of a mortgage,

then if, after the date of the creation of the mortgage ("the first mortgage"), the charge is registered under section 2 of the Land Charges Act 1972, the charge is, for the purposes of section 94 of the Law of Property Act 1925 (which regulates the rights of mortgagees to make further advances ranking in priority to subsequent mortgages), to be deemed to be a mortgage subsequent in date to the first mortgage.

(13) It is hereby declared that a charge under subsection (2) or (5) is not registrable under subsection 10 or under section 2 of the Land Charges Act 1972 unless it is a charge on a legal estate.

32 Further provisions relating to home rights

Schedule 4 (provisions supplementary to sections 30 and 31) has effect.

Occupation orders

33 Occupation orders where applicant has estate or interest etc or has home rights

(1) If—

(a) a person ("the person entitled")—

(i) is entitled to occupy a dwelling-house by virtue of a beneficial estate or interest or contract or by virtue of any enactment giving him the right to remain in occupation, or

(ii) has home rights in relation to a dwelling-house, and

(b) the dwelling-house—

(i) is or at any time has been the home of the person entitled and of another person with whom he is associated, or

(ii) was at any time intended by the person entitled and any such other person to be their home,the person entitled may apply to the court for an order containing any of the provisions specified in subsections (3), (4) and (5).

(2) If an agreement to marry is terminated, no application under this section may be made by virtue of section 62(3)(e) by reference to that agreement after the end of the period of three years beginning with the date on which it is terminated.

(2A) If a civil partnership agreement (as defined by section 73 of the Civil Partnership Act 2004) is terminated, no application under this section may be made by virtue of section 62(3)(eza) by reference to that agreement after the end of the period of three years beginning with the day on which it is terminated.

(3) An order under this section may—

(a) enforce the applicant's entitlement to remain in occupation as against the other person ("the respondent");

(b) require the respondent to permit the applicant to enter and remain in the dwelling-house or part of the dwelling-house;

(c) regulate the occupation of the dwelling-house by either or both parties;

(d) if the respondent is entitled as mentioned in subsection (1)(a)(i), prohibit, suspend or restrict the exercise by him of his right to occupy the dwelling-house;

(e) if the respondent has home rights in relation to the dwelling-house and the applicant is the other spouse or civil partner, restrict or terminate those rights;

(f) require the respondent to leave the dwelling-house or part of the dwelling-house; or

(g) exclude the respondent from a defined area in which the dwelling-house is included.

(4) An order under this section may declare that the applicant is entitled as mentioned in subsection (1)(a)(i) or has home rights.

(5) If the applicant has home rights and the respondent is the other spouse or civil partner, an order under this section made during the marriage or civil partnership may provide that those rights are not brought to an end by—

(a) the death of the other spouse or civil partner; or

(b) the termination (otherwise than by death) of the marriage or civil partnership.

(6) In deciding whether to exercise its powers under subsection (3) and (if so) in what manner, the court shall have regard to all the circumstances including—

(a) the housing needs and housing resources of each of the parties and of any relevant child;

(b) the financial resources of each of the parties;

(c) the likely effect of any order, or of any decision by the court not to exercise its powers under subsection (3), on the health, safety or well-being of the parties and of any relevant child; and

(d) the conduct of the parties in relation to each other and otherwise.

(7) If it appears to the court that the applicant or any relevant child is likely to suffer significant harm attributable to conduct of the respondent if an order under this section containing one or more of the provisions mentioned in subsection (3) is not made, the court shall make the order unless it appears to the court that—

(a) the respondent or any relevant child is likely to suffer significant harm if the order is made; and

(b) the harm likely to be suffered by the respondent or child in that event is as great as, or greater than, the harm attributable to conduct of the respondent which is likely to be suffered by the applicant or child if the order is not made.

(8) The court may exercise its powers under subsection (5) in any case where it considers that in all the circumstances it is just and reasonable to do so.

(9) An order under this section—

(a) may not be made after the death of either of the parties mentioned in subsection (1); and

(b) except in the case of an order made by virtue of subsection (5)(a), ceases to have effect on the death of either party.

(10) An order under this section may, in so far as it has continuing effect, be made for a specified period, until the occurrence of a specified event or until further order.

34 Effect of order under s 33 where rights are charge on dwelling-house

(1) If B's home rights are a charge on the estate or interest of A or of trustees for the other spouse—

(a) any order under section 33 against the other spouse has, except so far as a contrary intention appears, the same effect against persons deriving title under the other spouse or under the trustees and affected by the charge, and

(b) subsections 33(1), (3), (4) and (10) and 30(3) to (6) apply in relation to any person deriving title under the other spouse or under the trustees and affected by the charge as they apply in relation to the other spouse.

(2) The court may make an order under section 33 by virtue of subsection (1)(b) if it considers that in all the circumstances it is just and reasonable to do so.

35 One former spouse or former civil partner with no existing right to occupy

(1) This section applies if—

(a) one former spouse or former civil partner is entitled to occupy a dwelling-house by virtue of a beneficial estate or interest or contract, or by virtue of any enactment giving him the right to remain in occupation;

(b) the other former spouse or former civil partner is not so entitled; and

(c) the dwelling-house—

(i) in the case of former spouses, was at any time their matrimonial home or was at any time intended by them to be their matrimonial home, or

(ii) in the case of former civil partners, was at any time their civil partnership home or was at any time intended by them to be their civil partnership home.

(2) The former spouse or former civil partner not so entitled may apply to the court for an order under this section against the other former spouse or former civil partner ("the respondent").

(3) If the applicant is in occupation, an order under this section must contain provision—

(a) giving the applicant the right not to be evicted or excluded from the dwelling-house or any part of it by the respondent for the period specified in the order; and

(b) prohibiting the respondent from evicting or excluding the applicant during that period.

(4) If the applicant is not in occupation, an order under this section must contain provision—

(a) giving the applicant the right to enter into and occupy the dwelling-house for the period specified in the order; and

(b) requiring the respondent to permit the exercise of that right.

(5) An order under this section may also—

(a) regulate the occupation of the dwelling-house by either or both of the parties;

(b) prohibit, suspend or restrict the exercise by the respondent of his right to occupy the dwelling-house;

(c) require the respondent to leave the dwelling-house or part of the dwelling-house; or

(d) exclude the respondent from a defined area in which the dwelling-house is included.

(6) In deciding whether to make an order under this section containing provision of the kind mentioned in subsection (3) or (4) and (if so) in what manner, the court shall have regard to all the circumstances including—

(a) the housing needs and housing resources of each of the parties and of any relevant child;

(b) the financial resources of each of the parties;

(c) the likely effect of any order, or of any decision by the court not to exercise its powers under subsection (3) or (4), on the health, safety or well-being of the parties and of any relevant child;

(d) the conduct of the parties in relation to each other and otherwise;

(e) the length of time that has elapsed since the parties ceased to live together;

(f) the length of time that has elapsed since the marriage or civil partnership was dissolved or annulled; and

(g) the existence of any pending proceedings between the parties—

(i) for an order under section 23A or 24 of the Matrimonial Causes Act 1973 (property adjustment orders in connection with divorce proceedings etc);

(ia) for a property adjustment order under Part 2 of Schedule 5 to the Civil Partnership Act 2004;

(ii) for an order under paragraph 1(2)(d) or (e) of Schedule 1 to the Children Act 1989 (orders for financial relief against parents); or

(iii) relating to the legal or beneficial ownership of the dwelling-house.

(7) In deciding whether to exercise its power to include one or more of the provisions referred to in subsection (5) ("a subsection (5) provision") and (if so) in what manner, the court shall have regard to all the circumstances including the matters mentioned in subsection (6)(a) to (e).

(8) If the court decides to make an order under this section and it appears to it that, if the order does not include a subsection (5) provision, the applicant or any relevant child is likely to suffer significant harm attributable to conduct of the respondent, the court shall include the subsection (5) provision in the order unless it appears to the court that—

(a) the respondent or any relevant child is likely to suffer significant harm if the provision is included in the order; and

(b) the harm likely to be suffered by the respondent or child in that event is as great as or greater than the harm attributable to conduct of the respondent which is likely to be suffered by the applicant or child if the provision is not included.

(9) An order under this section—

(a) may not be made after the death of either of the former spouses or former civil partners; and

(b) ceases to have effect on the death of either of them.

(10) An order under this section must be limited so as to have effect for a specified period not exceeding six months, but may be extended on one or more occasions for a further specified period not exceeding six months.

(11) A former spouse or former civil partner who has an equitable interest in the dwelling-house or in the proceeds of sale of the dwelling-house but in whom there is not vested (whether solely or as joint tenant) a legal estate in fee simple or a legal term of years absolute in the dwelling-house is to be treated (but only for the purpose of determining whether he is eligible to apply under this section) as not being entitled to occupy the dwelling-house by virtue of that interest.

(12) Subsection (11) does not prejudice any right of such a former spouse or former civil partner to apply for an order under section 33.

(13) So long as an order under this section remains in force, subsections (3) to (6) of section 30 apply in relation to the applicant—

(a) as if he were B (the person entitled to occupy the dwelling-house by virtue of that section); and

(b) as if the respondent were A (the person entitled as mentioned in subsection (1)(a) of that section).

36 One cohabitant or former cohabitant with no existing right to occupy

(1) This section applies if—

(a) one cohabitant or former cohabitant is entitled to occupy a dwelling-house by virtue of a beneficial estate or interest or contract or by virtue of any enactment giving him the right to remain in occupation;

(b) the other cohabitant or former cohabitant is not so entitled; and

(c) that dwelling-house is the home in which they cohabit or a home in which they at any time cohabited or intended to cohabit.

(2) The cohabitant or former cohabitant not so entitled may apply to the court for an order under this section against the other cohabitant or former cohabitant ("the respondent").

(3) If the applicant is in occupation, an order under this section must contain provision—

(a) giving the applicant the right not to be evicted or excluded from the dwelling-house or any part of it by the respondent for the period specified in the order, and

(b) prohibiting the respondent from evicting or excluding the applicant during that period.

(4) If the applicant is not in occupation, an order under this section must contain provision—

(a) giving the applicant the right to enter into and occupy the dwelling-house for the period specified in the order; and

(b) requiring the respondent to permit the exercise of that right.

(5) An order under this section may also—

(a) regulate the occupation of the dwelling-house by either or both of the parties;

(b) prohibit, suspend or restrict the exercise by the respondent of his right to occupy the dwelling-house;

(c) require the respondent to leave the dwelling-house or part of the dwelling-house; or

(d) exclude the respondent from a defined area in which the dwelling-house is included.

(6) In deciding whether to make an order under this section containing provision of the kind mentioned in subsection (3) or (4) and (if so) in what manner, the court shall have regard to all the circumstances including—

(a) the housing needs and housing resources of each of the parties and of any relevant child;

(b) the financial resources of each of the parties;

(c) the likely effect of any order, or of any decision by the court not to exercise its powers under subsection (3) or (4), on the health, safety or well-being of the parties and of any relevant child;

(d) the conduct of the parties in relation to each other and otherwise;

(e) the nature of the parties' relationship and in particular the level of commitment involved in it;

(f) the length of time during which they have cohabited;

(g) whether there are or have been any children who are children of both parties or for whom both parties have or have had parental responsibility;

(h) the length of time that has elapsed since the parties ceased to live together; and

(i) the existence of any pending proceedings between the parties—

(i) for an order under paragraph 1(2)(d) or (e) of Schedule 1 to the Children Act 1989 (orders for financial relief against parents), or

(ii) relating to the legal or beneficial ownership of the dwelling-house.

(7) In deciding whether to exercise its powers to include one or more of the provisions referred to in subsection (5) ("a subsection (5) provision") and (if so) in what manner, the court shall have regard to all the circumstances including—

(a) the matters mentioned in subsection (6)(a) to (d); and

(b) the questions mentioned in subsection (8).

(8) The questions are—

(a) whether the applicant or any relevant child is likely to suffer significant harm attributable to conduct of the respondent if the subsection (5) provision is not included in the order; and

(b) whether the harm likely to be suffered by the respondent or child if the provision is included is as great as or greater than the harm attributable to conduct of the respondent which is likely to be suffered by the applicant or child if the provision is not included.

(9) An order under this section—

(a) may not be made after the death of either of the parties; and

(b) ceases to have effect on the death of either of them.

(10) An order under this section must be limited so as to have effect for a specified period not exceeding six months, but may be extended on one occasion for a further specified period not exceeding six months.

(11) A person who has an equitable interest in the dwelling-house or in the proceeds of sale of the dwelling-house but in whom there is not vested (whether solely or as joint tenant) a legal estate in fee simple or a legal term of years absolute in the dwelling-house is to be treated (but only for the purpose of determining whether he is eligible to apply under this section) as not being entitled to occupy the dwelling-house by virtue of that interest.

(12) Subsection (11) does not prejudice any right of such a person to apply for an order under section 33.

(13) So long as the order remains in force, subsections (3) to (6) of section 30 apply in relation to the applicant—

(a) as if he were B (the person entitled to occupy the dwelling-house by virtue of that section); and

(b) as if the respondent were A (the person entitled as mentioned in subsection (1)(a) of that section).

37 Neither spouse or civil partner entitled to occupy

(1) This section applies if—

(a) one spouse or former spouse and the other spouse or former spouse occupy a dwelling-house which is or was the matrimonial home; but

(b) neither of them is entitled to remain in occupation—

(i) by virtue of a beneficial estate or interest or contract; or

(ii) by virtue of any enactment giving him the right to remain in occupation.

(1A) This section also applies if—

(a) one civil partner or former civil partner and the other civil partner or former civil partner occupy a dwelling-house which is or was the civil partnership home; but

(b) neither of them is entitled to remain in occupation—

(i) by virtue of a beneficial estate or interest or contract; or

(ii) by virtue of any enactment giving him the right to remain in occupation.

(2) Either of the parties may apply to the court for an order against the other under this section.

(3) An order under this section may—

(a) require the respondent to permit the applicant to enter and remain in the dwelling-house or part of the dwelling-house;
(b) regulate the occupation of the dwelling-house by either or both of the parties;
(c) require the respondent to leave the dwelling-house or part of the dwelling-house; or
(d) exclude the respondent from a defined area in which the dwelling-house is included.

(4) Subsections (6) and (7) of section 33 apply to the exercise by the court of its powers under this section as they apply to the exercise by the court of its powers under subsection (3) of that section.

(5) An order under this section must be limited so as to have effect for a specified period not exceeding six months, but may be extended on one or more occasions for a further specified period not exceeding six months.

38 Neither cohabitant or former cohabitant entitled to occupy

(1) This section applies if—
(a) one cohabitant or former cohabitant and the other cohabitant or former cohabitant occupy a dwelling-house which is the home in which they cohabit or cohabited; but
(b) neither of them is entitled to remain in occupation—
(i) by virtue of a beneficial estate or interest or contract; or
(ii) by virtue of any enactment giving him the right to remain in occupation.

(2) Either of the parties may apply to the court for an order against the other under this section.

(3) An order under this section may—
(a) require the respondent to permit the applicant to enter and remain in the dwelling-house or part of the dwelling-house;
(b) regulate the occupation of the dwelling-house by either or both of the parties;
(c) require the respondent to leave the dwelling-house or part of the dwelling-house; or
(d) exclude the respondent from a defined area in which the dwelling-house is included.

(4) In deciding whether to exercise its powers to include one or more of the provisions referred to in subsection(3) ("a subsection (3) provision") and (if so) in what manner, the court shall have regard to all the circumstances including—
(a) the housing needs and housing resources of each of the parties and of any relevant child;
(b) the financial resources of each of the parties;
(c) the likely effect of any order, or of any decision by the court not to exercise its powers under subsection (3), on the health, safety or well-being of the parties and of any relevant child;
(d) the conduct of the parties in relation to each other and otherwise; and
(e) the questions mentioned in subsection (5).

(5) The questions are—
(a) whether the applicant or any relevant child is likely to suffer significant harm attributable to conduct of the respondent if the subsection (3) provision is not included in the order; and
(b) whether the harm likely to be suffered by the respondent or child if the provision is included is as great as or greater than the harm attributable to conduct of the respondent which is likely to be suffered by the applicant or child if the provision is not included.

(6) An order under this section shall be limited so as to have effect for a specified period not exceeding six months, but may be extended on one occasion for a further specified period not exceeding six months.

39 Supplementary provisions

(1) In this Part an 'occupation order' means an order under section 33, 35, 36, 37 or 38.

(2) An application for an occupation order may be made in other family proceedings or without any other family proceedings being instituted.

(3) If—

- (a) an application for an occupation order is made under section 33, 35, 36, 37 or 38, and
- (b) the court considers that it has no power to make the order under the section concerned, but that it has power to make an order under one of the other sections,

the court may make an order under that other section.

(4) The fact that a person has applied for an occupation order under sections 35 to 38, or that an occupation order has been made, does not affect the right of any person to claim a legal or equitable interest in any property in any subsequent proceedings (including subsequent proceedings under this Part).

40 Additional provisions that may be included in certain occupation orders

(1) The court may on, or at any time after, making an occupation order under section 33, 35 or 36—

- (a) impose on either party obligations as to—
  - (i) the repair and maintenance of the dwelling-house; or
  - (ii) the discharge of rent, mortgage payments or other outgoings affecting the dwelling-house;
- (b) order a party occupying the dwelling-house or any part of it (including a party who is entitled to do so by virtue of a beneficial estate or interest or contract or by virtue of any enactment giving him the right to remain in occupation) to make periodical payments to the other party in respect of the accommodation, if the other party would (but for the order) be entitled to occupy the dwelling-house by virtue of a beneficial estate or interest or contract or by virtue of any such enactment;
- (c) grant either party possession or use of furniture or other contents of the dwelling-house;
- (d) order either party to take reasonable care of any furniture or other contents of the dwelling-house;
- (e) order either party to take reasonable steps to keep the dwelling-house and any furniture or other contents secure.

(2) In deciding whether and, if so, how to exercise its powers under this section, the court shall have regard to all the circumstances of the case including—

- (a) the financial needs and financial resources of the parties; and
- (b) the financial obligations which they have, or are likely to have in the foreseeable future, including financial obligations to each other and to any relevant child.

(3) An order under this section ceases to have effect when the occupation order to which it relates ceases to have effect.

41

(*repealed*)

NON-MOLESTATION ORDERS

42 Non-molestation orders

(1) In this Part a "non-molestation order" means an order containing either or both of the following provisions—

(a) provision prohibiting a person ("the respondent") from molesting another person who is associated with the respondent;

(b) provision prohibiting the respondent from molesting a relevant child.

(2) The court may make a non-molestation order—

(a) if an application for the order has been made (whether in other family proceedings or without any other family proceedings being instituted) by a person who is associated with the respondent; or

(b) if in any family proceedings to which the respondent is a party the court considers that the order should be made for the benefit of any other party to the proceedings or any relevant child even though no such application has been made.

(3) In subsection (2) "family proceedings" includes proceedings in which the court has made an emergency protection order under section 44 of the Children Act 1989 which includes an exclusion requirement (as defined in section 44A(3) of that Act).

(4) Where an agreement to marry is terminated, no application under subsection (2)(a) may be made by virtue of section 62(3)(e) by reference to that agreement after the end of the period of three years beginning with the day on which it is terminated.

[(4ZA) If a civil partnership agreement (as defined by section 73 of the Civil Partnership Act 2004) is terminated, no application under this section may be made by virtue of section 62(3)(eza) by reference to that agreement after the end of the period of three years beginning with the day on which it is terminated.]

(4A) A court considering whether to make an occupation order shall also consider whether to exercise the power conferred by subsection (2)(b).

(4B) In this Part "the applicant", in relation to a non-molestation order, includes (where the context permits) the person for whose benefit such an order would be or is made in exercise of the power conferred by subsection (2)(b).

(5) In deciding whether to exercise its powers under this section and, if so, in what manner, the court shall have regard to all the circumstances including the need to secure the health, safety and well-being—

(a) of the applicant; and

(b) of any relevant child.

(6) A non-molestation order may be expressed so as to refer to molestation in general, to particular acts of molestation, or to both.

(7) A non-molestation order may be made for a specified period or until further order.

(8) A non-molestation order which is made in other family proceedings ceases to have effect if those proceedings are withdrawn or dismissed.

NOTES

Amendment

Prospectively amended by Civil Partnership 2004.

42A Offence of breaching non-molestation order

(1) A person who without reasonable excuse does anything that he is prohibited from doing by a non-molestation order is guilty of an offence.

(2) In the case of a non-molestation order made by virtue of section 45(1), a person can be guilty of an offence under this section only in respect of conduct engaged in at a time when he was aware of the existence of the order.

(3) Where a person is convicted of an offence under this section in respect of any conduct, that conduct is not punishable as a contempt of court.

(4) A person cannot be convicted of an offence under this section in respect of any conduct which has been punished as a contempt of court.

(5) A person guilty of an offence under this section is liable—

- (a) on conviction on indictment, to imprisonment for a term not exceeding five years, or a fine, or both;
- (b) on summary conviction, to imprisonment for a term not exceeding 12 months, or a fine not exceeding the statutory maximum, or both.

(6) A reference in any enactment to proceedings under this Part, or to an order under this Part, does not include a reference to proceedings for an offence under this section or to an order made in such proceedings.

"Enactment" includes an enactment contained in subordinate legislation within the meaning of the Interpretation Act 1978.

FURTHER PROVISIONS RELATING TO OCCUPATION AND NON-MOLESTATION ORDERS

43 Leave of court required for applications by children under sixteen

(1) A child under the age of sixteen may not apply for an occupation order or a non-molestation order except with the leave of the court.

(2) The court may grant leave for the purposes of subsection (1) only if it is satisfied that the child has sufficient understanding to make the proposed application for the occupation order or non-molestation order.

44 Evidence of agreement to marry or form a civil partnership

(1) Subject to subsection (2) the court shall not make an order under section 33 or 42 by virtue of section 62(3)(e) unless there is produced to it evidence in writing of the existence of the agreement to marry.

(2) Subsection (1) does not apply if the court is satisfied that the agreement to marry was evidenced by—

- (a) the gift of an engagement ring by one party to the agreement to the other in contemplation of their marriage, or
- (b) a ceremony entered into by the parties in the presence of one or more other persons assembled for the purpose of witnessing the ceremony.

(3) Subject to subsection (4), the court shall not make an order under section 33 or 42 by virtue of section 62(3)(eza) unless there is produced to it evidence in writing of the existence of the civil partnership agreement (as defined by section 73 of the Civil Partnership Act 2004).

(4) Subsection (3) does not apply if the court is satisfied that the civil partnership agreement was evidenced by—

- (a) a gift by one party to the agreement to the other as a token of the agreement, or
- (b) a ceremony entered into by the parties in the presence of one or more other persons assembled for the purpose of witnessing the ceremony.

45 Ex parte orders

(1) The court may, in any case where it considers that it is just and convenient to do so, make an occupation order or a non-molestation order even though the respondent has not been given such notice of the proceedings as would otherwise be required by rules of court.

(2) In determining whether to exercise its powers under subsection (1), the court shall have regard to all the circumstances including—

(a) any risk of significant harm to the applicant or a relevant child, attributable to conduct of the respondent, if the order is not made immediately;

(b) whether it is likely that the applicant will be deterred or prevented from pursuing the application if an order is not made immediately; and

(c) whether there is reason to believe that the respondent is aware of the proceedings but is deliberately evading service and that the applicant or a relevant child will be seriously prejudiced by the delay involved in effecting substituted service.

(3) If the court makes an order by virtue of subsection (1) it must afford the respondent an opportunity to make representations relating to the order as soon as just and convenient at a full hearing.

(4) If, at a full hearing, the court makes an occupation order ("the full order"), then—

(a) for the purposes of calculating the maximum period for which the full order may be made to have effect, the relevant section is to apply as if the period for which the full order will have effect began on the date on which the initial order first had effect; and

(b) the provisions of section 36(10) or 38(6) as to the extension of orders are to apply as if the full order and the initial order were a single order.

(5) In this section—

"full hearing" means a hearing of which notice has been given to all the parties in accordance with rules of court;

"initial order" means an occupation order made by virtue of subsection (1); and

"relevant section" means section 33(10), 35(10), 36(10), 37(5) or 38(6).

46 Undertakings

(1) In any case where the court has power to make an occupation order or non-molestation order, the court may accept an undertaking from any party to the proceedings.

(2) No power of arrest may be attached to any undertaking given under subsection (1).

(3) The court shall not accept an undertaking under subsection (1) instead of making an occupation order in any case where apart from this section a power of arrest would be attached to the order.

(3A) The court shall not accept an undertaking under subsection (1) instead of making a non-molestation order in any case where it appears to the court that—

(a) the respondent has used or threatened violence against the applicant or a relevant child; and

(b) for the protection of the applicant or child it is necessary to make a non-molestation order so that any breach may be punishable under section 42A.

(4) An undertaking given to a court under subsection (1) is enforceable as if the court had made an occupation order or a non-molestation order in terms corresponding to those of the undertaking.

(5) This section has effect without prejudice to the powers of the High Court and the family court apart from this section.

47 Arrest for breach of order

(1) *(repealed)*

(2) If—

(a) the court makes an occupation order; and

(b) it appears to the court that the respondent has used or threatened violence against the applicant or a relevant child,

it shall attach a power of arrest to one or more provisions of the order unless the court is satisfied that in all the circumstances of the case the applicant or child will be adequately protected without such a power of arrest.

(3) Subsection (2) does not apply in any case where the occupation order is made by virtue of section 45(1), but in such a case the court may attach a power of arrest to one or more provisions of the order if it appears to it—

- (a) that the respondent has used or threatened violence against the applicant or a relevant child; and
- (b) that there is a risk of significant harm to the applicant or child, attributable to conduct of the respondent, if the power of arrest is not attached to those provisions immediately.

(4) If, by virtue of subsection (3), the court attaches a power of arrest to any provisions of an occupation order, it may provide that the power of arrest is to have effect for a shorter period than the other provisions of the order.

(5) Any period specified for the purposes of subsection (4) may be extended by the court (on one or more occasions) on an application to vary or discharge the occupation order.

(6) If, by virtue of subsection (2) or (3), a power of arrest is attached to certain provisions of an order, a constable may arrest without warrant a person whom he has reasonable cause for suspecting to be in breach of any such provision.

(7) If a power of arrest is attached under subsection (2) or (3) to certain provisions of the order and the respondent is arrested under subsection (6)—

- (a) he must be brought before the relevant judicial authority within the period of 24 hours beginning at the time of his arrest; and
- (b) if the matter is not then disposed of forthwith, the relevant judicial authority before whom he is brought may remand him.

In reckoning for the purposes of this subsection any period of 24 hours, no account is to be taken of Christmas Day, Good Friday or any Sunday.

(8) If the court—

- (a) has made a non-molestation order, or
- (b) has made an occupation order but has not attached a power of arrest under subsection (2) or (3) to any provision of the order, or has attached that power only to certain provisions of the order,

then, if at any time the applicant considers that the respondent has failed to comply with the order, he may apply to the relevant judicial authority for the issue of a warrant for the arrest of the respondent.

(9) The relevant judicial authority shall not issue a warrant on an application under subsection (8) unless—

- (a) the application is substantiated on oath; and
- (b) the relevant judicial authority has reasonable grounds for believing that the respondent has failed to comply with the order.

(10) If a person is brought before a court by virtue of a warrant issued under subsection (9) and the court does not dispose of the matter forthwith, the court may remand him.

(11) Schedule 5 (which makes provision corresponding to that applying in magistrates' courts in civil cases under sections 128 and 129 of the Magistrates' Courts Act 1980) has effect in relation to the powers of the High Court and the family court to remand a person by virtue of this section.

(12) If a person remanded under this section is granted bail, he may be required by the relevant judicial authority to comply, before release on bail or later, with such requirements as appear to that authority to be necessary to secure that he does not interfere with witnesses or otherwise obstruct the course of justice.

48 Remand for medical examination and report

(1) If the relevant judicial authority has reason to consider that a medical report will be required, any power to remand a person under section 47(7)(b) or (10) may be exercised for the purpose of enabling a medical examination and report to be made.

(2) If such a power is so exercised, the adjournment must not be for more than 4 weeks at a time unless the relevant judicial authority remands the accused in custody.

(3) If the relevant judicial authority so remands the accused, the adjournment must not be for more than 3 weeks at a time.

(4) If there is reason to suspect that a person who has been arrested—

(a) under section 47(6), or

(b) under a warrant issued on an application made under section 47(8),

is suffering from mental disorder within the meaning of the Mental Health Act 1983, the relevant judicial authority has the same power to make an order under section 35 of that Act (remand for report on accused's mental condition) as the Crown Court has under that section in the case of an accused person within the meaning of that section.

49 Variation and discharge of orders

(1) An occupation order or non-molestation order may be varied or discharged by the court on an application by—

(a) the respondent, or

(b) the person on whose application the order was made.

(2) In the case of a non-molestation order made by virtue of section 42(2)(b), the order may be varied or discharged by the court even though no such application has been made.

(3) If B's home rights are, under section 31, a charge on the estate or interest of the other spouse or of trustees for A, an order under section 33 against A may also be varied or discharged by the court on an application by any person deriving title under the other spouse or under the trustees and affected by the charge.

(4) If, by virtue of section 47(3), a power of arrest has been attached to certain provisions of an occupation order, the court may vary or discharge the order under subsection (1) in so far as it confers a power of arrest (whether or not any application has been made to vary or discharge any other provision of the order).

. . .

TRANSFER OF TENANCIES

53 Transfer of certain tenancies

Schedule 7 makes provision in relation to the transfer of certain tenancies on divorce etc or on separation of cohabitants.

DWELLING-HOUSE SUBJECT TO MORTGAGE

54 Dwelling-house subject to mortgage

(1) In determining for the purposes of this Part whether a person is entitled to occupy a dwelling-house by virtue of an estate or interest, any right to possession of the dwelling-house conferred on a mortgagee of the dwelling-house under or by virtue of his mortgage is to be disregarded.

(2) Subsection (1) applies whether or not the mortgagee is in possession.

(3) Where a person ("A") is entitled to occupy a dwelling-house by virtue of an estate or interest, a connected person does not by virtue of—

(a) any home rights conferred by section 30, or

(b) any rights conferred by an order under section 35 or 36,

have any larger right against the mortgagee to occupy the dwelling-house than A has by virtue of his estate or interest and of any contract with the mortgagee.

(4) Subsection (3) does not apply, in the case of home rights, if under section 31 those rights are a charge, affecting the mortgagee, on the estate or interest mortgaged.

(5) In this section "connected person", in relation to any person, means that person's spouse, former spouse, civil partner, former civil partner, cohabitant or former cohabitant.

55 Actions by mortgagees: joining connected persons as parties

(1) This section applies if a mortgagee of land which consists of or includes a dwelling-house brings an action in any court for the enforcement of his security.

(2) A connected person who is not already a party to the action is entitled to be made a party in the circumstances mentioned in subsection (3).

(3) The circumstances are that—

- (a) the connected person is enabled by section 30(3) or (6) (or by section 30(3) or (6) as applied by section 35(13) or 36(13)), to meet the mortgagor's liabilities under the mortgage;
- (b) he has applied to the court before the action is finally disposed of in that court; and
- (c) the court sees no special reason against his being made a party to the action and is satisfied—
  - (i) that he may be expected to make such payments or do such other things in or towards satisfaction of the mortgagor's liabilities or obligations as might affect the outcome of the proceedings; or
  - (ii) that the expectation of it should be considered under section 36 of the Administration of Justice Act 1970.

(4) In this section "connected person" has the same meaning as in section 54.

56 Actions by mortgagees: service of notice on certain persons

(1) This section applies if a mortgagee of land which consists, or substantially consists, of a dwelling-house brings an action for the enforcement of his security, and at the relevant time there is—

- (a) in the case of unregistered land, a land charge of Class F registered against the person who is the estate owner at the relevant time or any person who, where the estate owner is a trustee, preceded him as trustee during the subsistence of the mortgage; or
- (b) in the case of registered land, a subsisting registration of—
  - (i) a notice under section 31(10);
  - (ii) a notice under section 2(8) of the Matrimonial Homes Act 1983; or
  - (iii) a notice or caution under section 2(7) of the Matrimonial Homes Act 1967.

(2) If the person on whose behalf—

- (a) the land charge is registered, or
- (b) the notice or caution is entered,

is not a party to the action, the mortgagee must serve notice of the action on him.

(3) If—

- (a) an official search has been made on behalf of the mortgagee which would disclose any land charge of Class F, notice or caution within subsection (1)(a) or (b),
- (b) a certificate of the result of the search has been issued, and
- (c) the action is commenced within the priority period,

the relevant time is the date of the certificate.

(4) In any other case the relevant time is the time when the action is commenced.

(5) The priority period is, for both registered and unregistered land, the period for which, in accordance with section 11(5) and (6) of the Land Charges Act 1972, a certificate on an official search operates in favour of a purchaser.

JURISDICTION AND PROCEDURE ETC

57 Jurisdiction of courts

(1) For the purposes of this Act "the court" means the High Court or the family court.

(2)–(12) (*repealed*)

58 Contempt proceedings

The powers of the court in relation to contempt of court arising out of a person's failure to comply with an order under this Part may be exercised by the relevant judicial authority.

. . .

GENERAL

62 Meaning of "cohabitants", "relevant child" and "associated persons"

(1) For the purposes of this Part—

- (a) "cohabitants" are two persons who are neither married to each other nor civil partners of each other but are living together as if they were a married couple or civil partners; and
- (b) "cohabit" and former cohabitants" is to be read accordingly, but the latter expression does not include cohabitants who have subsequently married each other or become civil partners of each other.

(2) In this Part, "relevant child", in relation to any proceedings under this Part, means—

- (a) any child who is living with or might reasonably be expected to live with either party to the proceedings;
- (b) any child in relation to whom an order under the Adoption Act 1976, the Adoption and Children Act 2002, or the Children Act 1989 is in question in the proceedings; and
- (c) any other child whose interests the court considers relevant.

(3) For the purposes of this Part, a person is associated with another person if—

- (a) they are or have been married to each other;
- (aa) they are or have been civil partners of each other;
- (b) they are cohabitants or former cohabitants;
- (c) they live or have lived in the same household, otherwise than merely by reason of one of them being the other's employee, tenant, lodger or boarder;
- (d) they are relatives;
- (e) they have agreed to marry one another (whether or not that agreement has been terminated);
- (eza) they have entered into a civil partnership agreement (as defined by section 73 of the Civil Partnership Act 2004) (whether or not that agreement has been terminated);
- (ea) they have or have had an intimate personal relationship with each other which is or was of significant duration;
- (f) in relation to any child, they are both persons falling within subsection (4); or
- (g) they are parties to the same family proceedings (other than proceedings under this Part).

(4) A person falls within this subsection in relation to a child if—

- (a) he is a parent of the child; or
- (b) he has or has had parental responsibility for the child.

(5) If a child has been adopted or falls within subsection (7), two persons are also associated with each other for the purpose of this Part if—

(a) one is a natural parent of the child or a parent of such a natural parent, and

(b) the other is the child or any person—

(i) who had become a parent of the child by virtue of an adoption order or has applied for an adoption order, or

(ii) with whom the child has at any time been placed for adoption.

(6) A body corporate and another person are not, by virtue of subsection (3)(f) or (g), to be regarded for the purposes of this Part as associated with each other.

(7) A child falls within this subsection if—

(a) an adoption agency, within the meaning of section 2 of the Adoption and Children Act 2002, has power to place him for adoption under section 19 of that Act (placing children with parental consent) or he has become the subject of an order under section 21 of that Act (placement orders), or

(b) he is freed for adoption by virtue of an order made—

(i) in England and Wales, under section 18 of the Adoption Act 1976,

. . .

63 Interpretation of Part IV

(1) In this Part—

"adoption order" means an adoption order within the meaning of section 72(1) of the Adoption Act 1976 or section 46(1) of the Adoption and Children Act 2002;

"associated", in relation to a person, is to be read with section 62(3) to (6);

"child" means a person under the age of eighteen years;

"cohabit", cohabitant" and "former cohabitant" have the meaning given by section 62(1);

"the court" is to be read with section 57;

"development" means physical, intellectual, emotional, social or behavioural development;

"dwelling-house" includes (subject to subsection (4))—

(a) any building or part of a building which is occupied as a dwelling,

(b) any caravan, house-boat or structure which is occupied as a dwelling,

and any yard, garden, garage or outhouse belonging to it and occupied with it;

"family proceedings" means any proceedings—

(a) under the inherent jurisdiction of the High Court in relation to children; or

(b) under the enactments mentioned in subsection (2),

"harm"—

(a) in relation to a person who has reached the age of eighteen years, means ill-treatment or the impairment of health; and

(b) in relation to a child, means ill-treatment or the impairment of health or development;

"health" includes physical or mental health;

"home rights" has the meaning given by section 30;

"ill-treatment" includes forms of ill-treatment which are not physical and, in relation to a child, includes sexual abuse;

"mortgage", "mortgagor" and "mortgagee" have the same meaning as in the Law of Property Act 1925;

"mortgage payments" includes any payments which, under the terms of the mortgage, the mortgagor is required to make to any person;

"non-molestation order" has the meaning given by section 42(1);
"occupation order" has the meaning given by section 39;
"parental responsibility" has the same meaning as in the Children Act 1989;
"relative", in relation to a person, means—

(a) the father, mother, stepfather, stepmother, son, daughter, stepson, stepdaughter, grandmother, grandfather, grandson or granddaughter of that person or of that person's spouse, former spouse, civil partner or former civil partner, or

(b) the brother, sister, uncle, aunt, niece nephew or first cousin (whether of the full blood or of the half blood or by marriage or civil partnership) of that person or of that person's spouse or former spouse,

and includes, in relation to a person who is cohabiting or has cohabited with another person, any person who would fall within paragraph (a) or (b) if the parties were married to each other or were civil partners of each other;
"relevant child", in relation to any proceedings under this Part, has the meaning given by section 62(2);
"the relevant judicial authority", in relation to any order under this Part, means—

(a) where the order was made by the High Court, a judge of that court;

(aa) where the order was made by the family court, a judge of that court.

(b), (c) (*repealed*)

(2) The enactments referred to in the definition of "family proceedings" are—

(a) . . .
(b) this Part;
(ba) Part 4A;
(c) the Matrimonial Causes Act 1973;
(d) the Adoption Act 1976;
(e) the Domestic Proceedings and Magistrates' Court Act 1978;
(f) Part III of the Matrimonial and Family Proceedings Act 1984;
(g) Parts I, II and IV of the Children Act 1989;
(h) section 30 of the Human Fertilisation and Embryology Act 1990;
(i) the Adoption and Children Act 2002;
(j) Schedules 5 to 7 to the CPA 2004.

(3) Where the question of whether harm suffered by a child is significant turns on the child's health or development, his health or development shall be compared with that which could reasonably be expected of a similar child.

(4) For the purposes of sections 31, 32, 53 and 54 and such other provisions of this Part (if any) as may be prescribed, this Part is to have effect as if paragraph (b) of the definition of "dwelling-house" were omitted.

(5) It is hereby declared that this Part applies as between the parties to a marriage even though either of them is, or has at any time during the marriage been, married to more than one person.

PART 4A
FORCED MARRIAGE

Forced marriage protection orders

63A Forced marriage protection orders

(1) The court may make an order for the purposes of protecting—

(a) a person from being forced into a marriage or from any attempt to be forced into a marriage; or

(b) a person who has been forced into a marriage.

(2) In deciding whether to exercise its powers under this section and, if so, in what manner, the court must have regard to all the circumstances including the need to secure the health, safety and well-being of the person to be protected.

(3) In ascertaining that person's well-being, the court must, in particular, have such regard to the person's wishes and feelings (so far as they are reasonably ascertainable) as the court considers appropriate in the light of the person's age and understanding.

(4) For the purposes of this Part a person ("A") is forced into a marriage if another person ("B") forces A to enter into a marriage (whether with B or another person) without A's free and full consent.

(5) For the purposes of subsection (4) it does not matter whether the conduct of B which forces A to enter into a marriage is directed against A, B or another person.

(6) In this Part—

"force" includes coerce by threats or other psychological means (and related expressions are to be read accordingly); and

"forced marriage protection order" means an order under this section.

63B Contents of orders

(1) A forced marriage protection order may contain—

(a) such prohibitions, restrictions or requirements; and

(b) such other terms;

as the court considers appropriate for the purposes of the order.

(2) The terms of such orders may, in particular, relate to—

(a) conduct outside England and Wales as well as (or instead of) conduct within England and Wales;

(b) respondents who are, or may become, involved in other respects as well as (or instead of) respondents who force or attempt to force, or may force or attempt to force, a person to enter into a marriage;

(c) other persons who are, or may become, involved in other respects as well as respondents of any kind.

(3) For the purposes of subsection (2) examples of involvement in other respects are—

(a) aiding, abetting, counselling, procuring, encouraging or assisting another person to force, or to attempt to force, a person to enter into a marriage; or

(b) conspiring to force, or to attempt to force, a person to enter into a marriage.

63C Applications and other occasions for making orders

(1) The court may make a forced marriage protection order—

(a) on an application being made to it; or

(b) without an application being made to it but in the circumstances mentioned in subsection (6).

(2) An application may be made by—

(a) the person who is to be protected by the order; or

(b) a relevant third party.

(3) An application may be made by any other person with the leave of the court.

(4) In deciding whether to grant leave, the court must have regard to all the circumstances including—

(a) the applicant's connection with the person to be protected;

(b) the applicant's knowledge of the circumstances of the person to be protected; and

(c) the wishes and feelings of the person to be protected so far as they are reasonably ascertainable and so far as the court considers it appropriate, in the light of the person's age and understanding, to have regard to them.

(5) An application under this section may be made in other family proceedings or without any other family proceedings being instituted.

(6) The circumstances in which the court may make an order without an application being made are where—

(a) any other family proceedings are before the court ("the current proceedings");

(b) the court considers that a forced marriage protection order should be made to protect a person (whether or not a party to the current proceedings); and

(c) a person who would be a respondent to any such proceedings for a forced marriage protection order is a party to the current proceedings.

(7) In this section—

"family proceedings" has the same meaning as in Part 4 (see section 63(1) and (2)) but also includes—

(a) proceedings under the inherent jurisdiction of the High Court in relation to adults;

(b) proceedings in which the court has made an emergency protection order under section 44 of the Children Act 1989 which includes an exclusion requirement (as defined in section 44A(3) of that Act); and

(c) proceedings in which the court has made an order under section 50 of the Act of 1989 (recovery of abducted children etc.); and

"relevant third party" means a person specified, or falling within a description of persons specified, by order of the Lord Chancellor.

(8) An order of the Lord Chancellor under subsection (7) may, in particular, specify the Secretary of State.

63CA Offence of breaching order

(1) A person who without reasonable excuse does anything that the person is prohibited from doing by a forced marriage protection order is guilty of an offence.

(2) In the case of a forced marriage protection order made by virtue of section 63D(1), a person can be guilty of an offence under this section only in respect of conduct engaged in at a time when the person was aware of the existence of the order.

(3) Where a person is convicted of an offence under this section in respect of any conduct, that conduct is not punishable as a contempt of court.

(4) A person cannot be convicted of an offence under this section in respect of any conduct which has been punished as a contempt of court.

(5) A person guilty of an offence under this section is liable—

(a) on conviction on indictment, to imprisonment for a term not exceeding five years, or a fine, or both;

(b) on summary conviction, to imprisonment for a term not exceeding 12 months, or a fine, or both.

(6) A reference in any enactment to proceedings under this Part, or to an order under this Part, does not include a reference to proceedings for an offence under this section or to an order made in proceedings for such an offence.

(7) "Enactment" includes an enactment contained in subordinate legislation within the meaning of the Interpretation Act 1978.

FURTHER PROVISION ABOUT ORDERS

63D Ex parte orders: Part 4A

(1) The court may, in any case where it considers that it is just and convenient to do so, make a forced marriage protection order even though the respondent has not been given such notice of the proceedings as would otherwise be required by rules of court.

(2) In deciding whether to exercise its powers under subsection (1), the court must have regard to all the circumstances including—

- (a) any risk of significant harm to the person to be protected or another person if the order is not made immediately;
- (b) whether it is likely that an applicant will be deterred or prevented from pursuing an application if an order is not made immediately; and
- (c) whether there is reason to believe that—
  - (i) the respondent is aware of the proceedings but is deliberately evading service; and
  - (ii) the delay involved in effecting substituted service will cause serious prejudice to the person to be protected or (if a different person) an applicant.

(3) The court must give the respondent an opportunity to make representations about any order made by virtue of subsection (1).

(4) The opportunity must be—

- (a) as soon as just and convenient; and
- (b) at a hearing of which notice has been given to all the parties in accordance with rules of court.

63E Undertakings instead of orders

(1) In any case where the court has power to make a forced marriage protection order, the court may accept an undertaking from the respondent instead of making the order.

(2) But a court may not accept an undertaking under subsection (1) if it appears to the court—

- (a) that the respondent has used or threatened violence against the person to be protected, and
- (b) that, for the person's protection, it is necessary to make a forced marriage protection order so that any breach of it by the respondent may be punishable under section 63CA.

(3) (*repealed*)

(4) An undertaking given to the court under subsection (1) is enforceable as if the court had made the order in terms corresponding to those of the undertaking.

(5) This section is without prejudice to the powers of the court apart from this section.

63F Duration of orders

A forced marriage protection order may be made for a specified period or until varied or discharged.

63G Variation of orders and their discharge

(1) The court may vary or discharge a forced marriage protection order on an application by—

- (a) any party to the proceedings for the order;
- (b) the person being protected by the order (if not a party to the proceedings for the order); or
- (c) any person affected by the order.

(2) In addition, the court may vary or discharge a forced marriage protection order made by virtue of section 63C(1)(b) even though no application under subsection (1) above has been made to the court.
(3) Section 63D applies to a variation of a forced marriage protection order as it applies to the making of such an order.
(4) Section 63E applies to proceedings for a variation of a forced marriage protection order as it applies to proceedings for the making of such an order.
(5) Accordingly, references in sections 63D and 63E to making a forced marriage protection order are to be read for the purposes of subsections (3) and (4) above as references to varying such an order.
(6), (7) (*repealed*)

ARREST FOR BREACH OF ORDERS

63H, 63I
(*repealed*)

63J Arrest under warrant
(1) (*repealed*)
(2) An interested party may apply to the relevant judge for the issue of a warrant for the arrest of a person if the interested party considers that the person has failed to comply with a forced marriage protection order or is otherwise in contempt of court in relation to the order.
(3) The relevant judge must not issue a warrant on an application under subsection (2) unless—

- (a) the application is substantiated on oath; and
- (b) the relevant judge has reasonable grounds for believing that the person to be arrested has failed to comply with the order or is otherwise in contempt of court in relation to the order.

(4) In this section "interested party", in relation to a forced marriage protection order, means—

- (a) the person being protected by the order;
- (b) (if a different person) the person who applied for the order; or
- (c) any other person;

but no application may be made under subsection (2) by a person falling within paragraph (c) without the leave of the relevant judge.

63K Remand: general
(1) The court before which an arrested person is brought by virtue of a warrant issued under section 63J may, if the matter is not then disposed of immediately, remand the person concerned.
(2) Schedule 5 has effect in relation to the powers of the court to remand a person by virtue of this section but as if the following modifications were made to the Schedule.
(3) The modifications are that—

- (a) in paragraph 2(1) of Schedule 5, the reference to section 47 is to be read as a reference to this section; and
- (b) in paragraph 2(5)(b) of the Schedule, the reference to section 48(1) is to be read as a reference to section 63L(1).

(4) Subsection (5) applies if a person remanded under this section is granted bail under Schedule 5 as modified above.
(5) The person may be required by the relevant judge to comply, before release on bail or later, with such requirements as appear to the relevant judge to be necessary to secure that the person does not interfere with witnesses or otherwise obstruct the course of justice.

63L Remand: medical examination and report

(1) Any power to remand a person under section 63K(1) may be exercised for the purpose of enabling a medical examination and report to be made if the relevant judge has reason to consider that a medical report will be required.

(2) If such a power is so exercised, the adjournment must not be for more than 4 weeks at a time unless the relevant judge remands the accused in custody.

(3) If the relevant judge remands the accused in custody, the adjournment must not be for more than 3 weeks at a time.

(4) Subsection (5) applies if there is reason to suspect that a person who has been arrested—

(a) . . .

(b) under a warrant issued on an application made under section 63J(2);

is suffering from mental illness or severe mental impairment.

(5) The relevant judge has the same power to make an order under section 35 of the Mental Health Act 1983 (remand for report on accused's mental condition) as the Crown Court has under section 35 of that Act in the case of an accused person within the meaning of that section.

JURISDICTION AND PROCEDURE

63M Jurisdiction of courts: Part 4A

(1) For the purposes of this Part "the court" means the High Court or the family court.

(2)–(4) (*repealed*)

63N

(*repealed*)

63O Contempt proceedings: Part 4A

The powers of the court in relation to contempt of court arising out of a person's failure to comply with a forced marriage protection order or otherwise in connection with such an order may be exercised by the relevant judge.

63P

(*repealed*)

SUPPLEMENTARY

63Q Guidance

(1) The Secretary of State may from time to time prepare and publish guidance to such descriptions of persons as the Secretary of State considers appropriate about –

(a) the effect of this Part or any provision of this Part; or

(b) other matters relating to forced marriages.

(2) A person exercising public functions to whom guidance is given under this section must have regard to it in the exercise of those functions.

(3) Nothing in this section permits the Secretary of State to give guidance to any court or tribunal.

63R Other protection or assistance against forced marriage

(1) This Part does not affect any other protection or assistance available to a person who—

(a) is being, or may be, forced into a marriage or subjected to an attempt to be forced into a marriage; or

(b) has been forced into a marriage.

(2) In particular, it does not affect—

(a) the inherent jurisdiction of the High Court;
(b) any criminal liability;
(c) any civil remedies under the Protection from Harassment Act 1997;
(d) any right to an occupation order or a non-molestation order under Part 4 of this Act;
(e) any protection or assistance under the Children Act 1989;
(f) any claim in tort; or
(g) the law of marriage.

63S Interpretation of Part 4A

In this Part—

"the court" is to be read with section 63M;

"force" (and related expressions), in relation to a marriage, are to be read in accordance with section 63A(4) to (6);

"forced marriage protection order" has the meaning given by section 63A(6);

"marriage" means any religious or civil ceremony of marriage (whether or not legally binding); and

"the relevant judge", in relation to any order under this Part, means—

(a) where the order was made by the High Court, a judge of that court; and
(b) where the order was made by the family court, a judge of that court.

. . .

SCHEDULE 4

PROVISIONS SUPPLEMENTARY TO SECTIONS 30 AND 31

1 Interpretation

In this Schedule "legal representative" means a person who, for the purposes of the Legal Services Act 2007, is an authorised person in relation to an activity which constitutes a reserved instrument activity (within the meaning of that Act).

2 Restriction on registration where spouse entitled to more than one charge

Where one spouse or civil partner is entitled by virtue of section 31 to a registrable charge in respect of each of two or more dwelling-houses, only one of the charges to which that spouse or civil partner is so entitled shall be registered under section 31(10) or under section 2 of the Land Charges Act 1972 at any one time, and if any of those charges is registered under either of those provisions the Chief Land Registrar, on being satisfied that any other of them is so registered, shall cancel the registration of the charge first registered.

3 Contract for sale of house affected by registered charge to include term requiring cancellation of registration before completion

(1) Where one spouse or civil partner is entitled by virtue of section 31 to a charge on an estate in a dwelling-house and the charge is registered under section 31(10) or section 2 of the Land Charges Act 1972, it shall be a term of any contract for the sale of that estate whereby the vendor agrees to give vacant possession of the dwelling-house on completion of the contract that the vendor will before such completion procure the cancellation of the registration of the charge at his expense.

(2) Sub-paragraph (1) shall not apply to any such contract made by a vendor who is entitled to sell the estate in the dwelling-house freed from any such charge.

(3) If, on the completion of such a contract as is referred to in sub-paragraph (1), there is delivered to the purchaser or his legal representative an application by the

spouse or civil partner entitled to the charge for the cancellation of the registration of that charge, the term of the contract for which sub-paragraph (1) provides shall be deemed to have been performed.

(4) This paragraph applies only if and so far as a contrary intention is not expressed in the contract.

(5) This paragraph shall apply to a contract for exchange as it applies to a contract for sale.

(6) This paragraph shall, with the necessary modifications, apply to a contract for the grant of a lease or underlease of a dwelling-house as it applies to a contract for the sale of an estate in a dwelling-house.

4 Cancellation of registration after termination of marriage or civil partnership etc

(1) Where a spouse's or civil partner's home rights are a charge on an estate in the dwelling-house and the charge is registered under section 31(10) or under section 2 of the Land Charges Act 1972, the Chief Land Registrar shall, subject to sub-paragraph (2), cancel the registration of the charge if he is satisfied—

- (a) in the case of a marriage—
  - (i) by the production of a certificate or other sufficient evidence, that either spouse is dead,
  - (ii) by the production of an official copy of a decree or order of a court, that the marriage has been terminated otherwise than by death, or
  - (iii) by the production of an order of the court, that the spouse's home rights constituting the charge have been terminated by the order, and
- (b) in the case of a civil partnership—
  - (i) by the production of a certificate or other sufficient evidence, that either civil partner is dead,
  - (ii) by the production of an official copy of an order or decree of a court, that the civil partnership has been terminated otherwise than by death, or
  - (iii) by the production of an order of the court, that the civil partner's home rights constituting the charge have been terminated by the order.

(2) Where—

- (a) the marriage or civil partnership in question has been terminated by the death of the spouse or civil partner entitled to an estate in the dwelling-house or otherwise than by death, and
- (b) an order affecting the charge of the spouse or civil partner not so entitled had been made under section 35(5),

then if, after the making of the order, registration of the charge was renewed or the charge registered in pursuance of sub-paragraph (3), the Chief Land Registrar shall not cancel the registration of the charge in accordance with sub-paragraph (1) unless he is also satisfied that the order has ceased to have effect.

(3) Where such an order has been made, then, for the purposes of sub-paragraph (2), the spouse or civil partner entitled to the charge affected by the order may—

- (a) if before the date of the order the charge was registered under section 31(10) or under section 2 of the Land Charges Act 1972, renew the registration of the charge, and
- (b) if before the said date the charge was not so registered, register the charge under section 31(10) or under section 2 of the Land Charges Act 1972.

(4) Renewal of the registration of a charge in pursuance of sub-paragraph (3) shall be effected in such manner as may be prescribed, and an application for such renewal or

for registration of a charge in pursuance of that sub-paragraph shall contain such particulars of any order affecting the charge made under section 33(5) as may be prescribed.

(5) The renewal in pursuance of sub-paragraph (3) of the registration of a charge shall not affect the priority of the charge.

(6) In this paragraph "prescribed" means prescribed by rules made under section 16 of the Land Charges Act 1972 or by land registration rules under the Land Registration Act 2002, as the circumstances of the case require.

5 Release of home rights

(1) A spouse or civil partner entitled to home rights may by a release in writing release those rights or release them as respects part only of the dwelling-house affected by them.

(2) Where a contract is made for the sale of an estate or interest in a dwelling-house, or for the grant of a lease or underlease of a dwelling-house, being (in either case) a dwelling-house affected by a charge registered under section 31(10) or under section 2 of the Land Charges Act 1972, then, without prejudice to sub-paragraph (1), the home rights constituting the charge shall be deemed to have been released on the happening of whichever of the following events first occurs—

- (a) the delivery to the purchaser or lessee, as the case may be, or his legal representative on completion of the contract of an application by the spouse or civil partner entitled to the charge for the cancellation of the registration of the charge; or
- (b) the lodging of such an application at Her Majesty's Land Registry.

6 Postponement of priority of charge

A spouse or civil partner entitled by virtue of section 31 to a charge on an estate or interest may agree in writing that any other charge on, or interest in, that estate or interest shall rank in priority to the charge to which that spouse or civil partner is so entitled.

SCHEDULE 5

POWERS OF HIGH COURT AND COUNTY COURT TO REMAND

1 Interpretation

In this Schedule "the court" means the High Court or the family court and includes—

- (a) in relation to the High Court, a judge of that court, and
- (b) in relation to the family court, a judge of that court.

2 Remand in custody or on bail

(1) Where a court has power to remand a person under section 47, the court may—

- (a) remand him in custody, that is to say, commit him to custody to be brought before the court at the end of the period of remand or at such earlier time as the court may require, or
- (b) remand him on bail—
  - (i) by taking from him a recognizance (with or without sureties) conditioned as provided in sub-paragraph (3), or
  - (ii) by fixing the amount of the recognizances with a view to their being taken subsequently in accordance with paragraph 4 and in the meantime committing the person to custody in accordance with paragraph (a).

(2) Where a person is brought before the court after remand, the court may further remand him.

(3) Where a person is remanded on bail under sub-paragraph (1), the court may direct that his recognizance be conditioned for his appearance—

(a) before that court at the end of the period of remand, or
(b) at every time and place to which during the course of the proceedings the hearing may from time to time be adjourned.

(4) Where a recognizance is conditioned for a person's appearance in accordance with sub-paragraph (1)(b), the fixing of any time for him next to appear shall be deemed to be a remand; but nothing in this sub-paragraph or sub-paragraph (3) shall deprive the court of power at any subsequent hearing to remand him afresh.

(5) Subject to paragraph 3, the court shall not remand a person under this paragraph for a period exceeding 8 clear days, except that—
(a) if the court remands him on bail, it may remand him for a longer period if he and the other party consent, and
(b) if the court adjourns a case under section 48(1), the court may remand him for the period of the adjournment.

(6) Where the court has power under this paragraph to remand a person in custody it may, if the remand for a period not exceeding 3 clear days, commit him to the custody of a constable.

3 Further remand

(1) If the court is satisfied that any person who has been remanded under paragraph 2 is unable by reason of illness or accident to appear or be brought before the court at the expiration of the period for which he was remanded, the court may, in his absence, remand him for a further time; and paragraph 2(5) shall not apply.

(2) Notwithstanding anything in paragraph 2(1), the power of the court under sub-paragraph (1) to remand a person on bail for a further time may be exercised by enlarging his recognizance and those of any sureties for him to a later time.

(3) Where a person remanded on bail under paragraph 2 is bound to appear before the court at any time and the court has no power to remand him under sub-paragraph (1), the court may in his absence enlarge his recognizance and those of any sureties for him to a later time; and the enlargement of his recognizance shall be deemed to be a further remand.

4 Postponement of taking of recognizance

Where under paragraph 2(1)(b)(ii) the court fixes the amount in which the principal and his sureties, if any, are to be bound, the recognizance may thereafter be taken by such person as may be prescribed by rules of court, and the same consequences shall follow as if it had been entered into before the court.

'prescribed by rules of court'—The relevant rule is FPR 2010, r 10.17. The persons prescribed in the High Court or the County Court are a district judge, a police officer of at least the rank of inspector or in charge of a police station, and (where the person making the application is in his custody) the governor or keeper of a prison.

. . .

SCHEDULE 7

TRANSFER OF CERTAIN TENANCIES ON DIVORCE ETC OR ON SEPARATION OF COHABITANTS

PART I
GENERAL

Interpretation

1

In this Schedule—

"civil partner", except in paragraph 2, includes (where the context requires) former civil partner;

"cohabitant", except in paragraph 3, includes (where the context requires) former cohabitant,

"the court" means the High Court or the family court,

"landlord" includes—

(a) any person from time to time deriving title under the original landlord; and

(b) in relation to any dwelling-house, any person other than the tenant who is, or (but for Part VII of the Rent Act 1977 or Part II of the Rent (Agriculture) Act 1976) would be, entitled to possession of the dwelling-house;

"Part II order" means an order under Part II of this Schedule;

"a relevant tenancy" means—

(a) a protected tenancy or statutory tenancy within the meaning of the Rent Act 1977;

(b) a statutory tenancy within the meaning of the Rent (Agriculture) Act 1976;

(c) a secure tenancy within the meaning of section 79 of the Housing Act 1985;

(d) an assured tenancy or assured agricultural occupancy within the meaning of Part I of the Housing Act 1988; or

(e) an introductory tenancy within the meaning of Chapter I of Part V of the Housing Act 1996;

"spouse", except in paragraph 2, includes (where the context requires) former spouse; and

"tenancy" includes sub-tenancy.

Cases in which court may make order

2

(1) This paragraph applies if one spouse or civil partner is entitled, either in his own right or jointly with the other spouse or civil partner, to occupy a dwelling-house by virtue of a relevant tenancy.

(2) The court may make a Part II order—

(a) on granting a decree of divorce, a decree of nullity of marriage or a decree of judicial separation or at any time thereafter (whether, in the case of a decree of divorce or nullity of marriage, before or after the decree is made absolute), or

[(a) on making a divorce, nullity of marriage or judicial separation order or at any time after making such an order (whether, in the case of a divorce or nullity of marriage order, before or after the order is made final), or]

(b) at any time when it has power to make a property adjustment order under Part 2 of Schedule 5 to the Civil Partnership Act 2004 with respect to the civil partnership.

3

(1) This paragraph applies if one cohabitant is entitled, either in his own right or jointly with the other cohabitant, to occupy a dwelling-house by virtue of a relevant tenancy.

(2) If the cohabitants cease to cohabit, the court may make a Part II order.

4

The court shall not make a Part II order unless the dwelling-house is or was—

(a) in the case of spouses, a matrimonial home;

(aa) in the case of civil partners, a civil partnership home; or
(b) in the case of cohabitants, a home in which they cohabited.

MATTERS TO WHICH THE COURT MUST HAVE REGARD

5

In determining whether to exercise its powers under Part II of this Schedule and, if so, in what manner, the court shall have regard to all the circumstances of the case including—

(a) the circumstances in which the tenancy was granted to either or both of the spouses, civil partners or cohabitants or, as the case requires, the circumstances in which either or both of them became tenant under the tenancy;
(b) the matters mentioned in section 33(6)(a), (b) and (c) and, where the parties are cohabitants and only one of them is entitled to occupy the dwelling-house by virtue of the relevant tenancy, the further matters mentioned in section 36(6)(e), (f), (g) and (h); and
(c) the suitability of the parties as tenants.

NOTES

Amendment

Prospectively amended by Divorce, Dissolution and Separation Act 2020.

PART II
ORDERS THAT MAY BE MADE

REFERENCES TO ENTITLEMENT TO OCCUPY

6

References in this Part of this Schedule to a spouse, a civil partner or a cohabitant being entitled to occupy a dwelling-house by virtue of a relevant tenancy apply whether that entitlement is in his own right or jointly with the other spouse, civil partner or cohabitant.

PROTECTED, SECURE OR ASSURED TENANCY OR ASSURED AGRICULTURAL OCCUPANCY

7

(1) If a spouse, civil partner or cohabitant is entitled to occupy the dwelling-house by virtue of a protected tenancy within the meaning of the Rent Act 1977, a secure tenancy within the meaning of the Housing Act 1985, an assured tenancy or assured agricultural occupancy within the meaning of Part I of the Housing Act 1988 or an introductory tenancy within the meaning of Chapter I of Part V of the Housing Act 1996, the court may by order direct that, as from such date as may be specified in the order, there shall, by virtue of the order and without further assurance, be transferred to, and vested in, the other spouse, civil partner or cohabitant—

(a) the estate or interest which the spouse or cohabitant so entitled had in the dwelling-house immediately before that date by virtue of the lease or agreement creating the tenancy and any assignment of that lease or agreement, with all rights, privileges and appurtenances attaching to that estate or interest but subject to all covenants, obligations, liabilities and incumbrances to which it is subject; and
(b) where the spouse or cohabitant so entitled is an assignee of such lease or agreement, the liability of that spouse or cohabitant under any covenant of indemnity by the assignee express or implied in the assignment of the lease or agreement to that spouse or cohabitant.

(2) If an order is made under this paragraph, any liability or obligation to which the spouse or cohabitant so entitled is subject under any covenant having reference to the

dwelling-house in the lease or agreement, being a liability or obligation falling due to be discharged or performed on or after the date so specified, shall not be enforceable against that spouse or cohabitant.

(3) If the spouse, civil partner or cohabitant so entitled is a successor within the meaning of Part 4 of the Housing Act 1985—

- (a) his former spouse (or, in the case of judicial separation, his spouse),
- (b) his former civil partner (or, if a separation order is in force, his civil partner), or
- (c) his former cohabitant,

is to be deemed also to be a successor within the meaning of that Part.

(3A) If the spouse, civil partner or cohabitant so entitled is a successor within the meaning of section 132 of the Housing Act 1996—

- (a) his former spouse (or, in the case of judicial separation, his spouse),
- (b) his former civil partner (or, if a separation order is in force, his civil partner), or
- (c) his former cohabitant,

is to be deemed also to be a successor within the meaning of that section.

(4) If the spouse, civil partner or cohabitant so entitled is for the purposes of section 17 of the Housing Act 1988 a successor in relation to the tenancy or occupancy—

- (a) his former spouse (or, in the case of judicial separation, his spouse),
- (b) his former civil partner (or, if a separation order is in force, his civil partner), or
- (c) his former cohabitant,

is to be deemed to be a successor in relation to the tenancy or occupancy for the purposes of that section.

(5) If the transfer under sub-paragraph (1) is of an assured agricultural occupancy, then, for the purposes of Chapter III of Part I of the Housing Act 1988—

- (a) the agricultural worker condition is fulfilled with respect to the dwelling-house while the spouse, civil partner or cohabitant to whom the assured agricultural occupancy is transferred continues to be the occupier under that occupancy, and
- (b) that condition shall be treated as so fulfilled by virtue of the same paragraph of Schedule 3 to the Housing Act 1988 as was applicable before the transfer.

(6) . . .

Statutory tenancy within the meaning of the Rent Act 1977

8

(1) This paragraph applies if the spouse, civil partner or cohabitant is entitled to occupy the dwelling-house by virtue of a statutory tenancy within the meaning of the Rent Act 1977.

(2) The court may by order direct that, as from the date specified in the order—

- (a) that spouse or cohabitant is to cease to be entitled to occupy the dwelling-house; and
- (b) the other spouse or cohabitant is to be deemed to be the tenant or, as the case may be, the sole tenant under that statutory tenancy.

(3) The question whether the provisions of paragraphs 1 to 3, or (as the case may be) paragraphs 5 to 7 of Schedule 1 to the Rent Act 1977, as to the succession by the surviving spouse or surviving civil partner of a deceased tenant, or by a member of the deceased tenant's family, to the right to retain possession are capable of having effect in the event of the death of the person deemed by an order under this paragraph to be the

tenant or sole tenant under the statutory tenancy is to be determined according as those provisions have or have not already had effect in relation to the statutory tenancy.

STATUTORY TENANCY WITHIN THE MEANING OF THE RENT (AGRICULTURE) ACT 1976

9

(1) This paragraph applies if the spouse or cohabitant is entitled to occupy the dwelling-house by virtue of a statutory tenancy within the meaning of the Rent (Agriculture) Act 1976.
(2) The court may by order direct that, as from such date as may be specified in the order—

- (a) that spouse or cohabitant is to cease to be entitled to occupy the dwelling-house; and
- (b) the other spouse or cohabitant is to be deemed to be the tenant or, as the case may be, the sole tenant under that statutory tenancy.

(3) A spouse, civil partner or cohabitant who is deemed under this paragraph to be the tenant under a statutory tenancy is (within the meaning of that Act) a statutory tenant in his own right, or a statutory tenant by succession, according as the other spouse, civil partner or cohabitant was a statutory tenant in his own right or a statutory tenant by succession.

PART III
SUPPLEMENTARY PROVISIONS

COMPENSATION

10

(1) If the court makes a Part II order, it may by the order direct the making of a payment by the spouse, civil partner or cohabitant to whom the tenancy is transferred ("the transferee") to the other spouse or cohabitant ("the transferor").
(2) Without prejudice to that, the court may, on making an order by virtue of sub-paragraph (1) for the payment of a sum—

- (a) direct that payment of that sum or any part of it is to be deferred until a specified date or until the occurrence of a specified event, or
- (b) direct that that sum or any part of it is to be paid by instalments.

(3) Where an order has been made by virtue of sub-paragraph (1), the court may, on the application of the transferee or the transferor—

- (a) exercise its powers under sub-paragraph (2), or
- (b) vary any direction previously given under that sub-paragraph,

at any time before the sum whose payment is required by the order is paid in full.
(4) In deciding whether to exercise its powers under this paragraph and, if so, in what manner, the court shall have regard to all the circumstances including—

- (a) the financial loss that would otherwise be suffered by the transferor as a result of the order;
- (b) the financial needs and financial resources of the parties; and
- (c) the financial obligations which the parties have, or are likely to have in the foreseeable future, including financial obligations to each other and to any relevant child.

(5) The court shall not give any direction under sub-paragraph (2) unless it appears to it that immediate payment of the sum required by the order would cause the transferee financial hardship which is greater than any financial hardship that would be caused to the transferor if the direction were given.

LIABILITIES AND OBLIGATIONS IN RESPECT OF THE DWELLING-HOUSE

11

(1) If the court makes a Part II order, it may by the order direct that both spouses, civil partners or cohabitants are to be jointly and severally liable to discharge or perform any or all of the liabilities and obligations in respect of the dwelling-house (whether arising under the tenancy or otherwise) which—

- (a) have at the date of the order fallen due to be discharged or performed by one only of them; or
- (b) but for the direction, would before the date specified as the date on which the order is to take effect fall due to be discharged or performed by one only of them.

(2) If the court gives such a direction, it may further direct that either spouse, civil partner or cohabitant is to be liable to indemnify the other in whole or in part against any payment made or expenses incurred by the other in discharging or performing any such liability or obligation.

DATE WHEN ORDER MADE BETWEEN SPOUSES IS TO TAKE EFFECT

12 Date when order made between spouses or civil partners takes effect

The date specified in a Part II order as the date on which the order is to take effect must not be earlier than—

- *(a) in the case of a marriage in respect of which a decree of divorce or nullity has been granted, the date on which the decree is made absolute;*
- [(a) in the case of a marriage in respect of which a decree of divorce or nullity has been granted, divorce or nullity of marriage order has been made, the date on which the decree is made absolute order is made final;]
- (b) in the case of a civil partnership in respect of which a dissolution or nullity order has been made, the date on which the order is made final.

REMARRIAGE OF EITHER SPOUSE

13 Effect of remarriage or subsequent civil partnership

(1) If after the grant of a decree dissolving or annulling a marriage either spouse remarries or forms a civil partnership, that spouse is not entitled to apply, by reference to the grant of that decree, for a Part II order.

[(1) If after the grant of a decree making of an order dissolving or annulling a marriage either spouse remarries or forms a civil partnership, that spouse is not entitled to apply, by reference to the grant of that decree, making of that order, for a Part II order.]

(2) If after the making of a dissolution or nullity order either civil partner forms a subsequent civil partnership or marries, that civil partner is not entitled to apply, by reference to the making of that order, for a Part II order.

(3) In sub-paragraphs (1) and (2)—

- (a) the references to remarrying and marrying include references to cases where the marriage is by law void or voidable, and
- (b) the references to forming a civil partnership include references to cases where the civil partnership is by law void or voidable.

[INCLUSION OF REFERENCES TO DECREES IN REFERENCES TO ORDERS

13A

In paragraphs 2 to 13—

- (a) a reference to a divorce order includes a decree of divorce;
- (b) a reference to a nullity of marriage order includes a decree of nullity of marriage;

(c) a reference to a judicial separation order includes a decree of judicial separation;

(d) a reference to making includes granting;

(e) a reference to an order being made final includes a decree being made absolute.

(2) If the court gives such a direction, it may further direct that either spouse, civil partner or cohabitant is to be liable to indemnify the other in whole or in part against any payment made or expenses incurred by the other in discharging or performing any such liability or obligation.]

Rules of court

14

(1) Rules of court shall be made requiring the court, before it makes an order under this Schedule, to give the landlord of the dwelling-house to which the order will relate an opportunity of being heard.

(2) Rules of court may provide that an application for a Part II order by reference to an order or decree may not, without the leave of the court by which that order was made or decree was granted, be made after the expiration of such period from the order or grant as may be prescribed by the rules.

Saving for other provisions of Act

15

(1) If a spouse or civil partner is entitled to occupy a dwelling-house by virtue of a tenancy, this Schedule does not affect the operation of sections 30 and 31 in relation to the other spouse's or civil partner's home rights.

(2) If a spouse, civil partner or cohabitant is entitled to occupy a dwelling-house by virtue of a tenancy, the court's powers to make orders under this Schedule are additional to those conferred by sections 33, 35 and 36.

NOTES

Amendment

Prospectively amended by Divorce, Dissolution and Separation Act 2020.

PROTECTION FROM HARASSMENT ACT 1997

England and Wales

A1.3

1 Prohibition of harassment

(1) A person must not pursue a course of conduct—

- (a) which amounts to harassment of another, and
- (b) which he knows or ought to know amounts to harassment of the other.

(1A) A person must not pursue a course of conduct—

- (a) which involves harassment of two or more persons, and
- (b) which he knows or ought to know involves harassment of those persons, and
- (c) by which he intends to persuade any person (whether or not one of those mentioned above)—
  - (i) not to do something that he is entitled or required to do, or
  - (ii) to do something that he is not under any obligation to do.

(2) For the purposes of this section or section 2A(2)(c), the person whose course of conduct is in question ought to know that it amounts to or involves harassment of another if a reasonable person in possession of the same information would think the course of conduct amounted to or involved harassment of the other.

(3) Subsection (1) or (1A) does not apply to a course of conduct if the person who pursued it shows—

- (a) that it was pursued for the purpose of preventing or detecting crime,
- (b) that it was pursued under any enactment or rule of law or to comply with any condition or requirement imposed by any person under any enactment, or
- (c) that in the particular circumstances the pursuit of the course of conduct was reasonable.

2 Offence of harassment

(1) A person who pursues a course of conduct in breach of section 1(1) or (1A) is guilty of an offence.

(2) A person guilty of an offence under this section is liable on summary conviction to imprisonment for a term not exceeding six months, or a fine not exceeding level 5 on the standard scale, or both.

(3) (*repealed*)

2A Offence of stalking

(1) A person is guilty of an offence if—

- (a) the person pursues a course of conduct in breach of section 1(1), and
- (b) the course of conduct amounts to stalking.

(2) For the purposes of subsection (1)(b) (and section 4A(1)(a)) a person's course of conduct amounts to stalking of another person if—

- (a) it amounts to harassment of that person,
- (b) the acts or omissions involved are ones associated with stalking, and
- (c) the person whose course of conduct it is knows or ought to know that the course of conduct amounts to harassment of the other person.

(3) The following are examples of acts or omissions which, in particular circumstances, are ones associated with stalking—

- (a) following a person,

(b) contacting, or attempting to contact, a person by any means,
(c) publishing any statement or other material—
  (i) relating or purporting to relate to a person, or
  (ii) purporting to originate from a person,
(d) monitoring the use by a person of the internet, email or any other form of electronic communication,
(e) loitering in any place (whether public or private),
(f) interfering with any property in the possession of a person,
(g) watching or spying on a person.

(4) A person guilty of an offence under this section is liable on summary conviction to imprisonment for a term not exceeding 51 weeks, or a fine not exceeding level 5 on the standard scale, or both.
(5) In relation to an offence committed before the commencement of section 281(5) of the Criminal Justice Act 2003, the reference in subsection (4) to 51 weeks is to be read as a reference to six months.
(6) This section is without prejudice to the generality of section 2.

2B Power of entry in relation to offence of stalking

(1) A justice of the peace may, on an application by a constable, issue a warrant authorising a constable to enter and search premises if the justice of the peace is satisfied that there are reasonable grounds for believing that—
(a) an offence under section 2A has been, or is being, committed,
(b) there is material on the premises which is likely to be of substantial value (whether by itself or together with other material) to the investigation of the offence,
(c) the material—
  (i) is likely to be admissible in evidence at a trial for the offence, and
  (ii) does not consist of, or include, items subject to legal privilege, excluded material or special procedure material (within the meanings given by sections 10, 11 and 14 of the Police and Criminal Evidence Act 1984), and
(d) either—
  (i) entry to the premises will not be granted unless a warrant is produced, or
  (ii) the purpose of a search may be frustrated or seriously prejudiced unless a constable arriving at the premises can secure immediate entry to them.

(2) A constable may seize and retain anything for which a search has been authorised under subsection (1).
(3) A constable may use reasonable force, if necessary, in the exercise of any power conferred by virtue of this section.
(4) In this section "premises" has the same meaning as in section 23 of the Police and Criminal Evidence Act 1984.

3 Civil remedy

(1) An actual or apprehended breach of section 1(1) may be the subject of a claim in civil proceedings by the person who is or may be the victim of the course of conduct in question.
(2) On such a claim, damages may be awarded for (among other things) any anxiety caused by the harassment and any financial loss resulting from the harassment.
(3) Where—
(a) in such proceedings the High Court or the county court grants an injunction for the purpose of restraining the defendant from pursuing any conduct which amounts to harassment, and

(b) the plaintiff considers that the defendant has done anything which he is prohibited from doing by the injunction,

the plaintiff may apply for the issue of a warrant for the arrest of the defendant.

(4) An application under subsection (3) may be made—

(a) where the injunction was granted by the High Court, to a judge of that court, and

(b) where the injunction was granted by the county court, to a judge of that court.

(5) The judge to whom an application under subsection (3) is made may only issue a warrant if—

(a) the application is substantiated on oath, and

(b) the judge has reasonable grounds for believing that the defendant has done anything which he is prohibited from doing by the injunction.

(6) Where—

(a) the High Court or the county court grants an injunction for the purpose mentioned in subsection (3)(a), and

(b) without reasonable excuse the defendant does anything which he is prohibited from doing by the injunction,

he is guilty of an offence.

(7) Where a person is convicted of an offence under subsection (6) in respect of any conduct, that conduct is not punishable as a contempt of court.

(8) A person cannot be convicted of an offence under subsection (6) in respect of any conduct which has been punished as a contempt of court.

(9) A person guilty of an offence under subsection (6) is liable—

(a) on conviction on indictment, to imprisonment for a term not exceeding five years, or a fine, or both, or

(b) on summary conviction, to imprisonment for a term not exceeding six months, or a fine not exceeding the statutory maximum, or both.

3A Injunctions to protect persons from harassment within section 1(1A)

(1) This section applies where there is an actual or apprehended breach of section 1(1A) by any person ("the relevant person").

(2) In such a case—

(a) any person who is or may be a victim of the course of conduct in question, or

(b) any person who is or may be a person falling within section 1(1A)(c),

may apply to the High Court or the county court for an injunction restraining the relevant person from pursuing any conduct which amounts to harassment in relation to any person or persons mentioned or described in the injunction.

(3) Section 3(3) to (9) apply in relation to an injunction granted under subsection (2) above as they apply in relation to an injunction granted as mentioned in section 3(3)(a).

4 Putting people in fear of violence

(1) A person whose course of conduct causes another to fear, on at least two occasions, that violence will be used against him is guilty of an offence if he knows or ought to know that his course of conduct will cause the other so to fear on each of those occasions.

(2) For the purposes of this section, the person whose course of conduct is in question ought to know that it will cause another to fear that violence will be used against him on any occasion if a reasonable person in possession of the same information would think the course of conduct would cause the other so to fear on that occasion.

(3) It is a defence for a person charged with an offence under this section to show that—

- (a) his course of conduct was pursued for the purpose of preventing or detecting crime,
- (b) his course of conduct was pursued under any enactment or rule of law or to comply with any condition or requirement imposed by any person under any enactment, or
- (c) the pursuit of his course of conduct was reasonable for the protection of himself or another or for the protection of his or another's property.

(4) A person guilty of an offence under this section is liable—

- (a) on conviction on indictment, to imprisonment for a term not exceeding ten years, or a fine, or both, or
- (b) on summary conviction, to imprisonment for a term not exceeding six months, or a fine not exceeding the statutory maximum, or both.

(5) If on the trial on indictment of a person charged with an offence under this section the jury find him not guilty of the offence charged, they may find him guilty of an offence under section 2 or 2A.

(6) The Crown Court has the same powers and duties in relation to a person who is by virtue of subsection (5) convicted before it of an offence under section 2 or 2A as a magistrates' court would have on convicting him of the offence.

4A Stalking involving fear of violence or serious alarm or distress

(1) A person ("A") whose course of conduct—

- (a) amounts to stalking, and
- (b) either—
  - (i) causes another ("B") to fear, on at least two occasions, that violence will be used against B, or
  - (ii) causes B serious alarm or distress which has a substantial adverse effect on B's usual day-to-day activities,

is guilty of an offence if A knows or ought to know that A's course of conduct will cause B so to fear on each of those occasions or (as the case may be) will cause such alarm or distress.

(2) For the purposes of this section A ought to know that A's course of conduct will cause B to fear that violence will be used against B on any occasion if a reasonable person in possession of the same information would think the course of conduct would cause B so to fear on that occasion.

(3) For the purposes of this section A ought to know that A's course of conduct will cause B serious alarm or distress which has a substantial adverse effect on B's usual day-to-day activities if a reasonable person in possession of the same information would think the course of conduct would cause B such alarm or distress.

(4) It is a defence for A to show that—

- (a) A's course of conduct was pursued for the purpose of preventing or detecting crime,
- (b) A's course of conduct was pursued under any enactment or rule of law or to comply with any condition or requirement imposed by any person under any enactment, or
- (c) the pursuit of A's course of conduct was reasonable for the protection of A or another or for the protection of A's or another's property.

(5) A person guilty of an offence under this section is liable—

- (a) on conviction on indictment, to imprisonment for a term not exceeding ten years, or a fine, or both, or
- (b) on summary conviction, to imprisonment for a term not exceeding twelve months, or a fine not exceeding the statutory maximum, or both.

(6) In relation to an offence committed before the commencement of section 154(1) of the Criminal Justice Act 2003, the reference in subsection (5)(b) to twelve months is to be read as a reference to six months.
(7) If on the trial on indictment of a person charged with an offence under this section the jury find the person not guilty of the offence charged, they may find the person guilty of an offence under section 2 or 2A.
(8) The Crown Court has the same powers and duties in relation to a person who is by virtue of subsection (7) convicted before it of an offence under section 2 or 2A as a magistrates' court would have on convicting the person of the offence.
(9) This section is without prejudice to the generality of section 4.

5 Restraining orders on conviction

(1) A court sentencing or otherwise dealing with a person ("the defendant") convicted of an offence may (as well as sentencing him or dealing with him in any other way) make an order under this section.
(2) The order may, for the purpose of protecting the victim or victims of the offence, or any other person mentioned in the order, from conduct which—

(a) amounts to harassment, or
(b) will cause a fear of violence,

prohibit the defendant from doing anything described in the order.
(3) The order may have effect for a specified period or until further order.
(3A) In proceedings under this section both the prosecution and the defence may lead, as further evidence, any evidence that would be admissible in proceedings for an injunction under section 3.
(4) The prosecutor, the defendant or any other person mentioned in the order may apply to the court which made the order for it to be varied or discharged by a further order.
(4A) Any person mentioned in the order is entitled to be heard on the hearing of an application under subsection (4).
(5) If without reasonable excuse the defendant does anything which he is prohibited from doing by an order under this section, he is guilty of an offence.
(6) A person guilty of an offence under this section is liable—

(a) on conviction on indictment, to imprisonment for a term not exceeding five years, or a fine, or both, or
(b) on summary conviction, to imprisonment for a term not exceeding six months, or a fine not exceeding the statutory maximum, or both.

(7) A court dealing with a person for an offence under this section may vary or discharge the order in question by a further order.

5A Restraining orders on acquittal

(1) A court before which a person ("the defendant") is acquitted of an offence may, if it considers it necessary to do so to protect a person from harassment by the defendant, make an order prohibiting the defendant from doing anything described in the order.
(2) Subsections (3) to (7) of section 5 apply to an order under this section as they apply to an order under that one.
(3) Where the Court of Appeal allow an appeal against conviction they may remit the case to the Crown Court to consider whether to proceed under this section.
(4) Where—

(a) the Crown Court allows an appeal against conviction, or
(b) a case is remitted to the Crown Court under subsection (3),

the reference in subsection (1) to a court before which a person is acquitted of an offence is to be read as referring to that court.

(5) A person made subject to an order under this section has the same right of appeal against the order as if—

- (a) he had been convicted of the offence in question before the court which made the order, and
- (b) the order had been made under section 5.

6 Limitation

In section 11 of the Limitation Act 1980 (special time limit for actions in respect of personal injuries), after subsection (1) there is inserted—

"(1A) This section does not apply to any action brought for damages under section 3 of the Protection from Harassment Act 1997."

7 Interpretation of this group of sections

(1) This section applies for the interpretation of sections 1 to 5.

(2) References to harassing a person include alarming the person or causing the person distress.

(3) A "course of conduct" must involve—

- (a) in the case of conduct in relation to a single person (see section 1(1)), conduct on at least two occasions in relation to that person, or
- (b) in the case of conduct in relation to two or more persons (see section 1(1A)), conduct on at least one occasion in relation to each of those persons.

(3A) A person's conduct on any occasion shall be taken, if aided, abetted, counselled or procured by another—

- (a) to be conduct on that occasion of the other (as well as conduct of the person whose conduct it is); and
- (b) to be conduct in relation to which the other's knowledge and purpose, and what he ought to have known, are the same as they were in relation to what was contemplated or reasonably foreseeable at the time of the aiding, abetting, counselling or procuring.

(4) "Conduct" includes speech.

(5) References to a person, in the context of the harassment of a person, are references to a person who is an individual.

8–11

(Applies to Scotland)

GENERAL

12 National security, etc

(1) If the Secretary of State certifies that in his opinion anything done by a specified person on a specified occasion related to—

- (a) national security,
- (b) the economic well-being of the United Kingdom, or
- (c) the prevention or detection of serious crime,

and was done on behalf of the Crown, the certificate is conclusive evidence that this Act does not apply to any conduct of that person on that occasion.

(2) In subsection (1), "specified" means specified in the certificate in question.

(3) A document purporting to be a certificate under subsection (1) is to be received in evidence and, unless the contrary is proved, be treated as being such a certificate.

13 Corresponding provision for Northern Ireland

An Order in Council made under paragraph 1(1)(b) of Schedule 1 to the Northern Ireland Act 1974 which contains a statement that it is made only for purposes corresponding to those of sections 1 to 7 and 12 of this Act—

(a) shall not be subject to sub-paragraphs (4) and (5) of paragraph 1 of that Schedule (affirmative resolution of both Houses of Parliament), but
(b) shall be subject to annulment in pursuance of a resolution of either House of Parliament.

14 Extent

(1) Sections 1 to 7 extend to England and Wales only.
(2) Sections 8 to 11 extend to Scotland only.
(3) This Act (except section 13) does not extend to Northern Ireland.

15 Commencement

(1) Sections 1, 2, 4, 5 and 7 to 12 are to come into force on such day as the Secretary of State may by order made by statutory instrument appoint.
(2) Sections 3 and 6 are to come into force on such day as the Lord Chancellor may by order made by statutory instrument appoint.
(3) Different days may be appointed under this section for different purposes.

16 Short title

This Act may be cited as the Protection from Harassment Act 1997.

CRIME AND SECURITY ACT 2010

Domestic violence

A1.4

24 Power to issue a domestic violence protection notice

(1) A member of a police force not below the rank of superintendent ("the authorising officer") may issue a domestic violence protection notice ("a DVPN") under this section.

(2) A DVPN may be issued to a person ("P") aged 18 years or over if the authorising officer has reasonable grounds for believing that—

- (a) P has been violent towards, or has threatened violence towards, an associated person, and
- (b) the issue of the DVPN is necessary to protect that person from violence or a threat of violence by P.

(3) Before issuing a DVPN, the authorising officer must, in particular, consider—

- (a) the welfare of any person under the age of 18 whose interests the officer considers relevant to the issuing of the DVPN (whether or not that person is an associated person),
- (b) the opinion of the person for whose protection the DVPN would be issued as to the issuing of the DVPN,
- (c) any representations made by P as to the issuing of the DVPN, and
- (d) in the case of provision included by virtue of subsection (8), the opinion of any other associated person who lives in the premises to which the provision would relate.

(4) The authorising officer must take reasonable steps to discover the opinions mentioned in subsection (3).

(5) But the authorising officer may issue a DVPN in circumstances where the person for whose protection it is issued does not consent to the issuing of the DVPN.

(6) A DVPN must contain provision to prohibit P from molesting the person for whose protection it is issued.

(7) Provision required to be included by virtue of subsection (6) may be expressed so as to refer to molestation in general, to particular acts of molestation, or to both.

(8) If P lives in premises which are also lived in by a person for whose protection the DVPN is issued, the DVPN may also contain provision—

- (a) to prohibit P from evicting or excluding from the premises the person for whose protection the DVPN is issued,
- (b) to prohibit P from entering the premises,
- (c) to require P to leave the premises, or
- (d) to prohibit P from coming within such distance of the premises as may be specified in the DVPN.

(9) An "associated person" means a person who is associated with P within the meaning of section 62 of the Family Law Act 1996.

(10) Subsection (11) applies where a DVPN includes provision in relation to premises by virtue of subsection (8)(b) or (8)(c) and the authorising officer believes that—

- (a) P is a person subject to service law in accordance with sections 367 to 369 of the Armed Forces Act 2006, and
- (b) the premises fall within paragraph (a) of the definition of "service living accommodation" in section 96(1) of that Act.

(11) The authorising officer must make reasonable efforts to inform P's commanding officer (within the meaning of section 360 of the Armed Forces Act 2006) of the issuing of the notice.

25 Contents and service of a domestic violence protection notice

(1) A DVPN must state—

- (a) the grounds on which it has been issued,
- (b) that a constable may arrest P without warrant if the constable has reasonable grounds for believing that P is in breach of the DVPN,
- (c) that an application for a domestic violence protection order under section 27 will be heard within 48 hours of the time of service of the DVPN and a notice of the hearing will be given to P,
- (d) that the DVPN continues in effect until that application has been determined, and
- (e) the provision that a magistrates' court may include in a domestic violence protection order.

(2) A DVPN must be in writing and must be served on P personally by a constable.

(3) On serving P with a DVPN, the constable must ask P for an address for the purposes of being given the notice of the hearing of the application for the domestic violence protection order.

26 Breach of a domestic violence protection notice

(1) A person arrested by virtue of section 25(1)(b) for a breach of a DVPN must be held in custody and brought before the magistrates' court which will hear the application for the DVPO under section 27—

- (a) before the end of the period of 24 hours beginning with the time of the arrest, or
- (b) if earlier, at the hearing of that application.

(2) If the person is brought before the court by virtue of subsection (1)(a), the court may remand the person.

(3) If the court adjourns the hearing of the application by virtue of section 27(8), the court may remand the person.

(4) In calculating when the period of 24 hours mentioned in subsection (1)(a) ends, Christmas Day, Good Friday, any Sunday and any day which is a bank holiday in England and Wales under the Banking and Financial Dealings Act 1971 are to be disregarded.

27 Application for a domestic violence protection order

(1) If a DVPN has been issued, a constable must apply for a domestic violence protection order ("a DVPO").

(2) The application must be made by complaint to a magistrates' court.

(3) The application must be heard by the magistrates' court not later than 48 hours after the DVPN was served pursuant to section 25(2).

(4) In calculating when the period of 48 hours mentioned in subsection (3) ends, Christmas Day, Good Friday, any Sunday and any day which is a bank holiday in England and Wales under the Banking and Financial Dealings Act 1971 are to be disregarded.

(5) A notice of the hearing of the application must be given to P.

(6) The notice is deemed given if it has been left at the address given by P under section 25(3).

(7) But if the notice has not been given because no address was given by P under section 25(3), the court may hear the application for the DVPO if the court is satisfied that the constable applying for the DVPO has made reasonable efforts to give P the notice.

(8) The magistrates' court may adjourn the hearing of the application.

(9) If the court adjourns the hearing, the DVPN continues in effect until the application has been determined.

(10) On the hearing of an application for a DVPO, section 97 of the Magistrates' Courts Act 1980 (summons to witness and warrant for his arrest) does not apply in relation to a person for whose protection the DVPO would be made, except where the person has given oral or written evidence at the hearing.

28 Conditions for and contents of a domestic violence protection order

(1) The court may make a DVPO if two conditions are met.

(2) The first condition is that the court is satisfied on the balance of probabilities that P has been violent towards, or has threatened violence towards, an associated person.

(3) The second condition is that the court thinks that making the DVPO is necessary to protect that person from violence or a threat of violence by P.

(4) Before making a DVPO, the court must, in particular, consider—

- (a) the welfare of any person under the age of 18 whose interests the court considers relevant to the making of the DVPO (whether or not that person is an associated person), and
- (b) any opinion of which the court is made aware—
  - (i) of the person for whose protection the DVPO would be made, and
  - (ii) in the case of provision included by virtue of subsection (8), of any other associated person who lives in the premises to which the provision would relate.

(5) But the court may make a DVPO in circumstances where the person for whose protection it is made does not consent to the making of the DVPO.

(6) A DVPO must contain provision to prohibit P from molesting the person for whose protection it is made.

(7) Provision required to be included by virtue of subsection (6) may be expressed so as to refer to molestation in general, to particular acts of molestation, or to both.

(8) If P lives in premises which are also lived in by a person for whose protection the DVPO is made, the DVPO may also contain provision—

- (a) to prohibit P from evicting or excluding from the premises the person for whose protection the DVPO is made,
- (b) to prohibit P from entering the premises,
- (c) to require P to leave the premises, or
- (d) to prohibit P from coming within such distance of the premises as may be specified in the DVPO.

(9) A DVPO must state that a constable may arrest P without warrant if the constable has reasonable grounds for believing that P is in breach of the DVPO.

(10) A DVPO may be in force for—

- (a) no fewer than 14 days beginning with the day on which it is made, and
- (b) no more than 28 days beginning with that day.

(11) A DVPO must state the period for which it is to be in force.

29 Breach of a domestic violence protection order

(1) A person arrested by virtue of section 28(9) for a breach of a DVPO must be held in custody and brought before a magistrates' court within the period of 24 hours beginning with the time of the arrest.

(2) If the matter is not disposed of when the person is brought before the court, the court may remand the person.

(3) In calculating when the period of 24 hours mentioned in subsection (1) ends, Christmas Day, Good Friday, any Sunday and any day which is a bank holiday in England and Wales under the Banking and Financial Dealings Act 1971 are to be disregarded.

30 Further provision about remand

(1) This section applies for the purposes of the remand of a person by a magistrates' court under section 26(2) or (3) or 29(2).

(2) In the application of section 128(6) of the Magistrates' Courts Act 1980 for those purposes, the reference to the "other party" is to be read—

- (a) in the case of a remand prior to the hearing of an application for a DVPO, as a reference to the authorising officer,
- (b) in any other case, as a reference to the constable who applied for the DVPO.

(3) If the court has reason to suspect that a medical report will be required, the power to remand a person may be exercised for the purpose of enabling a medical examination to take place and a report to be made.

(4) If the person is remanded in custody for that purpose, the adjournment may not be for more than 3 weeks at a time.

(5) If the person is remanded on bail for that purpose, the adjournment may not be for more than 4 weeks at a time.

(6) If the court has reason to suspect that the person is suffering from a mental disorder within the meaning of the Mental Health Act 1983, the court has the same power to make an order under section 35 of that Act (remand to hospital for medical report) as it has under that section in the case of an accused person (within the meaning of that section).

(7) The court may, when remanding the person on bail, require the person to comply, before release on bail or later, with such requirements as appear to the court to be necessary to secure that the person does not interfere with witnesses or otherwise obstruct the course of justice.

31 Guidance

(1) The Secretary of State may from time to time issue guidance relating to the exercise by a constable of functions under sections 24 to 30.

(2) A constable must have regard to any guidance issued under subsection (1) when exercising a function to which the guidance relates.

(3) Before issuing guidance under this section, the Secretary of State must consult—

- (a) the National Police Chiefs' Council, and
- (b) . . .
- (c) such other persons as the Secretary of State thinks fit.

DOMESTIC ABUSE BILL

PART 1
DEFINITION OF "DOMESTIC ABUSE"

A1.5

1 Definition of "domestic abuse"

(1) This section defines "domestic abuse" for the purposes of this Act.

(2) Behaviour of a person ("A") towards another person ("B") is "domestic abuse" if—

(a) A and B are each aged 16 or over and are personally connected to each other, and

(b) the behaviour is abusive.

(3) Behaviour is "abusive" if it consists of any of the following—

(a) physical or sexual abuse;

(b) violent or threatening behaviour;

(c) controlling or coercive behaviour;

(d) economic abuse (see subsection (4));

(e) psychological, emotional or other abuse;

and it does not matter whether the behaviour consists of a single incident or a course of conduct.

(4) "Economic abuse" means any behaviour that has a substantial adverse effect on B's ability to—

(a) acquire, use or maintain money or other property, or

(b) obtain goods or services.

(5) For the purposes of this Act A's behaviour may be behaviour "towards" B despite the fact that it consists of conduct directed at another person (for example, B's child).

(6) References in this Act to being abusive towards another person are to be read in accordance with this section.

(7) For the meaning of "personally connected", see section 2.

2 Definition of "personally connected"

(1) For the purposes of this Act, two people are "personally connected" to each other if any of the following applies—

(a) they are, or have been, married to each other;

(b) they are, or have been, civil partners of each other;

(c) they have agreed to marry one another (whether or not the agreement has been terminated);

(d) they have entered into a civil partnership agreement (whether or not the agreement has been terminated);

(e) they are, or have been, in an intimate personal relationship with each other;

(f) they each have, or there has been a time when they each have had, a parental relationship in relation to the same child (see subsection (2));

(g) they are relatives.

(2) For the purposes of subsection (1)(f) a person has a parental relationship in relation to a child if—

(a) the person is a parent of the child, or

(b) the person has parental responsibility for the child.

(3) In this section—

"child" means a person under the age of 18 years;

"civil partnership agreement" has the meaning given by section 73 of the Civil Partnership Act 2004;

"parental responsibility" has the same meaning as in the Children Act 1989 (see section 3 of that Act);

"relative" has the meaning given by section 63(1) of the Family Law Act 1996.

3 Children as victims of domestic abuse

(1) This section applies where behaviour of a person ("A") towards another person ("B") is domestic abuse.

(2) Any reference in this Act to a victim of domestic abuse includes a reference to a child who—

(a) sees or hears, or experiences the effects of, the abuse, and

(b) is related to A or B.

(3) A child is related to a person for the purposes of subsection (2) if—

(a) the person is a parent of, or has parental responsibility for, the child, or

(b) the child and the person are relatives.

(4) In this section—

"child" means a person under the age of 18 years;

"parental responsibility" has the same meaning as in the Children Act 1989 (see section 3 of that Act);

"relative" has the meaning given by section 63(1) of the Family Law Act 1996.

PART 2
THE DOMESTIC ABUSE COMMISSIONER

Domestic Abuse Commissioner

4 Appointment of Commissioner

(1) The Secretary of State must appoint a person as the Domestic Abuse Commissioner ("the Commissioner").

(2) The Commissioner is to hold and vacate office in accordance with the terms and conditions of the Commissioner's appointment.

(3) The Commissioner is not to be regarded as the servant or agent of the Crown or as enjoying any status, immunity or privilege of the Crown.

5 Funding

(1) The Secretary of State may make payments to the Commissioner out of money provided by Parliament for the purpose of enabling the Commissioner to meet expenditure incurred in the exercise of the Commissioner's functions.

(2) Payments are to be made at such times, and subject to any such conditions, as the Secretary of State considers appropriate.

(3) The Secretary of State may pay, or make provision for paying, to or in respect of the Commissioner—

(a) remuneration;

(b) allowances;

(c) sums by way of or in respect of pensions.

6 Staff etc

(1) The Secretary of State must provide the Commissioner with—

(a) such staff, and

(b) such accommodation, equipment and other facilities,

as the Secretary of State considers necessary for the carrying out of the Commissioner's functions.

(2) Before providing any staff, the Secretary of State must—
(a) consult the Commissioner, and
(b) obtain the Commissioner's approval as to the persons to be provided as staff.

(3) The Secretary of State must consult the Commissioner before providing any accommodation, equipment or other facilities.

FUNCTIONS OF COMMISSIONER

7 General functions of Commissioner

(1) The Commissioner must encourage good practice in—
(a) the prevention of domestic abuse;
(b) the prevention, detection, investigation and prosecution of offences involving domestic abuse;
(c) the identification of—
(i) people who carry out domestic abuse;
(ii) victims of domestic abuse;
(iii) children affected by domestic abuse;
(d) the provision of protection and support to people affected by domestic abuse.

(2) The things that the Commissioner may do in pursuance of the general duty under subsection (1) include—
(a) assessing, monitoring, and publishing information about, the provision of services to people affected by domestic abuse;
(b) making recommendations to any public authority about the exercise of its functions;
(c) undertaking or supporting (financially or otherwise) the carrying out of research;
(d) providing information, education or training;
(e) taking other steps to increase public awareness of domestic abuse;
(f) consulting public authorities, voluntary organisations and other persons;
(g) co-operating with, or working jointly with, public authorities, voluntary organisations and other persons, whether in England and Wales or outside the United Kingdom.

(3) Subject to subsection (4), the Commissioner may not do anything in pursuance of the general duty under subsection (1) that—
(a) relates to a devolved Welsh authority, or
(b) otherwise relates to Welsh devolved matters.

(4) Subsection (3) does not prevent the Commissioner from—
(a) doing anything falling within subsection (2)(c), (d) or (e), to the extent that the thing done does not relate to Welsh devolved matters;
(b) doing anything falling within subsection (2)(f) or (g);
(c) disclosing information to a devolved Welsh authority, or information which relates to Welsh devolved matters, under section 17.

(5) For the purposes of this section something relates to Welsh devolved matters so far as it relates to—
(a) any matter provision about which would be within the legislative competence of Senedd Cymru if it were contained in an Act of Senedd Cymru, or
(b) (so far as it is not within paragraph (a)), any matter functions with respect to which are exercisable by the Welsh Ministers, the First Minister for Wales, the Counsel General to the Welsh Government or the Senedd Commission.

(6) In this section—

"devolved Welsh authority" has the meaning given by section 157A of the Government of Wales Act 2006;

"public authority" means any public authority within the meaning of section 6 of the Human Rights Act 1998, other than a court or tribunal.

8 Reports

(1) The Commissioner may report to the Secretary of State on any matter relating to domestic abuse.

(2) The Commissioner must publish every report made under this section.

(3) Before publishing a report under this section, the Commissioner must send a draft of the report to the Secretary of State.

(4) The Secretary of State may direct the Commissioner to omit material from any report under this section before publication if the Secretary of State thinks the publication of that material—

(a) might jeopardise the safety of any person, or

(b) might prejudice the investigation or prosecution of an offence.

(5) The Secretary of State must consult the Commissioner before making any direction under subsection (4).

(6) The Commissioner must arrange for a copy of any report published under this section to be laid before Parliament.

9 Advice and assistance

(1) The Commissioner may provide the Secretary of State with any advice or assistance that the Secretary of State may request.

(2) The Commissioner may, at the request of any other person, provide the person with advice or assistance relating to the exercise of any of the person's functions, or the carrying out of any activities by the person, in relation to people affected by domestic abuse.

(3) The Commissioner may charge a person for providing the person with advice or assistance under subsection (2).

(4) The Commissioner must publish any advice given to a person under subsection (2).

(5) Before publishing any advice given under this section, the Commissioner must send a draft of what is proposed to be published to the Secretary of State.

(6) The Secretary of State may direct the Commissioner to omit anything contained in the advice before publication if the Secretary of State thinks the publication of that material—

(a) might jeopardise the safety of any person, or

(b) might prejudice the investigation or prosecution of an offence.

(7) The Secretary of State must consult the Commissioner before making any direction under subsection (6).

10 Incidental powers

(1) The Commissioner may do anything which the Commissioner considers will facilitate, or is incidental or conducive to, the carrying out of the Commissioner's functions.

(2) But the Commissioner may not borrow money.

Framework document

11 Framework document

(1) The Secretary of State must issue a document (a "framework document") that deals with matters relating to the Commissioner.

(2) The matters that may be dealt with by a framework document include (among other things)—

(a) matters relating to governance, funding and staffing;
(b) matters relating to the exercise of functions of the Commissioner;
(c) matters relating to scrutiny of the Commissioner's activities by Parliament or by Senedd Cymru.

(3) The Commissioner must have regard to the framework document when exercising any of the Commissioner's functions.

(4) The Secretary of State must have regard to the framework document when exercising any functions in relation to the Commissioner.

(5) The Secretary of State—
(a) must keep the framework document under review, and
(b) may issue a revised framework document.

(6) The Secretary of State—
(a) must consult the Commissioner in preparing or revising a framework document, and
(b) may not issue a framework document without the agreement of the Commissioner.

(7) The Secretary of State must consult the Welsh Ministers before issuing—
(a) the first framework document under this section, or
(b) any other framework document which is, in the opinion of the Secretary of State, significantly different from the framework document it replaces.

(8) The Secretary of State must—
(a) arrange for any framework document issued under this section to be published in the manner which the Secretary of State considers appropriate,
(b) send a copy of the framework document to the Welsh Ministers, and
(c) lay a copy of the framework document before Parliament.

(9) The Welsh Ministers must lay before Senedd Cymru a copy of any framework document sent to them under subsection (8)(b).

Advisory Board

12 Advisory Board

(1) The Commissioner must establish an Advisory Board ("the Board") for the purposes of providing advice to the Commissioner about the exercise of the Commissioner's functions.

(2) The Board is to consist of not fewer than six and not more than ten members appointed by the Commissioner.

(3) Each member of the Board is to hold and vacate office in accordance with the terms and conditions of the member's appointment.

(4) The members of the Board must include—
(a) at least one person appearing to the Commissioner to represent the interests of victims of domestic abuse;
(b) at least one person appearing to the Commissioner to represent the interests of charities and other voluntary organisations that work with victims of domestic abuse in England;
(c) at least one person appearing to the Commissioner to represent the interests of persons who provide, or have functions relating to, health care services in England;
(d) at least one person appearing to the Commissioner to represent the interests of persons who provide, or have functions relating to, social care services in England;
(e) at least one person appearing to the Commissioner to represent the interests of persons with functions relating to policing or criminal justice;

(f) at least one person appearing to the Commissioner to have academic expertise in relation to domestic abuse.

(5) The Commissioner may pay such remuneration or allowances to members of the Board as the Commissioner may determine.

(6) In this section—

"health care services" means services relating to health care (within the meaning of section 9 of the Health and Social Care Act 2008);

"social care services" means services relating to social care (within the meaning of that section).

STRATEGIC PLANS AND ANNUAL REPORTS

13 Strategic plans

(1) The Commissioner must, as soon as reasonably practicable after the Commissioner's appointment, prepare and publish a strategic plan.

(2) A strategic plan is a plan setting out how the Commissioner proposes to exercise the Commissioner's functions in the period to which the plan relates, which must be not less than one year and not more than three years.

(3) A strategic plan must in particular—

(a) state the Commissioner's objectives and priorities for the period to which the plan relates;

(b) state any matters on which the Commissioner proposes to report under section 8 during that period;

(c) state any other activities the Commissioner proposes to undertake during that period in the exercise of the Commissioner's functions.

(4) The Commissioner must, before the end of the period to which a strategic plan relates ("the current period")—

(a) prepare a strategic plan for a period immediately following the current period, and

(b) publish that plan.

(5) At any time during the period to which a strategic plan relates, the Commissioner—

(a) may revise the strategic plan, and

(b) must publish any revised plan.

(6) In preparing or revising a strategic plan, the Commissioner must consult—

(a) the Secretary of State,

(b) the Advisory Board established under section 12, and

(c) such other persons as the Commissioner considers appropriate.

(7) The Commissioner must arrange for a copy of any plan (or revised plan) published under this section to be laid before Parliament.

14 Annual reports

(1) As soon as reasonably practicable after the end of each financial year, the Commissioner must submit to the Secretary of State an annual report on the exercise of the Commissioner's functions during the year.

(2) The annual report must include—

(a) an assessment of the extent to which the Commissioner's objectives and priorities have been met in that year;

(b) a statement of the matters on which the Commissioner has reported under section 8 during the year;

(c) a statement of the other activities the Commissioner has undertaken during the year in the exercise of the Commissioner's functions.

(3) The Commissioner must arrange for a copy of every annual report under this section to be laid before Parliament (but see subsection (4)).

(4) The Secretary of State may direct the Commissioner to omit material from any report under this section before it is laid before Parliament if the Secretary of State thinks the publication of that material—

- (a) might jeopardise the safety of any person, or
- (b) might prejudice the investigation or prosecution of an offence.

(5) The Secretary of State must consult the Commissioner before making any direction under subsection (4).

(6) In this section "financial year" means—

- (a) the period beginning with the day on which the first Domestic Abuse Commissioner takes office and ending with the following 31 March, and
- (b) each successive period of 12 months.

DUTIES OF PUBLIC AUTHORITIES IN RELATION TO COMMISSIONER

15 Duty to co-operate with Commissioner

(1) The Commissioner may request a specified public authority to co-operate with the Commissioner in any way that the Commissioner considers necessary for the purposes of the Commissioner's functions.

(2) A specified public authority must, so far as reasonably practicable, comply with a request made to it under this section.

(3) In this section "specified public authority" means any of the following—

- (a) a chief officer of police of a police force maintained for a police area in England and Wales;
- (b) a local policing body;
- (c) the Chief Constable of the British Transport Police Force;
- (d) the British Transport Police Authority;
- (e) the Ministry of Defence Police;
- (f) an immigration officer or other official of the Secretary of State exercising functions in relation to immigration or asylum;
- (g) the Crown Prosecution Service;
- (h) the Parole Board;
- (i) the Criminal Cases Review Commission;
- (j) an English local authority;
- (k) an NHS body in England;
- (l) Her Majesty's Inspectors of Constabulary;
- (m) Her Majesty's Chief Inspector of the Crown Prosecution Service;
- (n) Her Majesty's Chief Inspector of Education, Children's Services and Skills;
- (o) a body approved as an independent inspectorate under section 106 of the Education and Skills Act 2008 (inspection of registered independent educational institutions);
- (p) the Care Quality Commission;
- (q) Monitor.

(4) The Secretary of State may by regulations amend this section so as to—

- (a) add a public authority as a specified public authority for the purposes of this section;
- (b) remove a public authority added by virtue of paragraph (a);
- (c) vary any description of a public authority.

(5) Before making regulations under subsection (4) the Secretary of State must consult the Commissioner.

(6) Regulations under subsection (4) may not contain provision adding a devolved Welsh authority as a specified public authority for the purposes of this section.

(7) In this section—

"devolved Welsh authority" has the meaning given by section 157A of the Government of Wales Act 2006;

"English local authority" means—

- (a) a county council or district council in England,
- (b) a London borough council,
- (c) the Greater London Authority,
- (d) the Common Council of the City of London in its capacity as a local authority, or
- (e) the Council of the Isles of Scilly;

"immigration officer" means a person appointed as an immigration officer under paragraph 1 of Schedule 2 to the Immigration Act 1971;

"NHS body in England" means—

- (a) a National Health Service trust in England established under section 25 of the National Health Service Act 2006,
- (b) an NHS foundation trust within the meaning given by section 30 of that Act,
- (c) the National Health Service Commissioning Board,
- (d) a clinical commissioning group established under section 14D of that Act, or
- (e) the National Health Service Trust Development Authority;

"public authority" means any public authority within the meaning of section 6 of the Human Rights Act 1998, other than a court or tribunal.

16 Duty to respond to Commissioner's recommendations

(1) This section applies where the Commissioner publishes a report under section 8 containing recommendations in relation to—

- (a) any public authority that is a specified public authority for the purposes of section 15;
- (b) any government department in the charge of a Minister.

(2) The relevant person must prepare comments on the report.

(3) In this section "the relevant person" means—

- (a) the public authority, or
- (b) the Minister in charge of the government department,

as the case may be.

(4) The comments must include, in respect of each recommendation made in the report, an explanation of—

- (a) the action which the relevant person has taken, or proposes to take, in response to the recommendation, or
- (b) why the relevant person has not taken, or does not propose to take, any action in response.

(5) The relevant person must arrange for the comments to be published in such manner as the person considers appropriate.

(6) The comments must be published before the end of the period of 56 days beginning with the day on which the report is published.

(7) The relevant person must send a copy of anything published under subsection (5) to—

- (a) the Commissioner, and
- (b) where the relevant person is a specified public authority for the purposes of section 15, the Secretary of State.

Disclosure of information

17 Disclosure of information

(1) The Commissioner may disclose to a person any information received by the Commissioner in connection with the Commissioner's functions if the disclosure is made for a purpose connected with a function of the Commissioner.

(2) A person may disclose any information to the Commissioner if the disclosure is made for the purposes of enabling or assisting the Commissioner to exercise any function.

(3) A disclosure of information authorised by this section does not breach—

- (a) any obligation of confidence owed by the person making the disclosure in relation to that information, or
- (b) any other restriction on the disclosure of information (however imposed).

(4) But nothing in this Part requires or authorises any of the following—

- (a) the disclosure of any patient information (see subsection (5));
- (b) the making of a disclosure which, although made in the exercise of a function under this Part, would contravene the data protection legislation (see subsection (6));
- (c) the making of a disclosure which is prohibited by any of Parts 1 to 7 or Chapter 1 of Part 9 of the Investigatory Powers Act 2016.

(5) "Patient information" means information (however recorded) which—

- (a) relates to—
  - (i) the physical or mental health or condition of an individual,
  - (ii) the diagnosis of an individual's condition, or
  - (iii) an individual's care or treatment,

  or is (to any extent) derived directly or indirectly from information relating to any of those matters, and
- (b) identifies the individual or enables the individual to be identified (either by itself or in combination with other information).

(6) In this section "the data protection legislation" has the same meaning as in the Data Protection Act 2018 (see section 3 of that Act).

(7) This section does not affect any power to disclose that exists apart from this section.

Miscellaneous and supplementary

18 Restriction on exercise of functions in individual cases

(1) The Commissioner may not exercise any function in relation to an individual case.

(2) But subsection (1) does not prevent the Commissioner considering individual cases and drawing conclusions about them for the purpose of, or in the context of, considering a general issue.

19 Amendments relating to Commissioner

(1) In Part 3 of Schedule 1 to the House of Commons Disqualification Act 1975 (offices disqualifying for membership), at the appropriate place insert—

> "Domestic Abuse Commissioner."

(2) In Part 6 of Schedule 1 to the Freedom of Information Act 2000 (other public bodies and offices: general), at the appropriate place insert—

> "The Domestic Abuse Commissioner."

(3) In section 37 of the Government of Wales Act 2006 (power of the Senedd to call witnesses etc), after subsection (6A) insert—

> "(6B) Subsection (1) applies in relation to things done by the Domestic Abuse Commissioner by virtue of section 7(4)(b) or (c) of the Domestic Abuse Act 2020 (functions exercisable in relation to

devolved Welsh authorities etc) as it applies in relation to the exercise by the Welsh Ministers of their functions."

PART 3
POWERS FOR DEALING WITH DOMESTIC ABUSE

Domestic abuse protection notices

20 Power to give a domestic abuse protection notice

(1) A senior police officer may give a domestic abuse protection notice to a person ("P") if conditions A and B are met.

(2) A domestic abuse protection notice is a notice prohibiting P from being abusive towards a person aged 16 or over to whom P is personally connected. (Section 21 contains further provision about the provision that may be made by notices.)

(3) Condition A is that the senior police officer has reasonable grounds for believing that P has been abusive towards a person aged 16 or over to whom P is personally connected.

(4) Condition B is that the senior police officer has reasonable grounds for believing that it is necessary to give the notice to protect that person from domestic abuse, or the risk of domestic abuse, carried out by P.

(5) It does not matter whether the abusive behaviour referred to in subsection (3) took place in England and Wales or elsewhere.

(6) A domestic abuse protection notice may not be given to a person who is under the age of 18.

(7) A domestic abuse protection notice has effect in all parts of the United Kingdom.

(8) In this Part—

"senior police officer" means a member of a relevant police force who is a constable of at least the rank of inspector;

"relevant police force" means—

(a) a force maintained by a local policing body;

(b) the British Transport Police Force;

(c) the Ministry of Defence Police.

21 Provision that may be made by notices

(1) A domestic abuse protection notice may provide that the person to whom the notice is given ("P")—

(a) may not contact the person for whose protection the notice is given;

(b) may not come within a specified distance of any premises in England or Wales in which that person lives.

"Specified" means specified in the notice.

(2) If P lives in premises in England or Wales in which the person for whose protection the notice is given also lives, the notice may also contain provision—

(a) prohibiting P from evicting or excluding that person from the premises;

(b) prohibiting P from entering the premises;

(c) requiring P to leave the premises.

22 Matters to be considered before giving a notice

(1) Before giving a domestic abuse protection notice to a person ("P"), a senior police officer must, among other things, consider the following—

(a) the welfare of any person under the age of 18 whose interests the officer considers relevant to the giving of the notice (whether or not that person and P are personally connected);

(b) the opinion of the person for whose protection the notice would be given as to the giving of the notice;

(c) any representations made by P about the giving of the notice;

(d) in a case where the notice includes provision relating to premises lived in by the person for whose protection the notice would be given, the opinion of any relevant occupant as to the giving of the notice.

(2) In subsection (1)(d) "relevant occupant" means a person other than P or the person for whose protection the notice would be given—

(a) who lives in the premises, and

(b) who is personally connected to—

(i) the person for whose protection the notice would be given, or

(ii) if P also lives in the premises, P.

(3) The officer must take reasonable steps to discover the opinions mentioned in subsection (1).

(4) It is not necessary for the person for whose protection a domestic abuse protection notice is given to consent to the giving of the notice.

23 Further requirements in relation to notices

(1) A domestic abuse protection notice must be in writing.

(2) A domestic abuse protection notice given to a person ("P") must state—

(a) the grounds on which it has been given,

(b) that a constable may arrest P without warrant if the constable has reasonable grounds for believing that P is in breach of the notice,

(c) that an application for a domestic abuse protection order under section 26 will be heard by a magistrates' court within 48 hours of the time of giving the notice (disregarding any days mentioned in section 27(3)) and a notice of the hearing will be given to P,

(d) that the notice continues in effect until that application has been determined or withdrawn, and

(e) the provision that a magistrates' court may include in a domestic abuse protection order.

(3) The notice must be served on P personally by a constable.

(4) On serving the notice on P, the constable must ask P for an address at which P may be given the notice of the hearing of the application for the domestic abuse protection order.

(5) Subsection (6) applies where—

(a) a senior police officer gives a domestic abuse protection notice to a person ("P") who the officer believes is a person subject to service law in accordance with sections 367 to 369 of the Armed Forces Act 2006,

(b) the notice includes provision by virtue of section 21(2) prohibiting P from entering premises, or requiring P to leave premises, and

(c) the officer believes that the premises are relevant service accommodation.

(6) The officer must make reasonable efforts to inform P's commanding officer of the giving of the notice.

(7) In this section—

"commanding officer" has the meaning given by section 360 of the Armed Forces Act 2006;

"relevant service accommodation" means premises which fall within paragraph (a) of the definition of "service living accommodation" in section 96(1) of that Act.

24 Breach of notice

(1) If a constable has reasonable grounds for believing that a person is in breach of a domestic abuse protection notice, the constable may arrest the person without warrant.

(2) A person arrested by virtue of subsection (1) must be held in custody and brought before the appropriate magistrates' court—

(a) before the end of the period of 24 hours beginning with the time of the arrest, or

(b) if earlier, at the hearing of the application for a domestic abuse protection order against the person (see section 26(3)).

(3) In subsection (2) "the appropriate magistrates' court" means the magistrates' court which is to hear the application mentioned in subsection (2)(b).

(4) In calculating when the period of 24 hours mentioned in subsection (2)(a) ends, the following days are to be disregarded—

(a) any Sunday,

(b) Christmas Day,

(c) Good Friday, and

(d) any day which is a bank holiday in England and Wales under the Banking and Financial Dealings Act 1971.

(5) If the person is brought before the court as mentioned in subsection (2)(a), the court may remand the person.

(For power to remand a person brought before the court as mentioned in subsection (2)(b), see section 27(8).)

(6) In the application of section 128(6) of the Magistrates' Courts Act 1980 to remand under subsection (5) above, the reference to the "other party" is to be read as a reference to the senior police officer who gave the notice.

(7) The court may, when remanding the person on bail, require the person to comply, before release on bail or later, with any requirements that appear to the court to be necessary to secure that the person does not interfere with witnesses or otherwise obstruct the course of justice.

(8) Sections 57A(2) and 57C of the Crime and Disorder Act 1998 (use of live link at preliminary hearings where accused is at police station) apply in relation to hearings arising by virtue of subsection (2)(a) as they apply in relation to preliminary hearings in a magistrates' court (within the meaning of section 57A(3) of that Act), but as if—

(a) any reference in section 57C of that Act to being in police detention in connection with an offence were a reference to being held in custody under subsection (2) above, and

(b) subsections (4), (10) and (11) of that section were omitted.

(9) In section 17(1) of the Police and Criminal Evidence Act 1984 (entry for purpose of arrest etc), after paragraph (c) insert—

"(cza) of arresting a person who the constable has reasonable grounds for believing is in breach of a domestic abuse protection notice given under section 20 of the Domestic Abuse Act 2020;".

Domestic abuse protection orders

25 Meaning of "domestic abuse protection order"

(1) In this Part a "domestic abuse protection order" is an order which, for the purpose of preventing a person ("P") from being abusive towards a person aged 16 or over to whom P is personally connected—

(a) prohibits P from doing things described in the order, or

(b) requires P to do things described in the order.

(2) A domestic abuse protection order may be made—

(a) on application (see section 26), or

(b) in the course of certain proceedings (see section 29).

(3) Section 30 sets out the conditions for making a domestic abuse protection order.

26 Domestic abuse protection orders on application

(1) A court may make a domestic abuse protection order under this section against a person ("P") on an application made to it in accordance with this section.

(2) An application for an order under this section may be made by—

- (a) the person for whose protection the order is sought;
- (b) the appropriate chief officer of police (see subsection (4));
- (c) a person specified in regulations made by the Secretary of State;
- (d) any other person with the leave of the court to which the application is to be made.

(3) Where P is given a domestic abuse protection notice by a member of a relevant police force under section 20, the chief officer of police in relation to that force must apply for a domestic abuse protection order against P.

(For further provision about such applications, see section 27.)

(4) The appropriate chief officer of police is—

- (a) in a case where subsection (3) applies, the chief officer of police referred to in that subsection;
- (b) in any other case, any of the following—
  - (i) the chief officer of police of the force maintained for any police area in which P resides;
  - (ii) the chief officer of police of any other force maintained for a police area who believes that P is in that police area or is intending to come to it;
  - (iii) the Chief Constable of the British Transport Police Force;
  - (iv) the Chief Constable of the Ministry of Defence Police.

(5) An application for an order under this section must be made to the family court, except where subsection (6) or (7) applies.

(6) An application made by a chief officer of police for an order under this section must be made by complaint to a magistrates' court.

(7) In a case where—

- (a) P, and the person for whose protection the order is sought, are parties to any family or civil proceedings, and
- (b) the court would have power to make a domestic abuse protection order under section 29 in those proceedings without an application being made,

an application for an order under this section may be made in those proceedings by the person for whose protection the order is sought.

(8) Where an application is made to a magistrates' court in accordance with this section—

- (a) the magistrates' court may adjourn the hearing of the application;
- (b) on the hearing of the application, section 97 of the Magistrates' Courts Act 1980 (summons to witness and warrant for arrest) does not apply in relation to the person for whose protection the order is sought, except where the person has given oral or written evidence at the hearing.

27 Applications where domestic abuse protection notice has been given

(1) This section applies where, as a result of a person ("P") being given a domestic abuse protection notice under section 20, a chief officer of police is required by section 26(3) to apply for a domestic abuse protection order against P.

(2) The application must be heard by the magistrates' court not later than 48 hours after the notice was given to P.

(3) In calculating when the period of 48 hours mentioned in subsection (2) ends, the following days are to be disregarded—

- (a) any Sunday,
- (b) Christmas Day,
- (c) Good Friday, and
- (d) any day which is a bank holiday in England and Wales under the Banking and Financial Dealings Act 1971.

(4) P must be given a notice of the hearing of the application.

(5) The notice under subsection (4) is to be treated as having been given if it has been left at the address given by P under section 23(4).

(6) But if the notice has not been given because P did not give an address under section 23(4), the court may hear the application if satisfied that the chief officer of police has made reasonable efforts to give P the notice.

(7) If the court adjourns the hearing of the application, the domestic abuse protection notice continues in effect until the application has been determined or withdrawn.

(8) If—

- (a) P is brought before the court at the hearing of the application as a result of P's arrest by virtue of section 24(1) (arrest for breach of domestic abuse protection notice), and
- (b) the court adjourns the hearing,

the court may remand P.

28 Remand under section 27(8) of person arrested for breach of notice

(1) This section applies where—

- (a) as a result of a person being given a domestic abuse protection notice under section 20, a chief officer of police has applied for a domestic abuse protection order against the person, and
- (b) the magistrates' court remands the person under section 27(8).

(2) In the application of section 128(6) of the Magistrates' Courts Act 1980 to such remand, the reference to the "other party" is to be read as a reference to the chief officer of police who applied for the order.

(3) If the court has reason to suspect that a medical report will be required, the power to remand the person may be exercised for the purpose of enabling a medical examination to take place and a report to be made.

(4) If the person is remanded in custody for that purpose, the adjournment may not be for more than 3 weeks at a time.

(5) If the person is remanded on bail for that purpose, the adjournment may not be for more than 4 weeks at a time.

(6) If the court has reason to suspect that the person is suffering from mental disorder within the meaning of the Mental Health Act 1983, the court has the same power to make an order under section 35 of that Act (remand to hospital for report on accused's mental condition) as it has under that section in the case of an accused person (within the meaning of that section).

(7) The court may, when remanding the person on bail, require the person to comply, before release on bail or later, with any requirements that appear to the court to be necessary to secure that the person does not interfere with witnesses or otherwise obstruct the course of justice.

29 Domestic abuse protection orders otherwise than on application

(1) A court may make a domestic abuse protection order under this section in any of the cases set out below.

Family proceedings

(2) The High Court or the family court may make a domestic abuse protection order against a person ("P") in any family proceedings to which both P and the person for whose protection the order would be made are parties.

Criminal proceedings

(3) Where a person ("P") has been convicted of an offence, the court dealing with P for that offence may (as well as sentencing P or dealing with P in any other way) make a domestic abuse protection order against P.

(4) But subsection (3) does not apply where the Court of Appeal is dealing with a person for an offence.

(5) A court by or before which a person is acquitted of an offence may make a domestic abuse protection order against the person.

(6) Where the Crown Court allows a person's appeal against a conviction for an offence, the Crown Court may make a domestic abuse protection order against the person.

Civil proceedings

(7) The county court may make a domestic abuse protection order against a person ("P") in any relevant proceedings to which both P and the person for whose protection the order would be made are parties.

(8) In subsection (7) "relevant proceedings" means proceedings of a description specified in regulations made by the Secretary of State.

30 Conditions for making an order

(1) The court may make a domestic abuse protection order under section 26 or 29 against a person ("P") if conditions A and B are met.

(2) Condition A is that the court is satisfied on the balance of probabilities that P has been abusive towards a person aged 16 or over to whom P is personally connected.

(3) Condition B is that the order is necessary and proportionate to protect that person from domestic abuse, or the risk of domestic abuse, carried out by P.

(4) It does not matter—

- (a) whether the abusive behaviour referred to in subsection (2) took place in England and Wales or elsewhere, or
- (b) whether it took place before or after the coming into force of this section.

(5) A domestic abuse protection order may not be made against a person who is under the age of 18.

31 Matters to be considered before making an order

(1) Before making a domestic abuse protection order against a person ("P"), the court must, among other things, consider the following—

- (a) the welfare of any person under the age of 18 whose interests the court considers relevant to the making of the order (whether or not that person and P are personally connected);
- (b) any opinion of the person for whose protection the order would be made—
  - (i) which relates to the making of the order, and
  - (ii) of which the court is made aware;
- (c) in a case where the order includes provision relating to premises lived in by the person for whose protection the order would be made, any opinion of a relevant occupant—
  - (i) which relates to the making of the order, and
  - (ii) of which the court is made aware.

(2) In subsection (1)(c) "relevant occupant" means a person other than P or the person for whose protection the order would be made—

- (a) who lives in the premises, and
- (b) who is personally connected to—
  - (i) the person for whose protection the order would be made, or
  - (ii) if P also lives in the premises, P.

(3) It is not necessary for the person for whose protection a domestic abuse protection order is made to consent to the making of the order.

32 Making of orders without notice

(1) A court may, in any case where it is just and convenient to do so, make a domestic abuse protection order against a person ("P") even though P has not been given such notice of the proceedings as would otherwise be required by rules of court.

(2) Subsection (1) does not apply in relation to the making of an order under section 26 on an application made in accordance with subsection (3) of that section (see instead section 27(4) to (6)).

(3) In deciding whether to exercise its powers under subsection (1), the court must have regard to all the circumstances, including—

- (a) any risk that, if the order is not made immediately, P will cause significant harm to the person for whose protection the order would be made,
- (b) in a case where an application for the order has been made, whether it is likely that the person making the application will be deterred or prevented from pursuing the application if an order is not made immediately, and
- (c) whether there is reason to believe that—
  - (i) P is aware of the proceedings but is deliberately evading service, and
  - (ii) the delay involved in effecting substituted service will cause serious prejudice to the person for whose protection the order would be made.

(4) If a court makes an order against a person by virtue of subsection (1), it must give the person an opportunity to make representations about the order—

- (a) as soon as just and convenient, and
- (b) at a hearing of which notice has been given to all the parties in accordance with rules of court.

33 Provision that may be made by orders

(1) A court may by a domestic abuse protection order impose any requirements that the court considers necessary to protect the person for whose protection the order is made from domestic abuse or the risk of domestic abuse.

"Requirement" includes any prohibition or restriction.

(2) The court must, in particular, consider what requirements (if any) may be necessary to protect the person for whose protection the order is made from different kinds of abusive behaviour.

(3) Subsections (4) to (6) contain examples of the type of provision that may be made under subsection (1), but they do not limit the type of provision that may be so made.

(4) A domestic abuse protection order may provide that the person against whom the order is made ("P")—

- (a) may not contact the person for whose protection it is made;
- (b) may not come within a specified distance of any premises in England or Wales in which that person lives.

  "Specified" means specified in the order.

(5) If P lives in premises in England or Wales in which the person for whose protection the order is made also lives, the order may contain provision—

- (a) prohibiting P from evicting or excluding that person from the premises;
- (b) prohibiting P from entering the premises;
- (c) requiring P to leave the premises.

(6) A domestic abuse protection order may require P to submit to electronic monitoring in England and Wales of P's compliance with other requirements imposed by the order.

In this Part a requirement imposed by virtue of this subsection is referred to as an "electronic monitoring requirement".

(7) Sections 34 and 35 contain further provision about the requirements that may be imposed by a domestic abuse protection order.

34 Further provision about requirements that may be imposed by orders

(1) Requirements imposed on a person by a domestic abuse protection order must, so far as practicable, be such as to avoid—

- (a) conflict with the person's religious beliefs;
- (b) interference with any times at which the person normally works or attends an educational establishment;
- (c) conflict with the requirements of any other court order or injunction to which the person may be subject.

(2) A domestic abuse protection order that imposes a requirement to do something on a person ("P") must specify the person who is to be responsible for supervising compliance with that requirement.

(3) Before including such a requirement in a domestic abuse protection order, the court must receive evidence about its suitability and enforceability from the person to be specified under subsection (2).

(4) Subsections (2) and (3) do not apply in relation to electronic monitoring requirements (see instead section 35(3) to (6)).

(5) It is the duty of a person specified under subsection (2)—

- (a) to make any necessary arrangements in connection with the requirements for which the person has responsibility (the "relevant requirements");
- (b) to promote P's compliance with the relevant requirements;
- (c) if the person considers that—
  - (i) P has complied with all the relevant requirements, or
  - (ii) P has failed to comply with a relevant requirement,

to inform the appropriate chief officer of police.

(6) In subsection (5)(c) the "appropriate chief officer of police" means—

- (a) the chief officer of police of the force maintained for the police area in which it appears to the person specified under subsection (2) that P resides,
- (b) if it appears to that person that P resides in more than one police area, whichever one of the relevant chief officers of police the person thinks it most appropriate to inform, or
- (c) if it appears to the person specified under subsection (2) that P does not reside in any police area, the chief officer of police of the force maintained for the police area in which the court that made the order is situated.

(7) A person ("P") who is subject to a requirement imposed by a domestic abuse protection order—

- (a) must keep in touch with the person specified under subsection (2) in relation to that requirement, in accordance with any instructions given by that person from time to time;
- (b) if P changes home address, must notify the person specified under subsection (2) of the new home address;
- (c) if P ceases to have any home address, must notify the person specified under subsection (2) of that fact.

These obligations have effect as requirements of the order.

35 Further provision about electronic monitoring requirements

(1) Subsections (2) to (4) apply for the purpose of determining whether a court may impose an electronic monitoring requirement on a person ("P") in a domestic abuse protection order.

(2) The requirement may not be imposed in P's absence.

(3) If there is a person (other than P) without whose co-operation it would be impracticable to secure the monitoring in question, the requirement may not be imposed without that person's consent.

(4) The court may impose the requirement only if—

(a) it has been notified by the Secretary of State that electronic monitoring arrangements are available in the relevant area, and
(b) it is satisfied that the necessary provision can be made under the arrangements currently available.

(5) In subsection (4)(a) "the relevant area" means—
(a) the local justice area in which it appears to the court that P resides or will reside, and
(b) in a case where it is proposed to include in the order—
(i) a requirement that P must remain, for specified periods, at a specified place, or
(ii) a provision prohibiting P from entering a specified place or area,
the local justice area in which the place or area proposed to be specified is situated.
"Specified" means specified in the order.

(6) A domestic abuse protection order that includes an electronic monitoring requirement must specify the person who is to be responsible for the monitoring.

(7) The person specified under subsection (6) ("the responsible person") must be of a description specified in regulations made by the Secretary of State.

(8) Where a domestic abuse protection order imposes an electronic monitoring requirement on a person, the person must (among other things)—
(a) submit, as required from time to time by the responsible person, to—
(i) being fitted with, or the installation of, any necessary apparatus, and
(ii) the inspection or repair of any apparatus fitted or installed for the purposes of the monitoring,
(b) not interfere with, or with the working of, any apparatus fitted or installed for the purposes of the monitoring, and
(c) take any steps required by the responsible person for the purpose of keeping in working order any apparatus fitted or installed for the purposes of the monitoring.

These obligations have effect as requirements of the order.

36 Duration and geographical application of orders

(1) A domestic abuse protection order takes effect on the day on which it is made. This is subject to subsection (2).

(2) If, on the day on which a domestic abuse protection order ("the new order") is made against a person, the person is subject to another domestic abuse protection order ("the previous order"), the new order may be made so as to take effect on the previous order ceasing to have effect.

(3) A domestic abuse protection order has effect—
(a) for a specified period,
(b) until the occurrence of a specified event, or
(c) until further order.

"Specified" means specified in the order.

(4) A domestic abuse protection order may also specify periods for which particular requirements imposed by the order have effect.

(5) But a domestic abuse protection order may not provide for an electronic monitoring requirement to have effect for more than 12 months.

(6) Subsection (5) is subject to any variation of the order under section 42.

(7) A requirement imposed by a domestic abuse protection order has effect in all parts of the United Kingdom unless expressly limited to a particular locality.

37 Breach of order

(1) A person who is subject to a domestic abuse protection order commits an offence if without reasonable excuse the person fails to comply with any requirement imposed by the order.

(2) In a case where the order was made against the person without that person being given notice of the proceedings, the person commits an offence under this section only in respect of behaviour engaged in at a time when the person was aware of the existence of the order.

(See also section 43(8) and (9), which makes similar provision where an order has been varied.)

(3) Where a person is convicted of an offence under this section in respect of any behaviour, that behaviour is not punishable as a contempt of court.

(4) A person may not be convicted of an offence under this section in respect of any behaviour which has been punished as a contempt of court.

(5) A person guilty of an offence under this section is liable—

- (a) on summary conviction—
  - (i) to imprisonment for a term not exceeding 12 months (or 6 months, if the offence was committed before the coming into force of paragraph 24(2) of Schedule 22 to the Sentencing Act 2020), or
  - (ii) to a fine,

  or both;
- (b) on conviction on indictment, to imprisonment for a term not exceeding 5 years or to a fine, or both.

(6) If a person is convicted of an offence under this section, it is not open to the court by or before which the person is convicted to make, in respect of the offence, an order under section 80 of the Sentencing Code (conditional discharge).

(7) If a person is convicted of an offence under section 42 of the Armed Forces Act 2006 as respects which the corresponding offence under the law of England and Wales (within the meaning given by that section) is an offence under this section, it is not open to the service court that convicted the person to make, in respect of the offence, an order under section 185 of that Act (conditional discharge).

In this subsection "service court" means the Court Martial or the Service Civilian Court.

(8) In proceedings for an offence under this section, a copy of the original domestic abuse protection order, certified by the proper officer of the court that made it, is admissible as evidence of its having been made and of its contents to the same extent that oral evidence of those matters is admissible in those proceedings.

38 Arrest for breach of order

(1) This section applies where a relevant court has made a domestic abuse protection order against a person ("P").

(2) In this section "relevant court" means—

- (a) the High Court,
- (b) the family court, or
- (c) the county court.

(3) A person mentioned in subsection (4) may apply to the relevant judge for the issue of a warrant for P's arrest if the person considers that P has failed to comply with the order or is otherwise in contempt of court in relation to the order.

(4) The persons referred to in subsection (3) are—

- (a) the person for whose protection the order was made;
- (b) where the order was made under section 26, the person who applied for the order (if different);
- (c) any other person with the leave of the relevant judge.

(5) The relevant judge may issue a warrant on an application under subsection (3) only if—

(a) the application is substantiated on oath, and

(b) the relevant judge has reasonable grounds for believing that P has failed to comply with the order or is otherwise in contempt of court in relation to the order.

(6) If—

(a) P is brought before a relevant court as a result of a warrant issued under this section, and

(b) the court does not immediately dispose of the matter,

the court may remand P.

(7) Schedule 1 contains further provision about remand under this section.

(8) In this section "the relevant judge" means—

(a) where the order was made by the High Court, a judge of that court;

(b) where the order was made by the family court, a judge of that court;

(c) where the order was made by the county court, a judge of that court.

(9) For the power of a constable to arrest P without warrant for breach of a domestic abuse protection order, see section 24 of the Police and Criminal Evidence Act 1984.

39 Notification requirements

(1) Subsections (2) to (6) apply where a person is subject to a domestic abuse protection order.

(2) The person must, within the period of three days beginning with the day on which the order is made, notify the police of the information in subsection (3).

(3) The information referred to in subsection (2) is—

(a) the person's name and, if the person uses one or more other names, each of those names;

(b) the person's home address.

(4) If the person uses a name which has not been notified under this section, the person must, within the period of three days beginning with the day on which the person first uses that name, notify the police of that name.

(5) If the person changes home address, the person must, before the end of the period of three days beginning with the day on which that happens, notify the police of the new home address.

(6) If the person ceases to have any home address, the person must, before the end of the period of three days beginning with the day on which that happens, notify the police of that fact.

(7) The Secretary of State may by regulations specify further notification requirements which a court may impose when making or varying a domestic abuse protection order.

In this subsection a "notification requirement" is a requirement for the person against whom the order is made to provide specified information to the police.

(8) The requirements imposed by subsections (2) to (6) do not apply where—

(a) the person is subject to another domestic abuse protection order (and accordingly those requirements already apply), or

(b) the person is subject to notification requirements under Part 2 of the Sexual Offences Act 2003 or section 9 of the Stalking Protection Act 2019.

(9) If on any day the person ceases to be subject to any notification requirements as mentioned in subsection (8)(a) or (b), the requirements imposed by subsections (2) to (6) apply to the person on and after that day, but as if the reference in subsection (2) to the day on which the order was made were a reference to that day.

(10) For provision about how to give a notification under subsection (2), (4), (5) or (6), see section 40.

40 Further provision about notification under section 39

(1) A person gives a notification under section 39(2), (4), (5) or (6) by—

(a) attending at a police station in the appropriate police area, and

(b) giving an oral notification to—

(i) a police officer, or

(ii) any person authorised for the purpose by the officer in charge of the station.

(2) In subsection (1) "the appropriate police area", in relation to a person, means—

(a) if the person's home address is in England and Wales, the police area in which that home address is situated;

(b) if the person does not have a home address in England and Wales, the police area in which the court that last made a domestic abuse protection order against the person is situated.

(3) In a case of a person giving a notification under section 39(5), any reference in subsection (2) to the person's home address is a reference to the person's home address at the time of giving the notification.

(4) A notification given in accordance with this section must be acknowledged—

(a) in writing, and

(b) in the form directed by the Secretary of State.

(5) When a person ("P") gives a notification under section 39, P must, if requested to do so by the person to whom notification is given, allow that person to do any of the following things—

(a) take P's fingerprints;

(b) photograph, or otherwise produce an image of, P or any part of P.

(6) The power in subsection (5) is exercisable for the purpose of verifying P's identity.

41 Offences relating to notification

(1) A person ("P") commits an offence if P—

(a) fails, without reasonable excuse, to comply with a requirement imposed by or under section 39, or

(b) notifies the police, in purported compliance with such a requirement, of any information which P knows to be false.

(2) A person who fails, without reasonable excuse, to comply with section 40(5) commits an offence.

(3) A person guilty of an offence under subsection (1) or (2) is liable—

(a) on summary conviction—

(i) to imprisonment for a period not exceeding 12 months (or 6 months, if the offence was committed before the coming into force of paragraph 24(2) of Schedule 22 to the Sentencing Act 2020), or

(ii) to a fine,

or both;

(b) on conviction on indictment, to imprisonment for a term not exceeding 5 years or to a fine, or both.

(4) A person commits an offence under subsection (1)(a) on the day on which the person first fails, without reasonable excuse, to comply with a requirement imposed by or under section 39.

(5) The person continues to commit the offence throughout any period during which the failure continues.

(6) But the person may not be prosecuted more than once in respect of the same failure.

42 Variation and discharge of orders

(1) A court may vary or discharge a domestic abuse protection order made by that or any other court.

This is subject to section 43.

(2) A court may vary or discharge a domestic abuse protection order under this section—

(a) on the application of a person mentioned in subsection (3), or

(b) in any case in which it could make a domestic abuse protection order under section 29.

(3) The persons referred to in subsection (2)(a) are—

(a) the person for whose protection the order was made;

(b) the person against whom the order was made ("P");

(c) where the order was made under section 26, the person who applied for the order;

(d) the chief officer of police of the force maintained for any police area in which P resides;

(e) the chief officer of police of any other force maintained for a police area who believes that P is in that police area or is intending to come to it.

(4) Before deciding whether to vary or discharge an order under this section, the court must hear from—

(a) any relevant chief officer of police who wishes to be heard, and

(b) in a case where the person for whose protection the order was made is seeking to discharge the order, or to remove or make less onerous any requirement imposed by the order, the person for whose protection it was made.

(5) For the purposes of subsection (4)(a) each of the following is a "relevant chief officer of police"—

(a) where the order was made on an application by a chief officer of police, that chief officer;

(b) the chief officer of police of the force maintained for any police area in which P resides;

(c) the chief officer of police of any other force maintained for a police area who believes that P is in that police area or is intending to come to it.

(6) Section 31 (matters to be considered before making an order) applies in relation to the variation or discharge of a domestic abuse protection order as it applies in relation to the making of such an order, but as if references to the person for whose protection the order would be made were references to the person for whose protection the order was made.

(7) Section 32 (making of orders without notice) applies in relation to the variation of a domestic abuse protection order as it applies in relation to the making of such an order, but as if—

(a) references to the person for whose protection the order would be made were references to the person for whose protection the order was made,

(b) subsection (2) were omitted, and

(c) the reference in subsection (4) to making representations about the order were a reference to making representations about the variation.

(8) The court may make any order varying or discharging a domestic abuse protection order that it considers appropriate.

This is subject to subsections (9) to (13).

(9) The court may include an additional requirement in the order, or extend the period for which the order, or a requirement imposed by the order, has effect, only if it is satisfied that it is necessary to do so in order to protect the person for whose protection the order was made from domestic abuse, or the risk of domestic abuse, carried out by P.

(10) The court may not extend the period for which an electronic monitoring requirement has effect by more than 12 months at a time.

(11) The court may remove any requirement imposed by the order, or make such a requirement less onerous, only if satisfied that the requirement as imposed is no longer necessary to protect the person for whose protection the order was made from domestic abuse, or the risk of domestic abuse, carried out by P.

(12) If it appears to the court that any conditions necessary for a requirement to be imposed are no longer met, the court—

- (a) may not extend the requirement, and
- (b) must remove the requirement.

(13) The court may discharge the order only if satisfied that the order is no longer necessary to protect the person for whose protection it was made from domestic abuse, or the risk of domestic abuse, carried out by P.

43 Variation and discharge: supplementary

(1) Any application to vary or discharge a domestic abuse protection order under section 42 must be made to the court that made the order.

This is subject to subsections (2) and (3).

(2) Where the order was made by a magistrates' court, an application to vary or discharge the order may be made to any other magistrates' court acting in the local justice area in which that court acts.

(3) Where—

- (a) the order was made under section 29 on an appeal in relation to a person's conviction or sentence for an offence, or
- (b) the order was made by a court under that section against a person committed or remitted to that court for sentencing for an offence,

any application to vary or discharge the order must be made to the court by or before which the person was convicted (but see subsection (4)).

(4) Where the person mentioned in subsection (3)(b) was convicted by a youth court, the reference in subsection (3) to the court by or before which the person was convicted is to be read as a reference to a magistrates' court acting in the local justice area in which the youth court acts.

(5) Except as provided for by subsection (3), a domestic abuse protection order made by the Crown Court may be varied or discharged under section 42 only by the Crown Court.

(6) A domestic abuse protection order made by the High Court may be varied or discharged under section 42 only by the High Court.

(7) An order that has been varied under section 42 remains an order of the court that first made it for the purposes of any further application under that section.

(8) Subsection (9) applies in a case where—

- (a) an order made against a person is varied under section 42 so as to include an additional requirement, or to extend the period for which the order, or a requirement imposed by the order, has effect, and
- (b) the person was not given notice of the proceedings.

(9) The person commits an offence under section 37 only if—

- (a) the behaviour constituting the offence was engaged in at a time when the person was aware of the making of the variation, and
- (b) the behaviour would not have constituted an offence under that section in the absence of the variation.

44 Appeals

(1) A person listed in subsection (2) may appeal against any decision of a court on an application for a domestic abuse protection order under section 26 (to the extent that it would not otherwise be so appealable).

(2) The persons referred to in subsection (1) are—

(a) the person for whose protection the order was sought,

(b) the person who applied for the order (if different), and

(c) where the court made a domestic abuse protection order under section 26, the person against whom it was made.

(3) A person against whom a domestic abuse protection order is made under subsection (3), (5) or (6) of section 29 may appeal against the making of the order (to the extent it would not otherwise be so appealable) as if it were a sentence passed on the person for the offence referred to in that subsection (assuming, in a case within section 29(5) or (6), that the person had been convicted of the offence).

(4) A person against whom a domestic abuse protection order is made may appeal against a variation of the order under section 42 that is made in a case within subsection (3), (5) or (6) of section 29 (to the extent it would not otherwise be so appealable) as if the varied order were a sentence passed on the person for the offence referred to in that subsection (assuming, in a case within section 29(5) or (6), that the person had been convicted of the offence).

(5) A person listed in subsection (6) may appeal against any decision of a court under section 42 in relation to a domestic abuse protection order (to the extent it would not otherwise be so appealable, whether under subsection (4) or otherwise).

(6) The persons referred to in subsection (5) are—

(a) the person for whose protection the order was made;

(b) the person against whom the order was made ("P");

(c) where the order was made under section 26, the person who applied for the order;

(d) the chief officer of police of the force maintained for any police area in which P resides;

(e) the chief officer of police of any other force maintained for a police area who believes that P is in that police area or is intending to come to it.

(7) An appeal arising by virtue of subsection (1) or (5)—

(a) in the case of a decision made by a magistrates' court, is to be made to the Crown Court;

(b) in the case of a decision made by the Crown Court, is to be made to the Court of Appeal.

For the powers of the Crown Court or Court of Appeal on such an appeal, see section 45(4).

(8) If, in the case of an appeal arising by virtue of subsection (1) or (5) in respect of a decision made by the High Court, the family court or the county court, the person making the appeal was not a party to the proceedings in that court, the person is to be treated for the purposes of that appeal as if the person had been a party to those proceedings.

(9) For further provision about appeals, see (in particular)—

(a) section 31K of the Matrimonial and Family Proceedings Act 1984 (appeals from the family court),

(b) section 16(1) of the Senior Courts Act 1981 (appeals from the High Court),

(c) section 77 of the County Courts Act 1984 (appeals from the county court),

(d) section 108(3) of the Magistrates' Courts Act 1980 (appeals against orders made on conviction in a magistrates' court),

(e) section 50(1) of the Criminal Appeal Act 1968 (appeals against orders made on conviction in the Crown Court), and

(f) rules of court.

45 Further provision about appeals

(1) Before determining any appeal relating to a domestic abuse protection order (whether or not an appeal under section 44), the court must hear from any relevant chief officer of police who wishes to be heard.

(2) For the purposes of subsection (1) each of the following is a "relevant chief officer of police"—

- (a) where the order was made on an application by a chief officer of police, that chief officer;
- (b) the chief officer of police of the force maintained for any police area in which the person ("P") against whom the order was made, or (in the case of an appeal against the decision of a court not to make an order under section 26) against whom it was sought, resides;
- (c) the chief officer of police of any other force maintained for a police area who believes that P is in that police area or is intending to come to it.

(3) Subsection (4) applies to—

- (a) an appeal made to the Crown Court by virtue of section 44(7)(a);
- (b) an appeal made to the Court of Appeal by virtue of section 44(7)(b).

(4) On an appeal to which this subsection applies, the court may, on a review of the decision appealed against—

- (a) confirm, vary or revoke any part of the decision;
- (b) refer the matter back to the court that made the decision with a direction to reconsider and make a new decision in accordance with its ruling;
- (c) make any order which the court that made the decision appealed against could have made;
- (d) make any incidental or consequential orders that appear to it to be just.

(5) For the purposes of section 43 (variation and discharge: supplementary)—

- (a) a domestic abuse protection order that has been confirmed or varied on an appeal (whether under subsection (4)(a) or otherwise) remains an order of the court that first made it, and
- (b) a domestic abuse protection order made by a court on an appeal (whether under subsection (4)(c) or otherwise) is to be treated as an order made by the court whose decision was appealed against.

46 Nature of certain proceedings under this Part

(1) Proceedings before a court arising by virtue of section 29(3), (5) or (6), and proceedings before a court arising by virtue of section 42(2)(b) in any case within section 29(3), (5) or (6), are civil proceedings (like proceedings before a magistrates' court under section 26 or 42(2)(a)).

(2) The court is not restricted in the proceedings to considering evidence that would have been admissible in the criminal proceedings in which the person concerned was convicted or (as the case may be) acquitted.

(3) The court may adjourn any proceedings arising by virtue of section 29(3), (5) or (6), or any proceedings arising by virtue of section 42(2)(b) in any case within section 29(3), (5) or (6), even after sentencing or acquitting the person concerned or allowing the person's appeal.

(4) A domestic abuse protection order may be made or varied in addition to an order discharging the person conditionally or absolutely in spite of anything in sections 79, 80 and 82 of the Sentencing Code (which relate to orders discharging a person conditionally or absolutely and their effect).

47 Special measures for witnesses

(1) Chapter 1 of Part 2 of the Youth Justice and Criminal Evidence Act 1999 (special measures directions in case of vulnerable and intimidated witnesses) applies to relevant proceedings under this Part as it applies to criminal proceedings, but with—

(a) the omission of the provisions of that Act mentioned in subsection (2) (which make provision only in the context of criminal proceedings), and

(b) any other necessary modifications.

(2) The provisions are—

(a) section 17(4) to (7);

(b) section 21(4C)(e);

(c) section 22A;

(d) section 32.

(3) Rules of court made under or for the purposes of Chapter 1 of Part 2 of that Act apply to relevant proceedings under this Part—

(a) to the extent provided by rules of court, and

(b) subject to any modifications provided by rules of court.

(4) Section 47 of that Act (restrictions on reporting special measures directions etc) applies with any necessary modifications—

(a) to a direction under section 19 of that Act as applied by this section;

(b) to a direction discharging or varying such a direction.

Sections 49 and 51 of that Act (offences) apply accordingly.

(5) In this section "relevant proceedings under this Part" means—

(a) proceedings under section 26, 29(2) or (7), 38 or 42(2)(a);

(b) proceedings arising by virtue of section 29(3), (5) or (6);

(c) proceedings arising by virtue of section 42(2)(b) in any case within section 29(3), (5) or (6);

(d) proceedings on an appeal relating to a domestic abuse protection order (whether or not an appeal under section 44).

Notices and orders: supplementary

48 Guidance

(1) The Secretary of State must issue guidance relating to the exercise by relevant persons of functions under or by virtue of this Part.

(2) In this section "relevant person" means—

(a) a constable;

(b) a person specified in regulations under subsection (2)(c) of section 26 for the purpose of making applications for orders under that section.

(3) A relevant person must have regard to any guidance issued under this section when exercising a function to which the guidance relates.

(4) The Secretary of State may from time to time revise any guidance issued under this section.

(5) Before issuing or revising guidance under this section, the Secretary of State must consult—

(a) the Domestic Abuse Commissioner, and

(b) such other persons as the Secretary of State considers appropriate.

(6) Subsection (5) does not apply in relation to any revisions of guidance issued under this section if the Secretary of State considers the proposed revisions of the guidance are insubstantial.

(7) The Secretary of State must publish—

(a) any guidance issued under this section, and

(b) any revisions of that guidance.

49 Data from electronic monitoring: code of practice

(1) The Secretary of State must issue a code of practice relating to the processing of data gathered in the course of electronic monitoring of individuals under electronic monitoring requirements imposed by domestic abuse protection orders.

(2) A failure to act in accordance with a code issued under this section does not of itself make a person liable to any criminal or civil proceedings.

50 Powers to make other orders in proceedings under this Part

(1) In section 8 of the Children Act 1989 (child arrangements orders and other orders with respect to children), in subsection (4), at the end insert—

> "(k) Part 3 of the Domestic Abuse Act 2020, where the proceedings are in the family court or the Family Division of the High Court."

(2) In Part 4 of the Family Law Act 1996 (family homes and domestic violence), in section 63(2) (definition of "family proceedings"), after paragraph (j) insert—

> "(k) Part 3 of the Domestic Abuse Act 2020, where the proceedings are in the family court or the Family Division of the High Court."

51 Proceedings not to be subject to conditional fee agreements

In section 58A of the Courts and Legal Services Act 1990 (conditional fee agreements: supplementary), in subsection (2), after paragraph (fd) (but before the "and" following it) insert—

> "(fe) proceedings under Part 3 of the Domestic Abuse Act 2020 (proceedings for domestic abuse protection order), where the proceedings are in the family court or the Family Division of the High Court;".

52 Consequential amendments of the Sentencing Code

(1) The Sentencing Code is amended as follows.

(2) In section 80 (order for conditional discharge), in subsection (3), at the end insert—

> "(f) section 37(6) (breach of domestic abuse protection order)."

(3) In Chapter 6 of Part 11 (other behaviour orders), before section 379 (but after the heading "Other orders") insert—

> **"378A Domestic abuse protection orders**
>
> See Part 3 of the Domestic Abuse Act 2020 (and in particular section 29(3) of that Act) for the power of a court to make a domestic abuse protection order when dealing with an offender for an offence."

53 Repeal of provisions about domestic violence protection notices and orders

(1) In the Crime and Security Act 2010, omit sections 24 to 33 (which make provision for domestic violence protection notices and domestic violence protection orders).

(2) In consequence of the repeal made by subsection (1), omit the following provisions—

- (a) in Schedule 8 to the Crime and Courts Act 2013, paragraph 179;
- (b) in Schedule 14 to the Policing and Crime Act 2017, paragraph 7(g).

54 Interpretation of Part 3

(1) In this Part—

"chief officer of police" means—

- (a) in relation to a police force maintained by a local policing body, the chief officer of police of that force;
- (b) in relation to the British Transport Police Force, the Chief Constable of the Force;
- (c) in relation to the Ministry of Defence Police, the Chief Constable of the Ministry of Defence Police;

"domestic abuse protection notice" has the meaning given by section 20(2);

"domestic abuse protection order" has the meaning given by section 25(1);

"electronic monitoring requirement" has the meaning given by section 33(6);

"family proceedings" means—

(a) proceedings in the family court (other than proceedings under or by virtue of this Part), and

(b) family proceedings within the meaning of Part 5 of the Matrimonial and Family Proceedings Act 1984;

"home address", in relation to a person, means—

(a) the address of the person's sole or main residence in the United Kingdom, or

(b) if the person has no such residence—

(i) the address or location of a place in the United Kingdom where the person can regularly be found;

(ii) if there is more than one such place, the address or location of whichever one of those places the person selects;

"relevant police force" has the meaning given by section 20(8);

"requirement", in relation to a domestic abuse protection order, is to be read in accordance with section 33(1);

"senior police officer" has the meaning given by section 20(8).

(2) Any reference to a member of a police force includes, in the case of a police force maintained by a local policing body, a reference to a special constable appointed by the chief officer of police of that force.

(3) Any reference to changing home address includes a reference to a case where—

(a) a person acquires a home address at any time, and

(b) immediately before that time, the person did not have a home address.

(4) See also—

(a) section 1 (definition of "domestic abuse");

(b) section 2 (definition of "personally connected").

PART 4
LOCAL AUTHORITY SUPPORT

55 Support provided by local authorities to victims of domestic abuse

(1) Each relevant local authority in England must—

(a) assess, or make arrangements for the assessment of, the need for domestic abuse support in its area,

(b) prepare and publish a strategy for the provision of such support in its area, and

(c) monitor and evaluate the effectiveness of the strategy.

(2) For the purposes of subsection (1)—

"domestic abuse support" means support, in relation to domestic abuse, provided to victims of domestic abuse, or their children, who reside in relevant accommodation;

"relevant accommodation" means accommodation of a description specified by the Secretary of State in regulations.

(3) A relevant local authority that publishes a strategy under this section must, in carrying out its functions, give effect to the strategy.

(4) Before publishing a strategy under this section, a relevant local authority must consult—

(a) the domestic abuse local partnership board appointed by the relevant local authority under section 56,

(b) any local authority for an area within the relevant local authority's area, and

(c) such other persons as the relevant local authority considers appropriate.

(5) A relevant local authority that publishes a strategy under this section—

(a) must keep the strategy under review,

(b) may alter or replace the strategy, and

(c) must publish any altered or replacement strategy.

(6) A relevant local authority may request any local authority for an area within the relevant local authority's area to co-operate with it in any way that the relevant local authority considers necessary for the purposes of its functions under this section.

(7) A local authority must, so far as reasonably practicable, comply with a request made to it under subsection (6).

(8) The Secretary of State may by regulations make provision about the preparation and publication of strategies under this section.

(9) The power to make regulations under subsection (8) may, in particular, be exercised to make provision about—

(a) the procedure to be followed by a relevant local authority in preparing a strategy;

(b) matters to which a relevant local authority must have regard in preparing a strategy;

(c) how a relevant local authority must publish a strategy;

(d) the date by which a relevant local authority must first publish a strategy;

(e) the frequency with which a relevant local authority must review its strategy.

(10) Before making regulations under this section, the Secretary of State must consult—

(a) the Domestic Abuse Commissioner,

(b) relevant local authorities, and

(c) such other persons as the Secretary of State considers appropriate.

56 Domestic abuse local partnership boards

(1) A relevant local authority in England must appoint a domestic abuse local partnership board for the purposes of providing advice to the authority about the exercise of the authority's functions under section 55.

(2) The members of the domestic abuse local partnership board must include—

(a) a representative of the relevant local authority;

(b) at least one person appearing to the authority to represent the interests of local authorities for areas within its area;

(c) at least one person appearing to the authority to represent the interests of victims of domestic abuse;

(d) at least one person appearing to the authority to represent the interests of children of domestic abuse victims;

(e) at least one person appearing to the authority to represent the interests of charities and other voluntary organisations that work with victims of domestic abuse in its area;

(f) at least one person appearing to the authority to represent the interests of persons who provide, or have functions relating to, health care services in its area;

(g) at least one person appearing to the authority to represent the interests of persons with functions relating to policing or criminal justice in its area.

(3) In this section "health care services" means services relating to health care (within the meaning of section 9 of the Health and Social Care Act 2008).

57 Annual reports

(1) As soon as reasonably practicable after the end of each financial year, a relevant local authority in England must submit to the Secretary of State an annual report in relation to the exercise of the authority's functions under this Part during the year.

(2) The Secretary of State may by regulations make provision about—

(a) the form of the report, and

(b) the content of the report.

(3) In this section "financial year" means—

(a) the period beginning with the day on which this section comes into force and ending with the following 31 March, and

(b) each successive period of 12 months.

58 Guidance

(1) The Secretary of State must issue guidance relating to the exercise by local authorities in England of functions under this Part.

(2) Local authorities in England must have regard to the guidance when exercising a function to which the guidance relates.

(3) The Secretary of State may from time to time revise any guidance issued under this section.

(4) Before issuing or revising guidance under this section, the Secretary of State must consult—

(a) the Domestic Abuse Commissioner,

(b) local authorities, and

(c) such other persons as the Secretary of State considers appropriate.

(5) Subsection (4) does not apply in relation to any revisions of guidance issued under this section if the Secretary of State considers the proposed revisions of the guidance are insubstantial.

(6) The Secretary of State must publish—

(a) any guidance issued under this section, and

(b) any revisions of that guidance.

59 Interpretation of Part 4

In this Part—

"local authority" means—

(a) a relevant local authority;

(b) a district council for an area for which there is a county council;

(c) a London borough council;

(d) the Common Council of the City of London in its capacity as a local authority;

"relevant local authority" means—

(a) a county council;

(b) a district council for an area for which there is no county council;

(c) the Greater London Authority;

(d) the Council of the Isles of Scilly.

PART 5
PROTECTION FOR VICTIMS AND WITNESSES IN COURT

SPECIAL MEASURES

60 Special measures in criminal proceedings for offences involving domestic abuse

(1) Chapter 1 of Part 2 of the Youth Justice and Criminal Evidence Act 1999 (giving of evidence or information for purposes of criminal proceedings: special measures directions in case of vulnerable and intimidated witnesses) is amended as follows.

(2) In section 17 (witnesses eligible for assistance on grounds of fear or distress about testifying)—

(a) in subsection (4), for "a sexual offence or an offence under section 1 or 2 of the Modern Slavery Act 2015" substitute "an offence listed in subsection (4A)";

(b) after subsection (4) insert—

"(4A) The offences are—

(a) a sexual offence;

(b) an offence under section 1 or 2 of the Modern Slavery Act 2015;

(c) any other offence where it is alleged that the behaviour of the accused amounted to domestic abuse within the meaning of the Domestic Abuse Act 2020 (see section 1 of that Act)."

(3) In section 25(4)(a) (evidence given in private), for "a sexual offence or an offence under section 1 or 2 of the Modern Slavery Act 2015" substitute "an offence listed in section 17(4A)".

61 Special measures in family proceedings: victims of domestic abuse

(1) This section applies where rules of court provide that the court may make a special measures direction in relation to a person ("P") who is a party or witness in family proceedings.

(2) Rules of court must provide that where P is, or is at risk of being, a victim of domestic abuse carried out by a person listed in subsection (3), it is to be assumed that the following matters are likely to be diminished by reason of vulnerability—

(a) the quality of P's evidence;

(b) where P is a party to the proceedings, P's participation in the proceedings.

(3) The persons referred to in subsection (2) are—

(a) a party to the proceedings;

(b) a relative of a party to the proceedings (other than P);

(c) a witness in the proceedings.

(4) Rules of court may provide for an exception to the provision made by virtue of subsection (2) where P does not wish to be deemed to be eligible for the making of a special measures direction by virtue of that subsection.

(5) In this section—

"family proceedings" has the meaning given by section 75(3) of the Courts Act 2003;

"relative" has the meaning given by section 63(1) of the Family Law Act 1996;

"special measures" means such measures as may be specified by rules of court for the purpose of assisting a person to give evidence or participate in proceedings;

"special measures direction" means a direction by the court granting special measures.

62 Special measures in civil proceedings: victims of specified offences

(1) Rules of court must make provision enabling the court to make a special measures direction in relation to a person who is a party or witness in civil proceedings where that person is the victim, or alleged victim, of a specified offence.

(2) Rules made by virtue of subsection (1) must, in particular, provide for the court to consider—

(a) whether—

(i) the quality of the person's evidence, or

(ii) where the person is a party to the proceedings, the person's participation in the proceedings,

is likely to be diminished by reason of vulnerability, and

(b) if so, whether it is necessary to make one or more special measures directions.

(3) For the purposes of this section—
  (a) a person is the victim of a specified offence if another person has been convicted of, or given a caution for, the offence;
  (b) a person is the alleged victim of a specified offence if another person has been charged with the offence.

(4) In this section—
"civil proceedings" means—
  (a) proceedings in the county court,
  (b) proceedings in the High Court, other than—
    (i) proceedings in the Family Division of the High Court which are business assigned, by or under section 61 of (and Schedule 1 to) the Senior Courts Act 1981, to that Division of the High Court and no other, and
    (ii) proceedings in the exercise of its jurisdiction under the Extradition Act 2003, and
  (c) proceedings in the civil division of the Court of Appeal;

"special measures" means such measures as may be specified by rules of court for the purpose of assisting a person to give evidence or participate in proceedings;

"special measures direction" means a direction by the court granting special measures;

"specified offence" means an offence which is specified, or of a description specified, in regulations made by the Lord Chancellor.

PROHIBITION OF CROSS-EXAMINATION IN PERSON

63 Prohibition of cross-examination in person in family proceedings

In the Matrimonial and Family Proceedings Act 1984, after Part 4A insert—

"PART 4B
FAMILY PROCEEDINGS: PROHIBITION OF CROSS-EXAMINATION IN PERSON

31Q Prohibition of cross-examination in person: introductory

In this Part—
"family proceedings" means—
  (a) proceedings in the family court,
  (b) proceedings in the Family Division of the High Court which are business assigned, by or under section 61 of (and Schedule 1 to) the Senior Courts Act 1981, to that Division of the High Court and no other, and
  (c) proceedings in the civil division of the Court of Appeal arising out of proceedings within paragraph (a) or (b);

"witness", in relation to any proceedings, includes a party to the proceedings.

31R Prohibition of cross-examination in person: victims of offences

(1) In family proceedings, no party to the proceedings who has been convicted of or given a caution for, or is charged with, a specified offence may cross-examine in person a witness who is the victim, or alleged victim, of that offence.

(2) In family proceedings, no party to the proceedings who is the victim, or alleged victim, of a specified offence may cross-examine in person a witness who has been convicted of or given a caution for, or is charged with, that offence.

(3) Subsections (1) and (2) do not apply to a conviction or caution that is spent for the purposes of the Rehabilitation of Offenders Act 1974, unless evidence in

relation to the conviction or caution is admissible in, or may be required in, the proceedings by virtue of section 7(2), (3) or (4) of that Act.

(4) Cross-examination in breach of subsection (1) or (2) does not affect the validity of a decision of the court in the proceedings if the court was not aware of the conviction, caution or charge when the cross-examination took place.

(5) In this section—

"caution" means—

(a) in the case of England and Wales—

(i) a conditional caution given under section 22 of the Criminal Justice Act 2003,

(ii) a youth conditional caution given under section 66A of the Crime and Disorder Act 1998, or

(iii) any other caution given to a person in England and Wales in respect of an offence which, at the time the caution is given, the person has admitted;

(b) in the case of Scotland, anything corresponding to a caution falling within paragraph (a) (however described) which is given to a person in respect of an offence under the law of Scotland;

(c) in the case of Northern Ireland—

(i) a conditional caution given under section 71 of the Justice Act (Northern Ireland) 2011, or

(ii) any other caution given to a person in Northern Ireland in respect of an offence which, at the time the caution is given, the person has admitted;

"conviction" means—

(a) a conviction before a court in England and Wales, Scotland or Northern Ireland;

(b) a conviction in service disciplinary proceedings (in England and Wales, Scotland, Northern Ireland, or elsewhere);

(c) a finding in any criminal proceedings (including a finding linked with a finding of insanity) that the person concerned has committed an offence or done the act or made the omission charged;

and "convicted" is to be read accordingly;

"service disciplinary proceedings" means—

(a) any proceedings (whether or not before a court) in respect of a service offence within the meaning of the Armed Forces Act 2006 (except proceedings before a civilian court within the meaning of that Act);

(b) any proceedings under the Army Act 1955, the Air Force Act 1955, or the Naval Discipline Act 1957 (whether before a court-martial or before any other court or person authorised under any of those Acts to award a punishment in respect of an offence);

(c) any proceedings before a Standing Civilian Court established under the Armed Forces Act 1976;

"specified offence" means an offence which is specified, or of a description specified, in regulations made by the Lord Chancellor.

(6) The following provisions (which deem a conviction of a person discharged not to be a conviction) do not apply for the purposes of this section to a conviction of a person for an offence in respect of which an order has been made discharging the person absolutely or conditionally—

(a) section 14 of the Powers of Criminal Courts (Sentencing) Act 2000;

(b) section 80 of the Sentencing Code;

(c) section 187 of the Armed Forces Act 2006 or any corresponding earlier enactment.

(7) For the purposes of this section "offence" includes an offence under a law that is no longer in force.

31S Prohibition of cross-examination in person: persons protected by injunctions etc

(1) In family proceedings, no party to the proceedings against whom an on-notice protective injunction is in force may cross-examine in person a witness who is protected by the injunction.

(2) In family proceedings, no party to the proceedings who is protected by an on-notice protective injunction may cross-examine in person a witness against whom the injunction is in force.

(3) Cross-examination in breach of subsection (1) or (2) does not affect the validity of a decision of the court in the proceedings if the court was not aware of the protective injunction when the cross-examination took place.

(4) In this section "protective injunction" means an order, injunction or interdict specified, or of a description specified, in regulations made by the Lord Chancellor.

(5) For the purposes of this section, a protective injunction is an "on-notice" protective injunction if—

- (a) the court is satisfied that there has been a hearing at which the person against whom the protective injunction is in force asked, or could have asked, for the injunction to be set aside or varied, or
- (b) the protective injunction was made at a hearing of which the court is satisfied that both the person who applied for it and the person against whom it is in force had notice.

31T Prohibition of cross-examination in person: evidence of domestic abuse

(1) In family proceedings, where specified evidence is adduced that a person who is a witness has been the victim of domestic abuse carried out by a party to the proceedings, that party to the proceedings may not cross-examine the witness in person.

(2) In family proceedings, where specified evidence is adduced that a person who is a party to the proceedings has been the victim of domestic abuse carried out by a witness, that party may not cross-examine the witness in person.

(3) In this section—

"domestic abuse" has the meaning given by section 1 of the Domestic Abuse Act 2020;

"specified evidence" means evidence specified, or of a description specified, in regulations made by the Lord Chancellor.

(4) Regulations under subsection (3) may provide that any evidence which satisfies the court that domestic abuse, or domestic abuse of a specified description, has occurred is specified evidence for the purposes of this section.

31U Direction for prohibition of cross-examination in person: other cases

(1) In family proceedings, the court may give a direction prohibiting a party to the proceedings from cross-examining (or continuing to cross-examine) a witness in person if—

- (a) none of sections 31R to 31T operates to prevent the party from cross-examining the witness, and
- (b) it appears to the court that—
  - (i) the quality condition or the significant distress condition is met, and
  - (ii) it would not be contrary to the interests of justice to give the direction.

(2) The "quality condition" is met if the quality of evidence given by the witness on cross-examination—

- (a) is likely to be diminished if the cross-examination (or continued cross-examination) is conducted by the party in person, and
- (b) would be likely to be improved if a direction were given under this section.

(3) The "significant distress condition" is met if—

- (a) the cross-examination (or continued cross-examination) of the witness by the party in person would be likely to cause significant distress to the witness or the party, and
- (b) that distress is likely to be more significant than would be the case if the witness were cross-examined other than by the party in person.

(4) A direction under this section may be made by the court—

- (a) on an application made by a party to the proceedings, or
- (b) of its own motion.

(5) In determining whether the quality condition or the significant distress condition is met in the case of a witness or party, the court must have regard to, among other things—

- (a) any views expressed by the witness as to whether or not the witness is content to be cross-examined by the party in person;
- (b) any views expressed by the party as to whether or not the party is content to cross-examine the witness in person;
- (c) the nature of the questions likely to be asked, having regard to the issues in the proceedings;
- (d) any behaviour by the party in relation to the witness in respect of which the court is aware that a finding of fact has been made in the proceedings or in any other proceedings;
- (e) any behaviour by the witness in relation to the party in respect of which the court is aware that a finding of fact has been made in the proceedings or in any other proceedings;
- (f) any behaviour by the party at any stage of the proceedings, both generally and in relation to the witness;
- (g) any behaviour by the witness at any stage of the proceedings, both generally and in relation to the party;
- (h) any relationship (of whatever nature) between the witness and the party.

(6) Any reference in this section to the quality of a witness's evidence is to its quality in terms of completeness, coherence and accuracy.

(7) For this purpose "coherence" refers to a witness's ability in giving evidence to give answers which—

- (a) address the questions put to the witness, and
- (b) can be understood, both individually and collectively.

31V Directions under section 31U: supplementary

(1) A direction under section 31U has binding effect from the time it is made until the witness in relation to whom it applies is discharged.

(2) But the court may revoke a direction under section 31U before the witness is discharged, if it appears to the court to be in the interests of justice to do so, either—

- (a) on an application made by a party to the proceedings, or
- (b) of its own motion.

(3) The court may revoke a direction under section 31U on an application made by a party to the proceedings only if there has been a material change of circumstances since—

(a) the direction was given, or
(b) if a previous application has been made by a party to the proceedings, the application (or the last application) was determined.

(4) The court must state its reasons for—
(a) giving a direction under section 31U;
(b) refusing an application for a direction under section 31U;
(c) revoking a direction under section 31U;
(d) refusing an application for the revocation of a direction under section 31U.

31W Alternatives to cross-examination in person

(1) This section applies where a party to family proceedings is prevented from cross-examining a witness in person by virtue of any of sections 31R to 31U.

(2) The court must consider whether (ignoring this section) there is a satisfactory alternative means—
(a) for the witness to be cross-examined in the proceedings, or
(b) of obtaining evidence that the witness might have given under cross-examination in the proceedings.

(3) If the court decides that there is not, the court must—
(a) invite the party to the proceedings to arrange for a qualified legal representative to act for the party for the purpose of cross-examining the witness, and
(b) require the party to the proceedings to notify the court, by the end of a period specified by the court, of whether a qualified legal representative is to act for the party for that purpose.

(4) Subsection (5) applies if, by the end of the period specified under subsection (3)(b), either—
(a) the party has notified the court that no qualified legal representative is to act for the party for the purpose of cross-examining the witness, or
(b) no notification has been received by the court and it appears to the court that no qualified legal representative is to act for the party for the purpose of cross-examining the witness.

(5) The court must consider whether it is necessary in the interests of justice for the witness to be cross-examined by a qualified legal representative appointed by the court to represent the interests of the party.

(6) If the court decides that it is, the court must appoint a qualified legal representative (chosen by the court) to cross-examine the witness in the interests of the party.

(7) A qualified legal representative appointed by the court under subsection (6) is not responsible to the party.

(8) For the purposes of this section—
(a) a reference to cross-examination includes a reference to continuing to conduct cross-examination;
(b) "qualified legal representative" means a person who, for the purposes of the Legal Services Act 2007, is an authorised person in relation to an activity which constitutes the exercise of a right of audience (within the meaning of that Act) in family proceedings.

31X Costs of legal representatives appointed under section 31W(6)

(1) The Lord Chancellor may by regulations make provision for the payment out of central funds of sums in respect of—

(a) fees or costs properly incurred by a qualified legal representative appointed under section 31W(6), and

(b) expenses properly incurred in providing such a person with evidence or other material in connection with the appointment.

(2) The regulations may provide for sums payable under subsection (1) to be determined by the Lord Chancellor or such other person as the regulations may specify.

(3) The regulations may provide for sums payable under subsection (1)—

(a) to be such amounts as are specified in the regulations;

(b) to be calculated in accordance with—

(i) a rate or scale specified in the regulations, or

(ii) other provision made by or under the regulations.

31Y Guidance for legal representatives appointed under section 31W(6)

(1) The Lord Chancellor may issue guidance in connection with the role which a qualified legal representative appointed under section 31W(6) in connection with any family proceedings is to play in the proceedings, including (among other things) guidance about the effect of section 31W(7).

(2) A qualified legal representative appointed under section 31W(6) must have regard to any guidance issued under this section.

(3) The Lord Chancellor may from time to time revise any guidance issued under this section.

(4) The Lord Chancellor must publish—

(a) any guidance issued under this section, and

(b) any revisions of that guidance.

31Z Regulations under Part 4B

(1) Any power of the Lord Chancellor to make regulations under this Part—

(a) is exercisable by statutory instrument,

(b) includes power to make different provision for different purposes, and

(c) includes power to make supplementary, incidental, consequential, transitional, transitory or saving provision.

(2) A statutory instrument containing regulations under this Part is subject to annulment in pursuance of a resolution of either House of Parliament."

64 Prohibition of cross-examination in person in civil proceedings

In the Courts Act 2003, after Part 7 insert—

"PART 7A

CIVIL PROCEEDINGS: PROHIBITION OF CROSS-EXAMINTION IN PERSON

85E Prohibition of cross-examination in person: introductory

In this Part—

"civil proceedings" means—

(a) proceedings in the county court,

(b) proceedings in the High Court, other than—

(i) proceedings in the Family Division of the High Court which are business assigned, by or under section 61 of (and Schedule 1 to) the Senior Courts Act 1981, to that Division of the High Court and no other, and

(ii) proceedings in the exercise of its jurisdiction under the Extradition Act 2003, and

(c) proceedings in the civil division of the Court of Appeal arising out of civil proceedings within paragraph (a) or (b);

"witness", in relation to any proceedings, includes a party to the proceedings.

85F Direction for prohibition of cross-examination in person

(1) In civil proceedings, the court may give a direction prohibiting a party to the proceedings from cross-examining (or continuing to cross-examine) a witness in person if it appears to the court that—

- (a) the quality condition or the significant distress condition is met, and
- (b) it would not be contrary to the interests of justice to give the direction.

(2) The "quality condition" is met if the quality of evidence given by the witness on cross-examination—

- (a) is likely to be diminished if the cross-examination (or continued cross-examination) is conducted by the party in person, and
- (b) would be likely to be improved if a direction were given under this section.

(3) The "significant distress condition" is met if—

- (a) the cross-examination (or continued cross-examination) of the witness by the party in person would be likely to cause significant distress to the witness or the party, and
- (b) that distress is likely to be more significant than would be the case if the witness were cross-examined other than by the party in person.

(4) A direction under this section may be made by the court—

- (a) on an application made by a party to the proceedings, or
- (b) of its own motion.

(5) In determining whether the quality condition or the significant distress condition is met in the case of a witness or party, the court must have regard to, among other things—

- (a) any views expressed by the witness as to whether or not the witness is content to be cross-examined by the party in person;
- (b) any views expressed by the party as to whether or not the party is content to cross-examine the witness in person;
- (c) the nature of the questions likely to be asked, having regard to the issues in the proceedings;
- (d) any conviction or caution of which the court is aware for an offence committed by the party in relation to the witness;
- (e) any conviction or caution of which the court is aware for an offence committed by the witness in relation to the party;
- (f) any behaviour by the party in relation to the witness in respect of which the court is aware that a finding of fact has been made in the proceedings or in any other proceedings;
- (g) any behaviour by the witness in relation to the party in respect of which the court is aware that a finding of fact has been made in the proceedings or in any other proceedings;
- (h) any behaviour by the party at any stage of the proceedings, both generally and in relation to the witness;
- (i) any behaviour by the witness at any stage of the proceedings, both generally and in relation to the party;
- (j) any relationship (of whatever nature) between the witness and the party.

(6) Any reference in this section to the quality of a witness's evidence is to its quality in terms of completeness, coherence and accuracy.

(7) For this purpose "coherence" refers to a witness's ability in giving evidence to give answers which—

(a) address the questions put to the witness, and
(b) can be understood, both individually and collectively.

85G Directions under section 85F: supplementary

(1) A direction under section 85F has binding effect from the time it is made until the witness in relation to whom it applies is discharged.

(2) But the court may revoke a direction under section 85F before the witness is discharged, if it appears to the court to be in the interests of justice to do so, either—

(a) on an application made by a party to the proceedings, or
(b) of its own motion.

(3) The court may revoke a direction under section 85F on an application made by a party to the proceedings only if there has been a material change of circumstances since—

(a) the direction was given, or
(b) if a previous application has been made by a party to the proceedings, the application (or the last application) was determined.

(4) The court must state its reasons for—

(a) giving a direction under section 85F;
(b) refusing an application for a direction under section 85F;
(c) revoking a direction under section 85F;
(d) refusing an application for the revocation of a direction under section 85F.

85H Alternatives to cross-examination in person

(1) This section applies where a party to civil proceedings is prevented from cross-examining a witness in person by virtue of a direction under section 85F.

(2) The court must consider whether (ignoring this section) there is a satisfactory alternative means—

(a) for the witness to be cross-examined in the proceedings, or
(b) of obtaining evidence that the witness might have given under cross-examination in the proceedings.

(3) If the court decides that there is not, the court must—

(a) invite the party to the proceedings to arrange for a qualified legal representative to act for the party for the purpose of cross-examining the witness, and
(b) require the party to the proceedings to notify the court, by the end of a period specified by the court, of whether a qualified legal representative is to act for the party for that purpose.

(4) Subsection (5) applies if, by the end of the period specified under subsection (3)(b), either—

(a) the party has notified the court that no qualified legal representative is to act for the party for the purpose of cross-examining the witness, or
(b) no notification has been received by the court and it appears to the court that no qualified legal representative is to act for the party for the purpose of cross-examining the witness.

(5) The court must consider whether it is necessary in the interests of justice for the witness to be cross-examined by a qualified legal representative appointed by the court to represent the interests of the party.

(6) If the court decides that it is, the court must appoint a qualified legal representative (chosen by the court) to cross-examine the witness in the interests of the party.

(7) A qualified legal representative appointed by the court under subsection (6) is not responsible to the party.

(8) For the purposes of this section—

(a) a reference to cross-examination includes a reference to continuing to conduct cross-examination;

(b) "qualified legal representative" means a person who, for the purposes of the Legal Services Act 2007, is an authorised person in relation to an activity which constitutes the exercise of a right of audience (within the meaning of that Act) in civil proceedings.

85I Costs of legal representatives appointed under section 85H(6)

(1) The Lord Chancellor may by regulations make provision for the payment out of central funds of sums in respect of—

(a) fees or costs properly incurred by a qualified legal representative appointed under section 85H(6), and

(b) expenses properly incurred in providing such a person with evidence or other material in connection with the appointment.

(2) The regulations may provide for sums payable under subsection (1) to be determined by the Lord Chancellor or such other person as the regulations may specify.

(3) The regulations may provide for sums payable under subsection (1)—

(a) to be such amounts as are specified in the regulations;

(b) to be calculated in accordance with—

(i) a rate or scale specified in the regulations, or

(ii) other provision made by or under the regulations.

(4) Regulations under this section may make different provision for different purposes.

85J Guidance for legal representatives appointed under section 85H(6)

(1) The Lord Chancellor may issue guidance in connection with the role which a qualified legal representative appointed under section 85H(6) in connection with any civil proceedings is to play in the proceedings, including (among other things) guidance about the effect of section 85H(7).

(2) A qualified legal representative appointed under section 85H(6) must have regard to any guidance issued under this section.

(3) The Lord Chancellor may from time to time revise any guidance issued under this section.

(4) The Lord Chancellor must publish—

(a) any guidance issued under this section, and

(b) any revisions of that guidance."

PART 6
OFFENCES INVOLVING VIOLENT OR ABUSIVE BEHAVIOUR

Offences against the person

65 Consent to serious harm for sexual gratification not a defence

(1) This section applies for the purposes of determining whether a person ("D") who inflicts serious harm on another person ("V") is guilty of a relevant offence.

(2) It is not a defence that V consented to the infliction of the serious harm for the purposes of obtaining sexual gratification (but see subsection (4)).

(3) In this section—

"relevant offence" means an offence under section 18, 20 or 47 of the Offences Against the Person Act 1861 ("the 1861 Act");

"serious harm" means—

(a) grievous bodily harm, within the meaning of section 18 of the 1861 Act,

(b) wounding, within the meaning of that section, or

(c) actual bodily harm, within the meaning of section 47 of the 1861 Act.

(4) Subsection (2) does not apply in the case of an offence under section 20 or 47 of the 1861 Act where—

(a) the serious harm consists of, or is a result of, the infection of V with a sexually transmitted infection in the course of sexual activity, and

(b) V consented to the sexual activity in the knowledge or belief that D had the sexually transmitted infection.

(5) For the purposes of this section it does not matter whether the harm was inflicted for the purposes of obtaining sexual gratification for D, V or some other person.

(6) Nothing in this section affects any enactment or rule of law relating to other circumstances in which a person's consent to the infliction of serious harm may, or may not, be a defence to a relevant offence.

OFFENCES COMMITTED OUTSIDE THE UK

66 Offences against the person committed outside the UK: England and Wales

(1) If—

(a) a person who is a United Kingdom national or is habitually resident in England and Wales does an act in a country outside the United Kingdom,

(b) the act constitutes an offence under the law in force in that country, and

(c) the act, if done in England and Wales, would constitute an offence to which this subsection applies,

the person is guilty in England and Wales of that offence.

(2) The offences to which subsection (1) applies are—

(a) murder;

(b) manslaughter;

(c) an offence under section 18, 20 or 47 of the Offences Against the Person Act 1861 (offences relating to bodily harm or injury);

(d) an offence under section 23 or 24 of that Act (administering poison);

(e) an offence under section 1 of the Infant Life (Preservation) Act 1929 (child destruction).

(3) Subsection (1) does not apply where a person would, in the absence of that subsection, be guilty of an offence of murder or manslaughter under the law of England and Wales.

(4) An act punishable under the law in force in any country constitutes an offence under that law for the purposes of subsection (1)(b) however it is described in that law.

(5) The condition in subsection (1)(b) is to be taken to be met unless, not later than rules of court may provide, the defendant serves on the prosecution a notice—

(a) stating that, on the facts as alleged with respect to the act in question, the condition is not in the defendant's opinion met,

(b) showing the grounds for that opinion, and

(c) requiring the prosecution to prove that it is met.

(6) But the court, if it thinks fit, may permit the defendant to require the prosecution to prove that the condition is met without service of a notice under subsection (5).

(7) In the Crown Court the question whether the condition is met is to be decided by the judge alone.

(8) In this section—

"act" includes a failure to act;

"country" includes territory;

"United Kingdom national" means an individual who is—

(a) a British citizen, a British overseas territories citizen, a British National (Overseas) or a British Overseas citizen,

(b) a person who under the British Nationality Act 1981 is a British subject, or

(c) a British protected person within the meaning of that Act.

67 Offences against the person committed outside the UK: Northern Ireland

(1) If—

(a) a person who is a United Kingdom national or is habitually resident in Northern Ireland does an act in a country outside the United Kingdom,

(b) the act constitutes an offence under the law in force in that country, and

(c) the act, if done in Northern Ireland, would constitute an offence to which this subsection applies,

the person is guilty in Northern Ireland of that offence.

(2) The offences to which subsection (1) applies are—

(a) murder;

(b) manslaughter;

(c) an offence under section 18, 20 or 47 of the Offences Against the Person Act 1861 (offences relating to bodily harm or injury);

(d) an offence under section 23 or 24 of that Act (administering poison);

(e) an offence under section 25 of the Criminal Justice Act (Northern Ireland) 1945 (child destruction).

(3) Subsection (1) does not apply where a person would, in the absence of that subsection, be guilty of an offence of murder or manslaughter under the law of Northern Ireland.

(4) An act punishable under the law in force in any country constitutes an offence under that law for the purposes of subsection (1)(b) however it is described in that law.

(5) The condition in subsection (1)(b) is to be taken to be met unless, not later than rules of court may provide, the defendant serves on the prosecution a notice—

(a) stating that, on the facts as alleged with respect to the act in question, the condition is not in the defendant's opinion met,

(b) showing the grounds for that opinion, and

(c) requiring the prosecution to prove that it is met.

(6) But the court, if it thinks fit, may permit the defendant to require the prosecution to prove that the condition is met without service of a notice under subsection (5).

(7) In the Crown Court the question whether the condition is met is to be decided by the judge alone.

(8) In this section—

"act" includes a failure to act;

"country" includes territory;

"rules of court" means—

(a) in relation to proceedings in a magistrates' court, magistrates' court rules;

(b) in relation to proceedings in the Crown Court, Crown Court rules;

"United Kingdom national" means an individual who is—

(a) a British citizen, a British overseas territories citizen, a British National (Overseas) or a British Overseas citizen,

(b) a person who under the British Nationality Act 1981 is a British subject, or

(c) a British protected person within the meaning of that Act.

(9) The Interpretation Act (Northern Ireland) 1954 applies for the purposes of this section as it applies to an Act of the Northern Ireland Assembly.

68 Amendments relating to offences committed outside the UK

(1) Part 1 of Schedule 2 contains amendments to provide for extra-territorial jurisdiction over certain other offences under the law of England and Wales.

(2) Part 2 of Schedule 2 contains amendments to provide for extra-territorial jurisdiction over certain offences under the law of Scotland.

(3) Part 3 of Schedule 2 contains amendments to provide for extra-territorial jurisdiction over certain other offences under the law of Northern Ireland.

PART 7
MISCELLANEOUS AND GENERAL

Management of offenders

69 Polygraph conditions for offenders released on licence

(1) In Part 3 of the Offender Management Act 2007 (other provisions about the management of offenders), section 28 (application of polygraph condition) is amended as follows.

(2) In subsection (2), for "a relevant sexual offence" substitute "an offence within subsection (3A)".

(3) In subsection (3)(a), for "for a term of twelve months or more" substitute "that is not for a term of less than twelve months".

(4) After subsection (3) insert—

"(3A) An offence is within this subsection if it is—

(a) a relevant offence involving domestic abuse (see subsections (3B) and (3C)), or

(b) a relevant sexual offence (see subsection (4)).

(3B) In this section "relevant offence involving domestic abuse" means—

(a) an offence listed in subsection (3C) which involved behaviour by the offender amounting to domestic abuse within the meaning of the Domestic Abuse Act 2020 (see section 1 of that Act);

(b) an offence under section 36 of that Act (breach of domestic abuse protection order).

(3C) The offences are—

(a) murder;

(b) an offence under section 5 of the Protection from Harassment Act 1997 (breach of a restraining order);

(c) an offence specified in Part 1 of Schedule 15 to the Criminal Justice Act 2003 (specified violent offences);

(d) an offence under section 76 of the Serious Crime Act 2015 (controlling or coercive behaviour in an intimate or family relationship)."

Disclosure of information by police

70 Guidance about the disclosure of information by police forces

(1) The Secretary of State must issue guidance to chief officers of police about the disclosure of police information by police forces for the purposes of preventing domestic abuse.

"Police information" means information held by a police force.

(2) Each chief officer of police of a police force must have regard to any guidance issued under this section.

(3) The Secretary of State may from time to time revise any guidance issued under this section.

(4) Before issuing or revising guidance under this section, the Secretary of State must consult—

(a) the Domestic Abuse Commissioner,
(b) the National Police Chiefs' Council, and
(c) such other persons as the Secretary of State considers appropriate.

(5) Subsection (4) does not apply in relation to any revisions of guidance issued under this section if the Secretary of State considers the proposed revisions of the guidance are insubstantial.

(6) The Secretary of State must publish—
(a) any guidance issued under this section, and
(b) any revisions of that guidance.

(7) In this section—
"chief officer of police" means—
(a) in relation to the British Transport Police Force, the Chief Constable of that Force;
(b) in relation to any other police force, the chief officer of police of that force;
"police force" means—
(a) a police force maintained by a local policing body, or
(b) the British Transport Police Force.

HOMELESSNESS

71 Homelessness: victims of domestic abuse

(1) Part 7 of the Housing Act 1996 (homelessness: England) is amended as follows.

(2) In section 177 (whether it is reasonable to continue to occupy accommodation)—
(a) in subsection (1), for "domestic violence or other violence" substitute "violence or domestic abuse";
(b) for subsection (1A) substitute—
"(1A) For this purpose—
(a) "domestic abuse" has the meaning given by section 1 of the Domestic Abuse Act 2020;
(b) "violence" means—
(i) violence from another person; or
(ii) threats of violence from another person which are likely to be carried out."

(3) Omit section 178 (meaning of associated person).

(4) In section 179 (duty of local housing authority in England to provide advisory services), in subsection (5)—
(a) for the definition of "domestic abuse" substitute—
""domestic abuse" has the meaning given by section 1 of the Domestic Abuse Act 2020;";
(b) omit the definition of "financial abuse".

(5) In section 189 (priority need for accommodation)—
(a) in subsection (1), after paragraph (d) insert—
"(e) a person who is homeless as a result of that person being a victim of domestic abuse.";
(b) after subsection (4) insert—
"(5) In this section "domestic abuse" has the meaning given by section 1 of the Domestic Abuse Act 2020."

(6) In section 198 (referral of case to another local housing authority)—
(a) in subsection (2), in paragraph (c), for "domestic violence" substitute "domestic abuse";
(b) in subsection (2ZA), in paragraph (b), for "domestic violence" substitute "domestic abuse";

(c) in subsection (2A), in paragraph (a), for "domestic violence" substitute "violence that is domestic abuse";

(d) for subsection (3) substitute—

"(3) For the purposes of subsections (2), (2ZA) and (2A)—

(a) "domestic abuse" has the meaning given by section 1 of the Domestic Abuse Act 2020;

(b) "violence" means—

(i) violence from another person; or

(ii) threats of violence from another person which are likely to be carried out."

(7) In section 218 (index of defined expressions: Part 7), in the table, omit the entry relating to section 178.

(8) In article 6 of the Homelessness (Priority Need for Accommodation) (England) Order 2002 (S.I. 2002/2051) (vulnerability: fleeing violence or threats of violence)—

(a) the existing text becomes paragraph (1);

(b) after that paragraph insert—

"(2) For the purposes of this article—

(a) "violence" does not include violence that is domestic abuse;

(b) "domestic abuse" has the meaning given by section 1 of the Domestic Abuse Act 2020."

(9) In consequence of the repeal made by subsection (3), omit the following provisions—

(a) in Schedule 8 to the Civil Partnership Act 2004, paragraph 61;

(b) in Schedule 3 to the Adoption and Children Act 2002, paragraphs 89 to 92.

Secure tenancies

72 Grant of secure tenancies in cases of domestic abuse

(1) Part 4 of the Housing Act 1985 (secure tenancies and rights of secure tenants) is amended as follows.

(2) After section 81 insert—

"81ZA Grant of secure tenancies in cases of domestic abuse

(1) This section applies where a local housing authority grants a secure tenancy of a dwelling-house in England before the day on which paragraph 4 of Schedule 7 to the Housing and Planning Act 2016 (grant of new secure tenancies in England) comes fully into force.

(2) The local housing authority must grant a secure tenancy that is not a flexible tenancy if—

(a) the tenancy is offered to a person who is or was a tenant of some other dwelling-house under a qualifying tenancy (whether as the sole tenant or as a joint tenant), and

(b) the authority is satisfied that—

(i) the person or a member of the person's household is or has been a victim of domestic abuse carried out by another person, and

(ii) the new tenancy is granted for reasons connected with that abuse.

(3) The local housing authority must grant a secure tenancy that is not a flexible tenancy if—

(a) the tenancy is offered to a person who was a joint tenant of the dwelling-house under a qualifying tenancy, and

(b) the authority is satisfied that—

(i) the person or a member of the person's household is or has been a victim of domestic abuse carried out by another person, and

(ii) the new tenancy is granted for reasons connected with that abuse.

(4) In this section—

"abuse" means—

(a) physical or sexual abuse;

(b) violent or threatening behaviour;

(c) controlling or coercive behaviour;

(d) economic abuse (within the meaning of section 1(4) of the Domestic Abuse Act 2020);

(e) psychological, emotional or other abuse;

"domestic abuse" means abuse carried out by a person who is personally connected to the victim of the abuse (within the meaning of section 2 of the Domestic Abuse Act 2020);

"qualifying tenancy" means a tenancy of a dwelling-house in England which is—

(a) a secure tenancy other than a flexible tenancy, or

(b) an assured tenancy—

(i) which is not an assured shorthold tenancy, and

(ii) which is granted by a private registered provider of social housing, by the Regulator of Social Housing or by a housing trust which is a charity.

(5) For the purposes of this section, a person may be a victim of domestic abuse despite the fact that the abuse is directed at another person (for example, the person's child)."

(3) In section 81B (cases where old-style English secure tenancies may be granted)—

(a) in subsection (2C)—

(i) for the definition of "abuse" substitute—

""abuse" means—

(a) physical or sexual abuse;

(b) violent or threatening behaviour;

(c) controlling or coercive behaviour;

(d) economic abuse (within the meaning of section 1(4) of the Domestic Abuse Act 2020);

(e) psychological, emotional or other abuse;";

(ii) for the definition of "domestic abuse" substitute—

""domestic abuse" means abuse carried out by a person who is personally connected to the victim of the abuse (within the meaning of section 2 of the Domestic Abuse Act 2020);";

(b) after subsection (2C) insert—

"(2D) For the purposes of this section, a person may be a victim of domestic abuse despite the fact that the abuse is directed at another person (for example, the person's child)."

Guidance

73 Power of Secretary of State to issue guidance about domestic abuse, etc

(1) The Secretary of State may issue guidance about—

(a) the effect of any provision made by or under—

(i) Parts 1 to 5,

(ii) section 66 or Part 1 of Schedule 2, or

(iii) section 69, 70, 71 or 72;

(b) other matters relating to domestic abuse in England and Wales.

(2) The Secretary of State must, in particular, issue guidance under this section about—

(a) the effect of sections 1 and 2, including guidance as to particular kinds of behaviour that amount to domestic abuse;

(b) the effect of domestic abuse on children.

(3) Any guidance issued under this section must, so far as relevant, take account of the fact that the majority of victims of domestic abuse in England and Wales (excluding children treated as victims by virtue of section 3) are female.

(4) A person exercising public functions to whom guidance issued under this section relates must have regard to it in the exercise of those functions. But nothing in this section permits the Secretary of State to issue guidance to a court or tribunal.

(5) The Secretary of State may from time to time revise any guidance issued under this section.

(6) Before issuing or revising guidance under this section, the Secretary of State must consult—

(a) the Domestic Abuse Commissioner,

(b) the Welsh Ministers, so far as the guidance relates to a devolved Welsh authority, and

(c) such other persons as the Secretary of State considers appropriate.

(7) In subsection (6)(b) "devolved Welsh authority" has the meaning given by section 157A of the Government of Wales Act 2006.

(8) Subsection (6) does not apply in relation to any revisions of guidance issued under this section if the Secretary of State considers the proposed revisions of the guidance are insubstantial.

(9) The Secretary of State must publish—

(a) any guidance issued under this section, and

(b) any revisions of that guidance.

Powers to make consequential or transitional provision, etc

74 Power of Secretary of State to make consequential amendments

(1) The Secretary of State may by regulations make provision that is consequential on any provision made by or under—

(a) Parts 1 to 5,

(b) section 65,

(c) section 66 or Part 1 of Schedule 2, or

(d) section 69, 70, 71 or 72.

(2) The power to make regulations under this section may, in particular, be exercised by amending, repealing, revoking or otherwise modifying any provision made by or under an Act passed before, or in the same session of Parliament as, this Act.

75 Power to make transitional or saving provision

(1) The Secretary of State may by regulations make such transitional or saving provision as the Secretary of State considers appropriate in connection with the coming into force of any provision of—

(a) Parts 1 to 5,

(b) section 65,

(c) section 66 or 68(1) or Part 1 of Schedule 2, or

(d) section 69, 70, 71, 72 or 73.

(2) The Department of Justice in Northern Ireland may by regulations make such transitional or saving provision as the Department considers appropriate in connection with the coming into force of any provision of section 67 or 68(3) or Part 3 of Schedule 2.

(3) Regulations under this section may (among other things) make any adaptations of provisions of this Act mentioned in subsection (1) or (2) (as the case may be) brought into force that appear to be appropriate in consequence of other provisions of this Act not yet having come into force.

FINAL PROVISIONS

76 Regulations

(1) Any power of the Secretary of State or Lord Chancellor to make regulations under this Act is exercisable by statutory instrument.

(2) Any power of the Department of Justice in Northern Ireland to make regulations under this Act is exercisable by statutory rule for the purposes of the Statutory Rules (Northern Ireland) Order 1979 (S.I. 1979/1573 (N.I. 12)).

(3) Regulations under this Act may—

- (a) make different provision for different purposes or in relation to different areas;
- (b) contain supplementary, incidental, consequential, transitional or saving provision.

(4) Subsection (3) does not apply to regulations under section 79 (see instead subsection (6) of that section).

(5) A statutory instrument containing regulations made by the Secretary of State or Lord Chancellor under this Act is subject to annulment in pursuance of a resolution of either House of Parliament, unless the instrument—

- (a) is required by subsection (6) or any other enactment to be laid in draft before, and approved by a resolution of, each House of Parliament, or
- (b) contains only regulations under section 35(7), 75 or 79.

(6) A statutory instrument that contains (with or without other provisions)—

- (a) regulations under section 39(7), or
- (b) regulations under section 74 that amend or repeal any Act,

may not be made unless a draft of the instrument has been laid before, and approved by a resolution of, each House of Parliament.

77 Financial provision

There is to be paid out of money provided by Parliament—

- (a) any expenditure incurred by a Minister of the Crown under or by virtue of this Act, and
- (b) any increase attributable to this Act in the sums payable under any other Act out of money so provided.

78 Extent

(1) Except as set out below, this Act extends to England and Wales only.

(2) Any amendment or repeal made by Part 2 or 3 has the same extent as the provision amended or repealed.

(3) Section 68(2) and Part 2 of Schedule 2 extend to Scotland only.

(4) Sections 67 and 68(3) and Part 3 of Schedule 2 extend to Northern Ireland only.

(5) The following provisions extend to England and Wales, Scotland and Northern Ireland—

- (a) section 37(7),
- (b) sections 74 to 77,
- (c) this section, and
- (d) sections 79 and 80.

(6) Section 37(7) and this subsection (and sections 74 to 76, 79 and 80, so far as relating to those provisions) extend to—

- (a) the Isle of Man, and

(b) the British overseas territories except Gibraltar;

and the power under section 384(2) of the Armed Forces Act 2006 may be exercised so as to modify section 37(7) as it extends to the Isle of Man or a British overseas territory other than Gibraltar.

(7) The power under section 384(1) of the Armed Forces Act 2006 may be exercised so as to extend section 37(7) of this Act to any of the Channel Islands (with or without modifications).

79 Commencement

(1) The following provisions of this Act come into force on the day on which this Act is passed—

(a) section 65;

(b) sections 74 to 78, this section and section 80;

(c) any power to make regulations under or by virtue of this Act.

(2) Sections 66 and 68(1) and Part 1 of Schedule 2 come into force at the end of the period of two months beginning with the day on which this Act is passed.

(3) Section 68(2) and Part 2 of Schedule 2 come into force in accordance with provision contained in regulations made by the Scottish Ministers.

(4) Sections 67 and 68(3) and Part 3 of Schedule 2 come into force in accordance with provision contained in an order made by the Department of Justice in Northern Ireland.

(5) The remaining provisions of this Act come into force in accordance with provision contained in regulations made by the Secretary of State.

(6) Regulations or an order under this section may make different provision for different purposes or in relation to different areas.

(7) Regulations under this section bringing any provision of Part 3 or section 69 into force only for a specified purpose or in relation to a specified area may—

(a) provide for that provision or section to be in force for that purpose or in relation to that area for a specified period;

(b) make transitional or saving provision relating to that provision or section ceasing to be in force at the end of the specified period.

(8) Regulations containing provision permitted by subsection (7)(a) may be amended by subsequent regulations under this section so as to continue any provision of Part 3 or section 69 in force for the specified purpose or in relation to the specified area for a further specified period.

(9) The power of the Department of Justice in Northern Ireland to make an order under this section is exercisable by statutory rule for the purposes of the Statutory Rules (Northern Ireland) Order 1979 (S.I. 1979/1573 (N.I. 12)).

(10) Any provision which the Department of Justice in Northern Ireland could make by regulations under section 75 may be made by the Department by an order under this section.

80 Short title

This Act may be cited as the Domestic Abuse Act 2020.

SCHEDULE 1

FURTHER PROVISION ABOUT REMAND UNDER SECTION 38

Section 38

1 Introductory

This Schedule applies where a court has power to remand a person ("P") under section 38.

2 Remand in custody or on bail

(1) The court may remand P in custody or on bail.

(2) If remanded in custody, P is to be committed to custody to be brought before the court—

(a) at the end of the period of remand, or

(b) at such earlier time as the court may require.

(3) The court may remand P on bail—

(a) by taking from P a recognizance (with or without sureties) conditioned as provided in paragraph 3, or

(b) by fixing the amount of the recognizances with a view to their being taken subsequently in accordance with paragraph 7 and, in the meantime, committing P to custody as mentioned in sub-paragraph (2).

(4) Where P is brought before the court after remand, the court may further remand P.

3

(1) Where P is remanded on bail, the court may direct that P's recognizance be conditioned for P's appearance—

(a) before the court at the end of the period of remand, or

(b) at every time and place to which during the course of the proceedings the hearing may from time to time be adjourned.

(2) Where a recognizance is conditioned for P's appearance as mentioned in sub-paragraph (1)(b), the fixing of a time for P next to appear is to be treated as a remand.

(3) Nothing in this paragraph affects the power of the court at any subsequent hearing to remand P afresh.

4

(1) The court may not remand P for a period exceeding eight clear days unless—

(a) the court adjourns proceedings for the purpose mentioned in paragraph 5(1), or

(b) P is remanded on bail and both P and the person who applied for the warrant under section 38 consent.

This is subject to paragraph 6.

(2) Where the court has power to remand P in custody, P may be committed to the custody of a constable if the remand is for a period not exceeding three clear days.

5 Remand for medical examination and report

(1) If the court has reason to suspect that a medical report will be required, the power to remand a person under section 38 may be exercised for the purpose of enabling a medical examination to take place and a report to be made.

(2) If the person is remanded in custody for that purpose, the adjournment may not be for more than 3 weeks at a time.

(3) If the person is remanded on bail for that purpose, the adjournment may not be for more than 4 weeks at a time.

(4) Sub-paragraph (5) applies if there is reason to suspect that a person who has been arrested under a warrant issued on an application made under section 38 is suffering from mental disorder within the meaning of the Mental Health Act 1983.

(5) The court has the same power to make an order under section 35 of that Act (remand to hospital for report on accused's mental condition) as the Crown Court has under that section in the case of an accused person (within the meaning of that section).

6 Further remand

(1) If the court is satisfied that a person ("P") who has been remanded is unable by reason of illness or accident to appear or be brought before the court at the end of the period of remand, the court may further remand P in P's absence.

(2) The power under sub-paragraph (1) may, in the case of a person who was remanded on bail, be exercised by enlarging the person's recognizance and those of any sureties for the person to a later time.

(3) Where a person ("P") remanded on bail is bound to appear before the court at any time and the court has no power to remand P under sub-paragraph (1), the court may (in P's absence) enlarge P's recognizance and those of any sureties for P to a later time.

(4) The enlargement of P's recognizance is to be treated as a further remand.

(5) Paragraph 4(1) (limit of remand) does not apply to the exercise of the powers conferred by this paragraph.

7 Postponement of taking of recognizance

Where under paragraph 2(3)(b) the court fixes the amount in which the principal and the sureties, if any, are to be bound, the recognizance may afterwards be taken by a person prescribed by rules of court, with the same consequences as if it had been entered into before the court.

8 Requirements imposed on remand on bail

The court may, when remanding a person on bail in accordance with this Schedule, require the person to comply, before release on bail or later, with any requirements that appear to the court to be necessary to secure that the person does not interfere with witnesses or otherwise obstruct the course of justice.

SCHEDULE 2

AMENDMENTS RELATING TO OFFENCES COMMITTED OUTSIDE THE UK

Section 68

PART 1

ENGLAND AND WALES

1 Protection from Harassment Act 1997

In the Protection from Harassment Act 1997, after section 4A insert—

> **"4B Offences under sections 4 and 4A committed outside the United Kingdom**
>
> (1) If—
>
> (a) a person's course of conduct consists of or includes conduct in a country outside the United Kingdom,
>
> (b) the course of conduct would constitute an offence under section 4 or 4A if it occurred in England and Wales, and
>
> (c) the person is a United Kingdom national or is habitually resident in England and Wales, the person is guilty in England and Wales of that offence.
>
> (2) In this section—
>
> "country" includes territory;
>
> "United Kingdom national" means an individual who is—
>
> (a) a British citizen, a British overseas territories citizen, a British National (Overseas) or a British Overseas citizen,
>
> (b) a person who under the British Nationality Act 1981 is a British subject, or
>
> (c) a British protected person within the meaning of that Act."

2 Sexual Offences Act 2003

(1) The Sexual Offences Act 2003 is amended as follows.

(2) In section 72 (offences outside the United Kingdom)—

(a) in subsections (1)(b) and (2)(c), for "section" substitute "subsection";

(b) after subsection (2) insert—

"(2A) If—

(a) a person who is a United Kingdom national or United Kingdom resident does an act in a country outside the United Kingdom,

(b) the act constitutes an offence under the law in force in that country, and

(c) the act, if done in England and Wales, would constitute a sexual offence to which this subsection applies,

the person is guilty in England and Wales of that sexual offence.";

(c) in subsection (3)(c), for "section" substitute "subsection";

(d) in subsection (5), after "(2)" insert ", (2A)";

(e) in subsection (6), after "(2)(b)" insert ", (2A)(b)";

(f) in subsection (10), for "this section applies" substitute "subsections (1) to (3) apply".

(3) In Schedule 2 (sexual offences to which section 72 applies)—

(a) in the heading, for "section 72" substitute "section 72(1) to (3)";

(b) in paragraph 1, in the opening words, for "section 72 applies" substitute "subsections (1), (2) and (3) of section 72 apply";

(c) after paragraph 1 insert—

"1A In relation to England and Wales, the sexual offences to which subsection (2A) of section 72 applies are an offence under any of sections 1 to 4 where the victim of the offence was 18 or over at the time of the offence.";

(d) in paragraph 3, after "paragraph 1" insert "or 1A".

3 Serious Crime Act 2015

In the Serious Crime Act 2015, after section 76 (controlling or coercive behaviour in an intimate or family relationship) insert—

"76A Offences under section 76 committed outside the United Kingdom

(1) If—

(a) a person's behaviour consists of or includes behaviour in a country outside the United Kingdom,

(b) the behaviour would constitute an offence under section 76 if it occurred in England and Wales, and

(c) the person is a United Kingdom national or is habitually resident in England and Wales, the person is guilty in England and Wales of that offence.

(2) In this section—

"country" includes territory;

"United Kingdom national" means an individual who is—

(a) a British citizen, a British overseas territories citizen, a British National (Overseas) or a British Overseas citizen,

(b) a person who under the British Nationality Act 1981 is a British subject, or

(c) a British protected person within the meaning of that Act."

(Pt 2 (which relates solely to Scotland) and Pt 3 (which relates solely to Northern Ireland) are not reproduced)

Appendix 2

EXTRACTS FROM FAMILY PROCEDURE RULES 2010 AND SUPPLEMENTARY PRACTICE DIRECTIONS

FAMILY PROCEDURE RULES 2010

SI 2010/2955

PART 10
APPLICATIONS UNDER PART 4 OF THE FAMILY LAW ACT 1996

A2.1

10.1 Scope and interpretation of this Part
The rules in this Part apply to proceedings under Part 4 of the 1996 Act.

10.2 Applications for an occupation order or a non-molestation order
(1) An application for an occupation order or a non-molestation order must be supported by a witness statement.
(2) An application for an occupation order or a non-molestation order may be made without notice.
(3) . . .
(4) Where an application is made without notice, the witness statement in support of the application must state the reasons why notice has not been given.
(Section 45 of the 1996 Act sets out the criteria for making an order without notice.)

10.3 Service of the application
(1) In an application made on notice, the applicant must serve—
- (a) a copy of the application together with any statement in support; and
- (b) notice of any hearing or directions appointment set by the court,

on the respondent personally—
- (i) not less than 2 days before the hearing; or
- (ii) within such period as the court may direct.

(1A) An application must not be served personally by the applicant himself or herself.
(2) Where the applicant is acting in person, the applicant may request the court officer to serve the application on the respondent.
(3) In an application for an occupation order under section 33, 35 or 36 of the 1996 Act, the applicant must serve on the mortgagee and any landlord of the dwelling-house in question—
- (a) a copy of the application; and
- (b) notice of the right to make representations in writing or orally at any hearing.

(4) The applicant must file a certificate of service after serving the application.

(Rule 6.23 makes provision for the different methods of serving a document and rule 6.35 provides for the court to authorise service by an alternative method.)

10.4

(Revoked)

10.5 Privacy

Any hearing relating to an application for an occupation order or a non-molestation order will be in private unless the court directs otherwise.

10.6 Service of an order

(1) The applicant must, as soon as reasonably practicable, serve on the respondent personally—

- (a) a copy of the order; and
- (b) where the order is made without notice—
  - (i) a copy of the application together with any statement supporting it; and
  - (ii) where the order is made by lay justices, a copy of the written record of the reasons for the court's decision.

(Rule 27.2 makes provision in respect of lay justices giving written reasons in the family court.)

(1A) The documents listed in paragraph (1) must not be served personally by the applicant himself or herself.

(2) The court must serve the documents listed in paragraph (1) if—

- (a) an applicant, acting in person, so requests; or
- (b) the court made the order of its own initiative.

(3) In an application for an occupation order under section 33, 35 or 36 of the 1996 Act, the applicant must serve a copy of any order made on the mortgagee and any landlord of the dwelling-house in question.

10.7 Representations made by a mortgagee or landlord

The court may direct that a hearing be held in order to consider any representations made by a mortgagee or a landlord.

10.8 Applications to vary, extend or discharge an order

Rules 10.5 to 10.7 apply to applications to vary, extend or discharge an order.

10.9 Orders containing provisions to which a power of arrest is attached

Where the court makes an occupation order containing one or more provisions to which a power of arrest is attached ("relevant provisions")—

- (a) each relevant provision must be set out in a separate paragraph in the order; and
- (b) a paragraph containing a relevant provision must not include a provision of the order to which the power of arrest is not attached.

10.10 Service of an order on the officer for the time being in charge of a police station

(1) Where the court makes—

- (a) an occupation order to which a power of arrest is attached; or
- (b) a non-molestation order,

a copy of the order must be delivered to the officer for the time being in charge of—

  - (i) the police station for the applicant's address; or
  - (ii) such other police station as the court may specify.

(2) A copy of the order delivered under paragraph (1) must be accompanied by a statement showing that the respondent has been served with the order or informed of

its terms (whether by being present when the order was made or by telephone or otherwise).

(3) The documentation referred to in paragraphs (1) and (2) must be delivered by—
  (a) the applicant; or
  (b) the court officer, where the order was served following a request under rule 10.6(2).

(4) Paragraph (5) applies where an order is made varying or discharging—
  (a) a provision of an occupation order to which a power of arrest is attached; or
  (b) a provision of a non-molestation order.

(5) The court officer must—
  (a) immediately inform—
    (i) the officer who received a copy of the order under paragraph (1); and
    (ii) if the applicant's address has changed, the officer for the time being in charge of the police station for the new address; and
  (b) deliver a copy of the order referred to in paragraph (4)(a) or (b) and the order referred to in paragraph (1) to any officer so informed.

10.11 Proceedings following arrest . . .

(1) This rule applies where a person is arrested pursuant to—
  (a) a power of arrest attached to a provision of an occupation order; . . .
  (b) a warrant of arrest issued on an application under section 47(8) of the 1996 Act; or
  (c) a warrant of arrest issued on an application for enforcement of an incoming protection measure.

  (The Civil Jurisdiction and Judgments (Protection Measures) Regulations 2014 make provision in relation to the powers of the family court and the High Court to enforce incoming protection measures under the Protection Measures Regulation.).

(2) The court before which a person is brought following arrest may—
  (a) determine whether the facts, and the circumstances which led to the arrest, amounted to disobedience of the order; or
  (b) adjourn the proceedings.

(3) Where the proceedings are adjourned and the arrested person is released—
  (a) unless the court directs otherwise, the matter must be dealt with within 14 days beginning with the date of arrest; and
  (b) the arrested person must be given not less than 2 days' notice of the hearing.

(4) An application notice seeking the committal for contempt of court of the arrested person may be issued if the arrested person is not dealt with within the period mentioned in paragraph (3)(a).

(The powers of the court to remand in custody or on bail are contained in section 47 of and Schedule 5 to the Family Law Act 1996.)

. . .

10.12 Enforcement of an order: requirement for a penal notice

At the time when the order is drawn up, the court officer will—
  (a) where the order made is (or includes) a non-molestation order; or
  (b) where the order made is an occupation order and the court so directs,

issue a copy of the order, endorsed with or incorporating a notice as to the consequences of disobedience, for service in accordance with rule 10.6.

(For enforcement of an order by way of committal see Part 37 (rule 37.9 concerns the requirement for a judgment or order to do or not to do an act to contain a penal notice if it is to be enforceable by way of committal).)

10.13 Enforcement of an undertaking

Part 37 applies where an application is made to commit a person for breach of an undertaking.

(Rule 37.4(2) includes requirements for the information to be contained in a contempt application in relation to breach of an undertaking.)

10.14 Power to adjourn the hearing for consideration of the penalty

The court may adjourn the hearing for consideration of the penalty to be imposed for any contempt of court found proved and such a hearing may be restored if the respondent does not comply with any conditions specified by the court.

. . .

10.15 Hospital orders or guardianship orders under the Mental Health Act 1983

(1) Where the court makes a hospital order under the Mental Health Act 1983 the court officer must—

- (a) send to the hospital any information which will be of assistance in dealing with the patient; and
- (b) inform the applicant when the respondent is being transferred to hospital.

(2) Where the court makes a guardianship order under the Mental Health Act 1983, the court officer must send any information which will be of assistance in dealing with the patient to—

- (a) the patient's guardian; and
- (b) where the guardian is a person other than the local services authority, the local services authority.

. . .

10.16 Transfer directions under section 48 of the Mental Health Act 1983

(1) Where a transfer direction given by the Secretary of State under section 48 of the Mental Health Act 1983 is in force in respect of a person remanded in custody by the court, the court officer must notify—

- (a) the governor of the prison to which that person was remanded; and
- (b) the hospital where that person is detained,

of any committal hearing which that person is required to attend.

(2) The court officer must also give notice in writing of any further remand to the hospital where that person is detained.

. . .

10.17 Recognizances

(1) Where, in accordance with paragraph 2(1)(b)(ii) of Schedule 5 to the 1996 Act, the court fixes the amount of any recognizance with a view to it being taken subsequently, the recognizance may be taken by—

- (a) a judge of the court;
- (b) a police officer of the rank of inspector or above or in charge of a police station; or
- (c) the governor or keeper of a prison where the arrested person is in custody.

(2) The person having custody of an applicant for bail must release that applicant if satisfied that the required recognizances have been taken.

. . .

PRACTICE DIRECTION 10A – PART 4 OF THE FAMILY LAW ACT 1996

A2.2

This Practice Direction supplements FPR Part 10

Applications for an occupation order or non-molestation order made by a child under the age of sixteen

2.1 If an application for an occupation order or non-molestation order is made by a child under the age of sixteen attention is drawn to section 43 of the 1996 Act. This provides that leave of the court is required for an application made by a child under the age of sixteen. The application should be made in accordance with Part 18.

Amendments—FPR Update 9.

Privacy

3.1 If at a hearing which has been held in private –

(a) a non-molestation order is made or an occupation order is made to which a power of arrest is attached; and
(b) the person to whom it is addressed was not given notice of the hearing and was not present at the hearing,

the terms of the order and the name of the person to whom it is addressed shall be announced in open court at the earliest opportunity.

3.2 This announcement may be either on the same day when the court proceeds to hear cases in open court or where there is no further business in open court on that day at the next listed sitting of the court.

3.3 When a person arrested under a power of arrest attached to an occupation order cannot conveniently be brought before the relevant judicial authority sitting in a place normally used as a courtroom within 24 hours after the arrest, that person may be brought before the relevant judicial authority at any convenient place. As the liberty of the subject is involved, the press and public should be permitted to be present, unless security needs make this impracticable.

Warrant of arrest on an application under section 47(8) of the 1996 Act

4.1 In accordance with section 47(9) of the 1996 Act, a warrant of arrest on an application under section 47(8) shall not be issued unless –

(a) the application is substantiated on oath; and
(b) the court has reasonable grounds for believing that the respondent has failed to comply with the order.

Attendance of arresting officer

5.1 Attention is drawn to section 47(7) of the 1996 Act. This provides that a person arrested under a power of arrest attached to an occupation order must be brought before a judge within the period of 24 hours beginning at the time of arrest.

5.2 When the arrested person is brought before the judge the attendance of the arresting officer will not be necessary, unless the arrest itself is in issue. A written statement from the arresting officer as to the circumstances of the arrest should normally be sufficient.

5.3 In those cases where the arresting officer was also a witness to the events leading to the arrest and his or her evidence regarding those events is required, arrangements should be made for the arresting officer to attend at a subsequent hearing to give evidence.

Application for Bail

6.1 An application for bail by a person arrested under –

(a) a power of arrest attached to an occupation order under section 47(2) or (3) of the 1996 Act; or
(b) a warrant of arrest issued on an application under section 47(8) or the 1996 Act,

may be made orally or in writing.

6.2 The court will require the following information, which an application in writing should therefore contain –

(a) the full name of the person making the application;
(b) the address of the place where the person making the application is detained at the time when the application is made;
(c) the address where the person making the application would reside if granted bail;
(d) the amount of the recognizance in which the person making the application would agree to be bound; and
(e) the grounds on which the application is made and, where a previous application has been refused, full particulars of any change in circumstances which has occurred since that refusal.

6.3 An application made in writing must be signed –

(a) by the person making the application or by a person duly authorised by that person in that behalf; or
(b) where the person making the application is a child or is for any reason incapable of acting, by a children's guardian or litigation friend acting on that person's behalf.

6.4 A copy of the application must be served on the person who obtained the injunction.

6.5 A copy of the bail notice must be given to a respondent who is remanded on bail.

Remand for Medical Examination and Report

7.1 Section 48(4) of the 1996 Act provides that the judge has power to make an order under section 35 of the Mental Health Act 1983 (remand to hospital for report on accused's mental condition) in certain circumstances. If the judge does so attention is drawn to section 35(8) of that Act, which provides that a person remanded to hospital under that section may obtain at his or her own expense an independent report on his or her mental condition from a registered medical practitioner or approved clinician of his or her choice and apply to the court on the basis of it for the remand to be terminated under section 35(7).

PART 12
CHILDREN PROCEEDINGS EXCEPT PARENTAL ORDER PROCEEDINGS AND PROCEEDINGS FOR APPLICATIONS IN ADOPTION, PLACEMENT AND RELATED PROCEEDINGS

CHAPTER 1

Interpretation and Application of this Part

A2.3

12.1 Application of this Part

(1) The rules in this Part apply to—

(a) emergency proceedings;

(b) private law proceedings;

(c) public law proceedings;

(d) proceedings relating to the exercise of the court's inherent jurisdiction (other than applications for the court's permission to start such proceedings);

(e) proceedings relating to child abduction and the recognition and enforcement of decisions relating to custody under the European Convention;

(f) proceedings relating to the *Council Regulation* or the 1996 Hague Convention in respect of children; and

(g) any other proceedings which may be referred to in a practice direction.

(Part 18 sets out the procedure for making an application for permission to bring proceedings.)

(Part 31 sets out the procedure for making applications for recognition and enforcement of judgments under the *Council Regulation* or the 1996 Hague Convention.)

(2) The rules in Chapter 7 of this Part also apply to family proceedings which are not within paragraph (1) but which otherwise relate wholly or mainly to the maintenance or upbringing of a minor.

(3) This Part is subject to any provision made by or pursuant to Part 41 (proceeding by electronic means).

NOTES

Amendment

Prospectively amended by SI 2019/517, as from IP completion day (as defined in the European Union (Withdrawal Agreement) Act 2020, s 39(1)–(5)).

12.2 Interpretation

In this Part—

"the 2006 Act" means the Childcare Act 2006;

"activity condition" has the meaning given to it by section 11C(2) of the 1989 Act;

"activity direction" has the meaning given to it by section 11A(3) of the 1989 Act;

"advocate" means a person exercising a right of audience as a representative of, or on behalf of, a party;

"care proceedings" means proceedings for a care order under section 31(1)(a) of the 1989 Act;

"Case Management Order" means an order in the form referred to in Practice Direction 12A;

"child assessment order" has the meaning assigned to it by section 43(2) of the 1989 Act;

. . .

. . .

"contribution order" has the meaning assigned to it by paragraph 23(2) of Schedule 2 to the 1989 Act;

"education supervision order" has the meaning assigned to it by section 36(2) of the 1989 Act;

"emergency proceedings" means proceedings for—

(a) the disclosure of information as to the whereabouts of a child under section 33 of the 1986 Act;

(b) an order authorising the taking charge of and delivery of a child under section 34 of the 1986 Act;

(c) an emergency protection order;

(d) an order under section 44(9)(b) of the 1989 Act varying a direction in an emergency protection order given under section 44(6) of that Act;

(e) an order under section 45(5) of the 1989 Act extending the period during which an emergency protection order is to have effect;

(f) an order under section 45(8) of the 1989 Act discharging an emergency protection order;

(g) an order under section 45(8A) of the 1989 Act varying or discharging an emergency protection order in so far as it imposes an exclusion requirement on a person who is not entitled to apply for the order to be discharged;

(h) an order under section 45(8B) of the 1989 Act varying or discharging an emergency protection order in so far as it confers a power of arrest attached to an exclusion requirement;

(i) warrants under sections 48(9) and 102(1) of the 1989 Act and under section 79 of the 2006 Act; or

(j) a recovery order under section 50 of the 1989 Act;

"emergency protection order" means an order under section 44 of the 1989 Act;

"enforcement order" has the meaning assigned to it by section 11J(2) of the 1989 Act;

"financial compensation order" means an order made under section 11O(2) of the 1989 Act;

"interim order" means an interim care order or an interim supervision order referred to in section 38(1) of the 1989 Act;

"Part 4 proceedings" means proceedings for—

(a) a care order, or the discharge of such an order, under section 39(1) of the 1989 Act;

(b) an order giving permission to change a child's surname or remove a child from the United Kingdom under section 33(7) of the 1989 Act;

(c) a supervision order, the discharge or variation of such an order under section 39(2) of the 1989 Act, or the extension of such an order under paragraph 6(3) of Schedule 3 to that Act;

(d) an order making provision regarding contact under section 34(2) to (4) of the 1989 Act or an order varying or discharging such an order under section 34(9) of that Act;

(e) an education supervision order, the extension of an education supervision order under paragraph 15(2) of Schedule 3 to the 1989 Act, or the discharge of such an order under paragraph 17(1) of Schedule 3 to that Act;
(f) an order varying directions made with an interim care order or interim supervision order under section 38(8)(b) of the 1989 Act;
(g) an order under section 39(3) of the 1989 Act varying a supervision order in so far as it affects a person with whom the child is living but who is not entitled to apply for the order to be discharged;
(h) an order under section 39(3A) of the 1989 Act varying or discharging an interim care order in so far as it imposes an exclusion requirement on a person who is not entitled to apply for the order to be discharged;
(i) an order under section 39(3B) of the 1989 Act varying or discharging an interim care order in so far as it confers a power of arrest attached to an exclusion requirement; or
(j) the substitution of a supervision order for a care order under section 39(4) of the 1989 Act;

"private law proceedings" means proceedings for—
(a) a section 8 order except a child arrangements order to which section 9(6B) of the 1989 Act applies with respect to a child who is in the care of a local authority;
(b) a parental responsibility order under sections 4(1)(c), 4ZA(1)(c) or 4A(1)(b) of the 1989 Act or an order terminating parental responsibility under sections 4(2A), 4ZA(5) or 4A(3) of that Act;
(c) an order appointing a child's guardian under section 5(1) of the 1989 Act or an order terminating the appointment under section 6(7) of that Act;
(d) an order giving permission to change a child's surname or remove a child from the United Kingdom under sections 13(1) or 14C(3) of the 1989 Act;
(e) a special guardianship order except where that order relates to a child who is subject of a care order;
(f) an order varying or discharging such an order under section 14D of the 1989 Act;
(g) an enforcement order;
(h) a financial compensation order;
(i) an order under paragraph 9 of Schedule A1 to the 1989 Act following a breach of an enforcement order;
(j) an order under Part 2 of Schedule A1 to the 1989 Act revoking or amending an enforcement order; or
(k) an order that a warning notice be attached to a child arrangements order;

"public law proceedings" means Part 4 proceedings and proceedings for—
(a) a child arrangements order to which section 9(6B) of the 1989 Act applies with respect to a child who is in the care of a local authority;
(b) a special guardianship order relating to a child who is the subject of a care order;
(c) a secure accommodation order under section 25 of the 1989 Act;
(d) . . .
(e) . . .
(f) . . .

(g) . . .
(h) . . .
(i) . . .
(j) . . .
(k) . . .
(l) . . .
(m) . . .
(n) a child assessment order, or the variation or discharge of such an order under section 43(12) of the 1989 Act;
(o) an order permitting the local authority to arrange for any child in its care to live outside England and Wales under paragraph 19(1) of Schedule 2 to the 1989 Act;
(p) a contribution order, or revocation of such an order under paragraph 23(8) of Schedule 2 to the 1989 Act;
(q) an appeal under paragraph 8(1) of Schedule 8 to the 1989 Act;

"special guardianship order" has the meaning assigned to it by section 14A(1) of the 1989 Act;

"supervision order" has the meaning assigned to it by section 31(11) of the 1989 Act;

"supervision proceedings" means proceedings for a supervision order under section 31(1)(b) of the 1989 Act;

"warning notice" means a notice attached to an order pursuant to section 8(2) of the Children and Adoption Act 2006.

(The 1980 Hague Convention, the 1996 Hague Convention, the Council Regulation, and the European Convention are defined in rule 2.3.)

CHAPTER 2

General Rules

12.3 Who the parties are

(1) In relation to the proceedings set out in column 1 of the following table, column 2 sets out who may make the application and column 3 sets out who the respondents to those proceedings will be.

Proceedings for	*Applicants*	*Respondents*
A parental responsibility order (section 4(1)(c), 4ZA(1)(c), or section 4A(1)(b) of the 1989 Act).	The child's father;	Every person whom the applicant believes to have parental responsibility for the child;
	the step parent; or	where the child is the subject of a care order, every person whom the applicant believes to have had parental responsibility immediately prior to the making of the care order;

	the child's parent (being a woman who is a parent by virtue of section 43 of the Human Fertilisation and Embryology Act 2008 and who is not a person to whom section 1(3) of the Family Law Reform Act 1987 applies) (sections 4(1)(c), 4ZA(1)(c) and 4A(1)(b) of the 1989 Act).	in the case of an application to extend, vary or discharge an order, the parties to the proceedings leading to the order which it is sought to have extended, varied or discharged;
		in the case of specified proceedings, the child.
An order terminating a parental responsibility order or agreement (section 4(2A), 4ZA(5) or section 4A(3) of the 1989 Act.	Any person who has parental responsibility for the child; or	As above.
	with the court's permission , the child (section 4(3), 4ZA(6) and section 4A(3) of the 1989 Act).	
An order appointing a guardian (section 5(1) of the 1989 Act).	An individual who wishes to be appointed as guardian (section 5(1) of the 1989 Act).	As above.
An order terminating the appointment of a guardian (section 6(7) of the 1989 Act).	Any person who has parental responsibility for the child; or	As above.
	with the court's permission, the child (section 6(7) of the 1989 Act).	
A section 8 order.	Any person who is entitled to apply for a section 8 order with respect to the child (section 10(4) to (7) of the 1989 Act); or	As above.
	with the court's permission, any person (section10(2)(b) of the 1989 Act).	
An enforcement order (section 11J of the 1989 Act).	A person who is, for the purposes of the child arrangements order, a person with whom the child concerned lives or is to live;	The person the applicant alleges has failed to comply with the child arrangements order.
	any person whose contact with the child concerned is provided for in the child arrangements order;	

	any individual subject to a condition under section 11(7)(b) of the 1989 Act or an activity condition imposed by a child arrangements order; or with the court's permission, the child (section 11J(5) of the 1989 Act).	
A financial compensation order (section 11O of the 1989 Act).	Any person who is, for the purposes of the child arrangements order, a person with whom the child concerned lives or is to live; any person whose contact with the child concerned is provided for in the child arrangements order; any individual subject to a condition under section 11(7)(b) of the 1989 Act or an activity condition imposed by a child arrangements order; or with the court's permission, the child (section 11O(6) of the 1989 Act).	The person the applicant alleges has failed to comply with the child arrangements order.
An order permitting the child's name to be changed or the removal of the child from the United Kingdom (section 13(1), 14C(3) or 33(7) of the 1989 Act).	Any person (section 13(1), 14C(3), 33(7) of the 1989 Act).	As for a parental responsibility order.
A special guardianship order (section 14A of the 1989 Act).	Any guardian of the child; any individual who is named in a child arrangements order as a person with whom the child is to live; any individual listed in subsection (5)(b) or (c) of section 10 (as read with subsection (10) of that section) of the 1989 Act; a local authority foster parent with whom the child has lived for a period of at least one year immediately preceding the application; or	As above, and if a care order is in force with respect to the child, the child.

	any person with the court's permission (section 14A(3) of the 1989 Act) (more than one such individual can apply jointly (section 14A(3) and (5) of that Act)).	
Variation or discharge of a special guardianship order (section 14D of the 1989 Act).	The special guardian (or any of them, if there is more than one); any individual who is named in a child arrangements order as a person with whom the child is to live; the local authority designated in a care order with respect to the child; any individual within section 14D(1)(d) of the 1989 Act who has parental responsibility for the child; the child, any parent or guardian of the child and any step-parent of the child who has acquired, and has not lost, parental responsibility by virtue of section 4A of that Act with the court's permission; or any individual within section 14D(1)(d) of that Act who immediately before the making of the special guardianship order had, but no longer has, parental responsibility for the child with the court's permission.	As above.
A secure accommodation order (section 25 section of the 1989 Act).	The local authority which is looking after the child; or	As above.

	the Health Authority, Secretary of State, National Health Service Commissioning Board, clinical commissioning group, National Health Service Trust established under section 25 of the National Health Service Act 2006 or section 18(1) of the National Health Service (Wales) Act 2006, National Health Service Foundation Trust or any local authority providing or arranging accommodation for the child (unless the child is looked after by a local authority).	
A care or supervision order (section 31 of the 1989 Act).	Any local authority; the National Society for the Prevention of Cruelty to Children and any of its officers (section 31(1) of the 1989 Act);or any authorised person.	As above.
An order varying directions made with an interim care or interim supervision order (section 38(8)(b) of the 1989 Act).	The parties to proceedings in which directions are given under section 38(6) of the 1989 Act; or any person named in such a direction.	As above.
An order discharging a care order (section 39(1) of the 1989 Act).	Any person who has parental responsibility for the child; the child; or the local authority designated by the order (section 39(1) of the 1989 Act).	As above.
An order varying or discharging an interim care order in so far as it imposes an exclusion requirement (section 39(3A) of the 1989 Act).	A person to whom the exclusion requirement in the interim care order applies who is not entitled to apply for the order to be discharged (section 39(3A) of the 1989 Act).	As above.
An order varying or discharging an interim care order in so far as it confers a power of arrest attached to an exclusion requirement (section 39(3B) of the 1989 Act).	Any person entitled to apply for the discharge of the interim care order in so far as it imposes the exclusion requirement (section 39(3B) of the 1989 Act).	As above.

An order substituting a supervision order for a care order (section 39(4) of the 1989 Act).	Any person entitled to apply for a care order to be discharged under section 39(1) (section 39(4) of the 1989 Act).	As above.
A child assessment order (section 43(1) of the 1989 Act).	Any local authority; the National Society for the Prevention of Cruelty to Children and any of its officers; or any person authorised by order of the Secretary of State to bring the proceedings and any officer of a body who is so authorised (section 43(1) and (13) of the 1989 Act).	As above.
An order varying or discharging a child assessment order (section 43(12) of the 1989 Act).	The applicant for an order that has been made under section 43(1) of the 1989 Act; or the persons referred to in section 43(11) of the 1989 Act (section 43(12) of that Act).	As above.
An emergency protection order (section 44(1) of the 1989 Act).	Any person (section 44(1) of the 1989 Act).	As for a parental responsibility order.
An order extending the period during which an emergency protection order is to have effect (section 45(4) of the 1989 Act).	Any person who— has parental responsibility for a child as the result of an emergency protection order; and is entitled to apply for a care order with respect to the child (section 45(4) of the 1989 Act).	As above.
An order discharging an emergency protection order (section 45(8) of the 1989 Act).	The child; a parent of the child; any person who is not a parent of the child but who has parental responsibility for the child; or	As above.

	any person with whom the child was living before the making of the emergency protection order (section 45(8) of the 1989 Act).	
An order varying or discharging an emergency protection order in so far as it imposes the exclusion requirement (section 45(8A) of the 1989 Act).	A person to whom the exclusion requirement in the emergency protection order applies who is not entitled to apply for the emergency protection order to be discharged (section 45(8A) of the 1989 Act).	As above.
An order varying or discharging an emergency protection order in so far as it confers a power of arrest attached to an exclusion requirement (section 45(8B) of the 1989 Act).	Any person entitled to apply for the discharge of the emergency protection order in so far as it imposes the exclusion requirement (section 45(8B) of the 1989 Act).	As above.
An emergency protection order by the police (section 46(7) of the 1989 Act).	The officer designated for the purposes of section 46(3)(e) of the 1989 Act (section 46(7) of the 1989 Act).	As above.
A warrant authorising a constable to assist in exercise of certain powers to search for children and inspect premises (section 48 of the 1989 Act).	Any person attempting to exercise powers under an emergency protection order who has been or is likely to be prevented from doing so by being refused entry to the premises concerned or refused access to the child concerned (section 48(9) of the 1989 Act).	As above.
A warrant authorising a constable to assist in exercise of certain powers to search for children and inspect premises (section 102 of the 1989 Act).	Any person attempting to exercise powers under the enactments mentioned in section 102(6) of the 1989 Act who has been or is likely to be prevented from doing so by being refused entry to the premises concerned or refused access to the child concerned (section 102(1) of that Act).	As above.
An order revoking an enforcement order (paragraph 4 of Schedule A1 to the 1989 Act).	The person subject to the enforcement order.	The person who was the applicant for the enforcement order; and,

		where the child was a party to the proceedings in which the enforcement order was made, the child.
An order amending an enforcement order (paragraphs 5 to 7 of Schedule A1 to the 1989 Act).	The person subject to the enforcement order.	The person who was the applicant for the enforcement order. (Rule 12.33 makes provision about applications under paragraph 5 of Schedule A1 to the 1989 Act.)
An order following breach of an enforcement order (paragraph 9 of Schedule A1 to the 1989 Act).	Any person who is, for the purposes of the child arrangements order, the person with whom the child lives or is to live; any person whose contact with the child concerned is provided for in the child arrangements order; any individual subject to a condition under section 11(7)(b) of the 1989 Act or an activity condition imposed by a child arrangements order; or with the court's permission, the child (paragraph 9 of Schedule A1 to the 1989 Act).	The person the applicant alleges has failed to comply with the unpaid work requirement imposed by an enforcement order; and where the child was a party to the proceedings in which the enforcement order was made, the child.
An order permitting the local authority to arrange for any child in its care to live outside England and Wales (Schedule 2, paragraph 19(1), to the 1989 Act).	The local authority (Schedule 2, paragraph 19(1), to the 1989 Act).	As for a parental responsibility order.
A contribution order (Schedule 2, paragraph 23(1), to the 1989 Act).	The local authority (Schedule 2, paragraph 23(1), to the 1989 Act).	As above and the contributor.
An order revoking a contribution order (Schedule 2, paragraph 23(8), to the 1989 Act).	The contributor; or the local authority.	As above.

An order relating to contact with the child in care and any named person (section 34(2) of the 1989 Act) or permitting the local authority to refuse contact (section 34(4) of that Act).	The local authority; or	As above; and
	the child (section 34(2) or 34(4) of the 1989 Act).	the person whose contact with the child is the subject of the application.
An order relating to contact with the child in care (section 34(3) of the 1989 Act).	The child's parents;	As above; and
	any guardian or special guardian of the child;	the person whose contact with the child is the subject of the application.
	any person who by virtue of section 4A of the 1989 Act has parental responsibility for the child;	
	where there was a child arrangements order in force with respect to the child immediately before the care order was made, any person named in that order as a person with whom the child was to live;	
	a person who by virtue of an order made in the exercise of the High Court's inherent jurisdiction with respect to children had care of the child immediately before the care order was made (section 34(3)(a) of the 1989 Act); or	
	with the court's permission, any person (section 34(3) (b) of that Act).	
An order varying or discharging an order for contact with a child in care under section 34 (section 34((9) of the 1989 Act).	The local authority;	As above; and
	the child; or	the person whose contact with the child is the subject of the application.
	any person named in the order (section 34(9) of the 1989 Act).	

An education supervision order (section 36 of the 1989 Act).	Any local authority (section 36(1) of the 1989 Act).	As above; and
		the child.
An order varying or discharging a supervision order (section 39(2) of the 1989 Act).	Any person who has parental responsibility for the child;	As above; and
	the child; or	the supervisor.
	the supervisor (section 39(2) of the 1989 Act).	
An order varying a supervision order in so far as it affects the person with whom the child is living (section 39(3) of the 1989 Act).	The person with whom the child is living who is not entitled to apply for the order to be discharged (section 39(3) of the 1989 Act).	As above; and
		the supervisor.
An order varying a direction under section 44(6) of the 1989 Act in an emergency protection order (section 44(9)(b) of that Act).	The parties to the application for the emergency protection order in respect of which it is sought to vary the directions;	As above, and
	the children's guardian;	the parties to the application for the order in respect of which it is sought to vary the directions;
	the local authority in whose area the child is ordinarily resident; or	any person who was caring for the child prior to the making of the order; and
	any person who is named in the directions.	any person named in a child arrangements order as a person with whom the child is to spend time or otherwise have contact and who is affected by the direction which it is sought to have varied.
A recovery order (section 50 of the 1989 Act).	Any person who has parental responsibility for the child by virtue of a care order or an emergency protection order; or	As above; and
	where the child is in police protection the officer designated for the purposes of section 46(3)(e) of the 1989 Act (section 50(4) of the 1989 Act).	the person whom the applicant alleges to have effected or to have been or to be responsible for the taking or keeping of the child.

An order discharging an education supervision order (Schedule 3, paragraph 17(1), to the 1989 Act).	The child concerned; a parent of the child; or the local authority concerned (Schedule 3, paragraph 17(1), to the 1989 Act).	As above; and the local authority concerned; and the child.
An order extending an education supervision order (Schedule 3, paragraph, 15(2), to the 1989 Act).	The local authority in whose favour the education supervision order was made (Schedule 3, paragraph 15(2), to the 1989 Act).	As above; and the child.
An appeal under paragraph (8) of Schedule 8 to the 1989 Act.	A person aggrieved by the matters listed in paragraph 8(1) of Schedule 8 to the 1989 Act.	The appropriate local authority.
An order for the disclosure of information as to the whereabouts of a child under section 33 of the 1986 Act.	Any person with a legitimate interest in proceedings for an order under Part 1 of the 1986 Act; or a person who has registered an order made elsewhere in the United Kingdom or a specified dependent territory.	Any person alleged to have information as to the whereabouts of the child.
An order authorising the taking charge of and delivery of a child under section 34 of the 1986 Act.	The person to whom the child is to be given up under section 34(1) of the 1986 Act.	As above; and the person who is required to give up the child in accordance with section 34(1) of the 1986 Act.
An order relating to the exercise of the court's inherent jurisdiction (including wardship proceedings).	A local authority (with the court's permission); any person with a genuine interest in or relation to the child; or the child (wardship proceedings only).	The parent or guardian of the child; any other person who has an interest in or relationship to the child; and the child (wardship proceedings only and with the court's permission as described at rule 12.37).

A warrant under section 79 of the 2006 Act authorising any constable to assist Her Majesty's Chief Inspector for Education, Children's Services and Skills in the exercise of powers conferred on him by section 77 of the 2006 Act.	Her Majesty's Chief Inspector for Education, Children's Services and Skills.	Any person preventing or likely to prevent Her Majesty's Chief Inspector for Education, Children's Services and Skills from exercising powers conferred on him by section 77 of the 2006 Act.
An order in respect of a child under the 1980 Hague Convention.	Any person, institution or body who claims that a child has been removed or retained in breach of rights of custody or claims that there has been a breach of rights of access in relation to the child.	The person alleged to have brought the child into the United Kingdom; the person with whom the child is alleged to be; any parent or guardian of the child who is within the United Kingdom and is not otherwise a party; any person in whose favour a decision relating to custody has been made if that person is not otherwise a party; and any other person who appears to the court to have sufficient interest in the welfare of the child.
An order concerning the recognition and enforcement of decisions relating to custody under the European Convention.	Any person who has a court order giving that person rights of custody in relation to the child.	As above.
An application for the High Court to request transfer of jurisdiction under *Article 15 of the Council Regulation or* Article 9 of the 1996 Hague Convention (rule 12.65).	Any person with sufficient interest in the welfare of the child and who would be entitled to make a proposed application in relation to that child, or who intends to seek the permission of the court to make such application if the transfer is agreed.	As directed by the court in accordance with rule 12.65.

An application under rule 12.71 for a declaration as to the existence, or extent, of parental responsibility under Article 16 of the 1996 Convention.	Any interested person including a person who holds, or claims to hold, parental responsibility for the child under the law of another State which subsists in accordance with Article 16 of the 1996 Hague Convention following the child becoming habitually resident in a territorial unit of the United Kingdom.	Every person whom the applicant believes to have parental responsibility for the child; any person whom the applicant believes to hold parental responsibility for the child under the law of another State which subsists in accordance with Article 16 of the 1996 Hague Convention following the child becoming habitually resident in a territorial unit of the United Kingdom; and where the child is the subject of a care order, every person whom the applicant believes to have had parental responsibility immediately prior to the making of the care order.
A warning notice.	The person who is, for the purposes of the child arrangements order, the person with whom the child concerned lives or is to live; the person whose contact with the child concerned is provided for in the child arrangements order; any individual subject to a condition under section 11(7)(b) of the 1989 Act or an activity condition imposed by the child arrangements order; or with the court's permission, the child.	Any person who was a party to the proceedings in which the child arrangements order was made. (Rule 12.33 makes provision about applications for warning notices).

(2) The court will direct that a person with parental responsibility be made a party to proceedings where that person requests to be one.

(3) Subject to rule 16.2, the court may at any time direct that—

- (a) any person or body be made a party to proceedings; or
- (b) a party be removed.

(4) If the court makes a direction for the addition or removal of a party under this rule, it may give consequential directions about—

(a) the service of a copy of the application form or other relevant documents on the new party;

(b) the management of the proceedings.

(5) In this rule—

"a local authority foster parent" has the meaning assigned to it by section 23(3) of the 1989 Act; and

"care home", "independent hospital", "local authority" and "clinical commissioning group" have the meanings assigned to them by section 105 of the 1989 Act.

(Part 16 contains the rules relating to the representation of children.)

NOTES

Amendment

Prospectively amended by SI 2019/517, as from IP completion day (as defined in the European Union (Withdrawal Agreement) Act 2020, s 39(1)–(5)).

12.4 Notice of proceedings to person with foreign parental responsibility

(1) This rule applies where a child is subject to proceedings to which this Part applies and—

(a) a person holds or is believed to hold parental responsibility for the child under the law of another State which subsists in accordance with Article 16 of the 1996 Hague Convention following the child becoming habitually resident in a territorial unit of the United Kingdom; and

(b) that person is not otherwise required to be joined as a respondent under rule 12.3.

(2) Subject to paragraph (2A) the applicant shall give notice of the proceedings to any person to whom the applicant believes paragraph (1) applies in any case in which a person whom the applicant believed to have parental responsibility under the 1989 Act would be a respondent to those proceedings in accordance with rule 12.3.

(2A) Notice shall not be given to a person to whom the applicant believes paragraph (1) applies if the court directs that such notice is not necessary.

(3) Unless a direction has been made under paragraph (2A), the applicant and every respondent to the proceedings shall provide such details as they possess as to the identity and whereabouts of any person they believe to hold parental responsibility for the child in accordance with paragraph (1) to the court officer, upon making, or responding to the application as appropriate.

(4) Where the existence of a person who is believed to have parental responsibility for the child in accordance with paragraph (1) only becomes apparent to a party at a later date during the proceedings, that party must notify the court officer of those details at the earliest opportunity.

(5) Where a person to whom paragraph (1) applies receives notice of proceedings, that person may apply to the court to be joined as a party using the Part 18 procedure.

12.5 What the court will do when the application has been issued

(1) When proceedings other than public law proceedings have been issued the court will consider—

(a) setting a date for—

(i) a directions appointment;

(ii) in private law proceedings, a First Hearing Dispute Resolution Appointment; or

(iii) . . .

(iv) the hearing of the application,

and if the court sets a date it will do so in accordance with rule 12.13 and Practice Direction 12B;

(b) giving any of the directions listed in rule 12.12 or, where Chapter 6, section 1 applies, rule 12.48; and

(c) doing anything else which is set out in Practice Direction 12B or any other practice direction.

(2) When Part 4 proceedings and in so far as practicable other public law proceedings have been issued the court will—

(a) set a date for the Case Management Hearing in accordance with Practice Direction 12A;

(b) set a date for the hearing of an application for an interim order if necessary;

(c) give any directions listed in rule 12.12; and

(d) do anything else which is set out in Practice Direction 12A.

(Practice Direction 12A sets out details relating to the Case Management Hearing. Practice Direction 12B supplementing this Part sets out details relating to the First Hearing Dispute Resolution Appointment.)

12.6 Children's guardian, solicitor and reports under section 7 of the 1989 Act

Within a day of the issue of Part 4 proceedings or the transfer of Part 4 Proceedings to the court and as soon as practicable after the issue of other proceedings or the transfer of the other proceedings to the court, the court will—

(a) in specified proceedings, appoint a children's guardian under rule 16.3(1) unless—

(i) such an appointment has already been made by the court which made the transfer and is subsisting; or

(ii) the court considers that such an appointment is not necessary to safeguard the interests of the child;

(b) where section 41(3) of the 1989 Act applies, consider whether a solicitor should be appointed to represent the child, and if so, appoint a solicitor accordingly;

(c) consider whether to ask an officer of the service or a Welsh family proceedings officer for advice relating to the welfare of the child;

(d) consider whether a report relating to the welfare of the child is required, and if so, request such a report in accordance with section 7 of the 1989 Act.

(Part 16 sets out the rules relating to representation of children.)

12.7 What a court officer will do

(1) As soon as practicable after the issue of proceedings the court officer will return to the applicant the copies of the application together with the forms referred to in Practice Direction 5A.

(2) As soon as practicable after the issue of proceedings or the transfer of proceedings to the court or at any other stage in the proceedings the court officer will—

(a) give notice of any hearing set by the court to the applicant; and

(b) do anything else set out in Practice Directions 12A or 12B or any other practice direction.

12.8 Service

(1) After the issue of proceedings under this Part, the documents specified in paragraph (5) must be served on the respondent or respondents.

(2) In section 8 private law proceedings, service under paragraph (1) will be effected by the court officer, unless—

(a) the applicant requests to do so; or

(b) the court directs the applicant to do so.

(3) In this Rule, "section 8 private law proceedings" are proceedings for a section 8 order except proceedings for a child arrangements order to which section 9(6B) of the 1989 Act applies with respect to a child who is in the care of a local authority.

(4) In any other proceedings to which this Part applies, service under paragraph (1) must be effected by the applicant.

(5) The documents are—

- (a) the application together with the documents referred to in Practice Direction 12C; and
- (b) notice of any hearing set by the court.

(6) Service under this rule must be carried out in accordance with Practice Direction 12C.

(7) The general rules about service in Part 6 apply but are subject to this rule.

(Practice Direction 12C (Service of Application in Children Proceedings) provides that in Part 4 proceedings (except proceedings for an interim order) the minimum number of days prior to the Case Management Hearing for service of the application and accompanying documents is 7 days. The Court has discretion to extend or shorten this time (see rule 4.1(3)(a)).

12.9–12.11
(*Revoked*)

12.12 Directions

(1) This rule does not apply to proceedings under Chapter 6 of this Part.

(2) At any stage in the proceedings, the court may give directions about the conduct of the proceedings including—

- (a) the management of the case;
- (b) the timetable for steps to be taken between the giving of directions and the final hearing;
- (c) the joining of a child or other person as a party to the proceedings in accordance with rules 12.3(2) and (3);
- (d) the attendance of the child;
- (e) the appointment of a children's guardian or of a solicitor under section 41(3) of the 1989 Act;
- (f) the appointment of a litigation friend;
- (g) the service of documents;
- (h) the filing of evidence including experts' reports; and
- (i) the exercise by an officer of the Service, Welsh family proceedings officer or local authority officer of any duty referred to in rule 16.38(1)

(3) Paragraph (4) applies where—

- (a) an officer of the Service or a Welsh family proceedings officer has filed a report or a risk assessment as a result of exercising a duty referred to in rule 16.38(1)(a); or
- (b) a local authority officer has filed a report as a result of exercising a duty referred to in rule 16.38(1)(b).

(4) The court may—

- (a) give directions setting a date for a hearing at which that report or risk assessment will be considered; and
- (b) direct that the officer who prepared the report or risk assessment attend any such hearing.

(5) The court may exercise the powers in paragraphs (2) and (4) on an application or of its own initiative.

(6) Where the court proposes to exercise its powers of its own initiative the procedure set out in rule 4.3(2) to (6) applies.

(7) Directions of a court which are still in force immediately prior to the transfer of proceedings to another court will continue to apply following the transfer subject to—

(a) any changes of terminology which are required to apply those directions to the court to which the proceedings are transferred; and

(b) any variation or revocation of the direction.

(8) The court or court officer will—

(a) take a note of the giving, variation or revocation of a direction under this rule; and

(b) as soon as practicable serve a copy of the note on every party.

(Rule 12.48 provides for directions in proceedings under the 1980 Hague Convention and the European Convention.)

12.13 Setting dates for hearings and setting or confirming the timetable and date for the final hearing

(1) At the—

(a) transfer to a court of proceedings;

(b) postponement or adjournment of any hearing; or

(c) conclusion of any hearing at which the proceedings are not finally determined,

the court will set a date for the proceedings to come before the court again for the purposes of giving directions or for such other purposes as the court directs.

(2) At any hearing the court may—

(a) confirm a date for the final hearing or the week within which the final hearing is to begin (where a date or period for the final hearing has already been set);

(b) set a timetable for the final hearing unless a timetable has already been fixed, or the court considers that it would be inappropriate to do so; or

(c) set a date for the final hearing or a period within which the final hearing of the application is to take place.

(3) The court officer will notify the parties of—

(a) the date of a hearing fixed in accordance with paragraph (1);

(b) the timetable for the final hearing; and

(c) the date of the final hearing or the period in which it will take place.

(4) Where the date referred to in paragraph (1) is set at the transfer of proceedings, the date will be as soon as possible after the transfer.

(5) The requirement in paragraph (1) to set a date for the proceedings to come before the court again is satisfied by the court setting or confirming a date for the final hearing.

12.14 Attendance at hearings

(1) This rule does not apply to proceedings under Chapter 6 of this Part except for proceedings for a declaration under rule 12.71.

(2) Unless the court directs otherwise and subject to paragraph (3), the persons who must attend a hearing are—

(a) any party to the proceedings;

(b) any litigation friend for any party or legal representative instructed to act on that party's behalf; and

(c) any other person directed by the court or required by Practice Directions 12A or 12B or any other practice direction to attend.

(3) Proceedings or any part of them will take place in the absence of a child who is a party to the proceedings if—

(a) the court considers it in the interests of the child, having regard to the matters to be discussed or the evidence likely to be given; and

(b) the child is represented by a children's guardian or solicitor.

(4) When considering the interests of the child under paragraph (3) the court will give—

- (a) the children's guardian;
- (b) the solicitor for the child; and
- (c) the child, if of sufficient understanding,

an opportunity to make representations.

(5) Subject to paragraph (6), where at the time and place appointed for a hearing, the applicant appears but one or more of the respondents do not, the court may proceed with the hearing.

(6) The court will not begin to hear an application in the absence of a respondent unless the court is satisfied that—

- (a) the respondent received reasonable notice of the date of the hearing; or
- (b) the circumstances of the case justify proceeding with the hearing.

(7) Where, at the time and place appointed for a hearing one or more of the respondents appear but the applicant does not, the court may—

- (a) refuse the application; or
- (b) if sufficient evidence has previously been received, proceed in the absence of the applicant.

(8) Where at the time and place appointed for a hearing neither the applicant nor any respondent appears, the court may refuse the application.

(9) Paragraphs (5) to (8) do not apply to a hearing where the court—

- (a) is considering—
  - (i) whether to make an activity direction or to attach an activity condition to a child arrangements order; or
  - (ii) an application for a financial compensation order, an enforcement order or an order under paragraph 9 of Schedule A1 to the 1989 Act following a breach of an enforcement order; and
- (b) has yet to obtain sufficient evidence from, or in relation to, the person who may be the subject of the direction, condition or order to enable it to determine the matter.

(10) Nothing in this rule affects the provisions of Article 18 of the Council Regulation in cases to which that provision applies.

(The Council Regulation makes provision in Article 18 for the court to stay proceedings where the respondent is habitually resident in another Member State of the European Union and has not been adequately served with the proceedings as required by that provision.)

NOTES

Amendment

Prospectively amended by SI 2019/517, as from IP completion day (as defined in the European Union (Withdrawal Agreement) Act 2020, s 39(1)–(5)).

12.15 Steps taken by the parties

If—

- (a) the parties or any children's guardian agree proposals for the management of the proceedings (including a proposed date for the final hearing or a period within which the final hearing is to take place); and
- (b) the court considers that the proposals are suitable,

it may approve them without a hearing and give directions in the terms proposed.

(Practice Direction 12A gives guidance as to the application of this rule to Part 4 proceedings in the light of the period that is for the time being allowed under section 32(1)(a)(ii) of the 1989 Act)

12.16 Applications without notice

(1) This rule applies to—

(a) proceedings for a section 8 order;
(b) emergency proceedings; and
(c) proceedings relating to the exercise of the court's inherent jurisdiction (other than an application for the court's permission to start such proceedings and proceedings for collection, location and passport orders where Chapter 6 applies).

(2) An application in proceedings referred to in paragraph (1) may. . . be made without notice in which case the applicant must file the application—
(a) where the application is made by telephone, the next business day after the making of the application; or
(b) in any other case, at the time when the application is made.

(3) . . .

(4) Where—
(a) a section 8 order;
(b) an emergency protection order;
(c) an order for the disclosure of information as to the whereabouts of a child under section 33 of the 1986 Act; or
(d) an order authorising the taking charge of and delivery of a child under section 34 of the 1986 Act,

is made without notice, the applicant must serve a copy of the application on each respondent within 48 hours after the order is made.

(5) Within 48 hours after the making of an order without notice, the applicant must serve a copy of the order on—
(a) the parties, unless the court directs otherwise;
(b) any person who has actual care of the child or who had such care immediately prior to the making of the order; and
(c) in the case of an emergency protection order and a recovery order, the local authority in whose area the child lives or is found.

(6) Where the court refuses to make an order on an application without notice it may direct that the application is made on notice in which case the application will proceed in accordance with rules 12.13 to 12.15.

(7) Where the hearing takes place outside the hours during which the court office is normally open, the court or court officer will take a note of the proceedings.

(Practice Direction 12E (Urgent Business) provides further details of the procedure for out of hours applications. See also Practice Direction 12D (Inherent Jurisdiction (including Wardship Proceedings).)

(Rule 12.47 provides for without-notice applications in proceedings under Chapter 6, section 1 of this Part, (proceedings under the 1980 Hague Convention and the European Convention).)

12.17 Investigation under section 37 of the 1989 Act

(1) This rule applies where a direction is given to an appropriate authority by the court under section 37(1) of the 1989 Act.

(2) On giving the direction the court may adjourn the proceedings.

(3) As soon as practicable after the direction is given the court will record the direction.

(4) As soon as practicable after the direction is given the court officer will—
(a) serve the direction on—
(i) the parties to the proceedings in which the direction is given; and
(ii) the appropriate authority where it is not a party;
(b) serve any documentary evidence directed by the court on the appropriate authority.

(5) Where a local authority informs the court of any of the matters set out in section 37(3)(a) to (c) of the 1989 Act it will do so in writing.

(6) Unless the court directs otherwise, the court officer will serve a copy of any report to the court under section 37 of the 1989 Act on the parties.

(Section 37 of the 1989 Act refers to the appropriate authority and section 37(5) of that Act sets out which authority should be named in a particular case.)

12.18 Disclosure of a report under section 14A(8) or (9) of the 1989 Act

(1) In proceedings for a special guardianship order, the local authority must file the report under section 14A(8) or (9) of the 1989 Act within the timetable fixed by the court.

(2) The court will consider whether to give a direction that the report under section 14A(8) or (9) of the 1989 Act be disclosed to each party to the proceedings.

(3) Before giving a direction for the report to be disclosed, the court must consider whether any information should be deleted from the report.

(4) The court may direct that the report must not be disclosed to a party.

(5) The court officer must serve a copy of the report in accordance with any direction under paragraph (2).

(6) In paragraph (3), information includes information which a party has declined to reveal under rule 29.1(1).

12.19 Additional evidence

(1) This rule applies to proceedings for a section 8 order or a special guardianship order.

(2) Unless the court directs otherwise, a party must not—

- (a) file or serve any document other than in accordance with these rules or any practice direction;
- (b) in completing a form prescribed by these rules or any practice direction, give information or make a statement which is not required or authorised by that form; or
- (c) file or serve at a hearing—
  - (i) any witness statement of the substance of the oral evidence which the party intends to adduce; or
  - (ii) any copy of any document (including any experts' report) which the party intends to rely on.

(3) Where a party fails to comply with the requirements of this rule in relation to any witness statement or other document, the party cannot seek to rely on that statement or other document unless the court directs otherwise.

12.20

(*Revoked*)

12.21 Hearings

(1) The court may give directions about the order of speeches and the evidence at a hearing.

(2) Subject to any directions given under paragraph (1), the parties and the children's guardian must adduce their evidence at a hearing in the following order—

- (a) the applicant;
- (b) any party with parental responsibility for the child;
- (c) other respondents;
- (d) the children's guardian;
- (e) the child, if the child is a party to proceedings and there is no children's guardian.

CHAPTER 3

Special Provisions about Public Law Proceedings

12.22 Timetable for the proceedings

In public law proceedings other than Part 4 proceedings, in so far as practicable the court will draw up the timetable for the proceedings or revise that timetable with a view to disposing of the application without delay and in any event within 26 weeks beginning with the date on which the application is issued.

(In relation to Part 4 proceedings, section 32(1)(a) of the 1989 Act requires the court to draw up a timetable with a view to disposing of the application without delay and in any event within 26 weeks beginning with the day on which the application is issued.)

12.23 Application of rules 12.24 to 12.26C

Rules 12.24 to 12.26C apply to Part 4 proceedings and in so far as practicable other public law proceedings.

12.24 Directions

The court will direct the parties to—

- (a) monitor compliance with the court's directions; and
- (b) tell the court or court officer about—
  - (i) any failure to comply with a direction of the court; and
  - (ii) any other delay in the proceedings.

12.25 The Case Management Hearing and the Issues Resolution Hearing

(1) The court will conduct the Case Management Hearing with the objective of—

- (a) confirming the level of judge to which the proceedings have been allocated;
- (b) drawing up a timetable for the proceedings including the time within which the proceedings are to be resolved;
- (c) identifying the issues; and
- (d) giving directions in accordance with rule 12.12 and Practice Direction 12A to manage the proceedings.

(2) The court may hold a further Case Management Hearing only where this hearing is necessary to fulfil the objectives of the Case Management Hearing set out in paragraph (1).

(3) The court will conduct the Issues Resolution Hearing with the objective of—

- (a) identifying the remaining issues in the proceedings;
- (b) as far as possible resolving or narrowing those issues; and
- (c) giving directions to manage the proceedings to the final hearing in accordance with rule 12.12 and Practice Direction 12A.

(4) Where it is possible for all the issues in the proceedings to be resolved at the Issues Resolution Hearing, the court may treat the Issues Resolution Hearing as a final hearing and make orders disposing of the proceedings.

(5) The court may set a date for the Case Management Hearing, a further Case Management Hearing and the Issues Resolution Hearing at the times referred to in Practice Direction 12A.

(6) The matters which the court will consider at the hearings referred to in this rule are set out in Practice Direction 12A.

(Rule 25.6 (experts: when to apply for the court's permission) provides that unless the court directs otherwise, parties must apply for the court's permission as mentioned in section 13(1), (3) and (5) of the 2014 Act as soon as possible and in Part 4 proceedings and in so far as practicable other public law proceedings no later than the Case Management Hearing.)

12.26 Discussion between advocates

(1) When setting a date for the Case Management Hearing or the Issues Resolution Hearing the court will direct a discussion between the parties' advocates to—

- (a) discuss the provisions of a draft of the Case Management Order; and
- (b) consider any other matter set out in Practice Direction 12A.

(2) Where there is a litigant in person the court will give directions about how that person may take part in the discussions between the parties' advocates.

(3) Unless the court directs otherwise—

- (a) any discussion between advocates must take place no later than 2 days before the Case Management Hearing; and
- (b) a draft of the Case Management Order must be filed with the court no later than 11am on the day before the Case Management Hearing.

(4) Unless the court directs otherwise—

- (a) any discussion between advocates must take place no later than 7 days before the Issues Resolution Hearing; and
- (b) a draft of the Case Management Order must be filed with the court no later than 11am on the day before the Issues Resolution Hearing.

(5) For the purposes of this rule "advocate" includes a litigant in person.

12.26A Application for extension of the time limit for disposing of the application

(1) An application requesting the court to grant an extension must state—

- (a) the reasons for the request;
- (b) the period of extension being requested; and
- (c) a short explanation of—
  - (i) why it is necessary for the request to be granted to enable the court to resolve the proceedings justly;
  - (ii) the impact which any ensuing timetable revision would have on the welfare of the child to whom the application relates;
  - (iii) the impact which any ensuing timetable revision would have on the duration and conduct of the proceedings; and
  - (iv) the reasons for the grant or refusal of any previous request for extension.

(2) Part 18 applies to an application requesting the grant of an extension.

(3) In this rule

"ensuing timetable revision" has the meaning given to it by section 32(6) of the 1989 Act;

"extension" means an extension of the period for the time being allowed under section 32(1)(a)(ii) of the 1989 Act which is to end no more than 8 weeks after the later of the times referred to in section 32(8) of that Act.

12.26B Disapplication of rule 4.1(3)(a) court's power to extend or shorten the time for compliance with a rule

Rule 4.1(3)(a) does not apply to any period that is for the time being allowed under section 32(1)(a)(ii) of the 1989 Act.

12.26C Extension of time limit: reasons for court's decision

(1) When refusing or granting an extension of the period that is for the time being allowed under section 32(1)(a)(ii) in the case of the application, the court will announce its decision and—

- (a) the reasons for that decision; and
- (b) where an extension is granted or refused, a short explanation of the impact which the decision would have on the welfare of the child.

(2) The court office will supply a copy of the order granting or refusing the extension including the reasons for the court's decision and the period of any extension and short explanation given under paragraph (1)(b) to—

(a) the parties; and

(b) any person who has actual care of the child who is the subject of the proceedings.

12.27 Matters prescribed for the purposes of the Act

(1) Proceedings for an order under any of the following provisions of the 1989 Act—

(a) a secure accommodation order under section 25;

(b) an order giving permission to change a child's surname or remove a child from the United Kingdom under section 33(7);

(c) an order permitting the local authority to arrange for any child in its care to live outside England and Wales under paragraph 19(1) of Schedule 2;

(d) the extension or further extension of a supervision order under paragraph 6(3) of Schedule 3;

(e) appeals against the determination of proceedings of a kind set out in sub-paragraphs (a) to (d);

are specified for the purposes of section 41 of that Act in accordance with section 41(6)(i) of that Act.

(2) The persons listed as applicants in the table set out in rule 12.3 to proceedings for the variation of directions made with interim care or interim supervision orders under section 38(8) of the 1989 Act are the prescribed class of persons for the purposes of that section.

(3) The persons listed as applicants in the table set out in rule 12.3 to proceedings for the variation of a direction made under section 44(6) of the 1989 Act in an emergency protection order are the prescribed class of persons for the purposes of section 44(9) of that Act.

12.28 Exclusion requirements: interim care orders and emergency protection orders

(1) This rule applies where the court includes an exclusion requirement in an interim care order or an emergency protection order.

(2) The applicant for an interim care order or emergency protection order must—

(a) prepare a separate statement of the evidence in support of the application for an exclusion requirement;

(b) serve the statement personally on the relevant person with a copy of the order containing the exclusion requirement (and of any power of arrest which is attached to it);

(c) inform the relevant person of that person's right to apply to vary or discharge the exclusion requirement.

(3) Where a power of arrest is attached to an exclusion requirement in an interim care order or an emergency protection order, the applicant will deliver—

(a) a copy of the order; and

(b) a statement showing that the relevant person has been served with the order or informed of its terms (whether by being present when the order was made or by telephone or otherwise),

to the officer for the time being in charge of the police station for the area in which the dwelling-house in which the child lives is situated (or such other police station as the court may specify).

(4) Rules 10.6(2) and 10.10 to 10.17 will apply, with the necessary modifications, for the service, variation, discharge and enforcement of any exclusion requirement to which a power of arrest is attached as they apply to an order made on an application under Part 4 of the 1996 Act.

(5) The relevant person must serve the parties to the proceedings with any application which that person makes for the variation or discharge of the exclusion requirement.

(6) Where an exclusion requirement ceases to have effect whether—

- (a) as a result of the removal of a child under section 38A(10) or 44A(10) of the 1989 Act;
- (b) because of the discharge of the interim care order or emergency protection order; or
- (c) otherwise,

the applicant must inform—

- (i) the relevant person;
- (ii) the parties to the proceedings;
- (iii) any officer to whom a copy of the order was delivered under paragraph (3); and
- (iv) (where necessary) the court.

(7) Where the court includes an exclusion requirement in an interim care order or an emergency protection order of its own motion, paragraph (2) will apply with the omission of any reference to the statement of the evidence.

(8) In this rule, "the relevant person" has the meaning assigned to it by sections 38A(2) and 44A(2) of the 1989 Act.

12.29 Notification of consent

(1) Consent for the purposes of the following provisions of the 1989 Act—

- (a) section 16(3);
- (b) section 38A(2)(b)(ii) or 44A(2)(b)(ii); or
- (c) paragraph 19(3)(c) or (d) of Schedule 2,

must be given either—

- (i) orally to the court; or
- (ii) in writing to the court signed by the person giving consent.

(2) Any written consent for the purposes of section 38A(2) or 44A(2) of the 1989 Act must include a statement that the person giving consent—

- (a) is able and willing to give to the child the care which it would be reasonable to expect a parent to give; and
- (b) understands that the giving of consent could lead to the exclusion of the relevant person from the dwelling-house in which the child lives.

12.30 Proceedings for secure accommodation orders: copies of reports

In proceedings under section 25 of the 1989 Act, the court will, if practicable, arrange for copies of all written reports filed in the case to be made available before the hearing to—

- (a) the applicant;
- (b) the parent or guardian of the child to whom the application relates;
- (c) any legal representative of the child;
- (d) the children's guardian; and
- (e) the child, unless the court directs otherwise,

and copies of the reports may, if the court considers it desirable, be shown to any person who is entitled to notice of any hearing in accordance with Practice Direction 12C.

CHAPTER 4

Special Provisions about Private Law Proceedings

12.31 The First Hearing Dispute Resolution Appointment

(1) The court may set a date for the First Hearing Dispute Resolution Appointment after the proceedings have been issued.

(2) The court officer will give notice of any of the dates so fixed to the parties.

(Provisions relating to the timing of and issues to be considered at the First Hearing Dispute Resolution Appointment are contained in Practice Direction 12B.)

12.32 Answer

A respondent must file and serve on the parties an answer to the application for an order in private law proceedings within 14 days beginning with the date on which the application is served.

12.33 Applications for warning notices or applications to amend enforcement orders by reason of change of residence

(1) This rule applies in relation to an application . . . for—

(a) a warning notice to be attached to a child arrangements order; or

(b) an order under paragraph 5 of Schedule A1 to the 1989 Act to amend an enforcement order by reason of change of residence.

(2) The application must be made without notice.

(3) The court may deal with the application without a hearing.

(4) If the court decides to deal with the application at a hearing, rules 12.5, 12.7 and 12.8 will apply.

12.34 Service of a risk assessment

(1) Where an officer of the Service or a Welsh family proceedings officer has filed a risk assessment with the court, subject to paragraph (2), the court officer will as soon as practicable serve copies of the risk assessment on each party.

(2) Before serving the risk assessment, the court must consider whether, in order to prevent a risk of harm to the child, it is necessary for—

(a) information to be deleted from a copy of the risk assessment before that copy is served on a party; or

(b) service of a copy of the risk assessment (whether with information deleted from it or not) on a party to be delayed for a specified period,

and may make directions accordingly.

12.35 Service of enforcement orders or orders amending or revoking enforcement orders

(1) Paragraphs (2) and (3) apply where the court makes—

(a) an enforcement order; or

(b) an order under paragraph 9(2) of Schedule A1 to the 1989 Act (enforcement order made following a breach of an enforcement order).

(2) As soon as practicable after an order has been made, a copy of it must be served by the court officer on—

(a) the parties, except the person against whom the order is made;

(b) the officer of the Service or the Welsh family proceedings officer who is to comply with a request under section 11M of the 1989 Act to monitor compliance with the order; and

(c) the responsible officer.

(3) Unless the court directs otherwise, the applicant must serve a copy of the order personally on the person against whom the order is made.

(4) The court officer must send a copy of an order made under paragraph 4, 5, 6 or 7 of Schedule A1 to the 1989 Act (revocation or amendment of an enforcement order) to—

- (a) the parties;
- (b) the officer of the Service or the Welsh family proceedings officer who is to comply with a request under section 11M of the 1989 Act to monitor compliance with the order;
- (c) the responsible officer; and
- (d) in the case of an order under paragraph 5 of Schedule A1 to the 1989 Act (amendment of enforcement order by reason of change of residence), the responsible officer in the former local justice area.

(5) In this rule, "responsible officer" has the meaning given in paragraph 8(8) of Schedule A1 to the 1989 Act.

. . .

PRACTICE DIRECTION 12J – CHILD ARRANGEMENTS AND CONTACT ORDERS: DOMESTIC ABUSE AND HARM FPR Pt 12

A2.4

This Practice Direction supplements FPR Part 12, and incorporates and supersedes the President's Guidance in Relation to Split Hearings (May 2010) as it applies to proceedings for child arrangements orders.

Summary

1 This Practice Direction applies to any family proceedings in the Family Court or the High Court under the relevant parts of the Children Act 1989 or the relevant parts of the Adoption and Children Act 2002 in which an application is made for a child arrangements order, or in which any question arises about where a child should live, or about contact between a child and a parent or other family member, where the court considers that an order should be made.

2 The purpose of this Practice Direction is to set out what the Family Court or the High Court is required to do in any case in which it is alleged or admitted, or there is other reason to believe, that the child or a party has experienced domestic abuse perpetrated by another party or that there is a risk of such abuse.

3 For the purpose of this Practice Direction –

'domestic abuse' includes any incident or pattern of incidents of controlling, coercive or threatening behaviour, violence or abuse between those aged 16 or over who are or have been intimate partners or family members regardless of gender or sexuality. This can encompass, but is not limited to, psychological, physical, sexual, financial, or emotional abuse. Domestic abuse also includes culturally specific forms of abuse including, but not limited to, forced marriage, honour-based violence, dowry-related abuse and transnational marriage abandonment;

'abandonment' refers to the practice whereby a husband, in England and Wales, deliberately abandons or 'strands' his foreign national wife abroad, usually without financial resources, in order to prevent her from asserting matrimonial and/or residence rights in England and Wales. It may involve children who are either abandoned with, or separated from, their mother;

'coercive behaviour' means an act or a pattern of acts of assault, threats, humiliation and intimidation or other abuse that is used to harm, punish, or frighten the victim;

'controlling behaviour' means an act or pattern of acts designed to make a person subordinate and/or dependent by isolating them from sources of support, exploiting their resources and capacities for personal gain, depriving them of the means needed for independence, resistance and escape and regulating their everyday behaviour;

'development' means physical, intellectual, emotional, social or behavioural development;

'harm' means ill-treatment or the impairment of health or development including, for example, impairment suffered from seeing or hearing the ill-treatment of another, by domestic abuse or otherwise;

'health' means physical or mental health;

'ill-treatment' includes sexual abuse and forms of ill-treatment which are not physical; and 'judge' includes salaried and fee-paid judges and lay justices sitting in the Family Court and, where the context permits, can include a justices' clerk or assistant to a justices' clerk in the Family Court.

General principles

4 Domestic abuse is harmful to children, and/or puts children at risk of harm, whether they are subjected to domestic abuse, or witness one of their parents being violent or abusive to the other parent, or live in a home in which domestic abuse is perpetrated (even if the child is too young to be conscious of the behaviour). Children may suffer direct physical, psychological and/or emotional harm from living with domestic abuse, and may also suffer harm indirectly where the domestic abuse impairs the parenting capacity of either or both of their parents.

5 The court must, at all stages of the proceedings, and specifically at the First Hearing Dispute Resolution Appointment ('FHDRA'), consider whether domestic abuse is raised as an issue, either by the parties or by Cafcass or CAFCASS Cymru or otherwise, and if so must –

- identify at the earliest opportunity (usually at the FHDRA) the factual and welfare issues involved;
- consider the nature of any allegation, admission or evidence of domestic abuse, and the extent to which it would be likely to be relevant in deciding whether to make a child arrangements order and, if so, in what terms;
- give directions to enable contested relevant factual and welfare issues to be tried as soon as possible and fairly;
- ensure that where domestic abuse is admitted or proven, any child arrangements order in place protects the safety and wellbeing of the child and the parent with whom the child is living, and does not expose either of them to the risk of further harm; and
- ensure that any interim child arrangements order (i.e. considered by the court before determination of the facts, and in the absence of admission) is only made having followed the guidance in paragraphs 25–27 below.

In particular, the court must be satisfied that any contact ordered with a parent who has perpetrated domestic abuse does not expose the child and/or other parent to the risk of harm and is in the best interests of the child.

6 In all cases it is for the court to decide whether a child arrangements order accords with Section 1(1) of the Children Act 1989; any proposed child arrangements order, whether to be made by agreement between the parties or otherwise must be carefully scrutinised by the court accordingly. The court must not make a child arrangements order by consent or give permission for an application for a child arrangements order to be withdrawn, unless the parties are present in court, all initial safeguarding checks have been obtained by the court, and an officer of Cafcass or CAFCASS Cymru has spoken to the parties separately, except where it is satisfied that there is no risk of harm to the child and/or the other parent in so doing.

7 In proceedings relating to a child arrangements order, the court presumes that the involvement of a parent in a child's life will further the child's welfare, unless there is evidence to the contrary. The court must in every case consider carefully whether the statutory presumption applies, having particular regard to any allegation or admission of harm by domestic abuse to the child or parent or any evidence indicating such harm or risk of harm.

8 In considering, on an application for a child arrangements order by consent, whether there is any risk of harm to the child, the court must consider all the evidence and information available. The court may direct a report under Section 7 of the Children Act 1989 to be provided either orally or in writing, before it makes its decision; in such a case, the court must ask for information about any advice given by the officer preparing the report to the parties and whether they, or the child, have been referred to any other agency, including local authority children's services. If the report

is not in writing, the court must make a note of its substance on the court file and a summary of the same shall be set out in a Schedule to the relevant order.

Before the FHDRA

9 Where any information provided to the court before the FHDRA or other first hearing (whether as a result of initial safeguarding enquiries by Cafcass or CAFCASS Cymru or on form C1A or otherwise) indicates that there are issues of domestic abuse which may be relevant to the court's determination, the court must ensure that the issues are addressed at the hearing, and that the parties are not expected to engage in conciliation or other forms of dispute resolution which are not suitable and/or safe.

10 If at any stage the court is advised by any party (in the application form, or otherwise), by Cafcass or CAFCASS Cymru or otherwise that there is a need for special arrangements to protect the party or child attending any hearing, the court must ensure so far as practicable that appropriate arrangements are made for the hearing (including the waiting arrangements at court prior to the hearing, and arrangements for entering and exiting the court building) and for all subsequent hearings in the case, unless it is advised and considers that these are no longer necessary. Where practicable, the court should enquire of the alleged victim of domestic abuse how best she/he wishes to participate.

First hearing/FHDRA

11 At the FHDRA, if the parties have not been provided with the safeguarding letter/report by Cafcass/CAFCASS Cymru, the court must inform the parties of the content of any safeguarding letter or report or other information which has been provided by Cafcass or CAFCASS Cymru, unless it considers that to do so would create a risk of harm to a party or the child.

12 Where the results of Cafcass or CAFCASS Cymru safeguarding checks are not available at the FHDRA, and no other reliable safeguarding information is available, the court must adjourn the FHDRA until the results of safeguarding checks are available. The court must not generally make an interim child arrangements order, or orders for contact, in the absence of safeguarding information, unless it is to protect the safety of the child, and/or safeguard the child from harm (see further paragraphs 25–27 below).

13 There is a continuing duty on the Cafcass Officer/Welsh FPO which requires them to provide a risk assessment for the court under section 16A Children Act 1989 if they are given cause to suspect that the child concerned is at risk of harm. Specific provision about service of a risk assessment under section 16A of the 1989 Act is made by rule 12.34 of the FPR 2010.

14 The court must ascertain at the earliest opportunity, and record on the face of its order, whether domestic abuse is raised as an issue which is likely to be relevant to any decision of the court relating to the welfare of the child, and specifically whether the child and/or parent would be at risk of harm in the making of any child arrangements order.

Admissions

15 Where at any hearing an admission of domestic abuse toward another person or the child is made by a party, the admission must be recorded in writing by the judge and set out as a Schedule to the relevant order. The court office must arrange for a copy of any order containing a record of admissions to be made available as soon as possible to any Cafcass officer or officer of CAFCASS Cymru or local authority officer preparing a report under section 7 of the Children Act 1989.

Directions for a fact-finding hearing

16 The court should determine as soon as possible whether it is necessary to conduct a fact-finding hearing in relation to any disputed allegation of domestic abuse –

(a) in order to provide a factual basis for any welfare report or for assessment of the factors set out in paragraphs 36 and 37 below;
(b) in order to provide a basis for an accurate assessment of risk;
(c) before it can consider any final welfare-based order(s) in relation to child arrangements; or
(d) before it considers the need for a domestic abuse-related Activity (such as a Domestic Violence Perpetrator Programme (DVPP)).

17 In determining whether it is necessary to conduct a fact-finding hearing, the court should consider –

(a) the views of the parties and of Cafcass or CAFCASS Cymru;
(b) whether there are admissions by a party which provide a sufficient factual basis on which to proceed;
(c) if a party is in receipt of legal aid, whether the evidence required to be provided to obtain legal aid provides a sufficient factual basis on which to proceed;
(d) whether there is other evidence available to the court that provides a sufficient factual basis on which to proceed;
(e) whether the factors set out in paragraphs 36 and 37 below can be determined without a fact-finding hearing;
(f) the nature of the evidence required to resolve disputed allegations;
(g) whether the nature and extent of the allegations, if proved, would be relevant to the issue before the court; and
(h) whether a separate fact-finding hearing would be necessary and proportionate in all the circumstances of the case.

18 Where the court determines that a finding of fact hearing is not necessary, the order must record the reasons for that decision.

19 Where the court considers that a fact-finding hearing is necessary, it must give directions as to how the proceedings are to be conducted to ensure that the matters in issue are determined as soon as possible, fairly and proportionately, and within the capabilities of the parties. In particular it should consider –

(a) what are the key facts in dispute;
(b) whether it is necessary for the fact-finding to take place at a separate (and earlier) hearing than the welfare hearing;
(c) whether the key facts in dispute can be contained in a schedule or a table (known as a Scott Schedule) which sets out what the applicant complains of or alleges, what the respondent says in relation to each individual allegation or complaint; the allegations in the schedule should be focused on the factual issues to be tried; and if so, whether it is practicable for this schedule to be completed at the first hearing, with the assistance of the judge;
(d) what evidence is required in order to determine the existence of coercive, controlling or threatening behaviour, or of any other form of domestic abuse;
(e) directing the parties to file written statements giving details of such behaviour and of any response;
(f) whether documents are required from third parties such as the police, health services or domestic abuse support services and giving directions for those documents to be obtained;
(g) whether oral evidence may be required from third parties and if so, giving directions for the filing of written statements from such third parties;
(h) where (for example in cases of abandonment) third parties from whom documents are to be obtained are abroad, how to obtain those documents in good time for the hearing, and who should be responsible for the costs of obtaining those documents;
(i) whether any other evidence is required to enable the court to decide the key issues and giving directions for that evidence to be provided;
(j) what evidence the alleged victim of domestic abuse is able to give and what support the alleged victim may require at the fact-finding hearing in order to give that evidence;
(k) in cases where the alleged victim of domestic abuse is unable for reasons beyond their control to be present at the hearing (for example, abandonment cases where the abandoned spouse remains abroad), what measures should be taken to ensure that that person's best evidence can be put before the court. Where

video-link is not available, the court should consider alternative technological or other methods which may be utilised to allow that person to participate in the proceedings;

(l) what support the alleged perpetrator may need in order to have a reasonable opportunity to challenge the evidence; and

(m) whether a pre-hearing review would be useful prior to the fact-finding hearing to ensure directions have been complied with and all the required evidence is available.

20 Where the court fixes a fact-finding hearing, it must at the same time fix a Dispute Resolution Appointment to follow. Subject to the exception in paragraph 31 below, the hearings should be arranged in such a way that they are conducted by the same judge or, wherever possible, by the same panel of lay justices; where it is not possible to assemble the same panel of justices, the resumed hearing should be listed before at least the same chairperson of the lay justices. Judicial continuity is important.

Reports under Section 7

21 In any case where a risk of harm to a child resulting from domestic abuse is raised as an issue, the court should consider directing that a report on the question of contact, or any other matters relating to the welfare of the child, be prepared under section 7 of the Children Act 1989 by an Officer of Cafcass or a Welsh family proceedings officer (or local authority officer if appropriate), unless the court is satisfied that it is not necessary to do so in order to safeguard the child's interests.

22 If the court directs that there shall be a fact-finding hearing on the issue of domestic abuse, the court will not usually request a section 7 report until after that hearing. In that event, the court should direct that any judgment is provided to Cafcass/CAFCASS Cymru; if there is no transcribed judgment, an agreed list of findings should be provided, as set out at paragraph 29.

23 Any request for a section 7 report should set out clearly the matters the court considers need to be addressed.

Representation of the child

24 Subject to the seriousness of the allegations made and the difficulty of the case, the court must consider whether it is appropriate for the child who is the subject of the application to be made a party to the proceedings and be separately represented. If the court considers that the child should be so represented, it must review the allocation decision so that it is satisfied that the case proceeds before the correct level of judge in the Family Court or High Court.

Interim orders before determination of relevant facts

25 Where the court gives directions for a fact-finding hearing, or where disputed allegations of domestic abuse are otherwise undetermined, the court should not make an interim child arrangements order unless it is satisfied that it is in the interests of the child to do so and that the order would not expose the child or the other parent to an unmanageable risk of harm (bearing in mind the impact which domestic abuse against a parent can have on the emotional well-being of the child, the safety of the other parent and the need to protect against domestic abuse including controlling or coercive behaviour).

26 In deciding any interim child arrangements question the court should–

(a) take into account the matters set out in section 1(3) of the Children Act 1989 or section 1(4) of the Adoption and Children Act 2002 ('the welfare check-list'), as appropriate; and

(b) give particular consideration to the likely effect on the child, and on the care given to the child by the parent who has made the allegation of domestic abuse, of any contact and any risk of harm, whether physical, emotional or psychological, which the child and that parent is likely to suffer as a consequence of making or declining to make an order.

27 Where the court is considering whether to make an order for interim contact, it should in addition consider –

(a) the arrangements required to ensure, as far as possible, that any risk of harm to the child and the parent who is at any time caring for the child is minimised and that the safety of the child and the parties is secured; and in particular:
   (i) whether the contact should be supervised or supported, and if so, where and by whom; and
   (ii) the availability of appropriate facilities for that purpose;

(b) if direct contact is not appropriate, whether it is in the best interests of the child to make an order for indirect contact; and

(c) whether contact will be beneficial for the child.

The fact-finding hearing or other hearing of the facts where domestic abuse is alleged

28 While ensuring that the allegations are properly put and responded to, the fact-finding hearing or other hearing can be an inquisitorial (or investigative) process, which at all times must protect the interests of all involved. At the fact-finding hearing or other hearing –

- each party can be asked to identify what questions they wish to ask of the other party, and to set out or confirm in sworn evidence their version of the disputed key facts; and
- the judge should be prepared where necessary and appropriate to conduct the questioning of the witnesses on behalf of the parties, focusing on the key issues in the case.

29 The court should, wherever practicable, make findings of fact as to the nature and degree of any domestic abuse which is established and its effect on the child, the child's parents and any other relevant person. The court must record its findings in writing in a Schedule to the relevant order, and the court office must serve a copy of this order on the parties. A copy of any record of findings of fact or of admissions must be sent by the court office to any officer preparing a report under Section 7 of the 1989 Act.

30 At the conclusion of any fact-finding hearing, the court must consider, notwithstanding any earlier direction for a section 7 report, whether it is in the best interests of the child for the court to give further directions about the preparation or scope of any report under section 7; where necessary, it may adjourn the proceedings for a brief period to enable the officer to make representations about the preparation or scope of any further enquiries. Any section 7 report should address the factors set out in paragraphs 36 and 37 below, unless the court directs otherwise.

31 Where the court has made findings of fact on disputed allegations, any subsequent hearing in the proceedings should be conducted by the same judge or by at least the same chairperson of the justices. Exceptions may be made only where observing this requirement would result in delay to the planned timetable and the judge or chairperson is satisfied, for reasons which must be recorded in writing, that the detriment to the welfare of the child would outweigh the detriment to the fair trial of the proceedings.

In all cases where domestic abuse has occurred

32 The court should take steps to obtain (or direct the parties or an Officer of Cafcass or a Welsh family proceedings officer to obtain) information about the facilities available locally (to include local domestic abuse support services) to assist any party or the child in cases where domestic abuse has occurred.

33 Following any determination of the nature and extent of domestic abuse, whether or not following a fact-finding hearing, the court must, if considering any form of contact or involvement of the parent in the child's life, consider –

(a) whether it would be assisted by any social work, psychiatric, psychological or other assessment (including an expert safety and risk assessment) of any party or the child and if so (subject to any necessary consent) make directions for such assessment to be undertaken and for the filing of any consequent report. Any such report should address the factors set out in paragraphs 36 and 37 below, unless the court directs otherwise;
(b) whether any party should seek advice, treatment or other intervention as a precondition to any child arrangements order being made, and may (with the consent of that party) give directions for such attendance.

34 Further or as an alternative to the advice, treatment or other intervention referred to in paragraph 33(b) above, the court may make an Activity Direction under section 11A and 11B Children Act 1989. Any intervention directed pursuant to this provision should be one commissioned and approved by Cafcass. It is acknowledged that acceptance on a DVPP is subject to a suitability assessment by the service provider, and that completion of a DVPP will take time in order to achieve the aim of risk-reduction for the long-term benefit of the child and the parent with whom the child is living.

Factors to be taken into account when determining whether to make child arrangements orders in all cases where domestic abuse has occurred

35 When deciding the issue of child arrangements the court should ensure that any order for contact will not expose the child to an unmanageable risk of harm and will be in the best interests of the child.

36 In the light of any findings of fact or admissions or where domestic abuse is otherwise established, the court should apply the individual matters in the welfare checklist with reference to the domestic abuse which has occurred and any expert risk assessment obtained. In particular, the court should in every case consider any harm which the child and the parent with whom the child is living has suffered as a consequence of that domestic abuse, and any harm which the child and the parent with whom the child is living is at risk of suffering, if a child arrangements order is made. The court should make an order for contact only if it is satisfied that the physical and emotional safety of the child and the parent with whom the child is living can, as far as possible, be secured before during and after contact, and that the parent with whom the child is living will not be subjected to further domestic abuse by the other parent.

37 In every case where a finding or admission of domestic abuse is made, or where domestic abuse is otherwise established, the court should consider the conduct of both parents towards each other and towards the child and the impact of the same. In particular, the court should consider –

(a) the effect of the domestic abuse on the child and on the arrangements for where the child is living;
(b) the effect of the domestic abuse on the child and its effect on the child's relationship with the parents;
(c) whether the parent is motivated by a desire to promote the best interests of the child or is using the process to continue a form of domestic abuse against the other parent;
(d) the likely behaviour during contact of the parent against whom findings are made and its effect on the child; and
(e) the capacity of the parents to appreciate the effect of past domestic abuse and the potential for future domestic abuse.

Directions as to how contact is to proceed

38 Where any domestic abuse has occurred but the court, having considered any expert risk assessment and having applied the welfare checklist, nonetheless considers that direct contact is safe and beneficial for the child, the court should consider what, if any, directions or conditions are required to enable the order to be carried into effect and in particular should consider –

(a) whether or not contact should be supervised, and if so, where and by whom;
(b) whether to impose any conditions to be complied with by the party in whose favour the order for contact has been made and if so, the nature of those conditions, for example by way of seeking intervention (subject to any necessary consent);
(c) whether such contact should be for a specified period or should contain provisions which are to have effect for a specified period; and
(d) whether it will be necessary, in the child's best interests, to review the operation of the order; if so the court should set a date for the review consistent with the timetable for the child, and must give directions to ensure that at the review the court has full information about the operation of the order.

Where a risk assessment has concluded that a parent poses a risk to a child or to the other parent, contact via a supported contact centre, or contact supported by a parent or relative, is not appropriate.

39 Where the court does not consider direct contact to be appropriate, it must consider whether it is safe and beneficial for the child to make an order for indirect contact.

The reasons of the court

40 In its judgment or reasons the court should always make clear how its findings on the issue of domestic abuse have influenced its decision on the issue of arrangements for the child. In particular, where the court has found domestic abuse proved but nonetheless makes an order which results in the child having future contact with the perpetrator of domestic abuse, the court must always explain, whether by way of reference to the welfare check-list, the factors in paragraphs 36 and 37 or otherwise, why it takes the view that the order which it has made will not expose the child to the risk of harm and is beneficial for the child.

. . .

PART 37
APPLICATIONS AND PROCEEDINGS IN RELATION TO CONTEMPT OF COURT

A2.5

37.1 Scope

(1) This Part sets out the procedure to be followed in proceedings for contempt of court ("contempt proceedings"). .

(2) This Part does not alter the scope and extent of the jurisdiction of courts determining contempt proceedings, whether inherent, statutory or at common law.

to pay a fine or to give security for good behaviour, as it applies in relation to an order of committal.

(3) This Part has effect subject to and to the extent that it is consistent with the substantive law of contempt of court.

37.2 Interpretation

"claimant" means a person making a contempt application;

"contempt application" means an application to the court for an order determining contempt proceedings;

"defendant" means the person against whom the application is made;

"order of committal" means the imposition of a sentence of imprisonment (whether immediate or suspended) for contempt of court;

"penal notice" means a prominent notice on the front of an order warning that if the person against whom the order is made (and, in the case of a corporate body, a director or officer of that body) disobeys the court's order, the person (or director or officer) may be held in contempt of court and punished by a fine, imprisonment, confiscation of assets or other punishment under the law.

37.3 How to make a contempt application

(1) A contempt application made in existing High Court or family court proceedings is made by an application under Part 18 in those proceedings, whether or not the application is made against a party to those proceedings.

(2) If the application is made in the High Court, it shall be determined by a High Court judge of the Division in which the case is proceeding. If it is made in the family court, it shall be determined by a judge of the family court. (The Family Court (Composition and Distribution of Business) Rules 2014(3) make provision for which level of judge may determine a contempt application.)

(3) A contempt application in relation to alleged interference with the due administration of justice, otherwise than in existing High Court or family court proceedings, is made by an application to the High Court under Part 19.

(4) Where an application under Part 19 is made under paragraph (3), the rules in Part 19 apply except as modified by this Part and the defendant is not required to acknowledge service of the application.

(5) Permission to make a contempt application is required where the application is made in relation to—

- (a) interference with the due administration of justice, except in relation to existing High Court or family court proceedings;
- (b) an allegation of knowingly making a false statement in any affidavit, affirmation or other document verified by a statement of truth or in a disclosure statement.

(6) If permission to make the application is needed, the application for permission shall be included in the contempt application, which will proceed to a full hearing only if permission is granted.

(7) If permission is needed and the application relates to High Court proceedings, the question of permission shall be determined by a single judge of the High Court. If permission is granted the contempt application shall be determined by a single judge or Divisional Court of that Division.

37.4 Requirements of a contempt application

(1) Unless and to the extent that the court directs otherwise, every contempt application must be supported by written evidence given by affidavit or affirmation.

(2) A contempt application must include statements of all the following, unless (in the case of (b) to (g)) wholly inapplicable—

- (a) the nature of the alleged contempt (for example, breach of an order or undertaking or contempt in the face of the court);
- (b) the date and terms of any order allegedly breached or disobeyed;
- (c) confirmation that any such order was personally served, and the date it was served, unless the court or the parties dispensed with personal service;
- (d) if the court dispensed with personal service, the terms and date of the court's order dispensing with personal service;
- (e) confirmation that any order allegedly breached or disobeyed included a penal notice;
- (f) the date and terms of any undertaking allegedly breached;
- (g) confirmation of the claimant's belief that the person who gave any undertaking understood its terms and the consequences of failure to comply with it;
- (h) a brief summary of the facts alleged to constitute the contempt, set out numerically in chronological order;
- (i) that the defendant has the right to be legally represented in the contempt proceedings;
- (j) that the defendant is entitled to a reasonable opportunity to obtain legal representation and to apply for legal aid which may be available without any means test;
- (k) that the defendant may be entitled to the services of an interpreter;
- (l) that the defendant is entitled to a reasonable time to prepare for the hearing;
- (m) that the defendant is entitled but not obliged to give written and oral evidence in their defence;
- (n) that the defendant has the right to remain silent and to decline to answer any question the answer to which may incriminate the defendant;
- (o) that the court may proceed in the defendant's absence if they do not attend but (whether or not they attend) will only find the defendant in contempt if satisfied beyond reasonable doubt of the facts constituting contempt and that they do constitute contempt;
- (p) that if the court is satisfied that the defendant has committed a contempt, the court may punish the defendant by a fine, imprisonment, confiscation of assets or other punishment under the law;
- (q) that if the defendant admits the contempt and wishes to apologise to the court, that is likely to reduce the seriousness of any punishment by the court;
- (r) that the court's findings will be provided in writing as soon as practicable after the hearing; and

(s) that the court will sit in public, unless and to the extent that the court orders otherwise, and that its findings will be made public.

37.5 Service of a contempt application

(1) Unless the court directs otherwise in accordance with Part 6 and except as provided in paragraph (2), a contempt application and evidence in support must be served on the defendant personally.

(2) Where a legal representative for the defendant is on the record in the proceedings in which, or in connection with which, an alleged contempt is committed—

(a) the contempt application and evidence in support may be served on the representative for the defendant unless the representative objects in writing within seven days of receipt of the application and evidence in support;

(b) if the representative does not object in writing, they must at once provide to the defendant a copy of the contempt application and the evidence supporting it and take all reasonable steps to ensure the defendant understands them;

(c) if the representative objects in writing, the issue of service shall be referred to a judge of the court dealing with the contempt application; and the judge shall consider written representations from the parties and determine the issue on the papers, without (unless the judge directs otherwise) an oral hearing.

37.6 Cases where no application is made

(1) If the court considers that a contempt of court (including a contempt in the face of the court) may have been committed, the court on its own initiative shall consider whether to proceed against the defendant in contempt proceedings.

(2) Where the court does so, any other party in the proceedings may be required by the court to give such assistance to the court as is proportionate and reasonable, having regard to the resources available to that party.

(3) If the court proceeds of its own initiative, it shall issue a summons to the defendant which includes the matters set out in rule 37.4(2)(a)–(s) (in so far as applicable) and requires the defendant to attend court for directions to be given.

(4) A summons issued under this rule shall be served on the defendant personally and on any other party, unless the court directs otherwise. If rule 37.5(2) applies, the procedure there set out shall be followed unless the court directs otherwise.

37.7 Directions for hearing of contempt proceedings

(1) The court shall give such directions as it thinks fit for the hearing and determination of contempt proceedings, including directions for the attendance of witnesses and oral evidence, as it considers appropriate.

(2) The court may issue a bench warrant to secure the attendance of the defendant at a directions hearing or at the substantive hearing.

(3) The court may not give any direction compelling the defendant to give evidence either orally or in writing.

37.8 Hearings and judgments in contempt proceedings

(1) All hearings of contempt proceedings shall, irrespective of the parties' consent, be listed and heard in public unless the court otherwise directs, applying the provisions of paragraph (4).

(2) In deciding whether to hold a hearing in private, the court must consider any duty to protect or have regard to a right to freedom of expression which may be affected.

(3) The court shall .take reasonable steps to ensure that all hearings are of an open and public character, save when a hearing is held in private.

(4) A hearing, or any part of it, must be held in private if, and only to the extent that, the court is satisfied of one or more of the matters set out in sub-paragraphs (a) to (g) and that it is necessary to sit in private to secure the proper administration of justice—

- (a) publicity would defeat the object of the hearing;
- (b) it involves matters relating to national security;
- (c) it involves confidential information (including information relating to personal financial matters) and publicity would damage that confidentiality;
- (d) a private hearing is necessary to protect the interests of any child or protected party;
- (e) it is a hearing of an application made without notice and it would be unjust to any respondent for there to be a public hearing;
- (f) it involves uncontentious matters arising in the administration of trusts or in the administration of a deceased person's estate; or
- (g) the court for any other reason considers this to be necessary to secure the proper administration of justice.

(5) The court must order that the identity of any party or witness shall not be disclosed if, and only if, it considers non-disclosure necessary to secure the proper administration of justice and in order to protect the interests of that party or witness.

(6) Unless and to the extent that the court otherwise directs, where the court acts under paragraph (4) or (5), a copy of the court's order shall be published on the website of the Judiciary of England and Wales (which may be found at www.judiciary.uk). Any person who is not a party to the proceedings may apply to attend the hearing and make submissions, or apply to set aside or vary the order.

(7) Advocates and the judge shall appear robed in all hearings of contempt proceedings, whether or not the court sits in public.

(8) Before deciding to sit in private for all or part of the hearing, the court shall notify the national print and broadcast media, via the Press Association.

(9) The court shall consider any submissions from the parties or media organisations before deciding whether and if so to what extent the hearing should be in private.

(10) If the court decides to sit in private it shall, before doing so, sit in public to give a reasoned public judgment setting out why it is doing so.

(11) At the conclusion of the hearing, whether or not held in private, the court shall sit in public to give a reasoned public judgment stating its findings and any punishment.

(12) The court shall inform the defendant of the right to appeal without permission, the time limit for appealing and the court before which any appeal must be brought.

(13) The court shall be responsible for ensuring that judgments in contempt proceedings are transcribed and published on the website of the judiciary of England and Wales.

37.9 Powers of the court in contempt proceedings

(1) If the court finds the defendant in contempt of court, the court may impose a period of imprisonment (an order of committal), a fine, confiscation of assets or other punishment permitted under the law.

(2) Execution of an order of committal requires issue of a warrant of committal. An order of committal and a warrant of committal have immediate effect unless and to the extent that the court decides to suspend execution of the order or warrant.

(3) An order or warrant of committal must be personally served on the defendant unless the court directs otherwise.

(4) To the extent that the substantive law permits, a court may attach a power of arrest to a committal order.

(5) An order or warrant of committal may not be enforced more than two years after the date it was made unless the court directs otherwise.

37.10 Applications to discharge committal orders

(1) A defendant against whom a committal order has been made may apply to discharge it.

(2) Any such application shall be made by an application notice under Part 18 in the contempt proceedings.

(3) The court hearing such an application shall consider all the circumstances and make such order under the law as it thinks fit."

PRACTICE DIRECTION 37A – APPLICATIONS AND PROCEEDINGS IN RELATION TO CONTEMPT OF COURT FPR Pt 37

A2.6

This Practice Direction supplements FPR Part 37.

CHAPTER 2 OF PART 37 – COMMITTAL FOR BREACH OF A JUDGMENT, ORDER OR UNDERTAKING TO DO OR ABSTAIN FROM DOING AN ACT

Requirement for a penal notice on judgments and orders – form of penal notice – Rule 37.9

1.1 A judgment or order which restrains a party from doing an act or requires an act to be done must, if disobedience is to be dealt with by proceedings for contempt of court, have a penal notice endorsed on it as follows (or in words to substantially the same effect) –

> 'If you the within-named [] do not comply with this order you may be held to be in contempt of court and imprisoned or fined, or your assets may be seized.'.

1.2 Where an order referred to in rule 37.9(3)(a) or (b) is to be endorsed with or have incorporated in it a penal notice in accordance with rule 37.9(3), the notice must be in the words set out in paragraph 1.1 of the Practice Direction, or words to substantially the same effect.

Requirement for a penal notice on judgments and orders – undertakings – Rule 37.9

2.1 Subject to rule 37.9(2) (which covers the case where the undertaking is contained in an order or judgment), the form of an undertaking to do or abstain from doing any act must be endorsed with a notice setting out the consequences of disobedience as follows (or in words to substantially the same effect) –

> 'You may be held to be in contempt of court and imprisoned or fined, or your assets may be seized, if you break the promises that you have given to the court.'.

2.2 The court may decline to –

(1) accept an undertaking; and
(2) deal with disobedience in respect of an undertaking by contempt of court proceedings,

unless the party giving the undertaking has made a signed statement to the effect that that party understands the terms of the undertaking and the consequences of failure to comply with it, as follows (or in words to substantially the same effect) –

> 'I understand the undertaking that I have given and that if I break any of my promises to the court I may be sent to prison, or fined, or my assets may be seized, for contempt of court.'.

2.3 The statement need not be given before the court in person. It may be endorsed on the court copy of the undertaking or may be filed in a separate document such as a letter.

CHAPTER 3 OF PART 37 – CONTEMPT IN THE FACE OF THE COURT

Committal for contempt in the face of the court – Rule 37.12

3.1 Where the committal proceedings relate to a contempt in the face of the court the matters referred to in paragraph 4.3 should be given particular attention. Normally, it will be appropriate to defer consideration of the respondent's actions and behaviour to allow the respondent time to reflect on what has occurred. The time needed for the following procedures should allow such a period of reflection.

3.2 The use of the Part 18 procedure is not required for contempt falling under Chapter 3 of Part 37, but other provisions of this Practice Direction should be applied, as necessary, or adapted to the circumstances.

3.3 The judge should –

(1) tell the respondent of the possible penalty that the respondent faces;
(2) inform the respondent in detail, and preferably in writing, of the actions and behaviour of the respondent which have given rise to the committal application;
(3) if the judge considers that an apology would remove the need for the committal application, tell the respondent;
(4) have regard to the need for the respondent to be –
  (a) allowed a reasonable time for responding to the committal application, including, if necessary, preparing a defence;
  (b) made aware of the possible availability of criminal legal aid and how to contact the Legal Aid Agency;
  (c) given the opportunity, if unrepresented, to obtain legal advice;
  (d) if unable to understand English, allowed to make arrangements, seeking the court's assistance if necessary, for an interpreter to attend the hearing; and
  (e) brought back before the court for the committal application to be heard within a reasonable time;
(5) allow the respondent an opportunity to –
  (a) apologise to the court;
  (b) explain the respondent's actions and behaviour; and
  (c) if the contempt is proved, to address the court on the penalty to be imposed on the respondent; and
(6) where appropriate, nominate a suitable person to give the respondent the information. (It is likely to be appropriate to nominate a person where the effective communication of information by the judge to the respondent was not possible when the incident occurred.)

3.4 If there is a risk of the appearance of bias, the judge should ask another judge to hear the committal application.

3.5 Where the committal application is to be heard by another judge, a written statement by the judge before whom the actions and behaviour of the respondent which have given rise to the committal application took place may be admitted as evidence of those actions and behaviour.

CHAPTER 5 OF PART 37 – COMMITTAL FOR MAKING A FALSE STATEMENT OF TRUTH

Committal application in relation to a false statement of truth – Rule 37.17

4.1 Rules 37.17(1)(b) and 37.17(2)(b) provide that a committal application may be made by the Attorney General. However, the Attorney General prefers a request that comes from the court to one made direct by a party to the proceedings in which the alleged contempt occurred without prior consideration by the court. A request to the Attorney General is not a way of appealing against, or reviewing, the decision of the judge.

4.2 Where the permission of the court is sought under rule 37.17(1)(a) or 37.17(2)(a) so that rule 37.15 is applied by rule 37.17(3), the affidavit evidence in support of the application must –

(1) identify the statement said to be false;
(2) explain –
  (a) why it is false; and
  (b) why the maker knew the statement to be false at the time it was made; and
(3) explain why contempt proceedings would be appropriate in the light of the overriding objective in Part 1.

4.3 The court may –

(1) exercise any of its powers under the rules (including the power to give directions under rule 37.15(6));
(2) initiate steps to consider if there is a contempt of court and, where there is, to punish it; or
(3) as provided by rule 37.17(4), direct that the matter be referred to the Attorney General with a request to consider whether to bring proceedings for contempt of court.

4.4 A request to the Attorney General to consider whether to bring proceedings for contempt of court must be made in writing and sent to the Attorney General's Office at 20 Victoria Street, London, SW1H 0NF.

Note—The Attorney-General's office is now at 5–8 The Sanctuary, London SW1P 3JS.

4.5 A request to the Attorney General must be accompanied by a copy of any order directing that the matter be referred to the Attorney General and must –

(1) identify the statement said to be false;
(2) explain –
  (a) why it is false; and
  (b) why the maker knew the statement to be false at the time it was made; and
(3) explain why contempt proceedings would be appropriate in the light of the overriding objective in Part 1.

4.6 Once the applicant receives the result of the request to the Attorney General, the applicant must send a copy of it to the court that will deal with the committal application, and the court will give such directions as it sees fit.

4.7 The rules do not change the law of contempt or introduce new categories of contempt. A person applying to commence such proceedings should consider whether the incident complained of does amount to contempt of court and whether such proceedings would further the overriding objective in Part 1.

CHAPTER 6 OF PART 37 – WRIT OF SEQUESTRATION TO ENFORCE A JUDGMENT, ORDER OR UNDERTAKING

Requirement for a penal notice on judgments and orders – form of penal notice – Rule 37.24

5 Paragraphs 1 and 2.1 to 2.3 apply to judgments and orders to be enforced by a writ of sequestration.

Levying execution on certain days

6 Unless the court orders otherwise, a writ of sequestration to enforce a judgment, order or undertaking must not be executed on a Sunday, Good Friday or Christmas Day.

CHAPTER 7 OF PART 37 – GENERAL RULES ABOUT COMMITTAL APPLICATIONS, ORDERS FOR COMMITTAL AND WRITS OF SEQUESTRATION

General rules

7.1 Subject to paragraph 7.2, this Section of the Practice Direction applies in relation to all matters covered by Part 37.

7.2 Where there is a conflict between the provisions in this Section of the Practice Direction and specific provisions elsewhere in this Practice Direction or in Part 37, the specific provisions prevail.

Human rights

8 In all cases the Convention rights of those involved should particularly be borne in mind. It should be noted that the standard of proof, having regard to the possibility that a person may be sent to prison, is that the allegation be proved beyond reasonable doubt.

(Section 1 of the Human Rights Act 1998 defines 'the Convention rights'.)

General rules about applications: applications which cannot be made without permission

9 If the committal application is one which cannot be made without permission –

(1) the permission may only be granted by a judge who would have power to hear the committal application if permission were granted;
(2) the date on which and the name of the judge by whom the requisite permission was granted must be stated on the application notice by which the committal application is commenced;
(3) the application notice may not be issued or filed until the requisite permission has been granted; and
(4) Rules 18.10 and 18.11 do not apply.

General rules about applications: using Part 18 procedure

10.1 Where the application is made using the Part 18 procedure in existing proceedings, the application notice must state that the application is made in the proceedings in question, and its title and reference number must correspond with the title and reference number of those proceedings.

10.2 If the application for permission to make a committal application or the committal application is commenced by the filing of an application notice –

(1) Part 18 will apply subject to the provisions of Part 37 and this Practice Direction, in particular sub-paragraphs (2) to (4);
(2) an amendment to the application notice may be made with the permission of the court but not otherwise;
(3) the court may not dispose of the application without a hearing; and
(4) the application notice must contain a prominent notice stating the possible consequences of the court making a committal order and of the respondent not attending the hearing. A form of notice which may be used is annexed to this Practice Direction.

Evidence and information

11.1 Written evidence in support of or in opposition to a committal application must be given by affidavit.

11.2 Written evidence served in support of or in opposition to a committal application must, unless the court otherwise directs, be filed.

11.3 The following rules do not apply to committal applications –

(1) rule 25.11 (Court's power to direct that evidence is to be given by a single joint expert);
(2) rule 25.12 (Instructions to single joint expert); and
(3) rule 25.13 (Power of court to direct a party to provide information).

The hearing – Rule 37.27

12.1 When issuing or filing the application notice for a committal application, the applicant must obtain from the court a date for the hearing of the committal application.

12.2 Unless the court otherwise directs, the hearing date of a committal application must not be less than 14 days after service of the application notice on the respondent. The hearing date must be specified in the application notice or in a Notice of Hearing attached to and served with the application notice.

12.3 The court may on the hearing date –

(1) give case management directions with a view to a hearing of the committal application on a future date; or
(2) if the committal application is ready to be heard, proceed to hear it.

12.4 In dealing with any committal application, the court will have regard to the need for the respondent to have details of the alleged acts of contempt and the opportunity to respond to the committal application.

12.5 The court will also have regard to the need for the respondent to be –

(1) allowed a reasonable time for responding to the committal application including, if necessary, preparing a defence;
(2) made aware of the possible availability of criminal legal aid and how to contact the Legal Aid Agency;
(3) given the opportunity, if unrepresented, to obtain legal advice; and
(4) if unable to understand English, allowed to make arrangements, seeking the assistance of the court if necessary, for an interpreter to attend the hearing.

Striking out, procedural defects and discontinuance

13.1 On application by the respondent or on its own initiative, the court may strike out a committal application if it appears to the court –

(1) that the application and the evidence served in support of it disclose no reasonable ground for alleging that the respondent is guilty of a contempt of court;
(2) that the application is an abuse of the court's process or, if made in existing proceedings, is otherwise likely to obstruct the just disposal of those proceedings; or
(3) that there has been a failure to comply with a rule, practice direction or court order.

13.2 The court may waive any procedural defect in the commencement or conduct of a committal application if satisfied that no injustice has been caused to the respondent by the defect.

13.3 A committal application may not be discontinued without the permission of the court.

ANNEX: PARAGRAPH 10.2(4)

Form of penal notice to be included on committal applications

IMPORTANT NOTICE

The Court has power to send you to prison, to fine you or seize your assets if it finds that any of the allegations made against you are true and amount to a contempt of court. **You must attend court** on the date shown on the front of this form. It is in your own interest to do so. You should bring with you any witnesses and documents which you think will help you put your side of the case. If you consider the allegations are not true you must tell the court why. If it is established that they are true, you must tell the court of any good reason why they do not amount to a contempt of court, or, if they do, why you should not be punished. If you need advice, you should show this document at once to your solicitor or go to a Citizens' Advice Bureau or similar organisation.

PRACTICE DIRECTION
26 MARCH 2015

Committal for Contempt of Court – Open Court

Preamble

A2.7

1 This Practice Direction applies to all proceedings for committal for contempt of court, including contempt in the face of the court, whether arising under any statutory or inherent jurisdiction and, particularly, supplements the provisions relating to contempt of court in the Civil Procedure Rules 1998, the Family Procedure Rules 2010, the Court of Protection Rules 2007, and the Criminal Procedure Rules 2014 and any related Practice Directions supplementing those various provisions. It applies in all courts in England and Wales, including the Court of Protection, and supersedes the Practice Guidance: Committal for Contempt [2013] 1 WLR 1326, dated 3 May 2013; Practice Guidance (Committal Proceedings: Open Court) (No 2) [2013] 1 WLR 1753, dated 4 June 2013; and President's Circular: Committals (The Family Court Practice 2014 at p 2976), dated 2 August 2013.

2 Any reference in this Practice Direction to a judgment includes reference to written reasons provided in accordance with rule 27.2 of the Family Procedure Rules 2010.

Open Justice

3 Open justice is a fundamental principle. The general rule is that hearings are carried out in, and judgments and orders are made in, public. This rule applies to all hearings, whether on application or otherwise, for committal for contempt irrespective of the court in which they are heard or of the proceedings in which they arise.

4 Derogations from the general principle can only be justified in exceptional circumstances, when they are strictly necessary as measures to secure the proper administration of justice. Derogations shall, where justified, be no more than strictly necessary to achieve their purpose.

Committal Hearings – in Public

5

(1) All committal hearings, whether on application or otherwise and whether for contempt in the face of the court or any other form of contempt, shall be listed and heard in public.

(2) They shall, except where paragraph 5(3) applies, be listed in the public court list as follows:
FOR HEARING IN OPEN COURT
Application by (*full name of applicant*) for
the Committal to prison of
(*full name of the person alleged to be in contempt*)

(3) In those cases where the person alleged to be in contempt is subject to arrest for an alleged breach of an order, including a location or collection order or an order made under the Family Law Act 1996, the hearing shall be listed in the public court list as follows:
FOR HEARING IN OPEN COURT [*add, where there has been a remand in custody*: in accordance with the order of (name of judge) dated (*date*)]
Proceedings for the Committal to prison of
(*full name of the person alleged to be in contempt*)

who was arrested on (*date*) in accordance with and for alleged breach of a [location/collection/Family Law Act 1996/other] order made by (*name of judge*) on (*date*).

6 Where it is not possible to publish the details required by paragraph 5(3) in the public court list in the usual way the day before the hearing ie, in such circumstances where the alleged contemnor is produced at court by the Tipstaff or a constable on the morning of the hearing, having been arrested over night, the following steps should be taken:

(1) Where, as in the Royal Courts of Justice, the public court list is prepared and accessible in electronic form, it should be updated with the appropriate entry as soon as the court becomes aware that the matter is coming before it;
(2) Notice of the hearing should at the same time be placed outside the door of the court in which the matter is being, or is to be heard, and at whatever central location in the building the various court lists are displayed;
(3) Notice should be given to the national print and broadcast media, via the Press Association's CopyDirect service, of the fact that the hearing is taking or is shortly due to take place.

If an alleged contemnor is produced at court, having been arrested overnight, the person shall immediately be produced before a judge who shall sit in public.

7 Where the committal hearing is brought by way of application notice, the court may authorise any person who is not a party to proceedings to obtain a copy of the application notice, upon request and subject to payment of any appropriate fee. Authorisation shall be granted in all but exceptional circumstances. Where authorisation is refused, the reasons for that refusal shall be set out in writing by the judge and supplied to the person who made the request.

Committal Hearings – in Private

8 Where the court, either on application or otherwise, is considering derogating from the general rule and holding a committal hearing in private, or imposing any other such derogation from the principle of open justice:

(1) it shall in all cases before the hearing takes place, notify the national print and broadcast media, via the Press Association's CopyDirect service, of the fact of the committal hearing (whether it is brought on application or otherwise) when and where it is listed for hearing, and the nature of the proposed derogation; and
(2) at the outset of the committal hearing the court shall hear submissions from the parties and/or the media on the question whether to impose the proposed derogation.

9 In considering the question whether there are exceptional circumstances justifying a derogation from the general rule, and whether that derogation is no more than strictly necessary the fact that the committal hearing is made in the Court of Protection or in any proceedings relating to a child does not of itself justify the matter being heard in private. Moreover the fact that the hearing may involve the disclosure of material which ought not to be published does not of itself justify hearing the application in private if such publication can be restrained by an appropriate order.

10 Where the court decides to exercise its discretion to derogate from the general rule, and particularly where it decides to hold a committal hearing in private, it shall, before it continues to do so, sit in public in order to give a reasoned public judgment setting out why it is doing so.

11 Where, having decided to exercise its discretion to hold a committal hearing in private, the court further decides that the substantive committal application is to be adjourned to a future date, the adjourned hearing shall be listed in the public court list

as follows:

FOR HEARING IN PRIVATE

In accordance with the order of (*name of judge*) dated (*date*)

[On the application of (*full name of applicant*)]

Proceedings for the Committal to prison of

(*full name of the person alleged to be in contempt*)

12 Orders directing a committal hearing be heard in private or of other such derogations from the principle of open justice shall not be granted by consent of the parties: see *JIH v News Group Newspapers* [2011] EWCA Civ 42, [2011] 1 WLR 1645 at [21].

Judgments

13

(1) In all cases, irrespective of whether the court has conducted the hearing in public or in private, and the court finds that a person has committed a contempt of court, the court shall at the conclusion of that hearing sit in public and state:
   (i) the name of that person;
   (ii) in general terms the nature of the contempt of court in respect of which the committal order, which for this purpose includes a suspended committal order, is being made;
   (iii) the punishment being imposed; and
   (iv) provide the details required by (i) to (iii) to the national media, via the CopyDirect service, and to the Judicial Office, at judicialwebupdates@judiciary.gsi.gov.uk, for publication on the website of the Judiciary of England and Wales.

(2) There are no exceptions to these requirements. There are never any circumstances in which any one may be committed to custody or made subject to a suspended committal order without these matters being stated by the court sitting in public.

14 In addition to the requirements at paragraph 13, the court shall, in respect of all committal decisions, also either produce a written judgment setting out its reasons or ensure that any oral judgment is transcribed, such transcription to be ordered the same day as the judgment is given and prepared on an expedited basis. It shall do so irrespective of its practice prior to this Practice Direction coming into force and irrespective of whether or not anyone has requested this.

15 Copies of the written judgment or transcript of judgment shall then be provided to the parties and the national media via the CopyDirect service. Copies shall also be supplied to BAILII and to the Judicial Office at judicialwebupdates@judiciary.gsi.gov.uk for publication on their websites as soon as reasonably practicable.

16 Advocates and the judge (except judges and justices of the peace in the Magistrates' courts) shall be robed for all committal hearings.

This Direction is made by the Lord Chief Justice, following consultation with the Master of the Rolls, President of the Queen's Bench Division, President of the Family Division and of the Court of Protection, and Chancellor of the High Court. It is issued in accordance with the procedure laid down in Part 1 of Schedule 2 to the Constitutional Reform Act 2005.

Lord Thomas LCJ

Appendix 3

SAMPLE FORMS AND ORDERS

FORM FL401

A3.1

Application for:
a non-molestation order
an occupation order

Family Law Act 1996 (Part IV)

The court

To be completed by the court
Date issued
Case number
Fee charged/Remission ID

Please read the accompanying notes as you complete this form.

1 About you (the applicant)

State your title (Mr, Mrs etc), full name, address, telephone number and date of birth (if under 18):

State your solicitor's name, address, reference, telephone, FAX and DX numbers:

Solicitor's fee account no.	

2 About the respondent

State the respondent's name, address and date of birth (if known):

3 The Order(s) for which you are applying

This application is for:

☐ a non-molestation order

☐ an occupation order

☐ Tick this box if you wish the court to hear your application without notice being given to the respondent. The reasons relied on for an application being heard without notice must be stated in the statement in support.

4 Your relationship to the respondent (the person to be served with this application)

Your relationship to the respondent is:

(Please tick only one of the following)

1 ☐ Married

2 ☐ Civil Partners

3 ☐ Were married

4 ☐ Former civil partners

5 ☐ Cohabiting

6 ☐ Were cohabiting

7 ☐ Both of you live or have lived in the same household

8 ☐ Relative
State how related:

9 ☐ Agreed to marry.
Give the date the agreement was made.
If the agreement has ended, state when.

10 ☐ Agreed to form a civil partnership.
Give the date the agreement was made.
If the agreement has ended, state when.

11 ☐ Both of you are parents of, or have parental responsibility for, a child

12 ☐ One of you is a parent of a child and the other has parental responsibility for that child

13 ☐ You are having, or have had an intimate personal relationship which is or was of significant duration

14☐ One of you is the natural parent or grandparent of a child adopted, placed or freed for adoption, and the other is:

(i) the adoptive parent

or (ii) a person who has applied for an adoption order for the child

or (iii) a person with whom the child has been placed for adoption

or (iv) the child who has been adopted, placed or freed for adoption.

State whether (i), (ii), (iii) or (iv):

15☐ Both of you are the parties to the same family proceedings (see also Section 11 below).

5 Application for a non-molestation order

If you wish to apply for a non-molestation order, state briefly in this section the order you want.

Give full details in support of your application in your supporting evidence.

6 Application for an occupation order

If you do not wish to apply for an occupation order, please go to section 9 of this form.

(A) State the address of the dwelling-house to which your application relates:

(B) State whether it is occupied by you or the respondent now or in the past, or whether it was intended to be occupied by you or the respondent:

(C) State whether you are entitled to occupy the dwelling-house: ☐ Yes ☐ No

If yes, explain why:

(D) State whether the respondent is entitled to occupy the dwelling-house: ☐ Yes ☐ No

If yes, explain why:

On the basis of your answers to (C) and (D) above, tick one of the boxes 1 to 6 below to show the category into which you fit

1 ☐ a spouse or civil partner who has home rights in the dwelling-house, or a person who is entitled to occupy it by virtue of a beneficial estate or interest or contract or by virtue of any enactment giving him or her the right to remain in occupation.

If you tick box 1, state whether there is a dispute or pending proceedings between you and the respondent about your right to occupy the dwelling-house.

2 ☐ a former spouse or former civil partner with no existing right to occupy, where the respondent spouse or civil partner is so entitled.

3 ☐ a cohabitant or former cohabitant with no existing right to occupy, where the respondent cohabitant or former cohabitant is so entitled.

4 ☐ a spouse or former spouse who is not entitled to occupy, where the respondent spouse or former spouse is also not entitled.

5 ☐ a civil partner or former civil partner who is not entitled to occupy, where the respondent civil partner or former civil partner is also not entitled.

6 ☐ a cohabitant or former cohabitant who is not entitled to occupy, where the respondent cohabitant or former cohabitant is also not entitled.

Home Rights

If you do have home rights please:

State whether the title to the land is registered or unregistered (if known):

If registered, state the Land Registry title number (if known):

If you wish to apply for an occupation order, state briefly here the order you want. Give full details in support of your application in your supporting evidence:

7 Application for additional order(s) about the dwelling-house

If you want to apply for any of the orders listed in the notes to this section, state what order you would like the court to make:

8 Mortgage and rent

Is the dwelling-house subject to a mortgage?

☐ Yes ☐ No

If yes, please provide the name and address of the mortgagee:

Is the dwelling-house rented?

☐ Yes ☐ No

If yes, please provide the name and address of the landlord:

9 At the court

Will you need an interpreter at court?

☐ Yes ☐ No

If yes, specify the language:

If you require an interpreter, you must notify the court immediately so that one can be arranged.

If you have a disability for which you require special assistance or special facilities, please state what your needs are. The court staff will get in touch with you about your requirements.

10 Other information

State the name and date of birth of any child living with or staying with, or likely to live with or stay with, you or the respondent:

State the name of any other person living in the same household as you and the respondent, and say why they live there:

11 Other Proceedings and Orders

If there are any other current family proceedings or orders in force involving you and the respondent, state the type of proceedings or orders, the court and the case number. This includes any application for an occupation order or non-molestation order against you by the respondent.

This application is to be served upon the respondent

Signed: Date:

6

Application for non-molestation order or occupation order
Notes for guidance

Section 1

If you do not wish your address to be made known to the respondent, leave the space on the form blank and complete Confidential Address Form C8. The court can give you this form.

If you are under 18, someone over 18 must help you make this application. That person, who might be one of your parents, is called a 'next friend'.

If you are under 16, you need permission to make this application. You must apply to the High Court for permission, using this form. If the High Court gives you permission to make this application, it will then either hear the application itself or transfer it to a county court.

Section 3

An urgent order made by the court before the notice of the application is served on the respondent is called an ex-parte order. In deciding whether to make an ex-parte order the court will consider all the circumstances of the case, including:

- any risk of significant harm to the applicant or a relevant child, attributable to conduct of the respondent, if the order is not made immediately
- whether it is likely that the applicant will be deterred or prevented from pursuing the application if an order is not made immediately
- whether there is reason to believe that the respondent is aware of the proceedings but is deliberately evading service and that the applicant or a relevant child will be seriously prejudiced by the delay involved.

If the court makes an ex-parte order, it must give the respondent an opportunity to make representations about the order as soon as just and convenient at a full hearing.

'Harm' in relation to a person who has reached the age of 18 means ill-treatment or the impairment of health, and in relation to a child means ill-treatment or the impairment of health and development.

'Ill-treatment' includes forms of ill-treatment which are not physical and, in relation to a child, includes sexual abuse. The court will require evidence of any harm which you allege in support of your application.

Section 4

For you to be able to apply for an order you must be related to the respondent in one of the ways listed in this section of the form. If you are not related in one of these ways you should seek legal advice.

Cohabitants are two persons who, although not married to each other, nor civil partners of each other, are living together as husband and wife or civil partners. People who have cohabited, but have then married or formed a civil partnership will not fall within this category but will fall within the category of married people or people who are civil partners of each other.

Those who live or have lived in the same household do not include people who share the same household because one of them is the other's employee, tenant, lodger or boarder.

You will only be able to apply as a relative of the respondent if you are:
(A) the father, mother, stepfather, stepmother, son, daughter, stepson, stepdaughter, grandmother, grandfather, grandson, granddaughter of the respondent or of the respondent's spouse, former spouse, civil partner or former civil partner.

(B) the brother, sister, uncle, aunt, niece, nephew or first cousin (whether of the full blood or of the half blood or by marriage or by civil partnership) of the respondent or of the respondent's spouse, former spouse, civil partner or former civil partner.

This includes, in relation to a person who is living or has lived with another person as husband and wife or as civil partners, any person who would fall within (A) or (B) if the parties were married to, or civil partners of, each other (for example, your cohabitee's father or brother).

Agreements to marry: You will fall within this category only if you make this application within three years of the termination of the agreement. The court will require the following evidence of the agreement:

evidence in writing

or the gift of an engagement ring in contemplation of marriage

or evidence that a ceremony has been entered into in the presence of one or more other persons assembled for the purpose of witnessing it.

Agreements to form a civil partnership: You will fall within this category only if you make this application within three years of the termination of the agreement. The court will require the following evidence of the agreement:

evidence in writing

or a gift from one party to the agreement to the other as a token of the agreement

or evidence that a ceremony has been entered into in the presence of one or more other persons assembled for the purpose of witnessing it.

Parents and parental responsibility:
You will fall within this category if

both you and the respondent are either the parents of the child or have parental responsibility for that child

or if one of you is the parent and the other has parental responsibility.

Section 4 continued

Under the Children Act 1989, parental responsibility is held automatically by a child's mother, and by the child's father if he and the mother were married to each other at the time of the child's birth or have married subsequently. Where, a child's father and mother are not married to each other at the time of the child's birth, the father may also acquire parental responsibility for that child, if he registers the birth after 1st December 2003, in accordance with section 4(1)(a) of the Children Act 1989. Where neither of these circumstances apply, the father, in accordance with the provisions of the Children Act 1989, can acquire parental responsibility.

From 30 December 2005, where a person who is not the child's parent ("the step-parent") is married to, or a civil partner of, a parent who has parental responsibility for that child, he or she may also acquire parental responsibility for the child in accordance with the provisions of the Children Act 1989.

From 1st September 2009, specific provision has been made in relation to parental responsibility in certain cases involving assisted reproduction. Parental responsibility is held automatically by a woman if—

- she and the child's mother were in a civil partnership with each other at the time of treatment unless that woman did not consent to the treatment; or
- she is a parent of the child by virtue of section 43 of the Human Fertilisation and Embryology Act 2008 and subsequently enters into a civil partnership with the mother.

A woman who is a parent of the child by virtue of section 43 of the 2008 Act but who does not subsequently enter into a civil partnership with the mother may acquire parental responsibility in accordance with the provisions of section 4ZA of the Children Act 1989

Section 5

A non-molestation order can forbid the respondent from molesting you or a relevant child. Molestation can include, for example, violence, threats, pestering and other forms of harassment. The court can forbid particular acts of the respondent, molestation in general, or both.

Section 6

If you wish to apply for an occupation order but you are uncertain about your answer to any question in this part of the application form, you should seek legal advice.

(A) A dwelling-house includes any building or part of a building which is occupied as a dwelling; any caravan, houseboat or structure which is occupied as a dwelling; and any yard, garden, garage or outhouse belonging to it and occupied with it.

(C) & (D) The following questions give examples to help you to decide if you or the respondent, or both of you, are entitled to occupy the dwelling-house:

(a) Are you the sole legal owner of the dwelling-house?

(b) Are you and the respondent joint legal owners of the dwelling-house?

(c) Is the respondent the sole legal owner of the dwelling-house?

(d) Do you rent the dwelling-house as a sole tenant?

(e) Do you and the respondent rent the dwelling-house as joint tenants?

(f) Does the respondent rent the dwelling-house as a sole tenant?

If you answer —

- **Yes** to (a), (b), (d) or (e) you are likely to be entitled to occupy the dwelling-house
- **Yes** to (c) or (f) you may not be entitled (unless, for example, you are a spouse or civil partner and have home rights – see notes under 'Home Rights' below)
- **Yes** to (b), (c), (e) or (f), the respondent is likely to be entitled to occupy the dwelling-house
- **Yes** to (a) or (d) the respondent may not be entitled (unless, for example, he or she is a spouse or civil partner and has home rights).

Box 1 For example, if you are sole owner, joint owner or if you rent the property. If you are not a spouse, former spouse, civil partner, former civil partner, cohabitant or former cohabitant of the respondent, you will only be able to apply for an occupation order if you fall within this category.

If you answer yes to this question, it will not be possible for a magistrates' court to deal with the application, unless the court decides that it is unnecessary for it to decide this question in order to deal with the application or make the order. If the court decides that it cannot deal with the application, it will transfer the application to a county court.

Box 2 For example, if the respondent is or was married to you, or if you and the respondent are or were civil partners, and he or she is sole owner or rents the property.

Box 3 For example, if the respondent is or was cohabiting with you and is sole owner or rents the property.

Home Rights
Where one spouse or civil partner "**(A)**" is entitled to occupy the dwelling-house by virtue of a beneficial estate or interest or contract or by virtue of any enactment giving him or her the right to remain in occupation, and the other spouse or civil partner "**(B)**" is not so entitled, then **B** (who is not entitled) has home rights.

The rights are—

(a) if **B** is in occupation, not to be evicted or excluded from the dwelling-house except with the leave of the court; and

(b) if **B** is not in occupation, the right, with the leave of the court, to enter into and occupy the dwelling-house.

Section 6 (continued)

Note: Home Rights do not exist if the dwelling-house has never been, and was never intended to be, the matrimonial or civil partnership home of the two spouses or civil partners. If the marriage or civil partnership has come to an end, home rights will also have ceased, unless a court order has been made during the marriage or civil partnership for the rights to continue after the end of that relationship.

Occupation Orders
The possible orders are:

If you have ticked box 1 above, an order under section 33 of the Act may:

- enforce the applicant's entitlement to remain in occupation as against the respondent
- require the respondent to permit the applicant to enter and remain in the dwelling-house or part of it
- regulate the occupation of the dwelling-house by either or both parties
- if the respondent is also entitled to occupy, the order may prohibit, suspend or restrict the exercise by him, of that right
- restrict or terminate any home rights of the respondent
- require the respondent to leave the dwelling-house or part of it
- exclude the respondent from a defined area around the dwelling-house
- declare that the applicant is entitled to occupy the dwelling-house or has home rights in it
- provide that the home rights of the applicant are not brought to an end by the death of the other spouse or civil partner or termination of the marriage or civil partnership.

If you have ticked box 2 or box 3 above, an order under section 35 or 36 of the Act may:

- give the applicant the right not to be evicted or excluded from the dwelling-house or any part of it by the respondent for a specified period
- prohibit the respondent from evicting or excluding the applicant during that period
- give the applicant the right to enter and occupy the dwelling-house for a specified period
- require the respondent to permit the exercise of that right
- regulate the occupation of the dwelling-house by either or both of the parties
- prohibit, suspend or restrict the exercise by the respondent of his right to occupy
- require the respondent to leave the dwelling-house or part of it
- exclude the respondent from a defined area around the dwelling-house.

If you have ticked box 4 or box 5 above, an order under section 37 or 38 of the Act may:

- require the respondent to permit the applicant to enter and remain in the dwelling-house or part of it
- regulate the occupation of the dwelling-house by either or both of the parties
- require the respondent to leave the dwelling-house or part of it
- exclude the respondent from a defined area around the dwelling-house.

You should provide any evidence which you have on the following matters in your evidence in support of this application. If necessary, further statements may be submitted after the application has been issued.

If you have ticked box 1, box 4 or box 5 above, the court will need any available evidence of the following:

- the housing needs and resources of you, the respondent and any relevant child
- the financial needs of you and the respondent
- the likely effect of any order, or any decision not to make an order, on the health, safety and well-being of you, the respondent and any relevant child
- the conduct of you and the respondent in relation to each other and otherwise.

If you have ticked box 2 above, the court will need any available evidence of:

- the housing needs and resources of you, the respondent and any relevant child
- the financial resources of you and the respondent
- the likely effect of any order, or of any decision not to make an order on the health, safety and well-being of you, the respondent and any relevant child
- the conduct of you and the respondent in relation to each other and otherwise
- the length of time that has elapsed since you and the respondent ceased to live together
- where you and the respondent were married, the length of time that has elapsed since the marriage was dissolved or annulled
- where you and the respondent were civil partners, the length of time that has elapsed since the dissolution or annulment of the civil partnership

Section 6 (continued)

- the existence of any pending proceedings between you and the respondent:

  under section 23A of the Matrimonial Causes Act 1973 (property adjustment orders in connection with divorce proceedings etc.)

  or under Part 2 of Schedule 5 to the Civil Partnership Act 2004 (property adjustment on or after dissolution, nullity or separation)

  or under Schedule 1 para 1(2)(d) or (e) of the Children Act 1989 (orders for financial relief against parents)

  or relating to the legal or beneficial ownership of the dwelling-house.

If you have ticked box 3 above, the court will need any available evidence of:

- the housing needs and resources of you, the respondent and any relevant child
- the financial resources of you and the respondent
- the likely effect of any order, or of any decision not to make an order, on the health, safety and well-being of you, the respondent and any relevant child
- the conduct of you and the respondent in relation to each other and otherwise
- the nature of your and the respondent's relationship
- the length of time during which you have lived together as husband and wife or civil partners
- whether you and the respondent have had any children, or have both had parental responsibility for any children
- the length of time that has elapsed since you and the respondent ceased to live together
- the existence of any pending proceedings between you and the respondent under Schedule 1 para 1(2)(d) or (e) of the Children Act 1989 or relating to the legal or beneficial ownership of the dwelling-house.

Section 7

Under section 40 of the Act the court may make the following additional orders when making an occupation order:

- impose on either party obligations as to the repair and maintenance of the dwelling-house
- impose on either party obligations as to the payment of rent, mortgage or other outgoings affecting it
- order a party occupying the dwelling-house to make periodical payments to the other party in respect of the accommodation, if the other party would (but for the order) be entitled to occupy it
- grant either party possession or use of furniture or other contents
- order either party to take reasonable care of any furniture or other contents
- order either party to take reasonable steps to keep the dwelling-house and any furniture or other contents secure.

Section 8

If the dwelling-house is rented or subject to a mortgage, the landlord or mortgagee must be served with notice of the proceedings in Form FL416. He or she will then be able to make representations to the court regarding the rent or mortgage.

Section 10

A person living in the same household may, for example, be a member of the family or a tenant or employee of you or the respondent.

Non-molestation order

A3.2
In the Family Court **No . . . . . .**
Sitting at [Place]

The Family Law Act 1996

The Marriage of XX and YY, or

The Civil Partnership of XX and YY, or

The Relationship of XX and YY, or

The Family of XX and YY

Adapt as necessary

After hearing [*name the advocate(s) who appeared*] . . . .

(In the case of an order made without notice) After reading the statement(s) and hearing the witness(es) specified in para [*insert*] of the Recitals below

NON-MOLESTATION ORDER MADE BY [NAME OF JUDGE] ON [DATE] SITTING IN PRIVATE

IMPORTANT NOTICE TO THE RESPONDENT, [YY] OF [*insert address*]

YOU MUST OBEY THIS ORDER. You should read it carefully. If you do not understand anything in this order you should go to a solicitor, Legal Advice Centre or Citizens Advice Bureau. You have a right to apply to the court to change or cancel the order.

WARNING: IF, WITHOUT REASONABLE EXCUSE, YOU DO ANYTHING WHICH YOU ARE FORBIDDEN FROM DOING BY THIS ORDER, YOU WILL BE COMMITTING A CRIMINAL OFFENCE AND LIABLE ON CONVICTION TO A TERM OF IMPRISONMENT NOT EXCEEDING FIVE YEARS OR TO A FINE OR BOTH.

ALTERNATIVELY, IF YOU DO NOT OBEY THIS ORDER, YOU WILL BE GUILTY OF CONTEMPT OF COURT AND YOU MAY BE SENT TO PRISON, BE FINED, OR HAVE YOUR ASSETS SEIZED.

The Parties

1. The applicant is XX

   The respondent is YY

   [The second respondent is ZZ]

   [*Specify if any party acts by a litigation friend*]

Definitions

2. The "children of the family" are:

  a. [forename and surname] born on [*date*];

  b. [forename and surname] born on [*date*]; and

  c. etc

3. The "family home" is [*insert full address including postcode*] / ["*insert*"] is [*insert full address including postcode*].

Recitals

4. This is a non-molestation order made against the respondent [YY] on [*insert date*] by [*insert name of judge*] on the application of the applicant [XX].

5. *(Where the order was made without notice)* The judge read the following witness statement(s) [*set out*] and heard oral evidence from [*insert name(s)*].

6. *(Where the order was made without or on short notice)* This order was made at a hearing [without notice]/[on short informal notice] to the respondent. The reason why the order was made [without notice]/[on short informal notice] to the respondent was [*set out*]. The respondent has the right to apply to the court to vary or discharge the order – see paragraph [*insert*] below.

Undertakings given to the court by the applicant XX

7. [By [insert time and date] the applicant shall:

  a. issue an application notice [in the form of the draft produced to the court] [claiming the appropriate relief]; and

  b. file a witness statement [substantially in the terms of the draft witness statement produced to the court] [confirming the substance of what was said to the court by the applicant's counsel/solicitor]].

8. By [insert time and date] the applicant shall serve upon the respondent, together with this order:

  a. a copy of the application;

  b. copies of the witness statement(s) and exhibits containing the evidence relied upon by the applicant, and any other documents provided to the court on the making of the application; and

  c. a note [prepared by [his]/[her] solicitor] recording the substance of the dialogue with the court at the hearing and the reasons given by the court for making the order, which note shall include (but not be limited to) any allegation of fact made orally to the court where such allegation is not contained in the witness statement(s) or draft witness statement(s) read by the judge.

IT IS ORDERED (BY CONSENT):

Non-Molestation Order – Applicant

9. The respondent, [YY], must not use or threaten violence against the applicant, [XX], and must not instruct, encourage or in any way suggest that any other person should do so.

10. The respondent, [YY], must not intimidate, harass or pester the applicant, [XX], and must not instruct, encourage or in any way suggest that any other person should do so.

11. The respondent, [YY], must not telephone, text, email or otherwise contact or attempt to contact the applicant, [XX], [except for the purpose of making arrangements for contact between the respondent and the children of the family] / [except through [his]/[her] solicitors [*insert name, address and telephone number*]].

12. The respondent, [YY], must not damage, attempt to damage or threaten to damage any property owned by or in the possession or control of the applicant, [XX], and must not instruct, encourage or in any way suggest that any other person should do so.

13. The respondent, [YY], must not damage, attempt to damage or threaten to damage the property or contents of [the family home]/[insert property], and must not instruct, encourage or in any way suggest that any other person should do so.

Non-Molestation Order - Zonal

14. The respondent, [YY], must not go to, enter or attempt to enter [the family home] / [*insert property*] / [any property where he knows or believes the applicant, [XX], to be living], and must not go [within [*insert*] metres of it] / [along the road(s) known as [*insert*]], except that the respondent may [go to the property [without entering it]] / [go along the road(s) known as [*insert*]] for the purpose of collecting the children of the family for, and returning them from, such contact with the children as may be agreed in writing between the applicant and the respondent or in default of agreement ordered by the court.

Non-Molestation Order - Children

15. The respondent, [YY], must not use or threaten violence against the child[ren] of the family, and must not instruct, encourage or in any way suggest that any other person should do so.

16. The respondent, [YY], must not intimidate, harass or pester the child[ren] of the family, and must not instruct, encourage or in any way suggest that any other person should do so.

17. The respondent, [YY], must not telephone, text, email or otherwise contact or attempt to contact the child[ren] of the family [except for such contact as may be agreed in writing between the applicant and the respondent or in default of agreement ordered by the court].

18. The respondent, [YY], must not [between the hours of 08:30 and 16:00] go to, enter or attempt to enter the school premises known as [*insert*], and must not go [within [*insert*] metres of it] / [along the road(s) known as [*insert*]], except [by prior written agreement with the applicant] / [by prior written invitation from the school authorities].

Duration of Non-Molestation Order

19. Paragraph(s) [*insert*] of this order shall be effective against the respondent [YY] once it is personally served on [him]/[her] [and/or] once [he]/[she] is made aware of the terms of this order whether by personal service or otherwise.

20. Paragraph(s) [*insert*] of this order shall last until [a further order is made] / [*insert date and time*] [unless before then it is varied or revoked by an order of the court].

21. The respondent may apply to the court at any time to vary or discharge this order on [*insert hours / days*] [written] notice to the [applicant]/[applicant's solicitors]. If any evidence is to be relied upon in support of [his]/[her] application, the substance of it must be communicated in writing to the [applicant]/[applicant's solicitors] in advance.

Hearings

22. The application(s) [is]/[are] listed for a further [directions] hearing in the Family Court sitting at [*place*] on [*insert date*] ('the return date'), at which hearing the court will reconsider the application [and whether the order should continue]. If you do not attend on the date and at the time shown the court may make an order in your absence.

Costs

23. The costs of this application are [reserved to the judge hearing the application on the return date] / [in the application], etc.

Dated

Note to Arresting Officer:

Under section 42A of the Family Law Act 1996, breach of a non-molestation order is a criminal offence punishable by up to five yeas' imprisonment. It is an arrestable offence and it is not necessary to obtain a warrant.

"A person who without reasonable excuse does anything that he is prohibited from doing by a non-molestation order is guilty of an offence".

Family Law Act 1996, section 42A(1).

Notice pursuant to PD 33A para 2.5

You XX, the applicant, may be sent to prison for contempt of court if you break the promises that have been given to the court

Statement pursuant to PD 33A para 1.5

I understand the undertakings that I have given, and that if I break any of my promises to the court I may be sent to prison for contempt of court

Signed

. . . .

XX [date]

Communications with the court

All communications to the court about this order should be sent to –

[Insert the address and telephone number of the appropriate Court Office]

Name and address of applicant's legal representatives

The applicant's legal representatives are –

[Name, address, reference, fax and telephone numbers both in and out of office hours and e-mail]

Occupation order

A3.3

In the Family Court **Sitting at [Place]**	No . . . . . .

The Family Law Act 1996

The Marriage of XX and YY, or

The Civil Partnership of XX and YY, or

The Relationship of XX and YY, or

The Family of XX and YY

Adapt as necessary

After hearing *[name the advocate(s) who appeared]* . . . .

(In the case of an order made without notice) After reading the statement(s) and hearing the witness(es) specified in para [*insert*] of the Recitals below

OCCUPATION ORDER MADE BY [NAME OF JUDGE] ON [DATE] SITTING IN PRIVATE

> **IMPORTANT NOTICE TO THE RESPONDENT, [YY] OF [*insert address*]**
> **YOU MUST OBEY THIS ORDER. You should read it carefully. If you do not understand anything in this order you should go to a solicitor, Legal Advice Centre or Citizens Advice Bureau. You have a right to apply to the court to change or cancel the order.**
> **WARNING: IF YOU DO NOT OBEY THIS ORDER, YOU WILL BE GUILTY OF CONTEMPT OF COURT AND YOU MAY BE SENT TO PRISON, BE FINED, OR HAVE YOUR ASSETS SEIZED.**

The Parties

1. The applicant is XX

   The respondent is YY

   [The second respondent is ZZ]

   [*Specify if any party acts by a litigation friend*]

Definitions

2. The "children of the family" are:

   a. [forename and surname] born on [*date*];

   b. [forename and surname] born on [*date*]; and

   c. etc

3. The "family home" is the property at [*insert full address including postcode*] [and its surrounding gardens, land and outbuildings] / ["*insert*"] is the property at [*insert full address including postcode*] [and its surrounding gardens, land and outbuildings]

Recitals

4. This is an occupation order made against the respondent [YY] on [*insert date*] by [*insert name of judge*] on the application of the applicant [XX].

5. *(Where the order was made without notice)* The judge read the following witness statement(s) [*set out*] and heard oral evidence from [*insert name(s)*].

6. *(Where the order was made without or on short notice)* This order was made at a hearing [without notice]/[on short informal notice] to the respondent. The reason why the order was made [without notice]/[on short informal notice] to the respondent was [*set out*]. The respondent has the right to apply to the court to set aside or vary the order – see paragraph [*insert*] below.

Undertakings given to the court by the applicant XX

7. *(Where the order was made without or on short notice)* [By [insert time and date] the applicant shall:

   a. issue an application notice [in the form of the draft produced to the court] [claiming the appropriate relief]; and

   b. file a witness statement [substantially in the terms of the draft witness statement produced to the court] [confirming the substance of what was said to the court by the applicant's counsel/solicitor]].

8. *(Where the order was made without or on short notice)* [By [insert time and date] the applicant shall [use [his]/[her] best endeavours personally to serve upon the respondent] / [serve upon the respondent, by [insert method of service – for example posting to the respondent's usual address]], together with this order:

   a. a copy of the application;

   b. copies of the witness statement(s) and exhibits containing the evidence relied upon by the applicant, and any other documents provided to the court on the making of the application; and

   c. a note [prepared by [his]/[her] solicitor] recording the substance of the dialogue with the court at the hearing and the reasons given by the court for making the order, which note shall include (but not be limited to) any allegation of fact made orally to the court where such allegation is not contained in the witness statement(s) or draft witness statement(s) read by the judge.]

9. The statement of service of this order on the respondent shall be filed at court and shall be in a form which complies with section 9 of the Criminal Justice Act 1967 [and shall include the following signed declaration:

"*This statement is true to the best of my knowledge and belief and I make it knowing that, if it were tendered in evidence, I would be liable to prosecution if I wilfully stated in it anything which I know to be false or did not believe to be true.*"]

IT IS ORDERED (BY CONSENT):

Occupation Order – Declaration under Section 33 **of the Family Law Act 1996**

10. The court declares that the applicant, [XX], is entitled to occupy [the family home] / [the property at [*insert full address including postcode*]] [and its surrounding gardens, land and outbuildings] as [his]/[her] home.

11. The court declares that the applicant, [XX], has home rights in [the family home] / [the property at [*insert full address including postcode*]], [and/or] the court declares that the applicant's, [XX's], home rights in [the family home] / [the property [at [*insert full address including postcode*]], shall not end when the respondent, [YY], dies or their [marriage/civil partnership] is dissolved and shall continue until [*insert date and time*] / [the determination of the applicant's financial provision claims under case number [*insert*]] or a further order is made.

Occupation Order under Section 33 **of the Family Law Act 1996**

12. The respondent, [YY], shall allow the applicant, [XX] to occupy [the family home] / [the property at [*insert full address including postcode*]] [and its surrounding gardens, land and outbuildings]] / [part of the property at [*insert full address including postcode*] [and its surrounding gardens, land and outbuildings], namely [*specify part*]].

13. The respondent, [YY], must not occupy [the family home] / [the property at [*insert full address including postcode*]] [and its surrounding gardens, land and outbuildings] / [*specify part of the property at* [*insert full address including postcode*]] [between [*specify dates and times*]].

14. The respondent, [YY], shall leave [the family home] / [the property at [*insert full address including postcode*]] [and its surrounding gardens, land and outbuildings] / [*specify part of the property* at [*insert full address including postcode*]] by [*insert date and time*] / [within [*insert hours/days*] of this order being personally served on [him]/[her] [and/or] of [him]/[her] being made aware of the terms of this order whether by personal service or otherwise].

15. Having left [the family home] / [the property] [and its surrounding gardens, land and outbuildings] / [*specify part of the property*], the respondent, [YY], must not return to, enter or attempt to enter [or go within [*insert*] metres of it], [except that the respondent may go to the property [without entering it] for the purpose of collecting the children of the family for, and returning them from, such contact as may be agreed in writing between the applicant and the respondent or in default of agreement ordered by the court].

16. The respondent, [YY], must not obstruct, harass, or interfere with the [applicant's], [XX's], peaceful occupation of [the family home] / [the property at [*insert full address including postcode*]] [and its surrounding gardens, land and outbuildings] / [*specify part of the property at* [*insert full address including postcode*]].

Occupation Order under Sections 35 and 36 of the Family Law Act 1996

17. The applicant, [XX], has the right to enter into and occupy [the family home] / [the property at [*insert full address including postcode*]] [and its surrounding gardens, land and outbuildings], and the respondent, [YY], shall allow the applicant to do so.

18. The applicant, [XX], has the right not to be evicted or excluded from, and the respondent, [YY], must not evict or exclude the applicant from, [the family

home] / [the property at [*insert full address including postcode*]] [and its surrounding gardens, land and outbuildings] or any part of it [except for [*specify part of the property*]].

19. The respondent, [YY], must not occupy [the family home] / [the property at [*insert full address including postcode*]] [and its surrounding gardens, land and outbuildings] / [*specify part of the property at* [*insert full address including postcode*]] [between [*specify dates and times*]].

20. The respondent, [YY], shall leave [the family home] / [the property at [*insert full address including postcode*]] [and its surrounding gardens, land and outbuildings] / [*specify part of the property* at [*insert full address including postcode*]] by [*insert date and time*] / [within [*insert hours/days*] of this order being personally served on [him]/[her] [and/or] of [him]/[her] being made aware of the terms of this order whether by personal service or otherwise].

21. Having left [the family home] / [the property] [and its surrounding gardens, land and outbuildings] / [*specify part of the property*], the respondent, [YY], must not return to, enter or attempt to enter [or go within [*insert*] metres of it], [except that the respondent may go to the property [without entering it] for the purpose of collecting the children of the family for, and returning them from, such contact as may be agreed in writing between the applicant and the respondent or in default of agreement ordered by the court].

22. The respondent, [YY], must not obstruct, harass, or interfere with the [applicant's], [XX's], peaceful occupation of [the family home] / [the property at [*insert full address including postcode*]] [and its surrounding gardens, land and outbuildings] / [*specify part of the property at* [*insert full address including postcode*]].

Occupation Order under Sections 37 and 38 of the Family Law Act 1996

23. The respondent, [YY], shall allow the applicant, [XX], to enter into and occupy [the family home] / [the property at [*insert full address including postcode*]] [and its surrounding gardens, land and outbuildings] / [part of the property at [*insert full address including postcode*] [and its surrounding gardens, land and outbuildings], namely [*specify part*]].

24. The respondent, [YY], must not occupy [the family home] / [the property at [*insert full address including postcode*]] [and its surrounding gardens, land and outbuildings] / [*specify part of the property at* [*insert full address including postcode*]] between [*specify dates and times*].

25. The respondent, [YY], shall leave [the family home] / [the property at [*insert full address including postcode*]] [and its surrounding gardens, land and outbuildings] / [*specify part of the property* at [*insert full address including postcode*]] by [*insert date and time*] / [within [*insert hours/days*] of this order being personally served on [him]/[her] [and/or] of [him]/[her] being made aware of the terms of this order whether by personal service or otherwise].

26. Having left [the family home] / [the property] [and its surrounding gardens, land and outbuildings] / [*specify part of the property*], the respondent, [YY], must not return to, enter or attempt to enter [or go within [*insert*] metres of it], [except that the respondent may go to the property [without entering it] for the purpose of collecting the children of the family for, and returning them from, such contact as may be agreed in writing between the applicant and the respondent or in default of agreement ordered by the court].

27. The respondent, [YY], must not obstruct, harass, or interfere with the [applicant's], [XX's], peaceful occupation of [the family home] / [the property at [*insert full address including postcode*]] [and its surrounding gardens, land and outbuildings] / [*specify part of the property at* [*insert full address including postcode*]].

Additional Provisions which may be included in Occupation Orders made under Sections 33, 35 or 36 of the Family Law Act 1996

28. [The applicant [XX]] and/or [The respondent [YY]] shall maintain and repair [the family home] / [the property at [*insert full address including postcode*]] [and its surrounding gardens, land and outbuildings].

29. [The applicant [XX]] and/or [The respondent [YY]] shall discharge the [mortgage payments]/[rental payments] in respect of [the family home] / [the property at [*insert full address including postcode*]].

30. [The applicant [XX]] and/or [The respondent [YY]] shall discharge the following outgoings in respect of [the family home] / [the property at [*insert full address including postcode*]]: [*insert outgoings*].

31. The applicant [XX] shall pay to the respondent [YY] £[*insert*] each week/month, for the use of [the family home] / [the property at [*insert full address including postcode*]].

32. The applicant [XX] shall keep and use the [furniture]/[contents]/[*specify if necessary*] of [the family home] / [the property at [*insert full address including postcode*]].

33. The respondent [YY] shall return to the applicant [XX] the [furniture]/ [contents]/ [*specify if necessary*] of [the family home] / [the property at [*insert full address including postcode*]] by no later than [*insert time and date*].

34. The applicant [XX] shall take reasonable care of the [furniture]/ [contents]/ [*specify if necessary*] of [the family home] / [the property at [*insert full address including postcode*]].

35. The applicant [XX] shall take all reasonable steps to keep secure [the family home] / [the property at [*insert full address including postcode*]] and the [furniture]/[contents]/[*specify if necessary*].

Duration of Occupation Order under Section 33 of the Family Law Act / Power of Arrest

36. Paragraph(s) [*insert*] of this order shall be effective against the respondent [YY] once it is personally served on [him]/[her] [and/or] once [he]/[she] is made aware of the terms of this order whether by personal service or otherwise.

37. Paragraph(s) [*insert*] of this order shall last until [*insert date and time*] unless it is set aside or varied before then by an order of the court.

38. The respondent has the right to apply to the court at any time, [(*where the order was made without notice)* and without waiting until the return date], to set aside or vary this order. [*Insert if appropriate:* The respondent must give [*insert hours / days*] [written] notice of the application to the [applicant]/[applicant's solicitors]]. If the respondent intends to rely on any evidence in support of [his]/[her] application to set aside or vary this order, [(*where the order was made without notice)* or intends to rely on any

evidence to oppose the continuation of the order at the return date], the substance of it must be provided in writing to the [applicant]/[applicant's solicitors] in advance.

39. *(Where the order was made without or on short notice)* [If the respondent intends to oppose the continuation of the order on the return date [he] / [she] must notify the court [in writing or by email] no later than [*insert date and time*] that [he] / [she] intends to attend the hearing on the return date and to oppose the continuation of the order. If the respondent does not notify the court then the court may, if appropriate, make an order dispensing with the need for any attendance by the [applicant] / [applicant's solicitors] on the return date and may, if appropriate, on the return date make an order extending the injunction.]

40. [A power of arrest is attached to paragraphs [*insert*] of this order].

Duration of Occupation Order under Sections 35 and 37 of the Family Law Act / Power of Arrest

41. Paragraph(s) [*insert*] of this order shall be effective against the respondent [YY] once it is personally served on [him]/[her] [and/or] once [he]/[she] is made aware of the terms of this order whether by personal service or otherwise.

42. Paragraph(s) [*insert*] of this order shall last until [*insert date and time – which must not be more than 6 months from the date of this order*] unless it is set aside or varied before then by an order of the court.

43. [Paragraph(s) [*insert*] of the occupation order made on [*insert date*] is extended until [*insert date and time – which must not be more than 6 months from the date of this extension*] unless it is set aside or varied before then by an order of the court].

44. The respondent has the right to apply to the court at any time, [*(where the order was made without notice)* and without waiting until the return date], to set aside or vary this order. [*Insert if appropriate:* The respondent must give [*insert hours / days*] [written] notice of the application to the [applicant]/[applicant's solicitors]] If the respondent intends to rely on any evidence in support of [his]/[her] application to set aside or vary this order, [*(where the order was made without notice)* or intends to rely on any evidence to oppose the continuation of the order at the return date], the substance of it must be provided in writing to the [applicant]/[applicant's solicitors] in advance.

45. *(Where the order was made without or on short notice)* [If the respondent intends to oppose the continuation of the order on the return date [he] / [she] must notify the court [in writing or by email] no later than [*insert date and time*] that [he] / [she] intends to attend the hearing on the return date and to oppose the continuation of the order. If the respondent does not notify the court then the court may, if appropriate, make an order dispensing with the need for any attendance by the [applicant] / [applicant's solicitors] on the return date and may, if appropriate, on the return date make an order extending the injunction.]

46. [A power of arrest is attached to paragraphs [*insert*] of this order.]

Duration of Occupation Order under Sections 36 and 38 of the Family Law Act / Power of Arrest

47. Paragraph(s) [*insert*] of this order shall be effective against the respondent [YY] once it is personally served on [him]/[her] [and/or] once [he]/[she] is made aware of the terms of this order whether by personal service or otherwise.

48. Paragraph(s) [*insert*] of this order shall last until [*insert date and time – which must not be more than 6 months from the date of this order*] unless it is set aside or varied before then by an order of the court.

49. [Paragraph(s) [*insert*] of the occupation order made on [*insert date*] is extended until [*insert date and time – which must not be more than 6 months from the date of this extension*] unless it is set aside or varied before then by an order of the court, and must end on that date.]

50. The respondent has the right to apply to the court at any time, [*(where the order was made without notice)* and without waiting until the return date], to set aside or vary this order. [*Insert if appropriate:* The respondent must give [*insert hours / days*] [written] notice of the application to the [applicant]/[applicant's solicitors]. If the respondent intends to rely on any evidence in support of [his]/[her] application to set aside or vary this order, [*(where the order was made without notice)* or intends to rely on any evidence to oppose the continuation of the order at the return date], the substance of it must be provided in writing to the [applicant]/[applicant's solicitors] in advance.

51. *(Where the order was made without or on short notice)* [If the respondent intends to oppose the continuation of the order on the return date [he] / [she] must notify the court [in writing or by email] no later than [*insert date and time*] that [he] / [she] intends to attend the hearing on the return date and to oppose the continuation of the order. If the respondent does not notify the court then the court may, if appropriate, make an order dispensing with the need for any attendance by the [applicant] / [applicant's solicitors] on the return date and may, if appropriate, on the return date make an order extending the injunction.]

52. [A power of arrest is attached to paragraphs [*insert*] of this order.]

Hearings

53. [The application(s) [is]/[are] listed for a further [directions] hearing in the Family Court sitting at [*insert place*] on [*insert date*] ('the return date'). At the hearing on the return date, the court will reconsider the application and decide whether [the order should continue] / [the application should be granted and the order should be made] (time estimate: [*insert time*]). If the respondent does not attend on the date and at the time shown the court may make an order in [his]/[her] absence.]

54. [The application(s) [is]/[are] listed for a Final Hearing in the Family Court sitting at [*insert place*] on [*insert date*]. At the hearing, the court will reconsider the application and decide whether [the order should continue] / [the application should be granted and the order should be made] (time estimate: [*insert days*]). If the respondent does not attend on the date and at the time shown the court may make an order in [his]/[her] absence.]

Costs

55. The costs of this application are [reserved to the judge hearing the application on the return date] / [in the application], etc.

Dated

Statements pursuant to PD 37A para 3.5

I understand the undertakings that I have given, and that if I break any of my promises to the court I may be sent to prison for contempt of court

. . . .

XX

I understand the undertakings that I have given, and that if I break any of my promises to the court I may be sent to prison for contempt of court

. . . .

YY

Communications with the court

All communications to the court about this order should be sent to –

[Insert the address and telephone number of the appropriate Court Office]

Name and address of applicant's legal representatives

The applicant's legal representatives are –

[Name, address, reference, fax and telephone numbers both in and out of office hours and e-mail]

Index